THE ORIGIN OF MAN
AND OF HIS SUPERSTITIONS

LECTOR HOUSE PUBLIC DOMAIN WORKS

THE ORIGIN OF MAN AND OF HIS SUPERSTITIONS

CARVETH READ

ISBN: 978-93-5614-352-4

Published: 1920

LECTOR HOUSE LLP
E-MAIL: lectorpublishing@gmail.com

THE ORIGIN OF MAN
AND OF HIS SUPERSTITIONS

BY

CARVETH READ, M.A.

LECTURER ON COMPARATIVE PSYCHOLOGY
(FORMERLY GROTE PROFESSOR OF PHILOSOPHY)
IN UNIVERSITY COLLEGE, LONDON

1920

PREFACE

The volume now published explains in its first part an hypothesis that the human race has descended from some ape-like stock by a series of changes which began and, until recently, were maintained by the practice of hunting in pack for animal food, instead of being content with the fruits and other nutritious products of the tropical forest. The hypothesis occurred to me many years ago, and was first published (in brief) in *The Metaphysics of Nature* (1805), Chap. XIII., and again in *Natural and Social Morals* (1909); but all it implied did not become clear until, in lecturing on Comparative Psychology, there was forced upon me the necessity of effecting an intelligible transition from the animal to the human mind, and of not being satisfied to say year after year that hands and brains were plainly so useful that they must have been developed by Natural Selection. Then one day the requisite ideas came to light; and an outline of the hypothesis was read at the Meeting of the British Association (Section H) at Birmingham in 1913, and printed in *Man*, November 1914. The Council of the Anthropological Institute has kindly consented to my using the substance of that article in the first chapter here following.

The article in *Man* dealt chiefly with the physical changes which our race has undergone. The correlative mental changes were explained in the *British Journal of Psychology* in an article which supplies the basis of the second chapter of this book.

The hunting-pack, then, was the first form of human society; and in lecturing on Ethnopsychology two questions especially interested me: (1) Under what mental conditions did the change take place from the organisation of the hunting-pack (when this weakened) to the settled life of the tribe or group? and (2) Why is the human mind everywhere befogged with ideas of Magic and Animism? They seemed at last to have the same answer: these superstitions were useful and (apparently) even necessary in giving to elders enough prestige to preserve tradition and custom when the leader of the hunt was no longer conspicuous in authority. A magic-working gerontocracy was the second form of society; and the third form was governed by a wizard-king or a priest-king, or by a king supported by wizards or priests. One must, therefore, understand the possibility of these beliefs in Magic and Animism, and how they arose and obtained a hold upon all tribes and nations; and hence the second part of this volume—on Superstition.

Some results of inquiry into these matters were also published in the *British Journal of Psychology* (namely, much of the substance of Chaps. III., IV., V., VI., and VIII.) and are here reproduced, with the editor's consent, enlarged and, for the most part, rewritten: the least altered are Chaps. VI. and VIII. Chaps. VII., IX. and X. have not hitherto been printed; but part of Chap. X. was read at the Meeting of the British Association at Bournemouth last year.

Messrs. Williams and Norgate have given permission to use the diagram in the footnote to p. 3, based on one of Prof. Keith's in his *Antiquity of Man*.

Extensive use has, of course, been made of the works of Darwin, Herbert Spencer and E. B. Tylor, and (among living authors) of the volumes of Sir J. G. Frazer and Prof. Ed. Westermarck. I am grateful to my friends and colleagues, Prof. Spearman, Prof. J. P. Hill and Prof. Arthur Keith for assistance in various ways. Mr. Pycraft, too, of the Natural History Museum has given me important information; and my old friend, Mr. Thomas Whittaker, has helped me, as usual, when my need was greatest.

CARVETH READ.

University College, London.
July 1920

CONTENTS

CHAPTER III

CHAPTER IV

CHAPTER V

CHAPTER VI

CHAPTER VII

CHAPTER VIII

CHAPTER IX

CHAPTER X

THE ORIGIN OF MAN
AND OF HIS SUPERSTITIONS

CHAPTER I

ON THE DIFFERENTIATION OF MAN
FROM THE ANTHROPOIDS

§ 1. THE HYPOTHESIS

§ 1. *The Hypothesis.*—That Man was differentiated from the anthropoid stock by becoming a hunter; perhaps in the Oligocene period

THAT the human species as we now see it, with its several races, Mongolian, Negro, Mediterranean, etc., represents a Family of the Primates is generally agreed; and there is evidence that the Family formerly comprised other species that have become extinct. Our nearest surviving zoological relatives are the Gorilla, Chimpanzee and Orang, and (at a further remove) the Siamang and Gibbons; and in spite of the fundamental anatomical resemblance between those apes and ourselves, the difference is so great that some explanation of how it came about is very desirable.

The differences between Man and his nearest relatives are innumerable; but taking the chief of them, and assuming that the minor details are correlated with these, it is the hypothesis of this essay that they may all be traced to the influence of one variation operating amongst the original anthropoid conditions. That variation was the adoption of a flesh-diet and the habits of a hunter in order to obtain it. Without the adoption of a flesh-diet there could have been no hunting; but a flesh-diet obtained without hunting (supposing it possible) could have done nothing for the evolution of our stock. The adoption of the hunting-life, therefore, is the essential variation upon which everything else depends. We need not suppose that a whole ancestral species varied in this way: it is enough that a few, or even one, of the common anthropoid stock should have done so, and that the variation was advantageous and was inherited.

Such a variation *must* have occurred at some time, since Man is everywhere more or less carnivorous; the earliest known men were hunters; weapons are among the earliest known artefacts. And it is not improbable that the change began at the anthropoid level; because although extant anthropoids are mainly frugivorous, yet they occasionally eat birds'-eggs and young birds; the gorilla has been said to eat small mammals; and other Primates (cebidæ, macaques and baboons) eat insects, arachnids, crabs, worms, frogs, lizards, birds; and the crab-eating macaque collects a large portion of its food on the Malay littoral. Why, then, should not one ape have betaken itself to hunting?

We need not suppose that our ancestors were ever exclusively carnivorous: that is very unlikely. A mixed diet is the rule even amongst hunting tribes, and everywhere the women collect and consume fruits and roots. But if at first nearly omnivorous, our ancestor (it is assumed) soon preferred to attack mammals, and advanced at a remote date to the killing of the biggest game found in his habitat. Everywhere savage hunters do so now: the little Semang kills the tiger, rhinoceros, elephant and buffalo; and many thousands of years ago, in Europe men slew the reindeer and the mammoth, the horse and the bison, the hyæna and the cave-bear. It is true they had weapons and snares, whilst the first hunter had only hands and teeth.

The change from a fruit-eating to a hunting life subserved the great utility of opening fresh supplies of food; and, possibly, a failure of the normal supply of the old customary food was the direct cause of the new habit. If our ape lived near the northern limits of the tropical forest, and a fall of temperature there took place, such as to reduce (especially in winter) the yield of fruit and other nutritious vegetation on which he had subsisted, famine may have driven him to attack other animals;[1] whilst more southerly anthropoids, not suffering from the change of climate, continued in their ancient manner of life. A large anthropoid (*Dryopithecus*) inhabited Central Europe in the Miocene, for his bones have been found; there may have been others; and during that period the climate altered from sub-tropical to temperate, with corresponding changes in fauna and flora. Hence it formerly occurred to me that perhaps the decisive change in the life of our Family happened there and then. It seems, however, that good judges put the probable date of the great differentiation much earlier, in the Oligocene;[2] and since I cannot find that any extensive alteration of climate is known to have happened during that period, it seems necessary to fall back upon "spontaneous" variation (as one must in many other cases); that is to say, from causes which are at present beyond our vision, the fateful ape did, in fact, prefer animal food so decidedly as to begin a-hunting for it. That being granted, the rest of the history was inevitable. The new pursuit was of a nature to engross the animal's whole attention and co-ordinate all his faculties;

---

[1] This was suggested to me by Mr. G. A. Garfitt.

[2] Estimated duration of the Cainozoic Period, assuming that the thickness of the deposits is about 63,000 feet, and that deposits accumulate at the rate of 1 foot in 100 years. Drawn to the scale of 1 mm. to 100,000 years. The estimate is given and explained by Prof. Sollas in the *Quarterly Journal of the Geological Society*, LXV. (1909). The "tree" is based on that given by Dr. A. Keith in *The Antiquity of Man*, p. 509.

and to maintain and reinforce it, his structure in body and mind may reasonably be supposed to have undergone rapid modification by natural selection; because those individuals that were in any organ or faculty best adapted to the new life had an advantage, which was inherited and gradually intensified.[3]

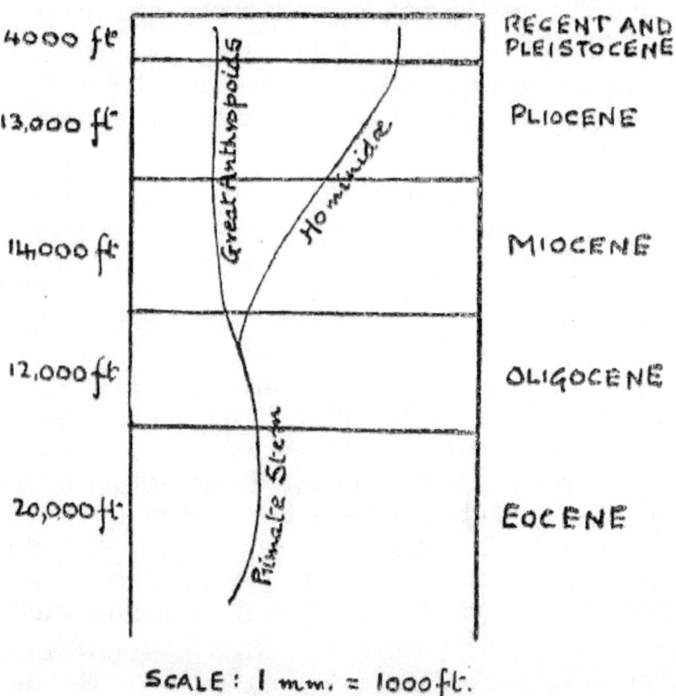

If we suppose the differentiation of the *Hominidæ* to have begun before the close of the Oligocene, about (say) 3,500,000 years are allowed for the evolution of the existing species of Man. All these reckonings are provisional.

[3] That Man was from the first a hunter has been suggested by several authors; but the consequences of the assumption have never (as far as I know) been worked out. A. R. Wallace, in *Darwinism* (p. 459), has the following passage: "The anthropoid apes, as well as most of the monkey tribe, are essentially arboreal in their structure, whereas the great distinctive character of man is his special adaptation to terrestrial locomotion. We can hardly suppose, therefore, that he originated in a forest region, where fruits to be obtained by climbing are the chief vegetable food. It is more probable that he began his existence on the open plains on high plateaux of the temperate or subtropical zone, where the seeds of indigenous cereals, numerous herbivora, rodents, game-birds, with fishes and molluscs in the lakes and rivers and seas supplied him with an abundance of varied food. In such a region he would develop skill as a hunter, trapper or fisherman, and later as a herdsman and cultivator—a succession of which we find indications in the palæolithic and neolithic races of Europe."

Prof. MacBride, in his popular introduction to *Zoology* (p. 84), also traces the specialisation of Man to the hunting life.

My friend Mr. Thomas Whittaker has sent me the following extract from Comte's *Politique Positive*, I. pp. 604-5: "L'obligation de se nourrir d'une proie qu'il faut atteindre et vaincre, perfectionne à la fois tous les attributs animaux, tant intérieurs qu'extérieurs. Son

§ 2. WHAT THE HYPOTHESIS EXPLAINS

§ 2. *What the Hypothesis Explains.* — World-wide range; why the earliest
known men were hunters; the erect gait; specialisation of hands;
reduction of arms; and of teeth and jaws; modification of skull; so-
cial co-operation; rudiments of speech; intelligence; control of fire

Let me run rapidly through the chief differences between Man and his nearest
congeners: some of them are obvious and can be stated very briefly; others I shall
return to in the next chapter. We shall see that they all follow naturally from the
above hypothesis.

(1) The anthropoids are never found out of the tropical forests of Africa and
Malaya (including Borneo and Sumatra). They feed chiefly on the fruits and other
highly nutritious vegetable products that, all the year round, are only there ob-
tainable. Although often coming to the ground, especially the chimpanzee and
gorilla, they are adapted to living in the trees: that is their home. In contrast with
their habits, Man is at home on the ground, with unlimited range over the whole
planet from beyond the Arctic Circle to Tasmania and Tierra del Fuego; because on
the ground (chiefly) he everywhere finds his food in the other animals whom he
hunts and slays. This, then, is the condition of his emancipation from the tropical
forest. It is, indeed, conceivable that a frugivorous animal, originally of the forest,
should obtain a wider range by taking to a coarser diet of roots and herbage, such
as suffices the Ungulates, browsing or grazing or digging with their snouts; but
this would not have led to the upright gait, or the big brain, or any of the marks
that distinguish Man. Not advance but retrogression must have followed such a
change.

(2) That the earliest men of whose condition of life we have any knowledge
were hunters agrees with the hypothesis. Any other view of Man's origin must
explain how and when he became a hunter. There seems to be no reason to put
the change of habits (which certainly occurred at some time) anywhere nearer
than the beginning of our differentiation. The further we put it back the better it
explains other modifications.

(3) The erect attitude was reached by the apes in the course of adaptation to

influence envers les sens et les muscles est trop évidente pour exiger ici aucun examen. Par
sa réaction habituelle sur les plus hautes fonctions du cerveau, elle développe également
l'intelligence et l'activité, dont le premier essor lui est toujours dû, même chez notre espèce.
A tous ces titres, cette nécessité modifie aussi les races qui en sont victimes, d'après les
efforts moins énergiques, mais plus continus, qu'elle y provoque pour leur défense. Dans
les deux cas, et surtout quant à l'attaque, elle détermine même les prémières habitudes
de co-opération active, au moins temporaire. Bornées à la simple famille chez les espèces
insociables, ces ligues peuvent ailleurs embrasser quelquefois de nombreuses troupes.
Ainsi commencent, parmi les animaux, des impulsions et des aptitudes qui ne pouvaient
se développer que d'après la continuité propre à la race la plus sociable et la plus intelli-
gente. Enfin, la condition carnassière doit aussi être appreciée dans sa réaction organique.
Une plus forte excitation, une digestion moins laborieuse et plus rapide, une assimilation
plus complète produisant un sang plus stimulant: telles sont ses propriétés physiologiques.
Toutes concourent à développer les fonctions supérieures, soit en augmentant l'énergie de
leurs organes, soit en procurant plus de temps pour leur exercice."

arboreal life;[4] but the erect gait as the normal mode of progression is (if we neglect the gibbons' imperfect performance) peculiar to ourselves; and such a gait was attained because the most successful hunters followed their prey afoot upon the ground. The feeble ineffective shuffle of the anthropoids upon the ground, supporting themselves with their arms where there are no overhanging boughs to swing by and help themselves along, could not have served the hunter, especially if he was to leave the forest. We may, indeed, suppose that at first prey was sometimes attacked by leaping upon it from the branch of a tree, as leopards sometimes do; but the less our ancestor in his new career trusted to trees the better for him. Such simple strategy could not make him a dominant animal throughout the world; nothing could do this but the gradual attainment of erect gait adapted to running down his prey. Hence the numerous modifications of structure necessary to it, whenever from time to time they occurred, were preserved and accumulated by natural selection: namely, the curving of the vertebral column, the balancing of the head upon a relatively slender neck, changes in the joints, bones and muscles of the legs, the lengthening of the leg and the specialisation of the foot (in which the heel is developed more than in the gorilla, and the great toe is lengthened and lies parallel with the other toes).

(4) The specialisation of the legs and feet, as it proceeded, made possible the specialisation of the hands: being gradually rid of the task of assisting locomotion, whether in trees or on the ground, they were used in grappling with prey, seconded by massive jaws and powerful canine teeth. In course of time they brought cudgels and stones to the encounter, and after many ages began to alter such means of offence into weapons that might be called artefacts. These simple beginnings probably occupied an immense time, perhaps more than half of the total period down to the present. The utility and consequent selection of hands had been great throughout; but their final development may be referred to the making and using of weapons fashioned according to a mental pattern. Those who had the best hands were selected because they made the best weapons and used them best; but we know from remains of several palæolithic stages of the art of manufacturing implements how very slowly the art improved.

(5) Along with specialisation of the hands went a reduction in the length and massiveness of the arms; and this must have been disadvantageous in directly grappling with prey. But it was necessary to the runner in order to lessen the weight and cumbersomeness of the upper part of the body and to improve his balance and agility. The change may also have been beneficial by affording physiological compensation for the lengthening and strengthening of the legs. And as soon as unwrought stones and clubs came into use there was mechanical compensation for the shortening of the arms. The result is an adaptive co-ordination of the total structure to the life of a two-footed hunter.

(6) Darwin says: "The early male forefathers of Man were, as previously stated, probably furnished with great canine teeth; but as they gradually acquired the habit of using stones, clubs, or other weapons, for fighting with their enemies or rivals, they would use their jaws and teeth less and less. In this case the jaws,

---

[4] F. Wood Jones, *Arboreal Man*, pp. 117-22.

together with the teeth, would become reduced in size, as we may feel almost sure from numerous analogous cases."

(7) Hence the profile began to approach the orthognathous type; and it progressed further in that direction on account of accompanying changes in the skull. The skull became less thick and rough, (*a*) because, as the hands (using weapons) superseded the teeth in fighting, jaws and neck grew less massive, and their muscles no longer needed such solid attachments; (*b*) because the head was less liable to injury when no longer used as the chief organ in combat. At the same time the skull slowly increased in capacity and became vaulted to make room for the brains of an animal, which (as we shall see) acquired much knowledge (parietal association area) and lived by the application of its knowledge to the co-ordination of increasingly complex and continuous activities (anterior association area).[5]

(8) Monkeys of most species, whether in the New World or in the Old, are social, living in bands of from ten to fifty or more, and may co-operate occasionally in mutual defence or in keeping watch. Baboons, indeed, are seen in herds of several hundreds; and they are credibly reported to co-operate in raiding plantations, and in defending themselves against leopards, other baboons and even human hunters.[6] Gibbons, again, are social, going in bands to the number of fifty. But the large anthropoids live only in families—the male orang being even of a somewhat solitary habit; three or four families of chimpanzees may for a time associate together. Man, however, is everywhere—with a few doubtful exceptions, probably degenerate—both social and co-operative; and the purpose of his co-operation at the level of the Australian or the Semang is instructive. It is not, as we might suppose, in industry, but in hunting, war, or tribal ceremonies that tribesmen work together—the last no doubt of comparatively recent origin: so that a few thousand years ago there was no co-operation except hunting and war (which come to the same thing).

That the large anthropoids are neither gregarious nor co-operative follows from their having no task in which co-operation would be useful, no common purpose: they are able alone to defend themselves and their families; and when families range apart through the woods their food is in better supply. But the ancestor of Man found an object for association and co-operation in the chase. Spencer, indeed, says that a large carnivore, capable of killing its own prey, profits by being solitary; and this may be true where game is scarce: in the Oligocene and Miocene periods game was not scarce. Moreover, when our ape first pursued game, especially big game (not being by ancient adaptation in structure and instinct a carnivore), he may have been, and probably was, incapable of killing enough prey single-handed; and, if so, he will have profited by becoming both social and co-operative as a hunter, like the wolves and dogs—in short, a sort of wolf-ape (*Lycopithecus*). The pack was a means of increasing the supply of food per unit; and gregariousness increased by natural selection up to the limit set by

[5] On these paragraphs—(3), (4), (5), (6), (7)—see Darwin's *Descent of Man*, 2nd ed., pp. 49-54: whence, of course, I have freely borrowed.

[6] Numerous references might be given, from which I select Hagenbeck, *Beasts and Men*, p. 63.

utility. Hence (as will be shown at length in the next chapter) Man is in character more like a dog or a wolf than he is like any other animal.

(9) Some development of the rudiments of speech may be confidently traced to social co-operation. The gibbon, most social, is also the most vocal of anthropoids; but having no common task in which united action is necessary, he uses his remarkable power of voice (apparently) merely to express his feelings and to keep the troop together. The chimpanzee and the gorilla enjoy probably a close and affectionate family life, but one that makes little or no demand for concerted effort. Hence their vocalisation is very rudimentary. According to R. L. Garner, it is true speech: a chimpanzee (he says) knows the meaning of the sounds he makes, and intends to convey it to some definite individual at whom he looks. But he has at command very few sounds, and those mainly expressive of natural wants.[7] If it be urged that anthropoids do not talk because their lower jaw and tongue have not the special adaptation to speech that is found in Man, it should be considered (a) that if such structure had been useful to them it would have been acquired, as at some time it must have been by Man himself; and (b) that even without any change they might have jabbered well enough to convey a good many discriminated, objective meanings if they had needed to do so: for Man must have begun in that way; he cannot have waited for the development of physical structure before trying to talk. Sufficient intelligence is not wanting to chimpanzees; for in captivity they learn to understand a good deal that is said to them. What they wanted was a sufficient motive for persistently trying to communicate, such that those who made any progress in the art had a living advantage over others. Man had such a motive; because co-operation was necessary to him, not (as we have seen) in industry, but in hunting. In hunting, in planning and directing the hunt, speech is plainly useful; and it is better than gesture, which probably preceded, and generally accompanied it; because, as speech became independent of gesture, it could go on whilst the hands and body were otherwise employed, or where comrades could not see one another—transferring, by a very profitable division of labour, the whole business of expression to organs not otherwise needed. It may not be much more than very simple beginnings of articulate speech that can be traced to early co-operative hunting; but in the beginning lies the whole difficulty. And the situation was particularly favourable to the beginning of language by onomatopœia, imitating the characteristic noises of different animals and of the weapons and actions employed in pursuing and slaying them.

(10) The intelligence and extensive knowledge (compared with anthropoids) that distinguish Man in his lowest known condition are clearly accounted for by his adoption of the hunting life. Already (as we may assume) the most intelligent of living animals, with great knowledge of the forest, he had everything to learn about the world beyond the forest as soon as he ventured into it, and everything to learn about the art of hunting. Depending chiefly upon sight and hearing, he had to learn by observation, and to remember, and to apply all and more than all

[7] R. L. Garner, *Gorillas and Chimpanzees*, ch. vi.: where mention is made of such meanings as "food," "calling to some one," "affection," "good" (said, I suppose, of food), "warning cries," "cold or discomfort," "drink," "illness," "dead": the entire vocabulary, perhaps, not more than twenty signs. The value of Garner's work is disputed.

that the carnivore knows and does instinctively, or learns by following its mother. He must have learned to discriminate all sorts of animals, many of them new in a strange country; their reactions to himself, manner of flight, or of attack, or defence; the spoor of each and its noises; its habits and haunts, where it reposed or went to drink, where to set snares or lie in wait for it. Advancing to the use of weapons, he must have adapted them to his prey; he must have discovered the best materials—wood, or stone, or bone—for making weapons, the best materials for snares, and where to find such things. He must have fixed in his mind this series: game, weapons, the making of them, materials, where found; and must have learned to attend to the items of the series in the necessary order without impatience or confusion: a task far beyond the power of any other animal.

Further, the hunting life supplied a stimulus that had formerly been wanting to our ape. There is some difficulty in comprehending why the anthropoid should be as intelligent as he is; and, similarly, it seemed to Wallace that the savage has intelligence above his needs—"in his large and well-developed brain he possesses an organ quite disproportionate to his actual requirements."[8] This illusion results from our not reflecting that the first task of increasing intelligence is to deal appropriately with details in greater and greater number and variety, and that the details of their life, with both savage and anthropoid, are just what we cannot appreciate. Still, the anthropoid seems to have a rather lazy time of it: especially, he seems to have hardly any occasion for following out a purpose needing some time for its accomplishment. This powerful stimulus the hunting life applies to carnivores, above all to dogs and wolves; and in the same way it affected our ape: compelling him to combine many activities for a considerable period of time, along with his fellows, and direct them to one end in the actual hunting, and (later) to prosecute still other activities for a longer period in preparing weapons and snares to make the hunting more effective. Add to these considerations the development of gesture and rudiments of speech, exacting intelligence for their acquisition and increasing intelligence by their attainment, and the superiority of the lowest savage to an anthropoid is sufficiently explained. Severe must have been the selection of those that were capable of such progress, and correspondingly rapid the advance and differentiation of the species.

(11) Using stones as weapons, and finding that broken stones do most damage, and breaking them for that purpose, the progressive hunter necessarily makes some sparks fly; and if these fall amongst dry leaves or grass, he may light a fire. "In making flint implements sparks would be produced; in polishing them it would not fail to be observed that they became hot; and in this way it is easy to see how the two methods of making fire may have originated."[9] But if the production of fire by friction had been suggested by the polishing of flints, it could hardly have been discovered before the neolithic stage; whereas hearths are known of much earlier date. And it may have happened earlier whilst some one was polishing an arrow or a spear with another piece of wood: a supposition which dispenses with the long inference from a warm flint to a flaming stick. It is a curious fact that to this day in Australia fire is sometimes made by rubbing a spear-thrower upon a

[8] *Natural Selection*, p. 193.
[9] Avebury, *Prehistoric Times*, 7th ed., p. 578.

shield;[10] but I lay no stress upon this, as if such a practice must be traditionary from the earliest discovery of the method. Either in the chipping of flints or in the polishing of spears it is far easier, and a more probable way, to learn the art of making fire than by observing that dried boughs or bamboos driven together by the wind sometimes catch fire; because those processes include the very actions which the art employs: imitation of nature is not called for. It is true that the natives of Nukufetan in the South Seas explain the discovery of fire by their having seen smoke arise from two crossed branches of a tree shaken in the wind;[11] but this, probably, is merely the speculation of some Polynesian philosopher. Volcanoes, too, have been pointed out as a possible source of fire; and, in the myth, Demeter is said to have lit her torches at the crater of Ætna—an action fit for a goddess. But were such an origin of fire conceivable with savages, it would not show how they came to make it themselves. Fire at first must have excited terror. Until uses were known for fire no one could have ventured to fetch it from a volcano, nor to make it by imitating the friction of boughs in the wind. Fires were accidentally lit by man again and again, and much damage done, before he could learn (a) the connection of events, (b) the uses of fire, (c) purposely to produce it, (d) how to control it. The second and fourth of these lessons are much more difficult than the mere making of fire; they are essential, yet generally overlooked. It seems necessary to suppose a series of accidents at each step, in order to show the effects of fire in hardening wood, hollowing wood, cooking game, baking and (later) glazing clay, and so forth. Perhaps a prairie-fire disclosed the advantages of cooking game, and many a prairie was afterwards burnt to that end before a more economical plan was discovered. As to the effect of fire on clay, Lord Avebury observes that clay-vessels may have been invented by (1) plastering gourds or coco-nuts with clay to resist the fire when boiling water in them; (2) observing the effect of fire on the clay; (3) leaving out the vegetable part.[12] This must have been a comparatively recent discovery; though there is some evidence of pottery having been made by palæolithic man. It is impossible to say when fire was discovered; but it was certainly known to the Mousterian culture—say, 50,000 years ago: probably very much earlier; and it was made by hunters.

§ 3. Minor and Secondary Consequences

> § 3. *Minor and Secondary Consequences.*—Alimentary canal; loss of seasonal marriage; naked skin; cannibalism; division into races; Nordic sub-race

(1) The extensive adoption by Man of a flesh-diet many hundreds of thousands of years ago might be expected to have shortened his alimentary canal in comparison with that of the anthropoids; but not much evidence of it is obtainable. Topinard, giving a proportionate estimate, says that in Man it is about six times the length of the body, in the gibbon about eight times. Dr. Arthur Keith, in a private communication with which he has favoured me, says that the adult chimpanzee's intestine is slightly longer than the adult man's, but that the measurements

[10] Spencer and Gillen, *Northern Tribes of Central Australia*, p. 619.

[11] Turner's *Samoa*, p. 285.

[12] Op. cit., p. 579.

are for certain reasons unsatisfactory, and that there have not been enough measurements of adult chimpanzees. We must remember that, on the one hand, the chimpanzee is not exclusively frugivorous, and that, on the other hand, it is not likely that Man has been at any time exclusively carnivorous; though the return of large populations to a vegetarian diet by means of agriculture is recent.

(2) Man has lost the restraint of seasonal marriage, common to the anthropoids with other animals, as determined by food-supply and other conditions of infantile welfare; though, according to Prof. Westermarck, traces of it may still be found in a few tribes.[13] That our domestic carnivores have also lost this wholesome restraint on passion and population points, probably, to some condition of a steadier food-supply as determining or permitting the change amongst ourselves. No growth of prudence, however, or habit of laying up stores can explain the steadier supply of food; since the lower savages have no prudence and no stores. On the whole, the change may be attributed (*a*) to an omnivorous habit being more steadily gratified than one entirely frugivorous or carnivorous; (*b*) to our ancestors having wandered in quest of game from country to country in which the seasons varied, so that the original correspondence of birth-time with favourable conditions of welfare was thrown out. There may also have been causes that kept down the normal numbers of the pack, so as to be equivalent, in scarce seasons, to more abundant food: the hunter's life, whilst securing a richer normal diet, involved many destructive incidents. And this (by the way) was favourable to rapid selection and adaptation; though if the destruction had been great enough to counterbalance the advantages of animal food, it must have frustrated the whole experiment.

(3) There is one characteristic difference of Man from the anthropoids which his hunting habits do not clearly explain—his relatively naked skin. Darwin attributed this condition to sexual selection.[14] He argued that, on the one hand, so far as Man has had the power of choice, women have been chosen for their beauty; and that, on the other hand, women have had more power of selection, even in the savage state, than is usually supposed, and "would generally choose not merely the handsomest men, according to their standard of taste, but those who were at the same time best able to defend and support them." Hence, if a partial loss of hair was esteemed ornamental by our ape-like progenitors, sexual selection, operating age after age, might result in relative nakedness. "The faces of several species of monkey and large surfaces at the posterior end of the body have been denuded of hair; and this we may safely attribute to sexual selection." The beard of the male, and the great length of the hair of the head in some races, especially seem due to this cause. The greater hairiness of Europeans, compared with other races, may be a case of reversion to remote ancestral conditions. But as all races are nearly naked, the common character was probably acquired before the several races had diverged from the common stock.

The species of monkey that have lost the hair on various parts of their bodies, and the beard of males (together with the longer head-hair of women) of our own

---

[13] *Primitive Marriage*, ch. ii.
[14] *Descent of Man*, 2nd ed., pp. 595-604.

race are cases that strongly support the ascription of such secondary sexual characters to sexual selection. Yet, going back to the time before the division of modern Man into races (say, 600,000 years), it seems incredible that any women then went unmarried, hair or no hair, if they were healthy (and the unhealthy soon ceased to exist); or that any man went unmarried, if he could do his share in the hunting-field (and, if not, he also soon ceased to exist). No facts observed amongst extant savages—the choice exerted by women, or the polygamy of chiefs—throw much light upon that ancient state of affairs. There were then no chiefs: the hunt-leader of pack or clan had no authority but his personal prowess, no tradition of ancestry or religion, nor probably the prestige of magic, to give him command of women. Unless, at that time, relative nakedness was strongly correlated with personal prowess in the male and efficiency in the female, it is difficult to understand how it can have been preserved and increased by sexual selection. Forgive me for adding an unkind remark: if the selection of women for their beauty has gone on for hundreds of thousands of years, and has had a cumulative effect upon the race, is not the result disappointing? Go into the street and look. That "women have become more beautiful, according to the general opinion, than men," is not an objective, truly æsthetic judgment, but one determined by causes of which "general opinion" is falsely unconscious. Schopenhauer[15] thought that men are better looking than women; and of average specimens this seems to be true; though, to be sure, he was a sort of misogynist.

Another explanation of Man's nakedness was suggested by Thomas Belt, based on the parallel case of certain races of naked dogs, namely, that he is the better able to free himself from parasites.[16] Darwin mentions this hypothesis and, in a footnote, cites in its favour "a practice with the Australians, when the vermin get troublesome, to singe themselves"; but he says, in the text, "whether this evil is of sufficient magnitude to have led to the denudation of the body through natural selection, may be doubted, since none of the many quadrupeds inhabiting the tropics have, as far as I know, acquired any specialised means of relief."[17] It appears, too, that against the probability of such a result must be set the actual disadvantage of nakedness, as insisted upon by Wallace, who says that savages feel the want of protection and try to cover their backs and shoulders.[18] Still, the disadvantage implied in occasionally feeling the want of protection would not prevent the loss of hair, if this would deliver the race from serious dangers from vermin; and the force of the argument from the condition of other tropical quadrupeds depends, at least in some measure, upon whether or not there is something peculiar in the case of naked dogs and men.

Belt argues that the naked dogs with dark, shining skins, found in Central America and also in Peru,[19] and which were found there at the Spanish conquest, have probably acquired their peculiar condition by natural selection, because they

[15] *Parerga and Paralipomena*, B. II, Kap. 27.

[16] *A Naturalist in Nicaragua*, ch. xi.

[17] Op. cit., p. 57.

[18] *Natural Selection*, pp. 195-7.

[19] Naked races of dogs have also been reported to exist in China, Manila and South Africa; but I can learn no particulars of them.

are despised by the natives, and no care is taken of their breeding, and yet they do not interbreed with the common hairy varieties, as usually happens with artificial stocks. The advantage of a naked skin being the greater freedom it gives from ticks, lice and other vermin, the advantage is especially great for a domestic animal living in the huts of savages, where, because they are inhabited year after year, vermin are extraordinarily abundant. The naked dog, then, differs from tropical quadrupeds which are adapted from a dateless antiquity to such vermin as infest them, by having been thrown by human companionship amongst not only strange vermin, but vermin in extraordinarily dense aggregation. Belt would have guarded a weak point in his case, had he explained why naked races of dogs are so scarce. Hairy races may have been more recently domesticated, or bred for their hairiness, or less addicted to an indoor life.

The case of our own forefather also differs somewhat from that of other tropical mammalia; because, by hypothesis, he underwent pretty rapidly such an extraordinary change of life; which may have brought him into circumstances where vermin, formerly negligible, became highly injurious. "Monkeys," as Belt observes, "change their sleeping-places almost daily"; the Orang is said to construct a fresh nest every night; this is also reported of the Gorilla. Not improbably, then, daily change of locality was the practice of the original anthropoid stock, whence we also are descended: thereby avoiding the accumulation of vermin. Did the hunting life introduce a new habit? In the old frugivorous forest life, the custom was to get up into some tree for the night, and within a short radius there were hundreds equally suitable; and, therefore, there was nothing to check the natural preference for a fresh one. When, however, the hunting pack began to make its lair on the ground, there was no such wide choice amongst caves, rock-shelters, or thickets: one might be better than any other for miles around. If, then, they settled down there as in a common lair, the circumstances were, for the time, favourable to the multiplication of vermin, and therefore to nakedness of skin, in order the more easily to be rid of them. Perhaps, then, this difference of Man from the anthropoids may be referred to one common cause with all the others—the hunting life. There, too, the defilement of blood made fur inconvenient to animals not apt to cleanse themselves, like those in the true carnivorous heredity and tradition.

When we consider how injurious some insects are to vertebrate life, being suspected of having caused in some cases the extinction of species, can it be said that facility in ridding oneself of such vermin as lice and ticks is an inadequate cause of human nakedness, or not one that might outweigh the drawbacks of cold and wet? It is not, however, incompatible with the action of sexual selection, tending to the same result; nor, again, with the preferential destruction of hairy children if ever infanticide was practised. A further possible ground of deliberate selection may have been the mere ambition of differing from other animals; for a tribe on the Upper Amazons is reported to depilate to distinguish themselves from the monkeys, and the wish to be superior to other animals led a tribe in Queensland to pretend that they, unlike kangaroos, etc., have no fathers according to the flesh.[20] Admitting that this last motive can hardly have been primitive, still, our nakedness may

---

[20] W. E. Ling Roth, *North Queensland Ethnology*, Bulletin V. § 81.

be a resultant of several causes.

(4) Cannibalism, where it has been found amongst extant peoples, or is known to have been formerly practised, was often justified by certain magical or animistic ideas, but sometimes frankly by dietetic taste, or by the satisfaction of revenge or of emphatic triumph over an enemy. Was it an ancient and perhaps general custom? The excavations at Krapina in Croatia disclosed along with remains of the Neanderthal species, which seems to have had a habitation there, those of rhinoceros and cave-bear and of some other kind of Man; and "some of the human bones had been apparently split open: on that slender basis the Krapina men have been suspected of cannibalism."[21] If the suspicion is valid, the practice existed (say) 50,000 years ago in one species of Man; and perhaps much earlier, if we consider how it was merely an extension of the practice of devouring game to include the slain members of a hostile pack; for as primitive Man, or Lycopithecus, his pre-human forebear, no doubt regarded other animals as upon the same level as himself, so he will have regarded human enemies as upon the same footing with other animals. That true carnivores are not generally cannibals may be put down to their more ancient and perfect adaptation to a predatory life. For them persistent cannibalism would have been too destructive, and for us it belongs to the experimental stage of history; though, of course, even in recent times, under stress of famine, reversion to the practice is not unknown to civilised men.

(5) The extraordinary variability of modern Man (considered as one species) in stature, shape of skull, size and power of brain, colour, hairiness, quality of hair, and other characters, physical and mental, may be referred chiefly to his having become adapted to various local conditions upon settling here or there for long periods of time after wandering over the world in quest of game. The settling of offshoots of the original stock in certain regions long enough for them to undergo adaptation to local circumstances is the simplest explanation of existing races: the Negro adapted to equatorial Africa; the Asiatic stock ("Mongolian") to Central Asia; the Mediterranean race to the neighbourhood of the sea after which it is named. As to the Nordic sub-race (of the Mediterranean, we may suppose), with its fair hair and skin, it has the appearance of an Arctic beast of prey, like the Polar bear. The snow-leopard of the Himalaya is found at a midway stage of such adaptation. Some geologists and zoologists now believe that, during the Glacial Period, the climate of Northern Europe was not everywhere such as necessarily to destroy the local fauna and flora, and in that case our ancestors may for ages have maintained themselves there; or, if that was impossible (as the absence of palæolithic remains in Scandinavia seems to indicate), they may have roamed for many ages along the borders of glaciation, perhaps as far as the Pacific Coast. Chinese annals refer to fair tribes in Eastern Siberia 200 years before the Christian era;[22] and it seems requisite to imagine some extensive reservoir of mankind in order to explain the origin of the vast hordes which in prehistoric as in historical times again and again invaded Europe—hordes

---

[21] A. Keith, *The Antiquity of Man*, p. 134.
[22] M. A. Czaplicka, *My Siberian Year*, p. 230.

> "which the populous North
> Poured ever from her frozen loins, to pass
> Rhene or the Danau; when her barbarous sons
> Came like a deluge on the South, and spread
> Beneath Gibraltar to the Libyan sands."

That the race was formerly fairer than it is now may be inferred from the whiteness of its children's hair: the trait has outlived its utility. The occurrence of a fair complexion in some mountain tribes, in the Alps, e. g., has occasioned the conjecture that it may be due in some way to mountainous conditions,[23] of which snow might be one; but, if we suppose that the Nordic race extended during the Glacial Period into Western Europe (having already acquired its distinctive characters), a fair complexion in the Alps may be understood by supposing that, whilst the greater number of them followed the ice-sheet back to the north-east, some followed it southward up into the mountains—if the complexion is really ancient there.

Two objections to this hypothesis will occur to every one: (i) Why are not the Esquimo fair? Because, I suppose, they are much more recent immigrants into the Arctic regions, and perhaps were fully clothed when they arrived there. (ii) Could the Nordic people have existed in such circumstances unclothed? Whether this was possible physiologists must judge. We see the Fuegians maintain themselves, practically naked, under very inclement conditions. And it is not necessary to assume that the Nordic hunters were entirely naked; since the correlation between the hair, eyes and all parts of the skin is such that, if the whitening of any part (say the hair) was sufficiently advantageous to determine natural selection, the remainder of the body would be similarly affected. And, no doubt, the Mediterranean race was always whitish.

The Amerinds seem to have been derived chiefly from the Asiatic race. Pygmies and Australians may represent separate and still older stocks. But, as a result of migrations and conquests, most peoples are of mixed descent; and hence (i) individuals in the same locality sometimes vary greatly, because they inherit the blood of different strains in different proportions; and (ii) classification is difficult, so that whilst some observers are content to find half a dozen races, Deniker enumerates twenty-nine.

Besides general racial differences, there exist within each race and within each national group further differences between individuals in their physical, and still more in their mental, stature and ability. As it was necessary that Man should vary greatly in undergoing adaptation to the hunting life (as well as to different local environments), he was in an organic condition favourable to further variation.[24] And this has been utilised in his adaptation to a certain special condition of his gregariousness, namely, life in the hunting-pack; for this requires a difference of personality between leaders and followers, first in the chase and later in war. A good democrat may think it would have been a better plan to make all men equal from the first; and I would it had been so; for then the head of the race would not

[23] Ripley, *The Races of Europe*, pp. 76-7.
[24] Darwin, *Animals and Plants under Domestication*, Pop. ed., II. p. 308.

have had to drag along such an altogether disproportionate tail: a tail so huge and unwieldy that one may doubt whether it can ever be extricated from the morass of barbarism. But in the early days of gregariousness, a pack could not have held together, or have hunted efficiently, if all had been equal and each had exercised the right of private judgment. So in successful packs one led and the rest followed; as they still do, and will continue to do, of whatever kind may be the leader. And of all structures that make up a human being the most variable is the brain: the differences between men in stature and physique are trifling compared with those in mental power. Whatever feat of strength your Samson can perform, half a dozen ordinary men can also accomplish; but in every generation tasks are carried out by intellectual athletes, toward which all the ordinary men in the world, uniting their efforts, could do nothing—absolutely nothing.

§ 4. Prey and Competitors

§ 4. *Prey and Competitors.* —Climate and landscape in Oligocene and
   Miocene; animals, herbivorous; anthropoids and their stature in
   late Oligocene; carnivorous contemporaries

If we suppose the differentiation of the *Hominidæ* from the *Anthropoidea* to have begun in the Upper Oligocene, and that the decisive change was initiated by some ape that adopted the life of a hunter, it is interesting to consider what the world was like in which he lived, what sort of animals surrounded him, what animals probably became his prey, and what were his rivals in the chase.[25]

The surface of the planet was less mountainous than at present; in Europe the Pyrenees had risen, but the Alps were only beginning to rise; and in Asia the Himalayas began to dominate the world only in the middle of the next epoch, the Miocene. The distribution of land and water, too, was very different in the Oligocene from that which we now see: Europe was divided from Asia by a broad gulf stretching from the Indian Ocean to the Arctic Circle, and an arm of this gulf toward the west submerged a great part of Central Europe; Asia was broadly connected with North America, where now the sea penetrates between Siberia and Alaska; Africa had no connection with either Europe or Asia; North and South America were separated—perhaps at Panama. In the Miocene, Europe, Asia and Africa became united. These physiographic changes may have affected climate; for during the Eocene tropical conditions prevailed far to the north, and coal-beds were laid down in Alaska; but from the Oligocene onwards there was a gradual fall of temperature, slow at first, but ending (for the present) in the cataclysms of the Glacial Period. There was also a decrease in some regions of atmospheric moisture, which determines the density of vegetation. In its general character the vegetation was similar to that which now prevails in tropical, subtropical and temperate regions of the world. The species of plants now existing had not yet

---

[25] The contents of this section lie outside my own studies, and have been taken from various books of Geology and Palæontology: I must especially mention Prof. Osborne's *Age of Mammals* (1910) and Prof. Scott's *Land Mammals in the Western Hemisphere* (1913). I have also profited by inspecting the Palæontological Gallery at South Kensington with the help of its excellent Guide-Book.

arrived; but of the same genera and families as those we see, conifers, palms and dicotyledonous flowering plants crowded the forests and overhung the rivers. The forests were more extensive and continuous than ours outside the tropics; for by degrees browsing animals, feeding down the young trees, check the renovation of forests and clear open spaces, where grasses grow; changes of temperature limit the northern or southern extension of certain kinds of plants, and a failure of humidity starves all the larger kinds; converting, at successive stages, forest into steppe and steppe into desert.

Animals, especially mammalia, with which chiefly we are concerned, were, at the close of the Oligocene, very different from any that now roam the lands; all the species, most genera, many families and some whole orders have since disappeared. But there were plenty to eat and a good many to dread. Until we know the neighbourhood in which our ape's adventures began, nothing precise can be said of his circumstances. Probably it was somewhere in the Old World, and probably it was in Asia. Unfortunately, we know nothing of the zoological antiquities of Asia until the early Miocene, and even then a very small selection of what must have existed, because geologists have hitherto explored a very small part of the continent—a few beds in north-western and northern India and in Burmah. But there is so much evidence of the migrations of animals in successive ages of the Tertiary Period, that any remains from the Oligocene and Miocene will help us to understand what sort of neighbours our remote ancestors had to live amongst.

For prey there was great variety of birds and reptiles (everywhere eaten by savages) and fishes; but we are most concerned with the mammalia, which he may be supposed to have pursued afoot. Of these the most important are the hoofed animals, which fall into two great groups, perhaps not closely connected—the odd-toed (Perissodactyls) and the even-toed (Artiodactyls). During the Oligocene there lived in Europe, or in North America, or in both—and, therefore, probably in Asia—numbers of the odd-toed group: tapirs; rhinoceroses of several species, some without horns, some with, some amphibious (Amynodonts), all smaller than their modern representatives; chalicotheres, strange beasts something like horses, but instead of hoofs they had claws on their toes—perhaps survived in China into the Pleistocene; small predecessors of the horse with three toes on each foot; titanotheres, hugest animals of their age, extinct in the middle of it—something like the rhinoceros and nearly as big as an elephant (*Brontotherium*). Of the even-toed group, pig-like animals abounded, and some true pigs appeared; entelodonts, or giant-pigs, were common; anthracotheres, somewhat pig-like in size and shape; ancestral camels about the size of sheep were to be had in North America; oreodonts, unfinished-looking creatures of many species; primitive deer and other ruminants, small in size and not having yet grown any horns. In Europe, during the Upper Oligocene, cœnotheres, small and graceful animals, lived in large herds around the lakes. There were also primitive proboscidia about half the size of modern elephants; many insectivores; and, amongst rodents, beavers and tailless hares. Generally, animals of this age that have left descendants were smaller than their modern representatives; and notably their brains were smaller.

In the Lower and Middle Miocene there appeared also horned cervuline deer, chevrotaines, and horned antelopes; dinotheres and mastodons, probably from Africa; primitive hedgehogs, moles and shrews; and in the Upper Miocene, hipparion, true hares, several varieties of hornless giraffe, true deer, and ancestral sheep. True horses and cattle are first known from Pliocene beds; but it is needless to follow the story further: the fauna becomes more and more modern in its character, and uncouth forms die out.

Anthropoids are first met with in the Miocene and in Europe: pliopithecus, allied to the gibbons, in the Lower; and dryopithecus, related to the chimpanzee, in the Middle Miocene; but they are believed to have come from Asia. There, in Pliocene beds of the Siwaliks (southern foot-hills of the Himalayas), occur the orang and chimpanzee, besides macaques, langurs and baboons. Since the orang is now found only in Borneo and Sumatra, and the chimpanzee only in Africa, southern Asia seems to have been the centre from which the anthropoids dispersed; and this seems to be the chief positive ground for believing that the human stock began to be differentiated in that region. Since, again, by the Middle Miocene a chimpanzee form had already migrated into Europe, it may be assumed that the orang was already distinct from it (and perhaps had spread eastward): the differentiation of these genera must, therefore, have happened earlier; and, therefore, also the differentiation of the human stock; so that this event cannot be put later than some time in the Oligocene.

How big was Lycopithecus to begin with? The answer to this question must affect our view of his relations both to prey and to enemies. Inasmuch as the three extant anthropoids and Man are all of about the same size, there is a presumption that their common ancestor was in stature superior to the gibbons and to the largest monkeys—in fact, a "giant" ape (to borrow a term from Dr. Keith). Dryopithecus "was smaller than the chimpanzee, but much larger than the gibbon."[26] Awaiting further evidence of fossils, which is much to be desired, it is probable, on the whole, that Lycopithecus weighed less on the average than modern man, but more than the wolf.

As to competitors and aggressive enemies, there were snakes and crocodiles; but, confining our attention to carnivorous mammals, the time seems to have been favourable to the enterprise of a new hunter. By the middle of the Oligocene, the ancient Creodonts (primitive flesh-eaters which had flourished in the Eocene) were nearly extinct, represented in the deposits by their last surviving family, the Hyœnodonts. Ancestors of the modern carnivores, such as may be called by anticipation dogs and cats, derived (according to Prof. Scott) from the Creodont Family of the Miacidæ, were becoming numerous, but for the most part were still of small size. Apparently, the primitive dogs and their allies must, for some time, have been more formidable adversaries than the primitive cats, especially if we suppose them to have already begun to hunt in pack; and this is not improbable, both on account of their structure and because several distinct varieties and even genera, now extant, have that habit—such as wolf, jackal, dingo, dhole, Cape hunting-dog, etc. In the Upper Oligocene of North America, occurs a dog as big as a large modern wolf, and in Europe the bear-like dog, Amphicyon, of about the same size,

---

[26] A. Keith, *The Human Body*, p. 58.

but said to have been clumsy and slow-moving. There were several other dog-like species; they continue in the Miocene, and some of them increase in bulk; but true modern dogs or wolves (*Canis*) do not appear before the Pliocene. Then, too, first occur true bears (*Ursus*); hyænas in the Upper Miocene. "Cats" belong to two sub-families: (i) the true felines, our modern species and their ancestors; and (ii) the machærodonts, or sabre-toothed cats. The latter first appear in North America in the Lower Oligocene; the former in Europe in the Middle Oligocene. The sabre-tooths are so called from their thin, curved upper canines; which were so long (3 to 6 inches) that it is not easy to understand how they could open their mouths wide enough to bite with them. That they were effective in some way is proved by the fact that machærodonts, first appearing in the Lower Oligocene, increased in numbers and diversity of species for ages, and some of them in bulk. In North America, in the Upper Oligocene, one species was as large as a jaguar, and some of the biggest and most terrifying were contemporary with Man, and only became extinct in the Pleistocene. Their limbs were relatively shorter and thicker than those of the *Felinæ*. These, the true cats, at first progressed more slowly than the *Machærodontidæ*; but in the Siwalik deposits (Pliocene) there occur, along with machærodonts, forms resembling the leopard and the lynx, with others as large as tigers. The largest of all this group seems to have been the cave-lion, perhaps a large variety of the common African lion, which also lived with Man in Europe in the Pleistocene. These were serious competitors in the hunting-life of Lycopithecus and of primitive Man; and the effect of such competition in exterminating inferior forms is shown by the fate of the carnivorous marsupials of South America (allied to *Thylacinus*), which were the predatory fauna of that region, until in the Pliocene, North and South America having become united by continuous land, cats and dogs came in from the northern continent and put an end to them; and also by the fate of the creodonts, which in the Oligocene seem everywhere to have been exterminated by the new carnivores. In both cases the beaten competitors were very inferior in the size and complexity of their brains; and if Man has succeeded in the struggle for life against the same foes, in spite of his inferior bodily adaptation, it is probably due to his very superior brains. This may also be the reason why modern Man (*Homo sapiens!*), wandering everywhere over the world, has everywhere exterminated such experiments in human nature as Pithecanthropus, Eoanthropus, and Neanderthalensis; as others are soon to follow them into the Hades of extinct species.

These few pages give a ridiculously faint sketch of the animal world amidst which our remote ancestors began their career. But it may serve to indicate that there was always plenty to eat if you could kill it, and plenty of rivals who wanted their share. After the disappearance of the dinosaurs at the close of the Cretaceous period, the mammalia, already numerous, developed rapidly, and spread in ever multiplying numbers and diverging shapes over the whole area of the land. We may take it that from the Middle Eocene (at least) onwards the earth has always been as full of wild beasts as it would hold. To understand what it was like in the Middle Oligocene, one should read the adventures of hunters in South Africa seventy or eighty years ago (their verisimilitude is vouched for by

Livingstone),[27] before a gun in the hands of every Kaffir had begun to thin the vast herds that then covered the whole landscape, and in whose numbers the wild hunters and the lions could make no appreciable diminution. The little Bushmen regarded themselves and the lions as joint owners and masters of all the game. The masters fought one another, indeed; but there was no necessity to fight, for there was more than enough for both: lions were then sometimes met in gangs of ten or a dozen. Game throughout the Cainozoic ages was abundant and of all sizes: many small, many middle-sized and some prodigious. Even in the Eocene, some of the Amblypoda (*Dinoceras*, Am.) and of the Barypoda (*Arsinotherium*, Af.) were as big as rhinoceroses; in the Oligocene, Titanotheres not much smaller than elephants; in South America, in Miocene and Pliocene times, the Toxodonts; in the Pleistocene, Ground-sloths of huge bulk, and Glyptodonts. Of Families still represented amongst living animals, dinotheres and mastodons occur in the Miocene; and elephant, rhinoceros, hippopotamus, giraffe have abounded from the Pliocene to recent times, in many species, over most of Africa and the northern hemisphere. Even the marsupials in Australia produced a species (*Diprotodon*) as large as a rhinoceros with a skull three feet long. Any one of these would have been a meal for a whole pack of hunters, if they could kill it—as we may be sure they could.

§ 5. CONCLUSION

§ 5. *Conclusion.* —Summary

From the addiction of some ancestral ape to animal food, and to the life of a hunter in order to obtain it, then, the special characteristics of Man seem to be natural consequences. The hypothesis from which everything follows is exceptionally simple and moderate. It is generally admitted that our ancestor was a large anthropoid—possibly more gregarious than others, possibly more apt to live upon the ground; but neither of these suppositions is requisite. He was adapted to his life, as the chimpanzee and gorilla are to theirs: in which, probably, they have gone on with little change for ages. But into his life a disturbing factor entered—the impulse to attack, hunt and eat animals, which extensively replaced his former peaceable, frugivorous habit. The cause of this change may have been a failure in the supply of his usual diet, or an "accidental variation" of appetite. Not a great number need have shared in the hunting impulse; it is enough that a few should have felt it, or even one. If advantageous and inheritable, it would spread through his descendants. It was advantageous (*a*) in enlarging their resources of nutrition, and (*b*) in enabling them to escape from the tropical forest. On the other hand, to those least fit for the new life it brought the disadvantages of more strenuous exertion and of competition with other carnivorous types. But with hands and superior intelligence, those that had the requisite character succeeded. There was rapid selection of those whose variations of structure, character, activity were most effective in dealing with game and with enemies; especially of those who combined and co-operated, and learned to direct co-operation by some rudimentary speech.

But, again, the hunting impulse here assumed to have possessed some anthropoid was not something entirely new; anthropoids and many other Primates are

---

[27] *Travels and Researches in Western Africa*, ch. vii.

known to seize and devour birds, lizards and even small mammals when chance offers an easy opportunity. It is merely a greater persistence in this behaviour that turns it into hunting. How very improbable that such a change should *not* sometimes occur! Is it not likely to have occurred often, and with many failures? Similarly, of the resulting changes: the differentiation of our hands and feet is only an advance upon what you see in the gorilla; as for our ground-life, can the adult male gorilla be fairly called arboreal? Several Primates use unwrought weapons; most of them lead a gregarious life, to which our own is a return; they are co-operative at least in defence; like many other animals, they communicate by gestures and inarticulate vocal cries. Co-operative hunting, indeed, seems to be new in our Order; but since wolves and dogs, or their ancestors, fell in with it some time or other, why should it be beyond the capacity of apes? On second thoughts, is the co-operative raiding of plantations by baboons something altogether different from hunting in pack? Thus at each occasion of change in structure or function, Lycopithecus merely carried some tendency of the other Primates a little further, and a little further; until, certainly, he went a long way. The whole movement can be distinctly pictured throughout, and it has an air of being natural or even inevitable. Few hypotheses ask us to grant less than this one.

Moreover, if the story is not true, Man is an exception to the rule of animal life, that the structure of every organism is made up of apparatus subserving its peculiar conditions of nutrition and reproduction. Indeed, conditions of nutrition are the ground of the differentiation of animals and plants. Conditions of reproduction need not here be considered, as the apparatus is the same in the anthropoids and in ourselves. With many species to avoid being eaten and to mate are the reasons for some secondary characters, such as protective armour or coloration, fleetness with its correlative structures, nuptial plumage, and so forth. But to avoid being eaten and to mate, it is first of all necessary to eat and live; and accordingly, for each sort of animal, starting from the organisation of some earlier stock, its structure and activities are determined by the kind of food it gets, and the conditions of getting it: in our case, the hunting of game afoot.

CHAPTER II

ON THE DIFFERENTIATION OF THE HUMAN FROM THE ANTHROPOID MIND

§ 1. Heredity, Adaptation, Accommodation

§ 1. *Heredity, Adaptation, Accommodation*

FOLLOWING the general belief that Man is descended from a stock nearly allied to the greater anthropoids—Orang, Chimpanzee, Gorilla—we may assume that his mental endowments were once much the same as theirs; and that, so far as they are still the same, *heredity* sufficiently explains his having them. Thus the senses, perception, the simpler forms of comparison and inference, the appetites and many of the instincts and emotions are common to us with the apes, are seen in our children under three years old, and (in short) constitute that generic consciousness (as I have called it) from which the human mind in general and the peculiar traits of races and individuals are differentiated.

So much for heredity; but the differences of the human from the anthropoid mind, alike in intelligence and in character, are enormous, and must be accounted for in some other way. Allowing for some original specific difference which we can hardly hope to discover, the changes that have taken place may be considered as the result of *adaptation* to those habits of life under which our species (now ranking zoologically as a Family) has been developed. And this adaptation I shall assume to have been brought about under conditions of natural selection: human races, as we now see them, being the survivors of many variations, more or less successful, and the others having been destroyed. For good judges are of opinion that, amongst the discovered remains of ancient specimens of the human family, some that exhibit marked deviations from the modern type—Neanderthalensis, Eoanthropus, Pithecanthropus—should be regarded not as belonging to our ancestral line, but rather as representing distinct species that have failed in the struggle for existence.[28]

But besides the innate dispositions of human nature determined by heredity and natural selection, which are found in some measure universally, because they are adaptations to conditions that, at one time and not long ago, weighed upon the ancestors of all of us, there are numerous traits (some of them quite superficial) that vary from country to country and from age to age, according to the economic or political type of the society in which a man lives, his place therein, geographical

---

[28] See *The Antiquity of Man,* by Arthur Keith.

circumstances, religious institutions and the countless causes that govern manners and customs. In the lives of most men these traits are not necessary; they may be adopted and cast aside more than once in an individual's career: they are temporary *accommodations* due to education, imitation, tradition; and, in fact, are often the disguises of human nature. Still, as society grows more and more complex, orderly and stable, there is, no doubt, again some natural selection of those individuals who are capable of undergoing the requisite accommodations. Those that cannot endure the restraints of civilisation, wander away; the extremely lazy, improvident, dishonest, or aggressive, in considerable numbers, perish.

§ 2. The Original Stock and the Conditions of Differentiation

§ 2. *The Original Stock and the Conditions of Differentiation.* — Mind of the higher apes the best clue to that of the original stock. Conditions of differentiation: the hunting life; geographical diffusion; social life; imaginations concerning Magic and Animism

To the original mentality of man we can only seek a clue in the higher Primates, and especially in the extant anthropoids. No doubt, during the long millennia that have elapsed since the separation of our own stock from those of other genera and species, they also have undergone some evolution, but probably much less change than we have. Unfortunately, our knowledge of their habits and abilities is still deplorably limited. It seems certain, however, that their intelligence is much greater than that of any other kind of animal. They must have extensive knowledge of their habitat, of all the forest can yield for food or shelter, and of its other denizens dangerous or otherwise. They construct for themselves some sort of sleeping-place, not much inferior to the Australians' "lean-to," by piling branches together in the trees. Toward men, anthropoids seem to be unaggressive, and usually retreat from them; but, when attacked, defend themselves with fury. From other animals the male gorilla has nothing to fear, and he defends his family against leopards; the chimpanzee is said to fight leopards with varying success; and, as for the orang, Dyak chiefs told Wallace that no animals dare attack him, except crocodiles and pythons, and that he kills both of them.[29] The food of these apes is chiefly fruit and the tender shoots of trees and bamboos; but they sometimes eat eggs and young birds; and the gorilla is said to eat small mammals: in confinement they all take cooked flesh freely. Socially, they hardly get beyond family life. Orangs male and female are even seen alone, and young ones together without parents; gorillas are seen in family parties; chimpanzees in families, and occasionally three or four families in company. It is said that gorillas and chimpanzees have been seen together in a large band. I have met with no report of these animals fighting amongst themselves, except that male gorillas sometimes fight for a wife. Gorillas have also been said, upon very slight evidence, to be polygamous; chimpanzees and orangs seem to be monogamous.[30] Their family life is probably, as amongst all the other Primates, affectionate: the long youth of their children implies much parental care. Whilst the smaller anthropoids — siamang and gibbon — go in troops, as also do the

[29] *Malay Archipelago*, pp. 46-7.

[30] According to R. L. Garner, however, both gorillas and chimpanzees are polygamous. See *Gorillas and Chimpanzees*, pp. 54 and 214.

baboons and most monkeys of both hemispheres, the less sociability of the great anthropoids may be understood to result (*a*) from the limited supply of the right sort of food for them, even in the tropical forest to which they are confined — since animals of their bulk must consume a great deal; and (*b*) from their having no need of combining for the purpose of defence.

From the type thus outlined the mentality of the human race has departed so widely that some even of those who believe that our bodies have been derived from some simian stock (e. g. Wallace) hesitate to admit that our minds can have had a similar history. But as everywhere else in the animal kingdom mind and body constitute one organism, it is reasonable to consider whether the differentiation of the mind of man may not be understood to have taken place under the same conditions as those which determined the transformation of his body. What were these conditions?

(*a*) In the foregoing chapter I have collected a number of facts and arguments pointing to the probability that the chief cause of the evolution of the human Family was the adoption by some anthropoid (or allied form) of the life of the hunter in order to obtain animal food. That the change from a frugivorous to a carnivorous diet may itself have had some effect upon our temperament and activity is possible; but I lay no stress upon that. Most monkeys are almost exclusively frugivorous; the only Primate, except man, that depends a good deal upon animal food is, I believe, the crab-eating macaque (*Macacus cynomolgus*), of the Burmese and Malay littoral; yet monkeys are the most alert and active of animals; some of them are amongst the most courageous; anthropoids are amongst the most powerful. A carnivorous diet alone would not explain any changes in the shape and proportions of our trunk and limbs, nor the upright gait, nor the gregarious habit, nor the development of the brain, nor the invention of weapons, nor the use of fire, nor any of the mental and emotional characteristics that distinguish man from the other Primates; but all these things readily follow from our remote ancestor's adoption of the life of the hunter.

Sociologists, surveying extant peoples, have usually distinguished four stages of culture, the hunting, pastoral, agricultural and manufacturing; and some have indicated what they suppose to have been a still earlier stage, the "collecting," such as may be seen, e. g., amongst the Fuegians. But the collecting state is plainly degenerate, the resource of tribes fallen into distress; it cannot have been the first stage, because it implies no conditions that tend in any way to develop body or mind or society. That hunting came first is a true intuition: and, to understand the development of human nature, we need only refer the hunting-life back to the very origin of the human stock.[31]

(*b*) The great anthropoids are all confined to the equatorial forests; and it is

---

[31] This view is not opposed to the suggestion I have somewhere seen that the collecting activities of women, whilst men hunted, may, at some stage, have led to property and domestication of plants and animals. Again, the pastoral and agricultural states are not necessarily successive: it depends upon local conditions. For an excellent survey of the gradual rise of primitive culture and the difficulties it encountered, see H. Spencer's *Industrial Institutions, Principles of Sociology*, Vol. III.

obvious that, with their diet, it is impossible to pass out of tropical or (at furthest) sub-tropical regions. But the adoption of a flesh diet enabled the human stock to extend the range of its hunting (allowing for gradual adaptation to climate or accommodation by clothing) to any country that supplied the requisite prey; and, accordingly, in course of time, it wandered to every part of the world. The settling of various off-shoots of the original stock in certain regions long enough for them to undergo adaptation to local conditions is (as we have seen) the simplest explanation of existing races.

(*c*) Whilst none of the great anthropoids has advanced socially beyond family life, man is everywhere (with few and doubtful exceptions) gregarious—living at the lowest grade in tribes or bands of about fifty; and the gregarious life is one of the most important conditions of his peculiar development. Possibly, he may originally have been more gregarious than any extant anthropoid, in spite of his not needing society for defence, and of its seeming to be for so large a frugivorous animal inconvenient in relation to nutrition. Moreover, if the great anthropoids and our own ancestors were descended from some stock of the lower monkeys, such as always go in troops, the gregarious instinct may have remained with them as a latent character. Still, it is my conjecture that man became gregarious, or recovered the social habit, because of the utility of co-operative hunting; so that he became at first a sort of wolf-ape. This will be discussed in the next section. I observe here, however, that the hypothesis helps us to understand why man is still imperfectly sociable; the purpose of the hunting-pack, each wolf-ape seeking prey, was unfavourable to social life in other relations. That in human life group-consciousness preceded self-consciousness is a groundless and fantastic notion: all known savages are fully self-conscious, as their sentiments and behaviour imply; and even the higher brutes are (in my judgment) self-conscious in their relations with others. Current speculations about fashion, imitation, tradition, crowd-psychology, are in danger of exaggeration, and overlook the patent facts of individualism, as shown by the hypocrite, the criminal, the vagrant, the contra-suggestible, the hermit, the sceptic, the saint. Some people—without being in any way morbid—find that a good deal of solitude is necessary to the complete life: by nature the student and the pioneer escape from the crowd.

(*d*) The later stages of human development have been considerably modified by certain imaginary conditions peculiar to Man; for he—we know not at what date—invented them. These may be summed up under the names of Magic and Animism; and in subsequent chapters they will be discussed, with their astonishing vagaries and still more astonishing reactions upon human life.

The chief conditions, then, to which man has been adapted, and thereby differentiated in body and mind from the anthropoid stock, I take to be four: the hunting life; geographical circumstances; social life; and his own imaginations.

§ 3. Primal Society

§ 3. *Primal Society.*—Forms of gregariousness amongst Mammalia; the hunting-pack most likely original of human society. Other conjectures

In looking for the probable form of the earliest human or (rather) prehuman society, one naturally makes a survey of other mammalian societies; and the task is soon accomplished. It is surprising how few and simple the types of them are, in contrast with the elaborate polities of some hymenoptera and of the termites: these have much greater superficial resemblance to modern human societies; but, in fact, they are families rather than societies; their interesting activities will one day probably be traced to relatively simple mechanisms; and in every way they are too remote from us for any useful comparison. As for mammalian societies, even using the term to include families, they may be classified under four or five types:

(1) Families: (*a*) Monogamous: of which the best examples seem to be found in some monkeys. Many of the cats are believed to pair monogamously; but it is doubtful whether, or in what measure, the male takes part in the rearing of the whelps.

(*b*) Polygamous: characteristic of many species of deer;—after the breeding-season, the stags often wander away by themselves.

(2) Associations of families without apparent structure or organisation, such as those of the vizcacha and the beaver. They have no leaders, and make no attempt at mutual defence; but their inco-ordinated activities, in making their burrows, dams, etc., have results which, especially in the case of the beavers, look as if the animals had worked upon a common, premeditated plan. Gregariousness exists widely in the animal kingdom without any utility in attack or defence, but merely for convenience of breeding, or for the advantage of signalling the approach of danger, from any direction, to the whole flock.

(3) Troops or herds, comprising several families. This type is common amongst monkeys: generally the families are monogamous, and both parents care for the offspring; they have leaders, and combine in mutual defence. This is especially effective with the baboons—who, however, are polygamous. A very similar type is characteristic of cattle; who also have leaders as the result of battle between the bulls, each trying to control and keep together as many cows as he can; and they often combine their forces against beasts of prey.

(4) Hunting-packs—most noticeable with wolves and wild dogs: they have leaders, and probably an order of precedence determined by battle. In the breeding-season (February to August) a pack of wolves breaks up into pairs; but whether their pairing is for life or merely seasonal is disputed; and it is also doubtful whether the male takes any share in caring for the puppies; such habits may vary in different localities.[32] The numbers of the pack depend on circumstances, and are now much smaller in Canada than in Russia.

---

[32] It is certainly believed by fox-hunters that a fox feeds his vixen when she is occupied with their family, and that "if the vixen is killed he will bring up the family by himself."—Thomas F. Dale, *The Fox*, pp. 12, 13.

Nothing incredible in this—nor of wolves. Can the vixen provide for herself and litter alone? If not, the dog must do it: else there could be no foxes or wolves.

However, de Canteleu denies that the he-wolf takes any part in rearing the young (*La Chasse du Loup*, p. 30).

Was our own primitive society, then, like any of these? Since direct evidence cannot be obtained, we must be guided in forming our hypothesis by two considerations: (*a*) what type of society gives the best explanation of human nature as we now find it? and (*b*) for which type can we give the best reason why it should have been adopted? So I point out (*a*) that man, in character, is more like a wolf or dog than he is like any other animal; and (*b*) that for the forming of a pack there was a clear ground in the advantage to be obtained by co-operative hunting.[33]

It must be admitted that Darwin, discussing sexual selection in man, suggests a different hypothesis. He says: "Looking far enough back in the stream of time, and judging from the social habits of man as he now exists, the most probable view is that he aboriginally lived in small communities, each with a single wife, or if powerful with several, whom he jealously guarded against all other men. Or he may not have been a social animal, and yet have lived with several wives, like the gorilla; for all the natives 'agree that but one adult male is seen in a band; when the young male grows up, a contest takes place for mastery, and the strongest, by killing and driving out the others, establishes himself as the head of the community.' The younger males, being thus expelled and wandering about, would, when at last successful in finding a partner, prevent too close inter-breeding within the limits of the same family."[34] The information concerning the polygamy of the gorilla, quoted here from Dr. Savage, who wrote in 1845, has not since (I believe) been confirmed, except by Prof. Garner.[35]

Naturally, the above passage has attracted the attention of anthropologists; and I am sorry to expose myself to the charge of immodesty in venturing to put forward a different view. Atkinson in his essay on *Primal Law*, edited with qualified approval by Andrew Lang, starts from Darwin's hypothesis, and merely modifies it by urging that the young males, when driven off by their father, did not wander away, but kept near the family, always on the watch to murder their father. This amendment he makes, because he had observed the same habits in cattle and horses. Then, through a row of hypotheses with little evidence or rational connection, he arrives at an explanation of certain savage laws of avoidance, exogamy, etc. More recently, Prof. Freud has produced a most ingenious and entertaining essay on *Totem und Tabu*, in which he builds upon the same foundations. You easily see how the "Œdipus complex" emerges from such a primitive state of things, but will hardly, without reading the work, imagine the wealth of speculation it contains or its literary attractiveness. Atkinson probably relied upon the supposed parallel case of wild cattle and horses, because those animals resemble the apes in being vegetarian: though the diets are, in fact, very different. But even if such a comparison indicates a possible social state of our original ape-like stock, what is there in such a state that can be supposed to have introduced the changes that

---

[33] W. P. Pycraft, in his entertaining *Courtship of Animals*, after assuming that Man became a hunter for the sake of the excitement such a life afforded, goes on (p. 23): "A little later the advantages of neighbourliness were borne in on him, largely for the sake of the greater ease wherewith the animals of the chase could be captured by their combined efforts; but this begat comradeship and some of the graces that follow therefrom."

[34] *Descent of Man*, ch. xx.

[35] See above, footnote on p. 22.

made our forebears no longer ape-like? Supposing those changes to have already taken place, what evidence is there that the same social state endured? None: for it was assumed to have been the social state of our forebears on the ground of their resemblance in diet and family economy to the gorilla.

Returning, then, to our hypothesis as to the chief cause of human differentiation, namely, that a certain Primate, more nearly allied to the anthropoids than to any other, became carnivorous and adopted the life of a hunter, there are (as I have said) two ways in which this may have happened: either by such a variation on the part of our ancestor that he felt a stronger appetite for animal food than the gorilla does—strong enough to make him hunt for prey; or by such a change of climate in the region he inhabited—say from sub-tropical to temperate—as to make his former diet scarce, especially in winter, so that he became a hunter to avoid starvation. Every one admits that he became a hunter at some time: why not at the earliest? Nothing less than some great change of life, concentrating all his powers and straining every faculty, can possibly account for the enormous differentiation of Man. The adoption of the hunting life is such a change; and the further back we put it, the better it explains the other changes that have occurred in our physical and mental nature.

From the outset, again, our ancestor may have attacked big game, probably Ungulates—to whom he owed much; for not only did they provide prey, but by clearing the forest over wide areas compelled him to run in pursuit remote from his native trees, thus giving great selective advantage to every variation of legs and feet adapted to running: though at the very first there may have been little need to run, as he was not yet an object of terror; "we must remember that if man was unskilful, animals were unsuspicious."[36] I suppose him, at first, to have fallen to with hands and teeth: combining with others in a hungry, savage onslaught. By attacking big game advantage was given to those individuals and families who co-operated in hunting: thus forming the primal society of the human stock; a society entirely different from that of any of the Primates, or of cattle, and most like that of the dogs and wolves—a hunting-pack.

As in the course of generations the hunting-pack developed, no doubt, it had recognised leaders, the most powerful males, one perhaps pre-eminent. But it was not subject to one old male who claimed all the females; for the more adult males it comprised, the stronger it was; and, for the same reason, pairing, as among wolves, was the most efficient form of sexual relationship. But, in my judgment, it is altogether vain to try to deduce from this form of society, which may have existed three or four million years ago, any of the known customs of savages concerning marriage, such as avoidance, totemism, exogamy; which would be of comparatively recent date if we put back their origin 500,000 years. Many such rules can only have arisen when there was already a tradition and a language capable of expressing relationships.

§ 4. PSYCHOLOGY OF THE HUNTING-PACK

§ 4. *Psychology of the Hunting-pack.*—Interest in the chase and in kill-

[36] Avebury, *Prehistoric Times*, 7th ed., p. 580.

> ing; gregariousness; various modes of sympathy; aggressiveness;
> claim to territory; recognition of leaders, submission to the pack,
> emulation, precedency; strategy and persistence; struggle to share
> the prey; intelligence. Different mentality of the herbivorous herd

Possibly our ape-like ancestor was more sociable than any of the anthropoids; but sociability in ape-life would in no way account for our present character as men: nothing accounts for it, except the early formation of the hunting-pack. Since, however, we can know nothing of that institution directly, we must try to learn something about it from the parallel case of dogs and wolves. Galton remarks how readily the proceedings of man and dog "are intelligible to one another. Every whine or bark of the dog, each of his fawning, savage, or timorous movements is the exact counterpart of what would have been the man's behaviour, had he felt similar emotions. As the man understands the thoughts of the dog, so the dog understands the thoughts of the man, by attending to his natural voice, his countenance, and his actions."[37] No more, if as much, could be said of the terms upon which we stand with a tame chimpanzee, in spite of greater physical and facial resemblance and nearer kinship. What can connect us so closely in mind with an animal so remote from us in lineage and anatomy as the dog is? Adaptation to the same social conditions, the life of the hunting-pack.

(1) The master-interest of every member of the pack lies in the chase, because success in it is necessary to life. To show how this passion actuates ourselves, I quote Mr. F. C. Selous; who, during an expedition in Canada, roused a caribou stag within twenty yards, saw "the dreadful terror" in his eyes, and shot him. "Did I feel sorry for what I had done? it may be asked. Well! no, I did not. Ten thousand years of superficial and unsatisfying civilisation have not altered the fundamental nature of man, and the successful hunter of to-day becomes a primeval savage, remorseless, triumphant, full of a wild, exultant joy, which none but those who have lived in the wilderness, and depended on their success as hunters for their daily food, can ever know or comprehend."[38] To the hunter my paradox must seem a truism. And that the hunter temporarily released from civilised restraints, who suffers such intoxication, merely renews old savage raptures is shown by the following curious parallel: a Bushman, returning from a successful hunt to the wagons of the traveller Baines—"Behold me!" he shouted, "the hunter! Yea, look on me, the killer of elephants and mighty bulls! Behold me, the big elephant, the lion! Look on me, ye Damaras and Makalaka; admire and confess that I am a great Bull-calf."[39]

Again, since the interest of the chase culminates in the kill—for this is the condition of making a meal—to kill becomes, in some predatory animals, a passion that is often gratified without regard to their needs. Wolves often slay many more sheep than they devour: a sheep-dog that undergoes reversion kills by night the sheep on neighbouring farms without any call of hunger; and, says Mr. Thompson Seton (writing of the natives of North Canada), "the mania for killing that is seen

---

[37] *Inquiries into Human Faculty*, p. 262.
[38] *Hunting Trips in North America*, p. 349.
[39] G. W. Stone, *Native Races of South Africa*, p. 91.

in so many white men, is evidently a relic of savagery; for all these Indians and half-breeds are full of it."[40] They fired at everything they saw. The manners of my own pack—now long dispersed—were very similar to the Indians'; and the sport of pigeon- or of pheasant-shooting has been reduced to its last element—skilful slaying.

The disposition to slay is reinforced, when prey makes serious resistance, by anger; and generally by a distinct tendency, sometimes called "destructiveness," perhaps a latent character derived from the monkeys, and which I take to be partly a play-impulse and partly an expression of curiosity.

(2) The gregariousness of the pack is variable; probably, amongst wolves, it was much greater anciently than it is to-day. There are conflicting statements about the gregariousness of wolves that have been studied in different countries. Couteulx de Canteleu (France) says: "The wolf is an enemy of all society; when they assemble it is not a pacific society, but a band of brigands."[41] Thompson Seton (Canada) says: "Wolves are the most sociable of beasts of prey; they arrange to render one another assistance. A pack seems to be an association of personal acquaintances, and would resent the presence of a total stranger."[42] Gregariousness of wolves must be reduced by failure of game (as by the destruction of bison in North America), and still more by the encroachments of civilisation (as in France). The primitive human pack, probably, was more constantly gregarious than wolves are: (a) because its individuals, having no instinctive or traditionary knowledge of hunting, were more dependent on co-operation; and (b) because the long youth of children made it necessary for parents to associate with the pack during their nurture—else no pack could have existed; for whilst wolves are nearly full-grown at eighteen months, apes are not mature until the eighth or ninth year. At a later period, after the invention of effective weapons, an individual became, for many kinds of game, less dependent on co-operation; but by that time, the hunting-grounds of a pack were circumscribed by those of other hostile packs; so that no one dared go far alone.

(3) With gregariousness went, of course, (a) perceptive sympathy—every animal read instantly in the behaviour of others their feelings and impulses; (b) contagious sympathy—the impulses of any animal, expressed in its behaviour, spread rapidly to all the rest; and (c) effective sympathy, so far (at least) as that all united to defend any associate against aggression from outside the pack. Perceptive and contagious sympathy, however, extend beyond the limits of the pack or the species. Most of the higher mammalia can read the state of mind of others, though of widely different kinds, in their expression and behaviour; and many are liable to have their actions immediately affected by signs of the emotional impulses of others, especially fear. These modes of sympathy, therefore, though liveliest amongst gregarious animals, are not dependent on specific gregariousness.

(4) The pack has a disposition to aggression upon every sort of animal outside the pack, either as prey or as a competitor for prey: limited no doubt by what we

---

[40] *The Arctic Prairies*, p. 20.
[41] *La Chasse du Loup*, p. 21.
[42] *Life Histories of Northern Animals*, p. 755.

should call considerations of prudence or utility; which must vary with the size of the pack, the prowess of its individuals, the possession of weapons, etc. After the invention of weapons and snares, many savage tribes can kill every sort of animal in their habitat, as the palæolithic Europeans did many thousands of years ago. From the outset the human pack must have come into competition with the true carnivores, must have defended itself against them, may have discovered that attack was the safest defence, and may have been victorious even without weapons. Mr. G. P. Sanderson writes: "It is universally believed by the natives (of South India) that the tiger is occasionally killed by packs of wild dogs.... From what I have seen of their style of hunting, and of their power of tearing and lacerating, I think there can be no doubt of their ability to kill a tiger.... Causes of hostility may occasionally arise between the tiger and wild dogs through attempted interference with each other's prey."[43]

(5) A hunting-pack, probably, always claims a certain territory. This is the first ground of the sense of property, so strongly shown by domestic dogs: the territorial claims of the half-wild dogs of Constantinople are well known. To nourish a pack the hunting-grounds must be extensive. Mr. Thompson Seton says that in Canada the wolf has a permanent home-district and a range of about fifty miles.[44] Very many generations must have elapsed before the deviation of our forebears from anthropoid habits resulted in the formation of so many packs as to necessitate the practical delimitation of hunting-grounds. Then the aggressiveness of the pack turned upon strangers of its own species; the first wars arose, and perhaps cannibalism on the part of the victors. It is certain that, in North America, wolves kill and eat foxes, dogs, coyotes; and it is generally believed that wolves will eat a disabled companion; though, according to Mr. W. H. Hudson, a wolf will only eat another when it has killed that other, and then only as the carrying out of the instinct to eat whatever it has killed.[45] It may be so.

(6) A pack must have a leader, and must devotedly follow him as long as he is manifestly the best of the pack; and here we have a rudimentary loyalty.

(7) Every individual must be subservient to the pack, as long as it works together; and this seems to be the ground of the "instinct of self-abasement" (McDougall), so far as the attitudes involved in such subserviency are due to a distinct emotional impulse, and are not rather expressive of fear or of devotion.

(8) The members of the pack must be full of emulation; in order that, when the present leader fails, others may be ready to take his place.

(9) For the internal cohesion of the pack, there must be the equivalent of a recognised table of precedence amongst its members; and this is reconciled with the spirit of emulation, by fighting until each knows his place, followed by complete submission on the part of the inferior. Mr. Th. Roosevelt says of a pack of dogs employed in bear-hunting, "at feeding-time each took whatever his strength permitted, and each paid abject deference to whichever animal was his known

[43] *Wild Beasts of India*, pp. 275-6. Cf. Casserly, *Life on an Indian Outpost*, pp. 94-5. Brehm says, in *Thierleben*, that in Russia wolves attack and kill the bear.
[44] *Life Histories of Northern Animals*, p. 754.
[45] *Naturalist in La Plata*, p. 346.

superior in prowess."[46] Mr. W. H. Hudson writes of dogs on cattle-breeding establishments on the pampas, that he presumes "they are very much like feral dogs and wolves in their habits. Their quarrels are incessant; but when a fight begins the head of the pack, as a rule, rushes to the spot," and tries to part the combatants—not always successfully. "But from the foremost in strength and power down to the weakest there is a gradation of authority; each one knows just how far he can go, which companion he can bully when in a bad temper or wishing to assert himself, and to which he must humbly yield in his turn."[47] The situation reminds one of a houseful of schoolboys, and of how ontogeny repeats phylogeny. Where political control is very feeble, as in mining camps or backwoods settlements, civilised men revert to the same conditions. Fifty years ago, "all along the frontier between Canada and the United States, every one knew whom he could lick, and who could lick him."[48] Amongst Australian aborigines, we are told that "precedence counts for very much."[49]

(10) A pack of wolves relies not merely upon running down its prey, but resorts to various stratagems to secure it: as by surrounding it; heading it off from cover; driving it over a precipice; arranging relays of pursuers, who take up the chase when the first begin to flag; setting some to lie in ambush while the rest drive the prey in their direction. Such devices imply intelligent co-operation, some means of communicating ideas, patience and self-control in the interests of the pack and perseverance in carrying out a plan. Failure to co-operate effectually is said to be punished with death. Primitive man, beginning with more brains than a wolf, may be supposed soon to have discovered such arts and to have improved upon them.

(11) When prey has been killed by a pack of wolves, there follows a greedy struggle over the carcass, each trying to get as big a meal as possible. Mr. Th. Roosevelt writes of dogs used in hunting the cougar (puma): "The relations of the pack amongst themselves (when feeding) were those of wild beast selfishness.... They would all unite in the chase and the fierce struggle which usually closed it. But the instant the quarry was killed, each dog resumed his normal attitude of greedy anger or greedy fear toward the others."[50] As this was a scratch pack of hounds, however, we cannot perhaps infer that a naturally formed pack of wolves is equally discordant, or that the human pack was ever normally like that. Galton, indeed, says: "Many savages are so unamiable and morose as to have hardly any object in associating together, besides that of mutual support;"[51] but this is by no means true of all savages. At any rate, the steadier supply of food obtained by our race since the adoption of pastoral or agricultural economy, with other circumstances, has greatly modified the greedy and morose attitude in many men and disguised it in others; though it reappears under conditions of extreme social dislocation, and it is a proverb that "thieves quarrel over their plunder." In the original pack

[46] *Outdoor Pastimes of an American Hunter*, p. 70.
[47] Op. cit., pp. 336-7.
[48] Hiram S. Maxim, *My Life*, p. 57.
[49] Spencer and Gillen, *Across Australia*, p. 388.
[50] Op. cit., pp. 6-7.
[51] Op. cit., p. 78.

such a struggle over the prey may have subserved the important utility of eliminating the weak, and of raising the average strength and ferocity. But some custom must have been established for feeding the women and children. No doubt when fruits were obtainable, the women and children largely subsisted upon them. But the strong instinct of parental care in Primates, the long youth of children, and the greater relative inferiority of females to males (common to anthropoids and savages) than is found amongst dogs and wolves, must have made the human pack from the first differ in many ways from a pack of wolves.

So much, then, as to the traits of character established in primitive man by his having resorted to co-operative hunting: they all plainly persist in ourselves.

On our intelligence life in the hunting-pack had just as revolutionary an influence, as already explained in the first chapter. The whole art of hunting had to be learned from its rudiments by this enterprising family. With them there was no inherited instinct or disposition, and no tradition or instruction, as there is with the true carnivores: they depended solely on observation, memory, inference. With poor olfactory sense (as usual in apes) prey must be followed and inconvenient enemies outwitted, by acquiring a knowledge of their footprints and other visible signs of neighbourhood, and by discrimination of all the noises they make. The habits and manners of prey and of enemies, their favourite lairs, feeding-grounds and watering-places, their paths through forest, marsh, thicket and high grass, must all be learnt: so must their speed, endurance, means and methods of attack and defence. The whole country within the range of the pack must be known, its resources and its difficulties; and whenever new territory was entered, new lessons in all these matters had to be learned. This must have entailed a rapid natural selection of brains. Only a rapidly developing, plastic brain could have been capable of the requisite accommodation of behaviour in such conditions: a mechanism was required by which more and more new lines of specialised reaction were related to numerous newly observed and discriminated facts.

The very crudest weapons may be handled with variable dexterity; the best handling must be discovered and practised; and this had a high selective value for the hands as well as for the brain. Probably crude weapons were very early used; for some monkeys (and baboons generally) throw sticks or stones, or roll stones down upon an enemy. In Borneo, Wallace came upon a female orang who, "as soon as she saw us, began breaking off branches and the great spiny fruits [of the durian] with every appearance of rage, causing such a shower of missiles as effectually kept us from approaching too near the tree. This habit of throwing down branches has been doubted; but I have, as here narrated, observed it myself on three separate occasions."[52] The importance of the observation consists in its proving the existence in an anthropoid of the impulse to use missiles under the occasional stress of anger; so that it might be expected rapidly to develop under the constant pressure of hunger. The use of clubs and stones induced the discrimination of the best materials for such weapons, and where they could be found; and, in process of time, brought in a rough shaping of them, the better to serve

---

[52] *Malay Archipelago*, p. 43.

their purposes. Then came the invention of snares and pitfalls and the discovery of poisons.

Thus the primitive human, or prehuman mind, was active in many new directions; and depending for its skill, not upon instinct or imitation, but upon observation and memory and inference, it was necessary for it to arrange ideas in a definite order before acting upon them, as in making weapons or planning a hunt; indefiniteness or confusion in such matters was fatal. The contrast between growing memory of the past and present experience, between practical ideas and the actions realising them that had been suspended until the right moment came, furthered the differentiation of self-consciousness amidst the world; the contrasts of co-operation and greed, of emulation and loyalty and submission, of honour and shame, furthered the differentiation of self-consciousness amidst the tribe.

If it be asked—how much of all this development attributed to the hunting-pack might have been brought about just as well by the formation of a defensive herd, such as we see in cattle and horses?—a definite answer can be given. The herd is, of course, marked by (2) gregariousness, (3) perceptive and contagious sympathy and sometimes effective sympathy in common defence, (7) recognition of leaders (all herds that travel have leaders), (8) emulation, (9) precedence; but not by (1) interest in the chase and in killing, nor (4) aggressiveness, nor (10) strategy and perseverance in attack, nor (11) greed; and herd-life affords no conditions for the development of intelligence and dexterity, nor for any of the physical characters that distinguish man. Herd-life does not involve the great and decisive change which is implied in the evolution of human nature. We must conceive, then, of the primitive human mind as a sort of chimpanzee mind adapted to the wolfish conditions of the hunting-pack. Wolves themselves have undergone no great development, compared (say) with cats, for want of hands and other physical advantages which we had to begin with. If some species of baboon had taken to the hunting-life, there might have been very interesting results.

§ 5. THE WOLF-TYPE OF MAN ESTABLISHED BY NATURAL SELECTION

§ 5. *The Wolf-type of Man established by Natural Selection.*—Keith's hypothesis as to epoch of differentiation. Slow progress of culture; full adaptation to hunting life prior to Neolithic culture

The differentiation of the human from the anthropoid stock must have begun a long time ago; as to when it began there is no direct evidence; and even if fossil remains of the earlier stages of our evolution had been discovered, we could only judge from the strata in which they occurred what must have been their relative antiquity. When it comes to reducing the chronology of past ages to figures, geologists either decline to make any estimate, or the results of their calculations may differ as 1 to 10. Since my own studies give me no claim to an opinion on such matters, whilst it is helpful to have clear ideas, however tentative, I shall adopt the views of Dr. Arthur Keith in his work on *The Antiquity of Man*, based on estimates published by Prof. Sollas.[53] On turning to p. 509 of that work, a genealogical tree will be found, showing the probable lines of descent of the higher Primates. The separation of the human from the great anthropoid stock is represented as having happened at about the last third of the Oligocene period—say 2,000,000 years ago (or, according to the later estimate, 3,500,000). Pithecanthropus (of Java) branched off as a distinct genus about the middle of the Miocene. Neanderthal man (*Homo Neanderthalensis*) and Piltdown man (*Eoanthropus Dawsoni*) separated as distinct species (or genera) from the stock of modern man (absurdly named *Homo sapiens*) early in the Pliocene, and became extinct respectively (say) 20,000 and 300,000 years ago. The races of modern man began to differentiate near the end of the Pliocene (say) 500,000 years from the present time. Such is the "working hypothesis."

The skull capacity of the great anthropoids averages 500 c.c.; that of Pithecanthropus is estimated at 900 c.c.; the Australian native average is 1200 c.c.; Eoanthropus, according to Dr. Keith, rises to 1400;[54] a Neanderthal skull has been measured at 1600 c.c.; the modern English average is under 1500 c.c. Of course, mental power depends not on size of the brain only, but also on its differentiation, which may have recently advanced.

As to culture, the Neolithic period extends in Western Europe from about 2000 to 10,000 B.C.: and to that age is usually attributed the introduction of agriculture, the domestication of animals, pottery, weaving, permanent constructed dwellings, and monuments requiring collective labour; but some of these improvements may be of earlier date. In other parts of the world, e. g. in the Eastern Mediterranean region, such culture is probably older, but still comparatively recent. What is known as the Palæolithic stage of culture is often supposed to have begun early in the second quarter of the Pleistocene period, giving us a retrospect of (say) 300,000 years. But if we include under "Palæolithic" all unpolished stone-work that shows clear signs of having been executed according to an idea or mental pattern (and this seems a reasonable definition), the "rostro-carinate" implements must be so called, and then the beginning of this culture must be pushed back into the Pliocene.[55] In Pliocene (and perhaps Miocene) deposits have further been discovered numerous "eoliths": stones so roughly chipped that they do not imply an idea-pattern; so that, whilst many archæologists accept them as of human workmanship, some experts dispute their claim to be considered artefacts. Of course, there must be eoliths; the only question is whether we have yet unearthed any of them. Our forefathers cannot have begun by shaping stones to a definite figure and special purpose. Beginning with stones taken up as they lay, they discovered that a broken stone with a sharp edge inflicted a worse wound than a whole one; then broke stones to obtain this advantage; used sharp fragments to weight clubs; and very slowly advanced to the manufacture of recognisable axes and spear-heads, mean-

---

[53] See the *Report of the British Association*, 1900, pp. 711-30. The author has since then revised his estimates, assigning much greater depth to the Pliocene and Miocene deposits and proportionally more time for their formation. See the *Quarterly Journal of the Geological Society*, LXV. (1909).

[54] Dr. Smith Woodward's reconstruction gives the skull of Eoanthropus a capacity of about 1300 c.c.

[55] See Ray Lankester's *Description of the Test-Specimen. R.A.I., Occasional Papers*, No. 4.

while discovering other uses for flaked stones; and it seems to have needed at least 1,400,000 (or 2,800,000) years to arrive at the poorest of known palæoliths. This strikingly agrees with the law, often stated, that the progress of culture is, by virtue of tradition, cumulative, and flows, as a stone falls, with accelerating velocity: in spite of the ebb, to which from age to age we see it to be liable. At any one time, moreover, the art of stone-working was, probably, even in adjacent tribes, at different stages of advancement; it depends partly upon the kind of stone obtainable; but it has been only recently that such contrasts could occur as Herodotus[56] describes among the hosts of Xerxes: when, beside the well-accoutred Persians and Medes, marched Libyans and Mysians armed with wooden javelins hardened in the fire, and Ethiopians with stone-tipped arrows and spears headed with the sharpened horns of antelopes.

The moral of all this is that there was abundant time before the rise of Neolithic culture (which may be called the beginning of civilisation) for the complete adaptation of mankind everywhere, by natural selection, to the life of hunters; and that, since then, there has not been time for the biological adaptation of any race to the civilised state. We shall see that natural selection has probably had some civilising influence; but any approach to complete adaptation has been impossible, not only for want of time, but also because of rapid changes in the structure of civilisation, the social protection of some eccentrics, the persistence of the hunting-life as a second resource or as a pastime, and by the frequent recurrence of warfare—that is to say, man-hunting. To civilisation we are, for the most part, merely accommodated by experience, education, tradition and social pressure. A few people seem to be adapted to civilised life from their birth, and others to the slavish life; but all inherit, more or less manifestly, the nature of the hunter and warrior. This is a necessary basis of general and social psychology; and perhaps tribal or national characters (so far as distinguishable) may be understood by assigning the conditions under which they have, in various directions, been modified from this type.

To avoid the appearance of overlooking an obvious objection, I may add that the life of the hunter does not imply an exclusively carnivorous diet, but merely that hunting is the activity upon which his faculties are bent and upon which his livelihood chiefly depends. It is most unlikely that a cousin of the frugivorous anthropoids should entirely give up his ancestral food, immediately, or perhaps at any time. Even the diet of the wolf, in North-East Canada, includes "much fruit, especially the uva-ursi"; and the coyote there also eats berries;[57] so does the jackal in India. Savage women everywhere subsist largely on roots and fruits. Dr. Keith says the teeth and jaws of the Neanderthal species were adapted to a coarse vegetable diet.[58] Yet the Neanderthal burials at La Ferrasie, La Chapelle aux Saints, Jersey and Krapina, with their implements and animal remains, leave no doubt that the species hunted the biggest game. At Krapina, besides mammoth and rhinoceros, "the cave-bear occurred abundantly, it was evidently a favourite article of diet": the inhabitants were not fanatical vegetarians.

---

[56] Book VII. chs. 69, 71, 74.

[57] E. Thompson Seton, *The Arctic Prairies*, pp. 304 and 352.

[58] Op. cit., pp. 151, 239, 476.

§ 6. Some further Consequences of the Hunting-life

§ 6. *Some further Consequences of the Hunting-life.*—Growth of constructiveness; language; customs—marriage; property; war; sports and games; laughter and lamentation

Between the remote age when our hypothetical ancestor became a hunter and the time to which probably belong the remains of the oldest known men, there lies a gap of (say) one (or two) and a half million years, concerning which we have not only no direct evidence but not even any parallel in the world by means of which to apply the comparative method. Just at the beginning, the parallel of the wolf-pack sheds some light upon our path; but the light soon grows faint; for the primitive human, from the first more intelligent than wolves, and inheriting from the ape-stock qualities of character which the new life greatly modified but could not extirpate, must under pressure of selection have become, after not many ages, an animal unlike any other. Just at the end, again, something concerning those who lived many thousand years before the beginning of history may be inferred from the parallel of existing savage customs; from their rock-dwellings, drawings, tools, weapons, hearths, something about their way of life; from evidence of their burial-customs, something of their beliefs. But what can be said of our ancestors during all those years that intervene between the beginning and the end?

Having been a hunter at the first and at the last, we may reasonably suppose that he had been so all the time. But, with our present knowledge, our chief guide as to other matters seems to be the fact that the most backward of existing savages possess powers of body and mind, and forms and products of culture, which must have been acquired gradually through a long course of development from no better origins than are traceable in apes and wolves. As the use of good stone weapons by living savages and the occurrence of stone weapons in deposits of various age in the Pleistocene—less and less perfectly made the further we go back—justify us in assuming that there must have been eoliths of even cruder workmanship at remoter dates, so the possession by savages of extensive languages, intricate customs, luxuriant myths, considerable reasoning powers and even humane sentiments, compel us to imagine such possessions as belonging to our prehistoric ancestors, in simpler and simpler forms, as we go back age by age toward the beginning. A tentative reconstruction of the lost series of events may sometimes be supported by what has been observed of the individual development of our children.

(*a*) For example, the constructive impulse, slightly shown by anthropoids that make beds and shelters in the trees, was called into activity in man especially in the making of weapons, tools and snares, and became an absorbing passion; so that a savage (often accused of being incapable of prolonged attention!) will sit for days working at a spear or an axe: they are inattentive only to what does not interest them. Many children from about the sixth year come under the same sort of fascination—digging, building, making bows and arrows, boats and so forth. This is a necessary preparation for all the achievements of civilised life; and it is reasonable to suppose that the stages of growth of such interest in construction are indicated by the improvement of ancient implements.

(*b*) As to language—in the most general sense, as the communication of emotions and ideas by vocal sounds—the rudiments of it are widespread in animal life. A sort of dog-language is recognised, and monkeys seem to have a still greater "vocabulary." Hence, a number of emotional vocal expressions was probably in use among the primitive human stock. And the new hunting-life was favourable to the development of communicative signs; for it depended on co-operation, which is wanting in ape-life, and in the lower extant savages hardly exists, except in hunting, war, and magical or religious rites. Hunting, moreover, is (as I have said) especially encouraging to onomatopœic expression in imitating the noises of animals, etc. It was still more favourable, perhaps, to the growth of gesture-language in imitating the behaviour of animals and the actions involved in circumventing and attacking them. Increasing powers of communication were extremely useful, and the pack must have tried to develop them. Without the endeavour to communicate, there could never have been a language better than the ape's; nor could there have been the endeavour without the need. That gesture alone was very helpful may be assumed; and it must have assisted in fixing the earliest vocal signs for things and actions and qualities, and probably determined the earliest syntax; but when, in hunting, members of the pack were hidden from one another, or when their hands were occupied, gesture was not available, and communication depended on the voice. The speech of children similarly emerges from emotional noises and impulsive babbling, assisted by gesture.

Passing to later ages, we cannot expect to learn much about the speech of prehistoric men, whom we know only by a few bones. As to the Java skull, Dr. Keith observes that "the region of the brain which subserves the essentially human gift of speech, was not ape-like in Pithecanthropus. The parts for speech are there; they are small, but clearly foreshadow the arrangement of convolutions seen in modern man." On the other hand, "the higher association areas ... had not reached a human level."[59] The jaw of this skull not having been found, nothing can be said of its fitness for carrying out the process of articulation. As to Eoanthropus, "if our present conception of the orbital part of the third frontal convolution is well founded, namely, that it takes part in the mechanism of speech, then we have grounds for believing that the Piltdown man had reached that point of brain-development when speech had become a possibility. When one looks at the lower jaw, however, and the projecting canine teeth, one hesitates to allow him more than a potential ability."[60] The jaw had not undergone the characteristic changes which in modern man give freedom to the tongue in the articulation of words.[61] But Dr. Keith "cannot detect any feature in the frontal, parietal or occipital areas which clearly separate this brain-cast from modern ones."[62] Eoanthropus, therefore, must have had a good deal to say and, being a social animal, must have felt the need of expression; and, though he was not a direct ancestor of ours, it can hardly be doubted that at some period the jaws of our own ancestors were no better adapted than his to articulate speech. May we not infer that articulate speech,

---

[59] *Antiquity of Man,* p. 268.
[60] A. Keith, op. cit., p. 408.
[61] Op. cit., p. 452.
[62] Op. cit., p. 414.

meeting a need of the stock, arose very gradually, and was slowly differentiated from some less definite and structural connection of expressive and onomatopœic vocables, such as we have seen may naturally have arisen amongst the earliest hunters? *Pari passu* the jaw was modified.

(*c*) All savages live by custom; gregarious animals have their customs; and in the primitive hunting-pack customs must have been early established as "conditions of gregariousness." M. Salomon Reinach, indeed, thinks that the anthropoid probably became human as the result of inventing taboos, especially in sexual relations; there was economy of nervous energy in the direction of the senses, and consequent enrichment of the intellect.[63] His hypothesis does not carry us far, perhaps, into the particulars of human form and faculty; but it contains this truth, that without the growth of customs there could have been no progress for human nature; and it certainly points to the probability that some custom was early established with regard to marriage. In Prof. Westermarck's opinion our species was originally monogamous.[64] Supposing this to have been the custom, as it is amongst many Primates, could it have persisted after the formation of the hunting-pack? According to Mr. Thompson Seton, wolves pair "probably for life";[65] but this is disputed; and so it is whether or no the male of a seasonal pair takes part in caring for the puppies.[66] Of the primitive human stock one may say that whilst, on the one hand, the association of many males and females in the same pack may have tended to break up the family, on the other hand, the long youth of the children and the parental care generally characteristic of Primates would have tended to preserve it; that the practice of pairing requires the largest number of males (setting aside polyandry), and lessens quarrelling, and is therefore favourable to the strength of the pack; and that any custom may have been established that was most favourable to the species in its new life. The least probable of all conditions is promiscuity; for the rearing of children with their ever-lengthening youth must have been difficult, taxing the care of both parents.

(*d*) The claim to property is instinctive in most animals—claim to a certain territory, or to a nest, or lair, or mate. Each early human pack probably claimed a certain hunting-range; and each family its lair, which it guarded, as our domestic dog guards the house. In Australia "every tribe has its own country, and its boundaries are well known; and they are respected by others";[67] and the Bushmen, who retained the ancient hunting-life more perfectly than any other known people, are said to have been formerly divided into large tribes with well-defined hunting-grounds.[68] As weapons or other implements, charms, or ornaments came into use, the attitude toward the territory or lair will have been extended to include them; indeed, it seems to be instinctive even in lower Primates. "In the Zoological Gardens," says Darwin, "a monkey, which had weak teeth, used to break open nuts with a stone; and I was assured by the keepers that, after using the stone,

---

[63] *Cultes, Mythes et Religion*, III. p. 430.
[64] *Primitive Marriage*, ch. iii.
[65] *Life Histories of Northern Animals*, p. 757.
[66] See above, § 3 (4), footnote, p. 25.
[67] Spencer and Gillen, *Across Australia*, p. 198.
[68] G. W. Stone, *Native Races of South Africa*, p. 33.

he hid it in the straw, and would not let any other monkey touch it. Here, then, we have the idea of property."[69] Among the half-wolf train-dogs of Canada, the claims of one to property seem to be recognised by others; for a dog will defend its *cache* of food against another that ordinarily it fears; and "the bigger dog rarely presses the point."[70] The utility of keeping the peace within the tribe, no doubt, led to the growth of customs concerning property, and to their protection by the social sanction, and later by the taboo.[71] For taboo cannot be the origin of respect for property or for any custom: it implies a custom already existing, which it protects by the growth of a belief in some magical penalty that is effective even when there are no witnesses. The same utility of order must have established customs of dividing the kill of the pack: later also protected by taboo, as we still see in many savage tribes.

The attitude towards property is very variable amongst the tribes now known to us. Still, considering how early and strongly it is manifested by children, we may infer with some plausibility its antiquity in the race. The urgent desire of property, and tenacity in holding it, displayed by many individuals, though not an amiable, has been a highly useful trait, to which is due that accumulation of capital that has made possible the whole of our material and much of our spiritual civilisation. Amongst barbarians it may be a necessary condition of social order. Had not wealth been highly prized amongst our own ancestors, it is hard to see how revenge could ever have been appeased by the wergeld. The payment, indeed, was not the whole transaction; it implied an acknowledgment of guilt and of the obligation to make amends; but these things would not have mollified an enemy nurtured in the tradition of the blood-feud, if silver had not been dear to him. It is still accepted as compensation for injuries that seem difficult to measure by the ounce. Wealth gives rank, and gratifies not only the greed but also the emulative spirit of the pack. Acquisitiveness is an essential trait of aristocracy, and adhesiveness of its perpetuity. Homespun prudence belongs, in our ancestry, to a more recent stratum of motives; we see it as a blind instinct in squirrels and beavers, a quasi-instinctive propensity in dogs and wolves (who hide food that they cannot immediately devour); but it is not known in any anthropoid, and is acquired at some stage by some human races—not by all; for it is not found in many extant savages. The only occasion on which Australian tribes show prudential foresight as to food is on the approach of the season of magical rites, when they lay in a stock of food before giving themselves up for weeks or months body and soul to thaumaturgy.[72] Prudence is not, however, merely a function of foresight or intelligence, or else the Irish would be as prudent as the Scotch.

(*e*) The first wars, probably, were waged for hunting-grounds; and this may have been a revival, for the carnivorous anthropoid pack, of a state of affairs that existed amongst their ancestors at a much earlier date; for battles for a feeding-ground have been witnessed between troops of the lower Primates. Such a

[69] *Descent of Man*, ch. iii.

[70] E. Thompson Seton, *Life Histories of Northern Animals*, p. 769.

[71] E. Westermarck, *Origin and Development of Moral Ideas*, II. p. 52.

[72] Spencer and Gillen, *Native Tribes of Northern Territory of Australia*, p. 27.

battle between two bands of langur (*Semnopithecus entellus*) has been described;[73] and Darwin relates after Brehm how "in Abyssinia, when baboons of one species (*C. gelada*) descend in troops from the mountains to plunder the fields, they sometimes encounter troops of another species (*C. hamadryas*), and then a fight ensues. The Geladas roll down great stones, which the Hamadryas try to avoid, and then both species, making a great uproar, rush furiously against each other."[74] As packs of the wolf-ape increased in numbers and spread over the world, they no doubt generally came to regard one another as rivals upon the same footing as the great cats and packs of dogs, and every attempt at expansion or migration provoked a battle. Wars strengthened the internal sympathies and loyalties of the pack or tribe and its external antipathies, and extended the range and influence of the more virile and capable tribes.

It is true that neighbouring tribes of savages are not now always mutually hostile. In Australia, we are told, local groups and adjacent tribes are usually friendly;[75] but with them the age of expansion seems to have closed some time ago, and a sort of equilibrium has been established. On the other hand, it is a shallow sort of profundity that insists upon interpreting every war as a struggle for nutrition, an effort to solve the social problem. Aggressiveness and insatiable greed are characteristic of many tribes — passions always easily exploited by their leaders, as in the civilised world by dynasts and demagogues. Plethora is more insolent than poverty. Lust of power, of glory, of mere fighting is a stronger incentive than solicitude for the poor.

However, in the development of society nothing has been so influential as war: an immense subject, for the outlines of which I refer to Herbert Spencer's *Political Institutions*.[76]

(*f*) Most of the amusements as well as the occupations of mankind depend for their zest upon the spirit of hunting and fighting, which they gratify and relieve, either directly or in a conventionalised and symbolical way, and at the same time keep alive. Sports and games involve the pursuit of some end by skill and strategy, often the seizing upon some sort of prey, or slaying outright, and they give scope to emulation. Emulation is a motive in the race for wealth, in every honourable career, even in addiction to science and learning: though here the main stress is upon an instinct older than the pack — curiosity, a general character of the Primates. That children at first play alone, later play together, and then "make up sides," repeats the change from the comparatively solitary life of anthropoids to the social life and combined activities of the hunting-pack. From the interest of the chase and the aggressiveness that is involved in it must be derived all that we call "enterprise," whether beneficent or injurious: a trait, certainly, which there is little reason to regard as inherited from the anthropoid stock.

(*g*) The great amusement and pastime of feeding has, no doubt, descended to us in unbroken tradition, through harvest and vintage festivals, from the unbri-

---

[73] *Royal Natural History*, I. pp. 72-3.

[74] *Descent of Man*, ch. iii.

[75] Spencer and Gillen, *Across Australia*, p. 200.

[76] *Principles of Sociology*, Vol. II.

dled indulgence that followed a successful hunt. And I offer the conjecture that the origin of laughter and the enjoyment of broad humour (so often discussed) may be traced to these occasions of riotous exhilaration and licence. We may suppose, indeed, that these conditions began to prevail not in the earliest days of the ravenous pack, but after some advance had been made in the customs of eating. Savages usually cram to repletion when possible, and with huge gusto, for there may not soon be another opportunity. If uproarious feasting was advantageous physically and socially (as till recently we all thought it was), addiction to the practice was a ground of survival; and laughter (a discharge of undirected energy, as Spencer says), being its natural expression and enhancement, shared in its perpetuation. This social origin agrees with the infectiousness of laughter, with its connection with triumph and cruelty, and with the quality of the jokes that still throughout the world excite most merriment—practical jokes and allusions to drunkenness, the indecorous, the obscene. Sir Robert Walpole preferred such humour as the most sociable; because in that everybody could take part. Many refinements have been introduced in polite circles; but it is in vain that one begins a theory of laughter with an analysis of the genius of Molière.

Similarly, I suppose that weeping, lamentation and the facial and bodily expressions of grief were developed by the social utility of common mourning in tribal defeat and bereavement.

§ 7. Moralisation of the Hunters

§ 7. *Moralisation of the Hunters.* —Character of Anthropoids; human benevolence; moral sense; effect of industry; of growing intelligence

We are left to speculate about the earliest growth of magnanimity, friendliness, compassion, general benevolence and other virtues. They cannot be explained merely by the hunting-life, which so easily accounts for greed, cruelty, pride and every sort of aggressiveness. Robert Hartmann writes: "It is well known that both rude and civilised peoples are capable of showing unspeakable and, as it is erroneously termed, inhuman cruelty towards each other. These acts of cruelty, murder and rapine are often the result of the inexorable logic of national characteristics and, unhappily, are truly human, since nothing like them can be traced in the animal world. It would, for instance, be a grave mistake to compare a tiger with a bloodthirsty executioner of the Reign of Terror, since the former only satisfies his natural appetite in preying on other animals. The atrocities of the trials for witchcraft, the indiscriminate slaughter committed by the Negroes on the coast of Guinea, the sacrifice of human victims by the Khonds, the dismemberment of living men by the Battus, find no parallel in the habits of animals in their savage state. And such a comparison is, above all, impossible in the case of anthropoids, which display no hostility toward men or other animals unless they are first attacked. In this respect the anthropoid ape stands upon a higher plane than many men."[77] Are we, then, to explain the more amiable side of human nature, partly at least, by derivation from the frugivorous Primates, extensively modified by our wolfish adaptation, but surviving as latent character?

---

[77] *Anthropoid Apes*, pp. 294-5.

(*a*) Several further considerations may be offered to account for the growth of what we call humanity, (i) The long non-age of human children is favourable to the attachments of family life, and such attachments may under certain conditions be capable of extension beyond the family; but I cannot trace the whole flood of altruistic regard to the sole source of maternal or parental love. (ii) Friendliness and the disposition to mutual aid are so useful to a hunting-pack that is not merely seasonal but permanent (as I take ours to have been), both to individuals and to the pack as a whole, within certain limits (as that the wounded, sick, or aged must not amount to an encumbrance), that we may suppose natural selection to have favoured the growth of effective sympathy, not merely in mutual defence, but so far as it is actually found at present in backward tribes. It nowhere seems to be excessive; and its manifestation in some civilised races seems to depend not upon a positive increase of benevolence in the generality, but (iii) upon the breaking down here and there of conditions that elsewhere oppose and inhibit it. Thus the generosity, mercy and magnanimity that constitute the chivalrous ideal, depend (I believe) upon the attainment by a class of such undisputed superiority that there is no occasion for jealousy or rivalry in relation to other classes; for should the superiority be disputed, these virtues quickly disappear. Similarly, what have been called the "slavish virtues" of charity, humility, long-suffering may arise amongst those who are free from rivalry, because they have no hope of aggrandisement in wealth or honour, and who have indeed suffered long. With the interfusion of classes, their virtues interfuse; for they have a common root, and are active, provided that circumstances do not inhibit them.

(iv) But since in individuals our complex nature varies in all directions, and amongst the rest in the direction of benevolence; and since any organ or quality that varies is apt to continue to do so, and may go on varying even beyond the limits of biological utility; why in human life may not this happen with benevolence (or with any other passion or virtue); so that in some men it expands with wonderful richness and beauty even to the sacrifice of themselves—nay, by excessive clemency or generosity, even to the injury of the tribe or of the race?

(*b*) The moral sense or conscience has been discussed by Darwin[78] "exclusively from the side of natural history"; so as this is the way of considering human nature in the present book, I shall epitomise his account of it; which seems to be true, and to which I see little to add. He finds four chief conditions of the growth of a moral sense: (*a*) the social instincts lead an animal to take pleasure in the society of its fellows, to sympathise with them and to help them. (*b*) When the mind is highly developed, images of past actions and motives continually recur; "and that feeling of dissatisfaction or even misery which invariably results ... from any dissatisfied instinct would arise as often as it was perceived that the enduring and always present social instinct had yielded to some other instinct, at the time stronger, but neither enduring in its nature nor leaving behind it a very vivid impression"—as with anger or greed. (*c*) After language has been acquired, public opinion can be expressed, and becomes the paramount guide of action; though still "our regard for the approbation and disapprobation of our fellows depends on sympathy." (*d*)

---

[78] *Descent of Man,* ch. iv.

Social instinct, sympathy and obedience to the judgment of the community are strengthened by the formation of habit. Darwin then proves successively these four positions.

Seeing the stress here laid upon sympathy, it may make the matter clearer if we observe that the word occurs in different senses—for the participation in another's satisfaction or distress (emotional sympathy) and readiness to help (effective sympathy); and these are the meanings under (*a*), the first of the above heads: and, again, for the knowledge that there are ideas or judgments in another's mind together with approval or disapproval of our actions; and this is the meaning under (*c*), the third head. But knowledge of another's thoughts is not sympathy, except so far as, being accompanied with assent to his judgment, there is participation in his feelings of approval or disapproval; and, if we dissent from his judgment, there may, indeed, be perceptive sympathy as to his feelings, but there is no emotional sympathy or participation in them—there is rather fear or resentment. It is necessary to bear in mind that perception of another's feelings, participation in them and impulse to help or relieve are separable processes, and that perceptive sympathy is as active in cruelty as in generosity or mercy.

It may be added that (*b*), the second of the four conditions assigned by Darwin as determining the growth of the moral sense or conscience, accounts more especially for "remorse of conscience"; and that (*c*), the third condition, explains that tone of authority attaching to conscience on which Bishop Butler laid so much stress.[79]

How early the moral sense began to form itself in our stock cannot be estimated because it must have been a very gradual process. Probably the rudiments of it appeared in the family life of the ape even before our differentiation; and the authoritative character of conscience established itself under the discipline of the hunting-pack before there was much development of mind (for dogs know what theft is), and under pressure of a public opinion that managed to express itself without language. In an original and suggestive book[80] Mr. Trotter has shown that a herd (pack, tribe or nation) necessarily approves of whatever actions are done in its interests as good or right, and disapproves of the contrary actions as bad or wrong. Confident that its beliefs and customs are good and right, the pack persecutes dissenters and nonconformists. "Good" is a relative idea. "'The good are good warriors and hunters,' said a Pawnee chief; whereupon the author who mentions the saying remarks that this would also be the opinion of a wolf if he could express it."[81] Hence we may guess the principal contents of the primitive categorical imperative. The study of Ethnology and History enables us to trace the modification and enrichment of those contents under varying conditions of culture, and for the results of such study I refer to Edward Westermarck's *Origin and Development of Moral Ideas*.

(*c*) After the introduction of agriculture, the stress of natural selection was in certain directions altered. At first, indeed, most agricultural work, probably,

[79] *Sermons on Human Nature.*
[80] *The Herd Instinct.*
[81] Tylor, *Primitive Culture*, II. p. 89.

was done by women; but in its progress it fell extensively into the hands of men; and then advantage accrued to those tribes that were capable of steady industry and prudence. The new employment decreased aggression on the principle that "had Alexander been holding the plough, he could not have run his friend Clitus through with a spear." The sick and aged were now less an encumbrance than they had been to hunters. Those who could not endure a settled life wandered away in their old pursuits. The more aggressive clans slaughtered one another in the vendetta. Social pressure and hanging eliminated many of the more idle, improvident, dishonest and unruly, whose instincts resisted "accommodation." The more neighbourly and co-operative tended to predominate. As civilisation intensifies, the numerous ways of getting a livelihood, which (as we have seen) derive their motive-force from the spirit of the pack, gratify that spirit under so many disguises and with so little direct personal collision, as to be compatible with a great deal of friendliness and benevolence; and co-operation, direct or indirect, steadily increases.

(*d*) Increasing capacity of forming ideas of remote ends and of co-ordinating many activities in their pursuit, implies the inhibition of many aggressive or distracting impulses, and constitutes an automatic control. And although it is now fashionable to depreciate the power of intelligence in human life, surely, its development has had great influence. As men come to foresee the many consequences of action they learn to modify and regulate it, as each foreseen consequence excites some impulse, either reinforcing or inhibiting action. Reflection upon our lot has done much to ameliorate it. The "conditions of gregariousness" (to use W. K. Clifford's definition of morality) have been expounded by the more penetrating and comprehensive minds—prophets, poets, philosophers; and some disciples have understood them and have persuaded many to believe. Nor have such luminaries arisen only in the later phases of culture when their writings have been delivered or their sayings recorded. Probably it was some one man who first pointed out to a tribe that had ignored the fact, that whether a wrong had been done by accident or on purpose affected the agent's guilt and ought to affect the penalty exacted. Some one man, probably, first saw what injustice is often disguised by the specious equality of the *lex talionis*; another first tried to assuage the bitterness of a vendetta by appointing compensation; another, perhaps first proposed to substitute animal for human sacrifice, or a puppet for a slave. And when we read the lists of sagacious proverbs that have been collected from many savage tribes, we must consider that it was by eminent individuals that those sayings were first uttered one by one: individuals with the gifts of insight and expression to summarise the experience of a whole tribe in memorable words, rude forerunners of our prophets and philosophers.

§ 8. Influence of the Imaginary Environment

§ 8. *Influence of the Imaginary Environment.*—Belief in Magic and Spirits often injurious; but on the whole advantageous; especially by establishing government

The necessity of learning the whole art of hunting from its rudiments, without the help of instinct or tradition, by sheer observation, memory and inference, put extraordinary stress upon the brain. At first by knowledge, strategy, co-operation and persistence of will, later by devising weapons and snares, evolving language and discovering the ways of making and utilising fire, man found means of entirely changing the conditions of his life; but this would have been impossible without a great development of his brain; and, accordingly, it appears that Eoanthropus, at the beginning of the Pleistocene, had a skull with three times the cubic capacity of the anthropoids. With the growth of the brain came a continually increasing fecundity of ideas. "Piltdown man saw, heard, felt, thought, and dreamt much as we do."[82] The use of ideas is to foresee events and prepare for them beforehand: the great advantage of distance-senses over contact-senses, is to give an animal time to adapt its actions to deferred events; and ideas give this power in a vastly higher degree. So far the utility of brains and ideas seems obvious. But in order that ideas may be useful in this way, they must (one would suppose) represent and anticipate the actual course of events. If they falsely indicate the order of nature, or even beings and actions that do not exist at all, ideas may seem to be worse than useless.

Now, when we turn to the lowest existing savages, they are found to possess, in comparison with apes, a considerable fecundity of ideas; constituting, on the one hand, a good stock of common sense, or knowledge of the properties and activities of the things and animals around them, and of how to deal with them, which enables them to carry on the affairs of a life much more complex and continuous than any animal's: but including, on the other hand, a strange collection of beliefs about magic and spirits, which entirely misrepresent the course of nature and the effective population of the world. These latter beliefs, or imaginative delusions, hamper them in so many ways, waste so much time, lead them sometimes into such dark and cruel practices, that one may be excused for wondering whether their bigger brains can have been, on the whole, of any biological advantage to them in comparison with the anthropoids. The anthropoids live by common sense. So do savages, and they have much more of it; but the anthropoids seem not to be troubled by magic and animism. We must suppose that the common sense of primitive man increased age by age, as he became more and more perfectly adapted to the hunting-life, and that at some stage his imagination began to falsify the relations of things and the powers of nature. It seems that imagination-beliefs depend chiefly upon the influence of desire and fear, suggestibility, hasty generalisation, and the seduction of reasoning by analogy. At what stage imaginations, thus divorced from reality, began to influence human life, it is impossible to say; but it cannot be less than half a million years ago, if (as Dr. Keith says) Eoanthropus, 400,000 years ago, "thought and dreamt much as we do." Why did not such delusions hinder our development? Or did they promote it?

The first consideration is, that biological adaptation is nearly always a compromise: if any organ or faculty be useful on the whole, in spite of some disutility, its increase favours the survival of those in whom it increases; and this is true of the brain and its thinking. The second is, that nearly all the magical and animistic beliefs and practices that are socially destructive, probably belong to a stage of

---

[82] A. Keith, op. cit., p. 429.

human life that is attained long after our differentiation has been established, and when some progress has been made in arts and customs. Savages of the lowest culture have few beliefs that can be called positively injurious. Talismans and spells, not by themselves relied upon, but only adscititious to common-sense actions, give confidence without weakening endeavour. To curse, or to "point the bone," does not create but merely expresses a malevolent purpose; and, although sometimes fatal by suggestion, is on the whole better than to assassinate. Taboos do more good by protecting person and property and custom than they do harm by restricting the use of foods. Belief in imaginary evils waiting upon secret sins exerts, whilst supported by social unanimity, a control upon all kinds of behaviour: it is the beginning of the "religious sanction," and one sort of conscience. The dread of spirits that prowl at night keeps people in the family-cave or by the camp-fire; and that is the best place for them. Many rites and observances are sanitary. Totemism rarely does any harm, and may once have usefully symbolised the unity of social groups. Totemic and magical dances give excellent physical training, promote the spirit of co-operation, are a sort of drill; and (like all art), whilst indulging, they also restrain imagination by imposing upon it definite forms. For a long time there was no special profession of wizard or priest, with whose appearance most of the evil of magic and animism originates; though probably even they generally do more good than harm by their courage and sagacity, by discovering drugs and poisons, by laying ghosts, and by their primitive studies in medicine and psychology.

The wizard, however, and the priest, who could never have existed but for the prevalent beliefs in Magic and Animism, have a further and far more important function in human life, namely, the organisation, or rather reorganisation of society. The organisation of the hunting-pack described above was liable through several causes to fall asunder. Some of these causes are obvious: (*a*) The improvement of weapons and snares and discovery of poisons made very small parties, or even single families, self-sufficing—as among the Bushmen (though they sometimes assembled for a grand hunt).[83] (*b*) Failure of game from desiccation, as in Australia, or because the tribe has been driven into a poor country like Tierra del Fuego; so that a small population is scattered over a wide area, and reduced to a greater or less dependence on "collecting." (*c*) The adoption of even a primitive agricultural or pastoral life may make hunting a secondary interest. In such cases the natural leaders of a clan are no longer (as in the old pack) plainly indicated; and if society is to be saved from anarchy, some new control must establish itself for the preservation of tradition and custom. Conceivably this happened in several ways; but in fact (I believe) we know of only one, namely: First, the rule of wizards, who are chiefly old men credited with mysterious power that makes the boldest tribesman quail, such as the headmen and elders of an Australian tribe. In New Guinea, too, and much of Melanesia, the power of rulers, even though recognised as of noble birth, depends chiefly upon their reputation for Magic. And among the Bushmen secrets about poisons and antidotes and colours for painting (probably considered magical) were heirlooms in certain families of chiefs, and gave them caste.[84]

[83] G. M. Theal, *History and Ethnology of South Africa*, p. 11.
[84] G. W. Stone, *Native Races of South Africa*, p. 76.

Secondly, at a later stage, as the belief in ghosts more and more prevails, and ancestral ghosts are worshipped, and ghosts of heroes or chiefs become veritable gods, the priests who celebrate their worship strengthen the position of chiefs or kings descended from these gods, and help to maintain more comprehensive and coherent governments than those established upon Magic only; though to these later forms, also, and to Religion itself magical beliefs contribute their support. The inevitable development of illusory imaginations along with common sense, then, assisted early and also later culture, because they preserved order and cohesion by re-arousing the ancient submission and loyalty of the pack. For common sense is always limited to present conditions, it could never have foreseen the dependence of human life upon order and the necessity of maintaining cohesion even at great immediate sacrifices. These interests were, therefore, served indirectly through delusions; natural selection must, within certain limits, have favoured the superstitious. Excessively imaginative and superstitious tribes may sometimes have been eliminated; for common sense also has biological utility. But, perverse as it may seem, imaginations utterly false have had their share in promoting "progress": co-operating with agriculture and trade, magic, religions and the fine arts have, by supporting government and civil order, helped in accommodating us, and even in some measure adapting us, to our present condition, such as it is.

CHAPTER III

BELIEF AND SUPERSTITION

§ 1. SUPERSTITION

§ 1. *"Superstition."* — Here used merely to include Magic and Animism
as imagination-beliefs

INASMUCH as the influence of superstition upon the history of society can hardly be exaggerated, it must be worth while to inquire into its origin and nature. But this inquiry leads into a quagmire of ambiguous words: and to attempt to define them for all purposes would entangle the discussion in endless controversies. So it will be best to explain merely in what sense certain words will be used in this book. "Superstition," for example, means in common use (I think) false beliefs concerning supernatural powers, especially such as are regarded as socially injurious, and particularly as leading to obscurantism or cruelty: but it is often extended to cover beliefs of a negligible or frivolous kind, such as stories about "fairy-rings," or the unluckiness of seeing the new moon for the first time through glass. Plainly the injuriousness of a false belief is often in dispute, and at any rate is a question of time and place. "Superstition," then, is here used merely as a collective term for the subjects of the ensuing chapters — Magic (or the belief in occult forces) and Animism (or the belief in the activity of spirits).

The consequences of a belief, again, whether good or evil, cannot affect its psychological character: in trying to explain its nature and origin, one cannot take account of its social values. The explanation of superstitions must hold of all false beliefs, whatever their utility or disutility. Nay, further, whether a belief is false or true does not necessarily affect its psychological character: for a man may hold two doctrines, one true and the other false, both derived from the sincere testimony of the same person, and he may not be able to discern any difference in the degrees of confidence with which he holds them or in their influence upon his conduct. The understanding of false belief, then, requires an examination of belief in general.

Still, whilst in the mind of any given man a true and a false belief may have the same character and origin, considered generally they must surely have different origins and grounds; and to make the sequel clearer, I will anticipate its conclusions so far as to say that true beliefs seem to rest on perception or inferences verified by perception, and false beliefs seem to depend upon imagination that cannot be verified. This general statement will need several qualifications. But I rely upon it at present so far as to say that superstitions are essentially imagination-beliefs.

We shall find that these superstitions, though often held by whole tribes with the utmost assurance, differ in some subtle way from the perception-beliefs of their common sense, as that "fire burns" and that "water quenches fire." They are unstable: (1) they become active on occasions, and otherwise are apt to be forgotten—as ghosts are only thought of at night. (2) They are modifiable merely for the sake of economy or other convenience. (3) They lose their hold on a tribe, fall off and die in course of time without any change in the evidence for them. (4) They depend a good deal upon the assent of a crowd. (5) They often vary in neighbouring countries or families, or amongst the members of a family. This is not like common sense. Superstitions or imagination-beliefs are unstable, in spite of being often held with great obstinacy (so that people die for them), and of their enduring, in the simpler forms and at a certain level of social life, for thousands of years. There is something wanting in the holdfast or anchorage of imagination-beliefs.

It is necessary to explain what I mean by "imagination."

§ 2. IMAGINATION

§ 2. *Imagination.*—Various uses of the word; mental "images"; in connection with reasoning; and with literary fiction. Here means unverifiable representation

Is it enough to define "imagination" as merely the having of mental "images," pictures before the mind's eye? This would confine imagination to visual representations, to the exclusion of auditory, olfactory, etc., which are all a man born blind can have, and which sometimes occur to those who can see, though the visual are commonest. The word "images," therefore, is sometimes used to cover all these modes of representation; though "phantasmata" would be better.

Again, a mental image or phantasm, visual or auditory, is improperly called an imagination, if there is nothing more than the reproduction of a single sense-quality. Imaginations represent not abstract sensations, but perceptions. To see an armed knight is not merely to have a visual impression of him, but to perceive a living, solid, heavy object definitely in space; and imagination reproduces the whole of this, and otherwise would be quite uninteresting. What would the tournament in *Ivanhoe* amount to if the knights were only phantoms?

Further, imagination, merely as a reproduction of perception, is not distinguished from memory; but, in use, the two are always contrasted. Memories are recognised (in their complete form) as returning to us from earlier experience, both their component pictures and the order of them, and they are relatively stable; imaginations are felt to be more or less novel, and can easily be modified. Probably all the elements of an imagination might have occurred in a memory; but the arrangement of these elements is often so different from any actual experience as to baffle every attempt to redistribute them amongst their sources. Hence, in normal cases, our attitudes toward a memory and toward an imagination are entirely different. If a seeming memory prove false, we say it was only an imagination.

But, once more, a good many men never have images or phantasmata (except words), or very few or faint ones, or only when falling asleep, and so on. Yet they are not wanting in imagination; words or other signs serve them instead of images to carry all meanings (the important matter); they enter into the spirit of poetry and literary fiction: so that imagination may be active without images. And the fact seems to be that the effectiveness of mental processes depends very little upon phantasmata, but upon something much deeper in the mind; and that there exist in men all degrees of concrete representative power, from those who picture everything they think of with vivid and definite detail, down, through many stages of decreasing realisation, to those who have only faint or fragmentary "images," or even none at all: without its being possible to say (at present) that one type of mind is better or worse than another; though they may be adapted to different tasks.

Expectation and reasoning, which are closely allied (for every definite expectation is a sort of inference), are often carried on in pictures—"picture thinking"—and this also is called imagination. Tyndall's brilliant address on *The Scientific Uses of the Imagination* is well known. It greatly helps some men in thinking to form pictures of what they think about, such as a machine or an anatomical specimen, as if they had the thing before them; or even of an atom, which no man ever has before him, and which cannot be imagined by reproducing the precept, but only by constructing a picture from much grosser materials according to concepts. The picture thus formed necessarily falls short in some ways of the thing thought or meant, and can only be prevented from misleading us by guarding it with definitions or rules or abstract ideas; and this shows that the effectiveness of thought, the deeper process mentioned above, is a concatenation or evolution of meanings or general ideas, and that it is, in part, by illustrating these that pictures are useful: they also serve to fix attention, as words do.

Thus reasoning may express itself by imagination. On the other hand, imagination is more frequently contrasted with reason, as dealing in fiction, not reality. Our confusion is shown thus: to call an historian imaginative is depreciatory; yet it is as bad to say he is wanting in imagination. In the latter case, we mean that he fails adequately to conceive the events he treats of; in the former, that he embellishes or distorts them with unverifiable representations.

Again, the term "imagination" is sometimes confined to intellectual processes in the fine arts: dramas, novels, etc., are works of imagination. Now dramas and novels all proceed upon one method, namely: they begin by stating or insinuating an hypothesis concerning certain persons in a given situation, and then deducing (that is reasoning out) the consequences, occasionally helping the plot by further assumptions: at least that is how it appears, though probably the main incident of the plot is thought of first, and then an hypothesis is framed that conveniently leads up to it. And if the reasoning is feeble, and if the subsidiary assumptions are too numerous or too facile, we say the work is flimsy or improbable—allowing for the *genre*; for a romance is not expected to be as probable as a modern novel. *Gulliver's Travels* afford the most perfect example of this method; for each voyage begins with a frank absurdity—men six inches or sixty feet high, a flying island, rational horses; but this being granted, the sequel makes tolerable logic. Well, many scientific investigations seem to follow exactly the same method—begin with an hypothesis, deduce the consequences, and occasionally help out the argument with further hypotheses (though that is not all): and here again the conclusion is usually thought of first, and the hypothesis invented to explain it. If it be said that the scientist believes his hypothesis to be true, whilst the romancer does not, it may be replied that the scientist sometimes expressly warns us that his assumption is only a "working hypothesis," which may not be true (though he thinks it may be), whereas early epic poets and minstrels often regarded their work as by no means without a foundation in fact.

Imagination and reasoning, then, are closely allied or interwoven, and the contrasting of them depends entirely upon this, that there is a sense in which imagination is not a presentation of truth or matter-of-fact, whether it is believed to be or not; and a sense in which reasoning is devoted solely to the discovery of truth concerning facts, and to that end is protected by a methodology, carefully comparing its premises, carefully verifying its conclusions; whereas the imagination that is contrasted with reasoning knows nothing of a methodology nor of verification. Even the modern novelist, a great part of whose hypothesis is usually true—the present state of society, facts of history or geography, etc.,—does not pretend to present a truth of fact. It belongs to his art to play at reasoning; he has learnt to play the game very well; but it remains play: he aims at and attains not truth but verisimilitude. And when we look back on the history of fiction we see (on the whole) the verisimilitude growing, age by age, slighter and fainter; till in early romance and poetry it is disturbed and broken and destroyed by stories about monsters, impossible heroes, magicians and gods, believed at one time to be true, and just the same as stories still believed by barbarians and savages, but which we believe no longer.

It is such stories as these last, including all superstitions, that I especially call "imagination-beliefs." The term includes all false beliefs, but with the rest I am not directly concerned. How are imagination-beliefs possible?

§ 3. Belief

§ 3. *Belief.*—Nature of belief; degrees of probability; tested by action; play-belief

Belief is here used to denote the attitude of mind in which perceptions are regarded as real, judgments as true of matters-of-fact, actions and events as about to have certain results. It is a serious and respectful attitude; for matter-of-fact compels us to adjust our behaviour to it, whether we have power to alter it or not. Hume describes belief as having a certain "force, vivacity, solidity, firmness, steadiness; influence and importance in governing our actions";[85] and these terms are quite just, but most of them are synonyms; and the whole dictionary will not make anybody understand what belief is who has never felt it. However, there is no such person.

The quality of this attitude (or the "feeling" of it) as a specific "state of consciousness" is difficult to observe, because (like pleasure or displeasure) it is al-

---

[85] *Treatise of Human Nature*, Part III. § 7. For the recent psychology of Belief see James Sully's *The Human Mind*, ch. xiii., and James Ward's *Psychological Principles*, ch. xiv.

ways marginal to something else in the focus of attention, some object, judgment or action; but we can appreciate it in its variations by considering the very different degrees of "force, steadiness," etc., which characterise several beliefs regarded as more or less probable. The degree of belief ought to correspond with the weight of evidence: if evidence for any judgment is complete and uncontradicted, it may be called 1, and the corresponding state of mind should be "certainty"; if evidence for it there is none, or if evidence for the contradictory judgment is complete, it may be called 0, and the state of mind "disbelief." Between these extremes there is room for an infinite series of fractions, and for corresponding shades of doubt (which, of course, do not really occur); and in the middle, at ½, there should be suspension of judgment. But most of these refined attitudes are the luxury of a few men severely trained in estimating evidence, and by them enjoyed only in the departments they have been trained in. For the mass of mankind, a very few shades of confidence or dubiety fill up their scale of judgment-values; and these may be far from corresponding as they should do with the quantity or quality of the evidence; and the nearest they get to suspension of judgment is a state of hesitation between alternatives that by turns seem equally likely. Disbelief, though the opposite logically to belief, as rejection to acceptance, has, nevertheless, much in common with it—the character of finality and positiveness, which is often (perhaps always) derived from belief in something else which is incompatible with the given judgment.

When the attitude of belief is established in one's mind by evidence clearly conceived, whether by the examination of facts or the weighing of arguments, it is called "conviction," and so is the process of bringing it about; but if it results from considerations imperfectly appreciated, and from emotional appeals, especially when urged by another person, it may be called "persuasion," though the word describes the process rather than the result. Most imagination-beliefs, including all superstitions, are persuasions.

It is generally admitted that the test of the strength of one's belief is its influence upon our actions—where the test is practicable. With full belief one acts "confidently" (a significant verbal proposition!); in doubt, hesitatingly or cautiously; in disbelief, not at all, or in the sense of the contrary belief. But we cannot always judge of a man's beliefs from his actions; for he may be actuated by several beliefs, and we do not know what they are. And popular actions that involve no loss or hardship may express mere assent without belief.

There is a kind of imagination-belief, and the purest kind, which has nothing to do with evidence: it is often called "make-believe" or "play-belief": the entering into or contemplating some activity, which we know to have no direct bearing on our necessary interests, with as much ardour and absorption as if it were the only important thing in the world: as in games and sports, especially in drama and romance. This is one of the many things that do not astonish because they are so common; and the usual (and probably the true) explanation of it is, that this state of mind is of the utmost utility in giving zest to play, especially during youth. For many animals share in this spirit; and the young of the higher animals, which enjoy a long protected youth, pass the time chiefly at play, and thereby develop and train all their faculties, physical and mental. It somewhat outlasts youth in many animals, and conspicuously in ourselves, some having nothing better to do (and they might do worse), and others relieving from time to time the strain or tedium of work and, in some sort, prolonging youth into middle age; till play becomes gradually less engrossing.

This play-belief depends entirely upon imaginative excitement; and it shows that the attitude of belief may be adopted voluntarily, or fall upon us (as it were) by surprise and maintain itself for a time in great strength: with many at a melodrama it runs to anxiety, weeping and anguish; and this not only without evidence, but in spite of the knowledge that this is London, whose magistrates would never permit such doings: only one forgets London, with all its dull conventions of law and order. Attention is engrossed by the play.

Play-belief has the same traits as were said above to mark superstitions: (1) it becomes active on occasions, and otherwise disappears; (2) it is always modifiable for convenience or by a change of taste; (3) it loses its hold and tends to die out in a man as time goes on; (4) it is strengthened by the assent of an excited crowd; (5) the objects of such beliefs are very variable. We shall find that in other ways there is a close alliance between superstition and play. But, certainly, superstition has a much deeper hold upon our nature; for it not only excites fear and anxiety, but itself is born of those passions: the desire of security and confidence, the dread of impending and unknown perils, these are its life and strength. So that the wonder is that superstitions are not more enduring. And the truth seems to be that the tendency to adopt superstitions does endure at a certain level of mentality, though particular superstitious beliefs are mutable; just as in the individual, a disposition to play outlasts many particular modes of recreation.

Belief, then, is an attitude of mind in which we may find ourselves for good reasons, or for bad reasons, or for none at all; sometimes even slipping into it voluntarily or involuntarily when we know the situation is unreal; indeed, an attitude in which, in play or earnest, we pass our lives, unless something happens to arouse doubt or criticism.

§ 4. Causes and Grounds of Belief

§ 4. *Causes and Grounds of Belief.*—Derived from perception. Evidentiary causes, or grounds, raising some probability; and non-evidentiary causes which are not grounds. Memory, testimony, inference so far as unverifiable are imagination. Influence of apperceptive masses and of methodology. Non-evidentiary causes have their own apperceptive masses—derived from bad observation, memory, testimony; influenced by emotion, desire and voluntary action; by sympathy and antipathy, and by suggestibility

The source, direct or indirect, of all belief is perception. In perception must be included, for subjective studies, introspection; though being difficult to keep steady, to repeat and to compare with the observation of other minds, it carries less conviction. As to perception we say that "seeing is believing"; and, in fact, an object holds the eye in a way that vouches for its own reality; but, if we suspect that our eyes deceive us, reassurance comes with the handling of the thing. Belief has sometimes been discussed as if it were chiefly concerned with ideas or the relations of ideas; and systems of philosophy have sought justification in the coherence of ideas, with little or no regard (not to say with contempt) for the coherence of ideas with perceptions. But nearly the whole of every man's life (savage or philosopher) passes in an attitude of unquestioning belief in the evidence of his senses; and it is thence that belief extends to ideas on a presumption of their representing reality. We know that a perception may be fallible, but perceptions and the comparison of perceptions in the long run overrule everything else; and experimental methods consist in taking precautions against the errors of perception, and in bringing every hypothesis to the test of perception.

Further causes of belief are either Evidentiary, which (though often misleading) may generally be justified on reflection as raising some degree of probability, and which may, therefore, be called "grounds"; or Non-evidentiary, which (though very influential) cannot, on reflection, be justified as having any logical value, and are, therefore, causes only and not grounds.

(1) Evidentiary grounds of belief are (*a*) memory, which is plainly indispensable if we are to learn by experience; and (*b*) testimony, which must be trusted if language is not to be useless and social co-operation impossible: both these grounds are supposed to rest upon the primary rock of previous perception, but are slippery and treacherous. Memory is only valid so far as it truthfully represents original experience, and testimony only so far as it presents (i) a valid memory, (ii) correctly reported. Hence in serious matters precautions must be taken against their fallibility: otherwise they are not good evidence. A specious memory, so far as it is false, is imagination; and false testimony, so far as it reports (i) a false memory or (ii) an invention of the reporter, is also imagination. Testimony gathers force, as a cause of belief, with the numbers and consideration of those who support it, and is especially strengthened by their unanimity; but, as a ground of belief, it depends only on their knowledge and truthfulness. A third ground of belief is (*c*) inference; which is necessary to all original adjustment of our conduct to the future or to unperceived circumstances, but highly fallible, and constituting the chief problem for the exercise of Logic when that science arises: especially to explain the conditions of valid observations and experiments, of probability, of the conclusion of an argument being covered by its premises, and of the sufficiency of verification. False inferences that cannot be verified are imaginations.

As the growing mind of society deals with true beliefs they are piled up and classified in systems of science and philosophy: in which systems each belief or judgment strengthens and is strengthened by the rest. Even without systematisation, the mere structural similarity of judgments, formed unconsciously on the same implicit principles of causation and classification, throws them into those loose apperceptive masses which we call "common sense." Such systems or masses, whether of science or of common sense, readily assimilate and confirm new inferences having the same character, and offer resistance to all inferences having a different structure, such as those about magic and spirits. The selective power of these apperceptive masses over novel ideas constitutes "understanding," and is the plain solid man's substitute for Logic; and so it is with many scientists, who often neglect the abstract study of Logic. For these systems or masses of experience are the substance of Logic and Methodology, which are their skeletons abstracted from them. They are the basis of all effective comparison and criticism; agreement or disagreement with them is the test of truth or error. It is the chief defect of common sense that the verification of its judgments depends almost entirely upon repetition of experiences (what Logicians call "simple enumeration"), without that analysis of observations which alone can show the necessary relations of facts; but this defect is in some measure remedied in good minds by that power of unformulated ideas of natural order, the result of unconscious analysis, which we call "good judgment" —a power which the fortunate possessor may be unable to explain.

(2) Non-evidentiary causes of belief are all reducible to bad observations, imaginations, and the causes that excite imagination; and bad observations are caused by false imaginations as to the meaning of sense-data. If it should seem to any one that since imagination consists of ideas it must be by nature incompatible with intense belief, we must consider that memory, the effects of testimony, and inferences also consist entirely of ideas; so that in that character they do not differ from imagination. Even perception depends for its meaning upon implicit ideas, and erroneous perception is due to erroneous ideas. The weakness of imagination-belief which (despite its frequent intensity) always in time becomes manifest, is due to its not being constantly confirmed by experience.

In detail the non-evidentiary causes of belief are as follows: (*a*) not only the truths of experience become massed or systematised in common sense and science, but the errors of misinterpreted experience and tradition form similar aggregates. Coincidences mistaken for causation, illusions, dreams, tales of thaumaturgy and ghost-stories, so far as they have anything in common in their outlines or emotional tone, form apperceptive masses which function in the same way as scientific systems: each of their constituent beliefs strengthens and is strengthened by the rest; and each mass (as a delusive "understanding") readily assimilates and confirms any new tale or illusion having its own character, and resists and repels every judgment having a different structure—and, therefore, refuses explanation. And just as science and common sense have a sort of internal skeleton of principles which has been exhibited as Logic, so some of these comparatively obscure and chaotic masses of illusion and tradition contain certain structural principles which, though unconscious at the lowest human level, obtain recognition as culture advances—for example, the principles of mimetic and contagious magic; and then, too, arise such caricatures of science as theogonies and cosmologies, chiromancy, astrology and so forth. But nothing ever emerges from them that can be called a test of truth or methodology; much less, of course, can such a thing be found at lower levels of culture. There you see the accumulating clouds of imagination-belief, which gather together from all the winds and pile themselves up to overshadow poor humanity age after age; which still, in our own world, are by no means dissipated; and to whose persistent influence we may (I suppose) attribute the mysticism that periodically infects philosophy itself.

(*b*) Contributory to these masses of error are bad observations, confused and distorted memories, dreams and corrupted testimony and tradition, all of them having their origin in some sort of experience and matter-of-fact, and all issuing in vain imaginations. For of course there is no such thing as imagination under-ived from experience; experience is distorted and corrupted by superstition, but it transfers to superstition the attitude of belief that always belongs to experience, and supplies materials from which (as we shall see) it is often possible to construct such a defence of superstition as, to an unsophisticated mind, must be very plausible and persuasive.[86] Direct experience is often interpreted by a story in such a way as to make the story more credible. If a stone is shown as marking the tomb of a hero, or a cleft in the mountain as proving the prowess of a wizard, one unconsciously transfers the attitude of belief involved in contemplating these relics to all the legends concerning those mighty men of old.

(*c*) The causes determining belief are reinforced in various ways by feeling and emotion. The agreeableness or disagreeableness of any judgment draws attention to, or diverts it from such a judgment and the evidence for it: except that some disagreeable emotions, especially fear, by a sort of fascination of attention, are favourable to belief in the reality of an imagined evil. They possess the whole mind.

(*d*) Every desire fixes attention upon beliefs favourable to it, and upon any evidence favourable to them, and diverts attention from conflicting beliefs and considerations. Thus every desire readily forms about itself a relatively isolated mass of beliefs, which resists comparison and, therefore (as Ribot says),[87] does not recognise the principle of contradiction. Incompatible desires may be cherished without our becoming aware of their incompatibility; or, if the fact obtrudes itself upon us, we repudiate it and turn away.

The more immature a mind, again, and the less knowledge it has, the less inhibition of desire is exerted by foresight of consequences that ought to awaken conflicting desires or fears; and the less compassion one has, the less is desire inhibited by its probable consequences to others: therefore, in both cases, the less check there is upon belief.

(*e*) Voluntary action in connection with any belief, whether of a rational kind or in the routine of rites and ceremonies, favours that belief: (1) by establishing the idea-circuit of means and end, the end suggesting the means to it, and the thought of means running forward to the end—a circuit that resists interruption: (2) by the general effect of habit and prejudice; for every habit of action or of thought has inertia, and, moreover, it is agreeable, and to break it is disagreeable; so that, again, a relatively isolated system is formed, which resists comparison and criticism.

On the influence of desire and of activities for an end depends "the will to believe." We cannot believe anything by directly willing it; but we can will what to attend to, or what to do, and that determines belief.

(*f*) Finally, belief is determined by certain social influences besides testimo-

[86] See below, ch. viii. § 5.
[87] *Logique des Sentiments*, II. § 4.

ny and tradition: especially by sympathy and antipathy between families, parties, tribes; and by imitativeness and suggestibility (qualified fortunately by contra-suggestibility); so that beliefs become fashionable, endemic, coercive, impassioned and intolerant. The power of a crowd to inflict its passions and beliefs upon the individual has recently been much explained: it has always been practically understood by wizards, priests and politicians who lead mankind by the ears. Suggestibility, in general, is the liability to follow example or testimony without criticising it; and for many people it is so easy to fall into the attitude of belief upon slight provocation, that this liability, to the extent of weakness, is very common. Contra-suggestibility in general is the opposite tendency. But special suggestibility (I should say) is the liability to adopt a belief on testimony not only in the absence of evidence, but against evidence; and contra-suggestibility is the liability to reject a belief against the evidence. They are merely extreme cases. If you draw two equal straight lines, A and B, and say, "It seems to me that B is longer than A," one person will reply "Certainly," another "Certainly not; A is the longer." The art of suggestion consists in reducing your audience to this state of imbecility; it requires you to bring them into such a condition of exclusive attention to your words that, comparison and criticism being excluded, their natural disposition to assent shall (for the time) have free play. The specially suggestible person is easily thrown into this state of exclusive attention, as if hypnotised. He who is suggestible by one man may not be so by another; or he may be more suggestible in the line of his prejudices than against them.

§ 5. The Beliefs of Immature Minds

§ 5. *The Beliefs of Immature Minds.* — Non-evidentiary causes more influential than with us; picture-thinking more vivid; no common standard of truth; feeble power of comparison, due perhaps to undeveloped brain

All these grounds and causes of belief, evidentiary and non-evidentiary (except Logic and Science) are common to both mature and immature minds: but their proportional influence with individuals or with societies is very different at different stages of development; and in immature minds and in the lower stages of culture, the power of the non-evidentiary causes is excessive. Probably the chief cause of the growth of common sense in the generality of men is an increasing regularity of social life, as (notably) in the bloom of the classical civilisations and in the last four hundred years.

Perception, in normal circumstances, is accepted by all as a matter of course or, rather, of necessity: it controls the activities of practical life in hunting and in industry, in making weapons, hoeing the ground, building houses: however, these labours may sometimes be modified or interrupted by the intrusion of beliefs derived from other sources. If a savage sings a spell to his prey, or weapon, or tool, or keeps the head of a slain enemy on a shelf that his victim's soul may assist him as a slave, he may thereby increase his own confidence in the work of hunting or gardening; but, otherwise, if his work be no better, neither need it be the worse for such fancies. The properties of matter exact practical recognition, without which nothing can be done. Even magical practices presuppose a sane perception of the central facts: as who is acting, for what purpose, when and where, with what and toward whom. Upon this basis there may be an astonishing superstructure of imagination-belief; but there are limits to the effectiveness of such beliefs.

M. Levy-Bruhl, indeed, in a very interesting book, maintains[88] that, under the influence of social ideas (*représentations collectives*), the primitive mind actually perceives things differently from what we do. Whilst we succeed in attaining an objective presentation, eliminating subjective associations, with primitives *propriétés mystique, forces occultes* are integral qualities of the object. He grants that, in certain cases of immediate practical interest, we find them very attentive and able to discriminate slight impressions, and to recognise the external signs of an object on which their subsistence or even their life depends; but holds that, in a very great majority of cases, their perceptions are over-weighted by subjective elements. This doctrine reverses (I venture to think) the real relations between perceptions and other causes of belief and their proportionate influence in savage life. It is not only where subsistence or life is at stake that backward peoples see things as they are: in merely experimental tests, Dr. Rivers found amongst both Papuans and Todas, that, as to suggestibility in perception, they showed a high degree of independence of judgment.[89] Their confidence in perception is not, like imagination-belief, occasional, modifiable for convenience, liable to lapse in course of time, dependent on the assent of a crowd. So far as occult or mystical attributes are by a savage assigned to things, such as magical force to a weapon, they constitute a secondary, imaginary integration with the percept. Such imaginary attributes cannot, like perception attributes, be verified by sensation: compare the hardness of a spearhead with its magical force.

The peculiarity of savage beliefs is due, not to corrupt and clouded perception, but to the influence of desire and anxiety upon their imagination, unrestrained by self-criticism and reinforced by the popular consensus. The savage's imagination is excited by the pressing needs of his life in hunting, love, war, agriculture, and therefore by hunger and emulation, hate and grief, fear and suspicion. Imaginations spring up in his mind by analogy with experience; but often by remote or absurd analogies; and there is no logic at hand and not enough common sense to distinguish the wildest imaginative analogies from trustworthy conclusions. The same pressing needs and the same emotional storms often affect a whole tribe, and simultaneously stimulate every one's imagination; and originating (no doubt) in ancient times and slowly accumulating and condensing, there grows up a mass of public imagination-beliefs, which are inculcated into every individual by tradition and common ceremonies. Such beliefs embodied in stories and formulæ, and associated with rites and customs, have for a long time the strength of custom in governing the behaviour of individuals and in tribal respect; but they prove at last to be weaker than custom, inasmuch as the observances may continue whilst the beliefs are forgotten or replaced by others, as the progress of culture makes it necessary to think of the old rites in a different way. In their flourishing period they extensively influence practical affairs, sometimes helpfully or harmlessly,

[88] *Les Fonctions Mentales dans les Sociétés Inférieures*, p. 40.
[89] *British Journal of Psychology*, Vol. I. p. 393.

sometimes injuriously and disastrously. In general, imaginations are prevented by biological necessity from modifying a tribe's conduct beyond certain limits; but, exceptionally, they result in tribal insanity, tending toward, if not accomplishing, the tribe's destruction, as in extreme cases of the practice of human sacrifice or of the ordeal by poison.

Indeed, so violent and tyrannous is the power of superstitious beliefs in many cases, that it may be difficult to understand how they are almost entirely born of the imagination. In a civilised country there are always current some beliefs as imaginative and absurd as any to be found in the middle of Africa; but surviving amidst a greater mass of perception-beliefs and positive ideas about industry and commerce, they have lost much of their driving power; and when the imaginative character of any belief has been recognised, it passes into the region of fine art or mythology, or even of ridicule. If such things have any place in our life, we turn to them of personal choice in the intervals of affairs. Under the influence of the fine arts or of literature treating of such things, our emotional states may be intense; but they are dissociated from action, exist for their own sake, have an appropriate tone (æsthetic) which marks their lack of energy, so that they require only an imaginary satisfaction. With a backward people there is much less "positive" opposition to their imaginative prepossessions and pursuits; what seems to us absurd, seems to them necessary; the actions and observances that express their beliefs are not performed as a matter of personal choice, but of public custom; the ends to be obtained (they think) are the same as those of what we call "business." And it must be so. Considering the function of superstition in promoting political evolution, it is plain that primitive man must have been capable of believing and doing those things which (within certain limits) had so much biological and social value.

To understand how the magical and religious beliefs of savages and the play-beliefs of civilised man, having a common source in imagination, are (in spite of strong contrasts) closely allied, we must call to mind the many degrees of intensity of play-belief in ourselves, varying from the momentary entertainment of playing with a child, through many grades of fiction or ceremony, down to a deeply serious frame of mind, a profound movement of dread or compassion that may long outlast our play. A child's absorption in such beliefs is more intense than ours; but circumstances prevent his attaining to the solid faith of a savage. The child of civilised people has little or no support in tradition (except from nurse-maids); he is not driven by the desires and anxieties of subsistence; and he is frequently interrupted by his seniors. The savage has an overwhelming tradition and authority, pressing anxieties and no seniors. Until the civilised sceptic reaches his shores, there is, for the average tribesman, nothing but tardy experience or social fatigue to check his vagaries. His imagination vies with the sense of reality, often overpowers it; yet his beliefs show many signs of their insecure foundations.

It is not only the influence of society and tradition that renders imagination-beliefs coercive to a savage; in the immature mind of the individual there are certain conditions favourable to their prevalence.

(*a*) The process of imagination itself, the memory and the picture-thinking of savages, seems to be more vivid, sensuous, stable, more like perception than our own normally is. "The Australians," says Spencer and Gillen, "have the most wonderful imagination."[90] They often die of it; and so do Hindoo peasants, Maories, Fijians, Negroes and others, if they know they have been cursed or have broken a taboo. With the Melanesians, says Dr. Coddrington, thinking is like seeing;[91] and Dr. Rivers has confirmed this statement. Hence there is a tendency to accept imaginations as perceptions are accepted; and to believe in the efficacy of rites, because the mere performing of them with an imagined purpose makes their purpose seem to be accomplished. When a man of intense and excited imagination makes an image of an enemy, and stabs it, that his enemy may suffer, his action gratifies the impulse to stab, as if he wounded the enemy himself, and revenge seems to be a present fact. Similar intensity of imagination is found in civilised children—greater than in ordinary adults. Savages, again, seem to dream more vividly and convincingly than is usual amongst ourselves, and are said to be more liable to hallucinations. Physiological conditions of the immature brain (childish or savage), in which excitement does not rapidly spread through many associated neurones, may be the basis of the vividness of imagination, dreaming and hallucination.

(*b*) But more important than any intensity of picture-thinking to the growth and persistence of imagination-beliefs, is the want of a mental standard, by which they might be discredited. It is true that even at a low level of culture individuals are found for whom common sense constitutes a private standard, and who are sceptics in relation to their tribal beliefs.[92] But such a private standard cannot be communicated, and for the great majority of the tribesmen common sense is no confident guide; and perhaps they are even incapable of effectively comparing their ideas. At any rate, one reason why we believe our memories and not our imaginations is that, whilst in both cases the images (or elements of images) entering into them are derived from experience, in memory the relations of images in place, time and context are also derived directly from experience; whereas in imagination images (or their elements) are reconstructed in relations in which they have never been experienced, by analogies of experience (often distorted) or by condensations the most capricious. Therefore, to make imaginations credible to us, even in play, the relations of experience must be faithfully imitated, as (e. g.) in *Robinson Crusoe*; or else our emotions must be so strongly excited as to possess our minds with the fiction to the exclusion of all criticism. But with immature minds observation of fact, outside the practical, repetitive, necessary course of life, is not exact and coherent; and, accordingly, their memories are not coherent, especially as to time-relations; so that, by comparison with such memories, irregular imaginations suffer little. There is not enough orderly memory or general knowledge to discredit even absurd imaginations; for so far as observation and memory are disorderly, generalisation, conscious or unconscious, is impossible. Hence not only traditionary myths may be monstrous and arbitrary, but occasional tales of private

------

[90] *Northern Tribes of Central Australia*, p. 462.
[91] *The Melanesians*, p. 247.
[92] Below, ch. viii. § 4.

invention, amongst both children and savages, usually exhibit disconnected transitions and impossible happenings. Yet they satisfy the immature mind.

(*c*) There are certain other conditions of the immature mind that hinder the comparison of ideas and, therefore, the criticism of beliefs. About every imperative need, such as success in hunting, with its desires and anxieties, rites and ceremonies grow up to gratify imaginatively the desires and relieve the anxieties; and ideas of these observances form relatively isolated systems. To us these ideas usually seem absurd and irrelevant when compared with the savage's own experiences and his other practices. We see a hunter, for example, endeavour to gain his ends by two distinct series of actions. In one he fasts, enchants his weapons, casts spells upon his expected prey; in the other he carefully prepares his weapons, patiently tracks his prey, warily approaches and slays it. The latter series we approve and appreciate as causation; the former we ridicule as hocus-pocus, contributing objectively nothing to the event (though probably it increases his confidence); and we pity "the heathen in his blindness." And, indeed, he may be said to be mind-blind; for in observing the rites, his attention is so occupied by means and end, and caught in the circuit in which these ideas revolve, and he is so earnest in carrying out the prescribed actions, that he cannot compare them with the really effective actions, so as to discover their absurdity and irrelevancy. In short, a state of mental dissociation is established for the system of magical ideas. So far does illusion go that he seems to regard the rites as the most important part of his proceedings. But that is not really his deepest conviction: he trusts in Magic and keeps his bowstring dry.

(*d*) In the case of children we may assume, and in the more backward races of men we may suspect, that the comparison of judgments is difficult, or sometimes even impossible, because of the imperfect development of the cerebral cortex. There must be some structural conditions of the free flow of energy through all organs of the brain, corresponding with the associability and comparability of all ideas. We may doubt if these conditions are complete even in good cultivated minds; since everybody finds one or another study or art especially difficult for him, or the freeing of himself from this or that sort of prejudice especially repugnant. And it is not only deliberate comparison that is hindered in the immaturity of the brain, but also that automatic process (more or less unconscious) of assimilation and discrimination to which (I think) we owe most of the results of abstraction and generalisation that may seem to have required purposive comparison. Such imperfections of structure, greatest at the lowest levels of organisation, and gradually decreasing as ideal rationality is approached, we may call "incoördination"; and, so far as it obtains, the results must be somewhat similar to the discoördination, the breaking down or interruption of organic efficiency, that occurs in hysteria, hypnosis and some forms of insanity. One of the results probably is suggestibility—the tendency to accept what is told, or insinuated, without examination; for freedom from this common liability depends (apart from the contra-suggestible disposition) upon the rapidity and definiteness with which one can compare that which is suggested with present fact or with one's knowledge and former experience; and this is hindered by incoördination.

Effective incoördination may, however, be merely functional for want of practice in thinking; and it exists often enough in civilised people, because they have not even the desire to be consistent. In either case, whether from defective structure or from the dull inertia of disuse, there will be failure of comparison and, therefore, of criticism, and also (we may suppose) a greater intensity of imagination and of dreaming and a liability to hallucination, such as is said to be frequently the case with immature minds.

§ 6. The Reasoning of Immature Minds

§ 6. *The Reasoning of Immature Minds.*—Fallacies of induction; ignorance of the minor premise in deduction; reasoning by analogy

We have seen that many beliefs result from inferences, and that inferences, when logically justifiable, may be considered as grounds (raising some degree of probability); but, when not justifiable, they are only causes of belief and their results are only imagination-beliefs. Since the general nature of reasoning is the same for Socrates and Sambo, we must inquire into the particular nature of the reasoning which leads immature minds into such bewildering mazes of error as we see (for example) in the world-wide prevalence of Magic and Animism.

On the inductive side of knowledge (the obtaining of premises) there is, of course, much imperfect observation and hasty generalisation; but, in spite of these faults, a savage learns by repeated experiences a great many narrow general truths about the physical world, plants, animals and his fellow-men, which constitute his stock of common sense and on the strength of which he lives as a very intelligent animal. We shall find from time to time errors of observation (such as the taking of a dream for reality) and of generalisation (such as the classing of worms with reptiles); but, strictly speaking, this is not reasoning: all reasoning is deductive, and the immature mind's deductive processes need a fuller analysis.

Our Logic consists of a few universal principles generally accepted, with which any more particular judgment may be compared in order to test its validity. The matter may be superficially acquired in a few hours; but the full comprehension of it implies the widest comparison of types of judgment from all departments of knowledge: Logic being (as I have said) a sort of skeleton of knowledge. Hence in any mind incapable of comparison and criticism—or so far as it is incapable—there must be an absence of Logic. So much effective comparison of experience, however, goes on without our specially attending to it that a man's logical power bears no proportion to his investigations into the structure of knowledge. One man may be a great student of Logic and a very inefficient reasoner from a want of discipline in the world of fact; another, who has never opened a text-book, may yet show by the definiteness of his judgments and the adequacy of his plans, that he is a sort of incarnate Logic, that his mind works according to reason or (in other words) according to the order of facts. It is the highest manifestation of common sense. Such men occur among backward peoples.

The only universal principles that need be considered here are the Law of Causation and the Form of Substance and Attribute (Mill's doctrine of Natural

Kinds): which may be called the principles of parallel reasoning; because the greater part of ordinary reasoning consists in drawing some inference parallel to one or the other of them, usually in some restricted shape. For example, a restriction of causation is the proposition that "exposure to intense daylight causes sun-burn," of substance and attribute that "the specific gravity of gold is about 19·5": whence we infer that if we expose ourselves to sunlight our faces or hands will suffer, or that any piece of gold will be relatively very heavy. But in such cases erroneous inferences are easy: for example, to expect that exposure to London sunshine will cause sunburn; for there the foul atmosphere cuts off the actinic rays: or to expect that a lump of brass will have specific gravity 19·5. A necessary precaution before trusting an inference, therefore, is the ascertaining that the inference deals with the very same sort of case as the premise describes: else there is no complete parallel. And Logicians show in the form of the syllogism this necessary precaution—to use their favourite example in a case of Substance and Attribute:

Major premise — *All men are mortal;*

Minor premise — *Socrates is a man;*

∴ Conclusion — *Socrates is mortal.*

The conclusion *Socrates is Mortal* is parallel to the major premise *All men are mortal;* and that it deals with the very same sort of case is secured by the minor premise, *Socrates is a man.* Whoever reasons must see to it that this premise is true. But the savage has never noticed that necessity; and thence come most of his errors.

The syllogism (it is now admitted) does not describe the way in which we reason, but is only a form which gives some help in testing the validity of reasoning if one should ever think of doing such a thing. In practice we do not think first of the major premise, then of the minor premise and lastly of the conclusion. As a rule we do not think of either premise at all: the "conclusion" comes first to mind. In certain circumstances of association, because of our hopes or our fears, it occurs to us that "Socrates is mortal." If some one should doubt this judgment and ask for proof, we might think of the major premise, and then put it into words for the first time—"All men die;" even then it might not seem necessary to add that "Socrates is a man." But although we may not have been at the time aware of these premises until we were asked for them, their presence in the mind in some way was necessary to determine the inference: the major premise was there as latent memory of one or more cases of people who had died; the minor premise was represented by the assimilation of the case of Socrates to those cases of mortal men. The former experiences have left an engram, which serves as a mould into which subsequent experience may run, and which conceivably may determine subsequent judgments even though the former experiences can no longer be remembered.

The phrase "form of thought" is most used for premises of high generality, such as the axioms of mathematics, causation, substance and attribute, space in three dimensions; and, undoubtedly, these are forms which determine the lines of all thinking to which they are relevant; but they would be useless, if there were not, under them, forms established in very concrete material by the repetition of simple experiences and ordinary events (or even by single impressive events), such as "men are mortal," "water quenches fire," which determine the lines of common-sense judgments. If there has been an experiential judgment—X is related to Y, when X again appears it is expected to be related to Y.

Amongst savages also, of course, experience settles in their minds such forms of thought; both the most general ones, which they never formulate but which necessarily control their thoughts, and many particular ones concerning the experience of daily life; which last control the details of their thoughts, and for practical purposes are true; but which, through ignorance of the minor premise, are allowed to assimilate many judgments of a very different nature. Thus, X being known to be related to Y, they are apt to infer that things that are like X, or which they suppose to be like X, are also in the same way related to Y; and this is disastrous. In civilised life, most occupations are so mechanical, and the general tradition is so positive, that there is little encouragement to think nonsense; so that the average man reasons tolerably about simple matters without having heard of the minor premise; but the savage's life is much less regular, and less fully occupied, and the tradition is full of magic and ghosts. Accordingly, he is always ready to think about magic and ghosts; and since his thoughts about such things can only run in the mould of his experiences (with some playroom for amplification, distortion and condensation), whilst he is also ignorant of the function of the minor premise, he seems to draw often from a very sound major premise a very absurd conclusion. For the minor premise is an invention of Logicians (perhaps their greatest): it does not occur to cursory, but only to critical thought.

For example, a savage judges that to put a lock of a man's hair in the fire injures and may destroy him: how comes he to think so? He has learnt by experience that for a man to put his hand in the fire, or to fall into it, hurts him; and this supplies the mould in which his inference about the lock of hair is cast. Similarly, he is apt to judge that to throw a man's image into the fire hurts him and may destroy him; and this clearly rests upon the same experience. His reasoning assumes the minor premise that (for the purpose of his revenge) a separated part of a man, or his image, is the same as the man himself; and this assumption is made explicit in the famous maxims of Magic, that in rites, whatever has been in contact with a man—or that any likeness of a man—may be substituted for him. But the generalisation of these maxims is left for an advanced stage of culture; the savage, who acts as if he held them, has never thought of, much less formulated them. They are derived, by later thought, entirely from an analysis of his conduct in magic. What the causes are that determine him to act as if he accepted the maxims of Magic will presently be discussed.[93]

There are certain other reasonings implied in savage practices, where the error lies not so much in the minor premise as in the minor term, thus: It is matter of experience that a sense of personal power and elation is produced by dancing and singing; and (perhaps without remembering such experience) a savage infers that magical power is increased by the same means. Or, again, it is matter of experience that men eat and use solid food and weapons; and a savage infers that ghosts eat ghostly food and use ghostly weapons; that is to say, that where food and spears

---

[93] Ch. iv. § 8.

are left at a tomb and remain untouched, the ghost has taken to himself the soul of these things which was his proper share. Now granting that there are such things as magical powers and ghosts, the reasoning that identifies them respectively with physical power and with men is, for the purpose of the inference, not unplausible; with a liberal examiner the minor premises might pass. But if magical powers and ghosts do not exist, the minor terms are imaginary.[94] In short, all these reasonings turn upon imaginations. The experiential major premises are true enough, but the minor premises are illusory, and as it is a maxim with Logicians that the force of reasoning follows the weaker premise, the conclusion is illusory. It is not in perception but in imagination that a part is the same as the whole, or that a likeness is the same as the thing itself; that magic controls events and that ghosts haunt their sepulchres.

These reasonings are fallacious imitations of parallel inferences according to cause and effect; but there are others of a kind peculiar to imagination: I mean reasonings by analogy—as when a Zulu, courting the dusky fair, chews a piece of wood, in the expectation that, as the wood is reduced to pulp, her heart, too, will be softened. These processes are not parallel; there is no resemblance between a lady's heart and a piece of wood, nor between mastication and court-ship; but the relation involved, the softening process, is felt to be the same in both connections and, therefore, the cases on the whole are thought to be the same. Many rites and observances depend upon such analogies—for this is the strict sense of analogy, "like relations of unlike terms"; and they have a leading part in the formation of myths in which natural events are represented as personal relations—Apollo chasing the Dawn, and so forth. And I formerly thought that such arguments as the foregoing, in which the actions of ghosts are identified with those of men, or the sufferings of a part are equated with those of the whole, were examples of analogical reasoning; for certainly, the terms involved are different: a ghost, or an image, or a nail-paring is not the same as a man. But, on reflection, I see that though these terms are really different, that has nothing to do with the psychology of the matter, for they are conceived by the savage to be the same; and, therefore, the inference is conceived as parallel to the experiential ground (even though this remain latent in consciousness).

Analogical thought is now understood to be imaginative only, and is confined to the metaphors and similes of poetry or rhetoric; though it is not very long ago that it was seriously trusted in argument, as in defending absolute monarchy in the State by the examples of patriarchy in the family, and even by the supposed "regiment" of bees and quails in their societies, of the lion over beasts and of the eagle over birds.

In this spirit, Malays, having identified the life of the rice plant with human life, regard the flowering rice as in its infancy, and proceed to feed it with pap: and carry out the analogy at further stages of its development. Similarly, to facilitate childbirth, or to liberate the struggling soul of the dying, it is a respected recipe to untie all knots, unfasten all buttons, unlock all doors, open all windows; for open-

---

[94] In assuming that there are no magical powers I do not mean that the magician has no professional powers, but that such real powers as he has are not magical.

ing or loosing, no matter what, is always the same process-relation.

These seem to be the chief modes of fallacious thinking—(1) false parallels and (2) analogies—which mislead the untutored mind and give to imagination-beliefs such coherence as they ever attain. Two accounts of superstitious reasoning have been given by those who admit that savages reason at all; one is that they reason correctly from absurd premises; the other that they reason absurdly from correct premises. If the foregoing analysis is sound, there is some truth and some error in both these doctrines. So far as primitive ratiocination is purely analogical, it is quite futile, whether its premises be true or false; for it cannot be cast in any admissible logical form. So far as in superstition it imitates parallel reasoning, according to cause and effect or substance and attribute, the major premise is, for the most part, empirically true; the minor premise is false; and the conclusion is a vain imagination. There are three types of ratiocination: (1) equations, as in mathematics; and here primitive man for a long time got no further than the counting of things by his fingers and toes. (2) Parallels of premise and inference, according to causation or substance and attribute, as in the physical and natural sciences; and here the savage collects by experience much common sense, and by inevitable fallacies much superstition. (3) Analogies of imagination. The natural progress of reason consists in relegating analogies to poetry and rhetoric; in introducing greater and greater accuracy into the judgments that serve as major premises, and greater caution in assuming minor premises; at last, in counting and measuring the facts reasoned about, and so preparing the beginnings of mathematical method. Such progress is promoted by the high biological value of greater definiteness of thought. Immature man in the necessary practical life—which may be called the biological life—has many definite perceptions and judgments and well-adjusted actions; outside that life, in the region of superstitious observance, he is not a rational, but an imaginative animal.

§ 7. GENERAL IDEAS AT THE SAVAGE LEVEL

§ 7. *General Ideas at the Savage Level.*—Savages have general ideas, though often not recognised or named; force; relations of causation and equality

The language of savages is often wanting in names of classes of things for which names are with us a matter of course, and it has been supposed that those who use the language must be without the corresponding general ideas. Thus it is reported that a tribe had a name for each kind of tree but none for tree in general; another had a name for coco-nuts at various stages of growth (when they serve different uses) but none for coco-nut at all times: therefore, it is inferred, they had no general idea of tree or of coco-nut. A Siberian example is still more remarkable. The Tunguses depend entirely upon reindeer for food, clothes, tents and locomotion, and keep herds of them; yet they have no name for the animal. But they have a name for wild and another for tame reindeer; a name for domestic reindeer that have been broken in, and another for the unbroken; a name for the female fawn, for the doe with young, for a doe with one fawn, a doe in the third year with two fawns; a name for each age-class of buck, and so on.[95] Are we to infer that the Tunguses have no general idea of reindeer?

It was, no doubt, natural to assume that we first perceive individuals, which now stand clearly before us, and then, having compared them, arrive at general ideas. But if knowledge grows by the assimilation and differentiation of experiences, the class on the one hand and the individual on the other, must be joint products of this process: classes becoming clearer as more and more individuals are discriminated. Classes, or class-ideas never stand before us as individuals do; but the greater part of the meaning of every perception of an individual is the kind of thing it is. And as to priority, to perceive the kind of thing is (biologically) far more important than its individuality. If the individual did not mean the class, to perceive it would be useless as a guide to action. The general idea derived from the assimilation of experiences is the apperceptive mass that converts sense-stimulation into cognition: when unconscious Romanes called it a "recept."

The primitiveness of general ideas is shown by gesture-language, which probably precedes speech, and which (except in direct indication of what is thought of) depends wholly upon general ideas suggested by imitative or significant actions. Primitive language must have described things by general characters, so far as it consisted in onomatopœia; to growl like a lion could only suggest the kind of animal. Primitive drawing (whether by children or savages) is nearly always generic: dog, horse, frigate-bird, hammer-headed shark, but not any individual.

There can be no doubt that savages are capable of general and abstract ideas; and no one now supposes that language is an adequate measure of thought. A language contains names only for things, groups, and aspects or actions of things which the people who use it need to discuss: if they do not need to speak of abstractions, there are no words for them. But we cannot assume of the contents of the mind, any more than of the outside world, that things do not exist unless we have noticed and named them. Professor Franz Boas has shown[96] that languages of the northern Amerinds, that do not idiomatically express abstract ideas, may be made to do so without violence, and that the abstract expression is intelligible to men native to the languages. "Every one who knows people of low culture," says Dr. Rivers, "must recognise the difficulty which besets the study of any abstract question, not so much because the savage does not possess abstract ideas as that he has no words of his own to express them."[97]

Amongst the ideas attained by savages, and having an important part in their lives, though often taken for granted and unexpressed, are some of the highest generality: for example "force." The notion of force is derived from the experience of effort in our own muscular exertions; but with the development of our perception of physical objects by the integration of sense-data—sight, touch, movement and resisted movement (kinæsthesis), smell, hearing—this sense of effort, being transferred to objects as equivalent to our own exertions about them, becomes the

---

[95] Czaplicka, *My Siberian Year*, p. 94. Other examples in Romanes, *Mental Evolution in Man*, pp. 351-3.

[96] *The Mind of Primitive Man*, V. pp. 150-52.

[97] *Sociological Review*, January 1910, p. 9.

all-important core of every object (or meaning of every perception of an object), without which the thing would be a mere show, neither useful nor injurious—sheep and tigers, rocks and pumpkins alike indifferent. Probably the perceptions of all the higher animals (down to reptiles) have this meaning. Force is reality, and by primitive man is thought of as the essence of whatever he conceives of as real, such as spells, talismans and ghosts. Having a subjective ground, from which it never becomes free, the notion of it is indefinite, varies for each of us with our constitution, age, health, and not only lends itself to the wildest whims of superstition, but has misled scientific investigations.

Relations are a class of general ideas familiar to savage thought, often appreciated with great subtlety and especially prominent in some magical operations. Relations are not only thought of by savages but compared, and likenesses discovered between them that may often surprise us. A gardener of New Guinea, having planted taro, ensured the growth of the crop by saying: "A muræna, left on the shore by the tide, was exhausted and on the point of expiring, when the tide returned, and it revived and swam away." And he struck the ground with a branch three times.[98] He saw that renewal of life in the muræna and in the taro were the same thing; so that to describe one must strengthen the other—such is the "force" of a spell!

The most important relation involved in knowledge and in its practical applications is causation. Savages who have no word for causation and have never thought of it in the abstract, must always act as if they assume it. This is apt to be misunderstood. It is written: "The natives [of Australia] have no idea of cause and effect. They notice that two things occur one after the other, and at once jump to the conclusion that one is cause and the other effect." They have, then, some idea of the relation, though ill-discriminated. Thus, having noticed that the plover often cries before rain, they imitate the cry when performing rites to bring on rain. We rather suppose that an atmospheric change, preceding the approaching rain, excites the plovers. But that does not occur to the natives: that "one after the other" is the same as effect after cause, or (as Logicians say) *post hoc, ergo propter hoc*, lies at the bottom of innumerable superstitions. The subconscious control exercised by this latent form of thought is very imperfect. The maxims of indirect Magic, that a likeness may be substituted for the thing itself, or a part of it for the whole, are merely formulæ of causation assumed under an erroneous belief as to what can be a cause. There are cases in which the like may be a substitute (one man for another) and a part may nearly serve for the whole (part of a broken knife). Hence these principles were stated and avowed by physicians and alchemists of the Middle Ages, and observed in their practice.

The quantitative axiom of mediate relation—"Magnitudes equal to the same magnitude are equal"—is, of course, never expressed by savages; but it is practically understood and applied by them whenever they use a common measure—the fingers for counting, the pace, or hand or arm-stretch to measure distance. These devices are gesture language; and the truth which the gestures assume has been forced upon the observation of primitive men whenever they saw three or

---

[98] Quoted by Frazer, *Spirits of the Corn and of the Wild*, I. p. 105.

more nearly equal things together—men in a row, birds in a flock, eggs in a nest. We need not suppose that conscious analysis is necessary to determine the relations between such things; the brain has its own method of analysis; and some day we learn the results. It was late in the day that the results became known; not, apparently, till the Greeks gave scientific form to the rudiments of mathematics. For then, for the first time, articulate axioms were wanted—to satisfy the form of science. The innumerable exact calculations of Egypt and Assyria could go on very well without them. Their discovery required the specific purpose of a scientist in search of them, the state of profound meditation and abstraction, excluding all irrelevant ideas, when in the emptiness and darkness of the mind their light became visible, like a faint sound in a silent room. Thus an idea, whose functioning has for ages controlled thought without being recognised, suddenly takes its place in the organisation of knowledge.

§ 8. The Weakness of Imagination-beliefs

§ 8. *The Weakness of Imagination-beliefs.*—Superficial resemblance to perception-beliefs; more nearly allied to play-belief

With immature minds their superstitions seem to rest on good evidence. Some of those who pray to Neptune are saved from shipwreck, and the drowned are forgotten: all confirmatory coincidences are deeply impressive, and failures are overlooked or excused. By suggestion the sick are often healed, and the hale are struck down. Curses and incantations, if known to the intended victim, fulfil themselves. So do good omens that give confidence, and bad omens that weaken endeavour. If a magician has the astuteness to operate for rain only when the wet season approaches, the event is likely to confirm his reputation. Sleight of hand, ventriloquism and the advantages of a dark séance are not unknown to sorcerers tutored in an old tradition of deceit, and their clients take it for demonstration. The constant practice by a whole village of both magic and industry for the same end, makes it impossible for ordinary mortals to see which of them is the real agent of success. For the failures of magic or of sacrifice the practitioners always have plausible explanations. Hence between imagination-beliefs and perception-beliefs, as to their causes, there may be, for the believers, no apparent difference.

But in character, also, imagination-beliefs may seem indistinguishable from perception-beliefs; in immediate feeling-quality they are certainly very much like them; and, on a first consideration, they appear to have as much influence over men's actions: but this is not true. We must not infer that to suffer martyrdom for a cult (as witches have done) can be a sign of nothing but unalterable faith in it: besides fanaticism and other abnormal states of mind, one must allow for loyalty to a party or leader, for oppositeness and hatred of the persecutor, for display, self-assertion and (in short) for a strong will. Those who take part in a religious war—are they driven wholly by enthusiasm for the supernatural, and not at all by hatred of aliens, love of fighting and hope of plunder? Discounting the admixture of other motives, the power of imagination-beliefs is, with most people, much less than we are apt to suppose. They are unstable, and in course of time change, though the "evidence" for them may remain the same. Moulded from the first by desire and anxiety, they remain plastic under the varying stress of these and other passions. In a primitive agricultural community, preparation of the soil, hoeing, reaping and harvesting go on (though with inferior tools and methods) just as they do with us; and from age to age the processes are generally confirmed or slowly improved. At the same time, every such employment is surrounded by a sort of aura of rites, which seem to be carried out with equal, or greater, scrupulosity and conviction; yet, age by age, these rites slowly atrophy and lose their importance and their ancient meaning, which is explained by new myths; or other rites may be learnt from neighbours or from invaders; for some rites may be necessary to their life, though not any particular ones.

The unstable character of superstitions and their close alliance with play-beliefs may be shown in various ways:

(*a*) The rites which express them are often carried out with deception, practised on the crowd in a public performance, as by obtaining from heaven a shower of rice, which (over night) has been lodged in the tree-tops, and is shaken down at the decisive moment; or, in private practice, played off on the patient, by bringing a stone in one's waist-belt and then extracting it from his body. Half the tribe may deceive the rest, the men mystifying the women and children, or the old the young.

(*b*) Religious beliefs often comprise incompatible attitudes: the worshippers of a god acknowledge in prosperity his superior wisdom and power—at the same time, perhaps, employing devices to cheat him; or, in long continuing distress from drought or war, they may threaten to punish him, withhold his sacrifices and desecrate his shrine. In Raiatea, when a chief of rank fell ill, extravagant rites and sacrifices were practised; but if these failed, "the god was regarded as inexorable, and was usually banished from the temple, and his image destroyed."[99]

(*c*) Imagination-beliefs break down under various trials—such as economy, selling the Rice-mother when the price of grain rises; offering the gods forged paper-money instead of good, or leaving many things at a grave and taking back the more precious; self-preservation, as in substituting the king's eldest son for himself in sacrifice; compassion, in burying with the dead puppets instead of slaves (though in this economy may have some part), or substituting in sacrifice a bull for a man.

In such cases as these we see how any desire, whose satisfaction is incompatible with a given belief or observance, tends to create a limiting belief and to modify the rites. Social indolence and fatigue—the product of many individual fatigues and occasional levity, whereby the meaning of rites is forgotten, and the rites themselves are gradually slurred and abbreviated—must be an important condition of the degeneration of rites, as it is of language. Foreign influence through trade or war introduces disturbing ideas that appeal to lovers of novelty, and show that other people with other beliefs are as well off as ourselves. Even repeated experience of failure may shake a man's confidence and make him throw away his fetish: though usually he gets another.

---

[99] W. Ellis, *Polynesian Researches*, II. p. 216.

(*d*) The beliefs of Magic and Animism are generally supported by intense emotional excitement during the incantations and ceremonies that express them. Emotion is artificially stimulated and, probably, is felt to be necessary in order to sustain illusion. It excludes criticism and increases suggestibility.

(*e*) The specific connexion of such beliefs with the play attitude is shown: by their rites including games, such as leaping, swinging, spear-throwing—supposed to have some magical efficacy; the ceremonies themselves are often dances, dramas, choruses; and with the degeneration of belief, the rites remain as dramatic or musical pastimes, whilst the myths survive in epic poems, fairy-tales and ghost-stories. When rites and incantations are not intended to incite to immediate action, it is necessary that the emotions generated in their performance shall subside with only an imaginary satisfaction: they, therefore, acquire the æsthetic tone of beauty, or sublimity, or pathos (or some rudimentary form of these feelings); so that the performance, thus experienced, becomes an end in itself.

These beliefs with their correlative ceremonies have a further resemblance to play in the indirectness of their utility. Play develops faculty; but no child thinks of that. Magic and Animism (as we have seen) tend to maintain custom and order; but this is not known to any one at first and hardly now to the generality. Rites of public interest, to procure rain or to encourage the crops, though useless for such purposes, gratify the desire to do something, or to feel as if something were being done toward the end desired, especially in the intervals when really effective work cannot be carried on, as whilst the crops are growing or after harvest: they allay anxiety and give hope and confidence. Moreover, they are organised pastimes— not that they are designed to pass the time, but that they have in fact that valuable function. The men of backward societies, during a considerable part of their lives, have not enough to do. Social ceremonies keep people out of mischief, and, at the same time, in various ways exercise and develop their powers. With us industry is a sufficient occupation, or even too engrossing, and circumstances keep us steady; so that, in leisure, pastimes may be treated lightly. With the savage some pastimes must present themselves as necessary periodical religious duties, whose performance (in his belief) encourages and enhances industry. So far, again, as needs and interests are common to a tribe, village or other group, these ceremonies ensure social co-operation and unity and also emulation in their performance; and they preserve tradition and the integration of successive generations. Our games are free from practical hopes and anxieties; but the more elaborate, such as horse-racing, have still a social function; or, like cricket and football, a tribal character: the school, college, county or even the nation feels deeply concerned about them. The Olympic Games, which interested the Greek world throughout all its scattered cities, have been traced back to primitive religious observances.[100]

As for the dark side of superstition, it needs no other explanation than crime, fanaticism and insanity: which also are diseases of the imagination. Jealousy, hatred, greed, ferocious pride and the lust of power are amongst the causes that mould belief. Any calling pursued in secret, like that of the sorcerer, under a social ban, is of course demoralised. Where the interest of an organised profession stands

---

[100] F. M. Cornford in Miss Jane Harrison's *Themis*, ch. vii.

in a certain degree of antagonism to the public interest, it may become the starting-point of unlimited abominations; and of this truth the interests of magicians and priests have supplied the most terrific examples. Dwelling upon what you know of black magic and red religion, the retrospect of human culture fills you with dismay; but need not excite astonishment; for human nature is less adapted to its environment (chiefly social) than anything else in the world; the development of the mind and of society has been too recent for us reasonably to expect anything better.

CHAPTER IV

MAGIC

"The histories I borrow, I refer them to the consciences of those I take them from." —*Montaigne*, I. 20.

§ 1. Antiquity of Magic

§ 1. *Antiquity of Magic*

Magic, until recently, was somewhat neglected by those who treated of savage ideas. In Sir E. B. Tylor's *Primitive Culture* only one chapter is given to Magic, against seven to Animism (belief in the agency of spirits). In Spencer's *Sociology*, Part I. is almost wholly devoted to the genesis and development of Animism, without a single chapter on Magic. The importance of early Animism became such an obsession, that travellers observed and reported upon it wherever they went, making only casual references to Magic—much to our loss. The tradition of this way of thinking seems to run back to Hume's *Natural History of Religion*, where he traces the development of religion from a primitive belief that all natural activities are like our own, and that everything is possessed and actuated by a spirit. This idea was adopted by Comte, and elaborated in his celebrated law of the three stages of the explanation of Nature as determining the growth of human culture: Fetichism, which ascribes all causation to the particular will of each object, and which by generalisation leads through polytheism to monotheism; Metaphysics, which, giving up the notion of personal will, attributes the activities of things to abstract forces; and Positivism, which, discarding the variety of forces that can never be known, turns to the exact description of the order of phenomena. Mill, in turn, adopted these doctrines from Comte, and gave them currency amongst us, as part of the extraordinary influence which for many years he exerted upon all our thoughts. Hence the priority of Animism to every other theory of things seemed at that time a matter of course.

Recently there have been signs that this conception of primitive thought is giving way to another, namely, that Animism was preceded by Magic. Sir J. G. Frazer puts it, that the idea of Magic is simpler than that of Animism; that Magic is found in full force amongst people whose Animism is feebly developed, and that its beliefs are more uniform throughout the world.[101] Substantially—with qualifications that will appear hereafter—this view of the matter is here accepted.

---

[101] *History of the Kingship*, p. 38; cf. also *The Magic Art*, I. p. 235, and footnote: "faith in magic is probably older than a belief in spirits."

When one comes to argue it, to produce the primitive facts is, of course, impossible. It must even be admitted that such evidence as we have amongst the few facts collected of late years concerning ancient races of men, gives the earlier date to animistic ideas; for if some of the cave-paintings of Aurignacian origin, in which, for example, wild cattle are shown pierced with arrows, may be interpreted as of magical significance; on the other hand, the burial at Le Moustier, still more ancient, shows a regard for the corpse, in the disposal of it and in the things left with it, such as usually goes with the ghost-theory. These discoveries take us back some thousands of years before Menes; but probably leave us far from the beginning of human ideas concerning the supernatural.

If Magic preceded Animism, we must insert a stage of thought at the beginning of Comte's series, making four instead of three; and the suggestion may perhaps be made to appear plausible, that the Metaphysical stage, the reign of occult forces in explanation, is not a mere residue of Fetichism after the spirit has departed, but rather the re-emergence into daylight of magical ideas of force, that always persisted, but for ages were kept in comparative obscurity by the vogue of Animism.

§ 2. WHAT IS MAGIC?

§ 2. *What is Magic?*—Magic defined; imaginary impersonal force contrasted with power of spirits; its action uniform like laws of nature. Kinds of Magic

In his *Development of Moral Ideas* (II. 47) Prof. Westermarck observes that savages distinguish two classes of phenomena; the natural or familiar, and the supernatural or mysterious. The latter again are divided into the mechanical (Magic) and the volitional (Animism). This seems to be true: it corrects the notion, still common, that the savage explains all natural activities by Animism; recognises that he takes some phenomena as a matter of course, as the animals do; and, as to events that are not a matter of course, rightly marks the distinction between his conceptions of them as either mechanical (due to some uniformly acting force) or volitional (that is, arbitrary or capricious). With the savage, then, there are on-goings of things around him that are *perceived* to be regular and continuous; and there are others between which connections are *imagined* to take place, and these either regularly or capriciously: for thus I venture to interpret the difference between the natural and the supernatural; it is the difference between perception-belief and imagination-belief. Common sense, Magic, Animism—these are the three great congeries of ideas that compete for the control of his thoughts and in his interpretation of the world.

Magic may be defined as a connexion of events imagined to be constant and to depend upon the agency of some thing or activity possessing an efficacious quality or force (in fact unreal), and not to depend (as a connexion) upon the will of any particular person.

Whether Magic is ever wrought by the bare wish or will of a human being will be discussed below (§ 6). Here, the proviso that a magical connexion does not depend upon the will of a person, is meant to exclude Animism. For pure Animism involves the belief that a ghost, spirit, or god (though he may work by Magic) can produce an effect by his direct action, without using any visible or invisible means other than his own spiritual body and force. This is not what a magician does: he works by means of a connexion of events known (so he thinks) to himself and often to others. The magical implement (talisman or spell) that he uses has qualities that are magical facts, just as the qualities of his spear are physical facts. He can make a stone spear-head by means of another stone; and he may be able to make a talisman by means of a spell; but the powers of the talisman or of the spell are their own; he cannot create Magic, but only discover and use it. Whether he shall use it, depends upon his choice; but its powers do not; they are inherent, like physical forces. Faust can conjure the devil; but so can Wagner, if he knows the spell: the power of the spell is indifferent to the conjuror. A man may, indeed, be a source of magical power because he is a chief, or has the evil eye, or is taboo for unpurged homicide; but these things do not depend upon his will; he is in the same class with impersonal things that are magical.

A rule of Magic, as describing a uniform connexion of events, resembles what we call a law of nature; and further in this, that it is not supposed to be absolute or unconditional, but a tendency, subject to counteraction by hostile Magic or (perhaps) by demonic force. But it differs from a law of nature in being wholly imaginary and incapable of verification.

To practise Magic is to use some such rule in order to obtain an end desired. This can be attempted by any man, so far as his knowledge reaches; and the greater his knowledge the greater his power, provided he have the courage to act upon it. All stages of proficiency may be traced from the simple layman who swings a bull-roarer to raise the wind, to the wizard who lives by his art, and is feared by all his tribe and far beyond it, or to the erudite magician who controls the demons and vies with the gods.

Magical things, objects or actions, in their simplest forms, are charms, spells and rites; and since the ends for which they can be used are either to protect oneself or to exert power over other persons or things, each of these kinds of magic-thing may be defensive or offensive. A defensive charm is called an amulet; an offensive charm is a talisman. For a defensive spell (say, against sickness or accident) there is, I believe, no appropriate name; offensive spells (say, to control the weather or to curse an enemy) may be called incantations (but the usage is not fixed). Rites (that is, any magic actions that are not spells) may also be defensive (as to touch wood), or offensive (as to point at a man); but we have no names for these different intentions. From these simplest beginnings the whole learning and mystery of Magic seems to have developed.

§ 3. The Beginnings of Magic

§ 3. *The Beginnings of Magic.* — A matter of speculation. The earliest were probably the simplest, and the kinds that have prevailed most widely by tradition and hereditary predisposition. The chief source of belief in Magic is the mistaking of coincidence for causation

The quest of origins is fascinating, because, if successful, it will help us to frame that outline of the history of the world which the philosophic mind regards as a necessary of life. To discuss the beginnings of Magic must necessarily be, in some measure, a speculative undertaking; because the facts are lost. If Magic was practised in the Aurignacian culture (say) 20,000 years ago, how can we get to the back of it? But speculation is not guess-work, if we always keep in view such facts as we have; if we are careful to give notice whenever the facts fail us; if we guide ourselves by scientific principles; and if we make no assumptions merely to suit our case, but only such as are generally admitted in all departments. For example:

(1) We may reasonably assume that the simplest magical beliefs and practices are of the earliest type: and nothing can be simpler than the belief in charms, rites and spells. It is, indeed, difficult to find many of these practices—though some can be produced—in their simplest forms in our records of backward peoples; partly because they have not been enough observed; partly because Magic is apt everywhere to become saturated with Animism; partly because charms, rites and spells are generally, for greater efficacy, compounded with one another. But these considerations do not affect the simplicity of the idea involved in the magical beliefs; which is merely this, that a certain object by its presence, or that an action, or an utterance, by merely entering into the course of events, will serve our purpose. A bare uniformity of connexion—if *A*, then *B*—in accordance with the familiar on-goings of Nature and our common activities, is all that is assumed. Many kinds of obstacles stop an arrow or a dart; carrion collects the vultures: so a patterned comb in one's hair stops the demon of disease; a patterned quiver, or a certain song, brings the monkeys down from the tree-tops.[102] A spell assumes merely that certain objects, or animals, or spirits, must always comply with a wish or command expressed in words, just as another human being often does. It is their supposed uniform coerciveness that makes the words magical. If any form of words ever seems to have been successful, it must be repeated; because to have the same effect the action must be the same. Immersed in an indefinite mass of experiences, the postulate that we call "cause and effect" (unformulated, of course) underlies every action, and therefore underlies Magic; it is the ground of all expectation and of all confidence.

(2) The types of Magic that are the most prevalent are probably the earliest; and these are charms, rites and spells. They are found not only amongst savages, but the world over: even in civilised countries most of the uneducated, many of the half-educated, and not a few of those who have "finished their education," employ them; whereas more complicated magical practices, except such as have been taken up into religious celebrations, are apt to fall into desuetude. What is universal must be adapted to very simple conditions of existence; these beliefs, therefore, to mental wants and proclivities that are probably primitive; and what conditions can be more simple, or more primitive, or more universal than ignorance of our fate and eagerness to clutch at anything that may give us confidence.

And not only are charms, rites and spells in all ages and everywhere employed in their simplest forms; but analysis of the most elaborate ritual and of

---

[102] Skeat and Blagden, *Pagan Races of the Malay Peninsula*, I. p. 417.

nominally animistic practices will discover the same beliefs at the bottom of them. The idea of the amulet or the talisman is found in fetiches, beads, praying-wheels, and equally in a long mimetic dance or a passion-play; whose central purpose always is to avert some evil or to secure some good—success in hunting, or war, or agriculture. Similarly, the spell is involved in all rites, so far as verbal formulæ are used in them; and in all curses or prayers, so far as their efficacy depends upon a sound form of words.

The persistence of magical beliefs amongst civilised people is, in some measure, due to tradition; though the tradition could not continue effective if there were not in every generation a predisposition to accept it; and how far it is due to tradition, how far to a spontaneous proclivity, in any one who is inclined to believe in charms, rites and spells, he himself must judge as best he can. Superstition having been at one time extremely useful socially, there is some presumption that tribes addicted to it (within limits) had an advantage, and that the disposition became hereditary. It is a recent acquisition compared with the love of climbing; but once ingrained, it must remain till disutility breeds it out. Meanwhile, it is a stain on the human soul. So much of one's early life is always forgotten that no one can be sure that he was not inoculated with such notions in childhood; especially when we consider that religious practices, taught before they can be well understood, must often wear a magical habit to a child; and that medicines, whose operations nobody used to understand, were on the same foot with Magic. For my own part, bating the last considerations, I cannot remember ever to have heard in childhood any sort of Magic spoken of except with amusement; yet magical beliefs have always haunted me. With Animism it was otherwise. When six or seven years old, I was told by a nursemaid—a convinced adherent of one of the many little sects that have ramified out of Wesleyanism in Cornwall—the most appalling ghost-stories; and these stories, exciting no doubt an ancient disposition, and reinforced by a visualising faculty that nightly peopled the darkness with innumerable spectres, entirely overpowered the teachings of those whom there was better reason to trust, that ghosts are a superstition from which true religion has for ever set us free. The effects lasted into middle age. Andrew Lang said of ghosts that "he did not believe, but he trembled"; and that precisely describes my own state of mind for many years. Now, as to Magic, my impression is that had it been suggested to me in a serious way, and not merely by casual allusions to "luck," the experience would have stuck in my memory. The first time that I can remember practising rites, I was between ten and eleven years old, living at a small boarding-school. To keep off a dreaded event, I used to go every morning to the pump, fill my mouth with water and spurt it out in a violent stream—three times. This went on for some weeks. To the best of my recollection, the impulse was spontaneous, and I cannot remember why the particular rite was adopted: to spout water out of the mouth may have been symbolic of a pushing away of what was feared; but I do not think I was conscious of that meaning. Nothing further of the kind recurs to me until about the age of fifteen, when, at another school, the master-passion of my life was cricket; and I always practised some rite before going on the field, and carried a charm in my pocket; but I cannot recall what they were. At present, a day rarely passes without my experiencing some impulse to practise Magic. In lighting my first pipe in the morning (for example), if I remember how I lit it, where I struck the match, etc., yesterday, and if no misfortune has happened since, I feel an unmistakable impulse to "light up" again in the same way. No reason is distinctly present to me for acting so, and therefore it is hazardous to analyse the attitude; but it is not merely incipient habit: to the best of my judgment it is this, that such a way of lighting my pipe was one amongst the antecedents of a quiet time, and that it will be well to reinstate as many of them as possible. It is more comfortable to do it than to alter it: one feels more confident.

Inquiry amongst my friends shows that some have similar experiences, and others (both men and women) have not. A *questionnaire* on such a point might be useful; but difficult to arrange without giving suggestion or exciting bias.[103]

(3) There are causes originating the belief in charms, rites and spells so simple that nothing could be more natural to the primitive human mind. What is more universally powerful in producing belief in the connexion of events, and consequent expectancy of repetition, than an interesting coincidence? If, says Sir E. F. im Thurn,[104] a Carib sees a rock in any way abnormal or curious, and if shortly afterwards any evil happens to him, he regards rock and evil as cause and effect, and perceives in the rock a spirit. This is animistic; but the same tendency to be impressed by coincidence underlies Magic. For example: A hunting party of Esquimos met with no game. One of them went back to the sledges and got the ham-bone of a dog to eat. Returning with this in his hand, he met and killed a seal. Ever afterwards he carried a ham-bone in his hand when hunting.[105] The ham-bone had become a talisman. Such a mental state as the Esquimo's used to be ascribed to the association of ideas; but it is better to consider it as an empirical judgment. Other circumstances of the event may have been associated in his mind; but as to the ham-bone and the kill, he thinks of them together, and judges that they are connected. Then, having judged that the ham-bone influenced the kill, he carries it with him in future in order to repeat the conditions of success.

We may perhaps discern the moment when Magic first fastened upon the human mind by considering how the use of weapons and snares by the primitive hunter impaired his sense of the mechanical continuity of the work. In a struggle with prey body to body, success or failure was thoroughly understood; but with the use of weapons and snares it became conditional upon the quality of these aids and upon his skill with them: more and more conditional as the number of steps increased between the first preparation and the event; at any one of which unforeseen occurrences might frustrate his plans. Hence an irresistible desire to

---

[103] In the *American Journal of Psychology*, p. 83 (1919), E. S. Conkling has an instructive article on *Superstitious Belief and Practice among College Students*. Of a large group examined 53 per cent. entertained some superstition (40 per cent. M., 66 per cent. F.). At some time, now or formerly, 82 per cent. had been so affected (73 per cent. M., 90 per cent. F.). Half assigned their former superstitions to the age from twelve to sixteen. Twenty-two per cent. attributed the disposition to the suggestion of elders, 47 per cent. to social suggestion, 15 per cent. to social inheritance, and 15 per cent. to emotions and feelings beyond the control of reason.

[104] *Among the Indians of Guiana*, p. 354.

[105] Quoted by Ames, *Psychology of Religious Experience*, p. 60.

strengthen and insure every step of his task; and to gratify this desire Magic arose.

That Magic should depend upon the assumption that "things connected in thought are connected in fact" seems unintelligible, until we consider that the thought in which they are connected is a judgment concerning the facts. But how is it possible to judge so foolishly? Absurd association is intelligible; it cannot be helped; but judgment is not a passive process. Well: a logician might interpret the case as a fallacy in applying the inductive canons: the Esquimo had two instances: (*a*) no ham-bone, no seal; (*b*) ham-bone, seal: or, again, into the circumstances of his expedition he introduced a ham-bone, and the seal followed. Therefore, the carrying of a ham-bone was the cause of getting a seal. He had not read Mill, and did not know what precautions should be taken before adopting such conclusions. The mind must have begun in this way; and after many thousands of years, the opportunities of error in empirical judgment began to be appreciated, and the canons were formulated. The experience of every man at every stage of life, personal or social (probably evoking an inherited disposition), continually impresses him with the belief in some connexion of antecedent and consequent, that each event arises out of others. But what it is in the antecedent that determines the event can never, in practical affairs, be exactly known. In definite cases, where method is applicable, we may analyse the consequent into the tendencies of forces in amount and direction; or we may sometimes reproduce it by an experiment exactly controlled. But where these resources fail us, as they often do in practical affairs, we are little confident of grasping all, or even the chief conditions of any event that interests us. The savage knows nothing of method, and, therefore, feels less distrust. He learns something of the conditions of success in hunting; this is biologically necessary to him as it is to a tiger; only those survive that learn them. He knows that he must have weapons as efficient as possible, must go to the habitat of his prey, must not be heard, or seen, or smelt. But with all precautions he sometimes fails; therefore there must be some other condition which he does not understand. Hence anything observed, or any word or action, that happens to be followed by success, may have been a means to that success.

And if it once has been, it always will be: not that he thinks of it in this general way. But even animals, as soon as they have learnt a sequence, trust to it. Dogs and cats learn faster than guinea-pigs; monkeys faster than dogs and cats; man quicker still. But in no case would there be any use in learning, if it did not lead to action as if the experience had been generalised. There is no mystery in generalisation; it is spontaneous, and only waits for language to express itself; the difficult thing to acquire is caution. In default of method, the only test of truth is relative constancy in experience—*per enumerationem simplicem*—faulty but broadly effective; which requires time and practice. Primitive Magic is an incautious, unexpressed generalisation; and the conditions are such that the error cannot be easily detected. As long as a savage follows the instinctive, traditionary and acquired knowledge that he has of hunting, practices based on wrong judgments, but not interfering with the traditionary art, such as the carrying about of a bone, or a crystal, or having a special pattern on his quiver, cannot impair his success; may add to it by increasing his confidence: so that as long as success lasts there is nothing to suggest the falsity of the judgment. A series of failures may make the hunter throw away his talisman, or (at a later stage of Magic) take it to a medicine-man to be redoctored. How many thousands of times may Magic have begun in this way and lost its hold again, before the human mind became chronically infected with it!

Similarly with amulets, anything unusual that a man happens to have about him, when attacked by a leopard or snake, from which he escapes, may be kept as a safeguard against future perils. And with rites: any gesture or action, however irrelevant, that happens to precede a successful effort, may be repeated in order to reinstate all the antecedents of success. So, too, with the origin of spells. It is a common impulse, and quite spontaneous, to accompany an action with words, incentive or expletive. If a hunter does so in driving home his spear successfully, he will next time repeat the words: they then become a spell.[106] First, then, there are practices of carrying about charms, repeating words, repeating actions; next, along with these practices, beliefs grow up as to the nature of their efficacy, their virtue; and much later it is discovered that some of the practices seem to involve certain common principles which the savage had never thought of.

In trying to imagine ourselves in the place of such a man, we must not omit the emotional excitement that determines his judgment. It is the intensity of his desire for success, his anxiety about it, that makes him snatch at, and cling to, whatever may possibly be a means to it: he does not see how it acts, but will take no risks by omitting it. Since what is true of primitive hunting is true of all undertakings—that we know some conditions of success but far from all—and since we are all of us frequently in this position—the wonder is that we resort so little to Magic. That many people do so in London is notorious.

§ 4. Magical Force and Primitive Ideas of Causation

> § 4. *Magical Force and Primitive Ideas of Causation.*—Idea of magical
> force derived from physical force (empathy, Animatism, invisible
> action at a distance, mana). How Animism and Magic corrupt the
> ideas of causation

Magic is a uniform connexion of events, depending on some impersonal force that has no real existence. What causes make men believe in such force? In the first place, everything is necessarily conceived of by everybody (and probably in some dim way by the higher animals) as a centre of forces. Its weight, when we try to lift it; inertia, when we push it, or when it is moving and we try to stop it; degree of hardness, when we strike or grasp it; elasticity, when the bent bough of a tree recoils; the sway of torrents and the lift of waves; falling trees, avalanches,

---

[106] Charms (and possibly rites and spells) are sometimes revealed in dreams (Howitt, *The Native Tribes of South-East Australia*, p. 378; and Hose and McDougall, *Pagan Tribes of Borneo*, I. p. 110). But this can only happen either where the belief in charms already exists (as in the cases cited), or by the coincidence of the dream with good or bad fortune. The connexion of events must first of all present itself as something observed: whether waking or dreaming is indifferent.

For further illustrations of the influence of coincidences in establishing a belief in Magic, see ch. viii. § 5.

water-spouts, hurricanes: all these things a man must think of, as he does of other men and animals, in comparison with his own strength or impotence. Into their actions and reactions he reads such tension and effort as he himself feels in struggling with them, or in grappling one of his own hands with the other; and as their action is full of surprises he does not suppose himself to know all that they can do.

But, further, the strain exhibited by some objects, especially trees; the noises they make, creaking and groaning in the wind; the shrieking and moaning of the wind itself, the threatening and whispering of the sea, thunder and the roar of torrents: all excite *Einfühlung* or empathy, illusory sympathy with things that do not feel. Their voices, more than anything else, I believe, endow them for our imaginations with an inward life, which Mr. Marett has well called Animatism,[107] and which must not be confounded with the Animism that used to be attributed to all children and all savages—the belief that every object is actuated by a spirit, or even that it has a consciousness like our own. What truth there was in that doctrine is fully covered by Animatism.

Again, the savage is acquainted with invisible forces some of which seem to act at a distance. The wind is the great type of invisible force; heat, sound, odour are also invisible, and act at a distance; the light of the camp-fire acts at a distance, spreading across the prairie or into the recesses of the forest; and lightnings issue from the clouds. In dreams, one visits some remote hunting-ground and returns instantly; distance and time are distorted or annihilated; and if you can act where you dream, why not where you intensely imagine yourself?

Hence there are abundant analogues in experience by which the savage can conceive of his talisman as a force-thing that acts invisibly and acts at a distance. Australian medicine-men "threw their joïas (evil magic) invisibly, 'like the wind,' as they said."[108] The talisman acts at a distance, like a missile; it acts for the person who owns it as his spear does, and is dangerous to others who have not practised with it. Sometimes, indeed, magic things have no owners, and are dangerous to everybody: malignant influence radiating from them, like the heat of a fire or the stench of a corpse. Such are two stones described by Messrs. Spencer and Gillen[109] as marking the place where an old man and two women died for breaking a marriage-taboo. "They are so full of evil magic that if any but old men go near, it kills them. Now and then a very old man goes and throws stones and bushes upon the spot to keep down the evil magic." It is as if one covered up a fire or a corpse. And, further, magical force may exist in a diffused way, like darkness, heat, cold, epidemic disease, tribal unrest, without necessarily attaching to any particular thing. In the Western Isles of Torres Straits[110] mishaps may be signs of an unlucky state of things in general. A fisherman, usually successful, having once failed at his task, was depressed; but on two women dying in his village soon after, he was consoled; since this showed that failure was not his fault. Currents of this magical force, favourable or unfavourable to things in general, may be seen

[107] R. R. Marett, *Preanimistic Religion, Folk-Lore*, 1900.
[108] A. W. Howitt, *The Native Tribes of South-East Australia*, p. 371.
[109] *Northern Tribes of Central Australia*, p. 472.
[110] A. C. Haddon, *Reports of the Cambridge Expedition to Torres Straits*, V. p. 361.

in the flow and ebb of the tide, the waxing and waning of the moon, and in the course of the seasons. From this way of thinking it is but a step to the conception of *mana*, as it is called in Melanesia:[111] *orenda* of the Iroquois, *manitou* of the Algonquin, *wakanda* of the Omaha.[112] It is the power of the wonderful and mysterious in the world, which becomes especially manifest in Magic and in the agency of spirits. Similar notions are found in many regions at various stages of culture, but nowhere (I believe) at the lowest stages; so that it is unreasonable to treat it as the first source of ideas of the supernatural. It is too comprehensive a generalisation to find expression amongst savages. The Arunta have got as far as the generalisation of evil Magic under the name of *arungquiltha*.[113] But *mana* is a generalisation of all the imaginary forces of superstition, vague and mysterious; as "cause," in popular use, is a generalisation of all the supposed "forces" of nature.

Rites also act at a distance by invisible force; for this power belongs to gesture-language, and the simplest rites are gestures. And so do spells; for wishes, commands, threats expressed in words, act upon men at a distance by invisible force; and spells are nothing but such expressions conceived of in a particular way, as having that uniform efficacity which is Magic. Spells, being thought of as forces, are reified; so that blessings or curses cling to their objects like garlands, or like contaminating rags.

Magical force, then, is a notion derived from experience of natural forces and employed to account for events that are unusual, wonderful, mysterious, not to be interpreted by that common sense which is the cumulative result of usual occurrences. It is superimposed upon the older and wider presumption of causation, and is expected to manifest itself with the same uniformity; so that, if the laws of it can be discovered, it supplies a basis for the Art of Magic. So far is Magic from being the source of the belief in causation! But I have spoken of the "older and wider *presumption* of causation"; for (as has been shown) the definite postulate that all the ongoings of the world may be analysed upon the principal of cause and effect, can never come into the minds of primitive men; and even to ourselves it rarely occurs, except in scientific discussions or logical exercises; but we always act as if we trusted in it, and so does a savage, and so does a dog. The presumption is reinforced by every moment's ordinary experience; and without it no consistency of life is possible. This ungeneralised presumption determines all thoughts and actions, mechanical, animistic, or magical. That the forces implied in superstition are generalised in such concepts as *mana* before the principle of causation obtains expression, is due to the prepotency of the unusual, wonderful, mysterious in attracting attention.

In our modern analysis of mechanical causation there are four requirements: (1) every event has a cause; (2) causation is uniform; (3) the cause is the assemblage of the indispensable conditions of the effect (and no others); (4) the cause is proportional to the effect. In the savage's mind these requirements are also obscurely

---

[111] Coddrington, *The Melanesians*, pp. 118-19.

[112] For a comparison of these allied notions see E. S. Hartland's *Ritual and Belief*, pp. 36-51.

[113] Spencer and Gillen, *Native Tribes of Central Australia*, p. 548.

recognised: (1) he seeks a cause for everything: (2) he expects it to act uniformly: (3) he believes in reinstating all the conditions of the effect, as appears from his preparations for hunting, or war, or marriage, or whatever he may have in hand; but he is much more ignorant than we are as to what conditions are indispensable and decisive: (4) he knows vaguely that the cause is proportional to the effect; for (a) he succeeds in making effective weapons, etc., by mechanical means; (b) he is very susceptible to the "size-weight illusion," twice as much as we are,[114] and this implies the adjustment of effort to a supposed weight; (c) he repeats a spell in order to strengthen it, or unites a talisman, a rite and a spell in one assault, implying that greater force must be directed against greater resistance; and so on.

Causation, then, is universally assumed: how do Animism and Magic influence the latent conception? As to Animism, (1) it palters with the uniformity of causation; for though the ghost or spirit acts from human motives, no one knows exactly what its motives are. It may be cajoled, implored, even threatened; but the result does not always answer desire: there is apparent caprice or free will, with consequent loss of confidence, and an uncomfortable feeling that leads to a reaction in favour of controlling the god, or ghost, by Magic. (2) The ghost is at first merely a man-force disengaged from the visible body, but still having its own body through which it can produce various effects. But the fear of a ghost immediately endows it with superhuman power; and in course of time it becomes more and more powerful, even to omnipotence; so that it can of itself bring about any event; and, therefore, the "assemblage of conditions" becomes unnecessary to causation: there need be no visible conditions: miracles occur; creation out of nothing is possible. (3) For such a power the "proportionality of cause and effect" becomes almost meaningless; but not quite, for there are degrees of spirit-force; and what one cannot do a stronger can.

As to Magic, it has the great merit of (1) preserving the uniformity of causation. But (2) it vitiates the presumption of causation by including in the total antecedent unreal conditions, namely, the forces of rites and spells; and by generating a frame of mind that makes it impossible to eliminate them. The hunter uses all the resources of his art in hunting; he also practises rites and spells. To which does he owe his success? We might suggest that he should try the hunting without the rites; but he is afraid to; and should he try, his positivism would probably break down at the first failure to kill. Well, then, let him try the rites without the hunting; but he is not such a fool: and, if he were, the medicine-man would tell him that, of course, he must "use the means." (3) Magic impairs the sense of proportionality between cause and effect, by recognising antecedents which are, in their nature, immeasurable. In their admirable work, *The Pagan Tribes of Borneo*, Messrs. Hose and McDougall remark[115] that it is sometimes said, that people of lowly culture have "no conception of mechanical causation, and that every material object is regarded by them as animated"; but they do not think that this could be truthfully said about any of the peoples of Borneo. In the construction of houses, boats, weapons, traps, they have a nice appreciation of the principles involved. Yet we

---

[114] W. McDougall, *Reports of the Cambridge Expedition to Torres Straits*, II. p. 199.
[115] Vol. II. p. 2.

find[116] that these skilled artisans believe that they can retard an enemy's boat by hanging under one of its benches a quartz pebble. Similarly, the Boloki of the Congo, having made a good canoe, before launching, strike it on the stern with an axe "to take away the weight."[117] And the Fijians, still better boat-builders, believe that to put a basket of bitter oranges on a canoe reduces its speed.[118]

Inasmuch as the possibility of action at a distance is still in debate, the savage cannot perhaps upon that tenet be confidently corrected.

If there is any truth in the foregoing account of the latent ideas, or presumptions, of savages concerning causation, it is plain that Magic (and likewise Animism) did not help, but hindered the development of these ideas. Notwithstanding (or, perhaps, because of) certain specious resemblances to science, Magic is, and always has been, the enemy of science.

§ 5. Magic and Mystery

§ 5. *Magic and Mystery*

Magic begins with ignorance of some of the conditions of a desired event, and the adoption (on account of coincidence) of anything that fixes one's attention as contributing to the total antecedent. As the supposed conditions of events grow more and more miscellaneous, the disposition increases to regard anything as a possible cause of anything else. Hence unbounded suspicion whenever an interesting event occurs whose antecedents are not familiar and manifest. The more unusual any occurrence, the more it must excite attention and be apt to arouse suspicion; and the first arrival of travellers or missionaries amongst a wild tribe is an event so unprecedented, that it is likely enough to occasion exaggerated suspicions and behaviour which, when reported, misrepresent the tribe's normal attitude of mind. For this allowance should be made.

However, in Magic the causation is never traceable; therefore it becomes mysterious. The sense of mystery arises when something excites wonder, wonder gives place to curiosity, curiosity is baffled, and wonder returns with fear. The magical power of an inert object, such as a black pebble or a shark's tooth, or of a bone that is pointed towards a victim, or of a spear that is swung but not thrown, and nevertheless inflicts a wound, though an invisible one, is something unknown, or mysterious. That is to say, it is a merely imagined action which remains obscure and inscrutable, in comparison with the perceived action of a spear thrown at a deer and slaying it with a visible wound. The savage has adequate practical knowledge of the latter process; of the former only a vague analogical image. He feels the difference, and that the Magic is mysterious; and mystery, being common to all magical processes, and deeply impressive (especially in black Magic), becomes what we call a "fundamental attribute" of Magic, pervading the whole apperceptive mass that is formed by a man's magic-beliefs. Therefore whatever excites the sense of mystery tends to be assimilated[119] by this apperceptive mass and confirmed as

[116] Vol. II. p. 124.
[117] Weeks, *Among Congo Cannibals*, p. 311.
[118] Thomas Williams, *Fiji and the Fijians*, p. 79.
[119] *Tends to be* assimilated—for if the presentation have some special character of An-

magical; just as the mass of our scientific knowledge assimilates and confirms any proposition that has the attributes of a scientific law. Hence the savage accepts the mysterious remedies of an European doctor as magical; and he is ready to regard as magical, and to fear, anything—a rock, tree, or water-spout—that by any trait excites his sense of mystery. Magic, then, does not arise from mystery; but having come into existence, it appeals to the feeling of mystery; and then whatever else is mysterious tends to become magical.[120]

Magic being mysterious, the more mysterious the more powerful it must be. Hence foreign Magic is more dreaded than the home-made; ancient Magic is more powerful than modern; muttered spells, or formulæ in a strange language, or in one whose meaning has been lost, are more efficacious than intelligible speech; written characters and numbers have a subduing prestige; verse is more subtle than prose (for poets are everywhere respected); a wizard is more impressive in a mask than when bare-faced, in a fit than when sober; and operations in the dark, that ought to excite scepticism, enhance credulity.

Masses of ideas having this mysterious quality form relatively dissociated systems, which offer resistance to all ideas that want it, and therefore to what we call "explanation." Hence the conservative, inexpugnable character of Magic and its easy alliance with Mysticism. Resistance to explanation may go the length of denying present experience; as when a man is seen to be slain by a weapon or by a falling tree, and yet his death is ascribed to sorcery: the fear of sorcery having become a fixed idea.

§ 6. Volitional Magic

§ 6. *Volitional Magic.*—A relatively late idea

Magical power inheres in things, rites and spells without regard to the man who uses them; they may be sold or taught, and then serve the new possessor. But much the greater part of all known magical operation depends upon the agency of some person, man or spirit, who sets it going; and rites and spells are from the first, by their nature, personal actions.

In the later stages of Magic, no doubt, it is held that a mere wish or volition may be efficacious: in Cornwall they still tell you, when you are cold or tired, that you "look wisht," that is, as if you had been ill-wisht and were pining away (this meaning is generally forgotten). But it seems to me improbable that such an idea should be primitive. People who, in inflicting penalties, do not discriminate

---

imism, it will be assimilated to the animistic system; or if Animism be the more active and fashionable theory in a man's social group.

[120] It has been thought strange that such a thing as a whirlwind may excite in the savage either fear or anger. To explain this we must consider the nature of wonder: it is an imaginative expansion of surprise, temporary paralysis of the imagination, with emotional disturbance, but no progressive instinct of its own. It either subsides helplessly, or gives place to curiosity, or passes into some other emotion that is connected with an instinct. Accordingly, it usually passes into curiosity or else fear, but sometimes into anger: which of these emotions shall be aroused depends, partly, upon the character of the person who wonders, partly, upon circumstances.

between accidental and intentional offences, cannot be supposed to ascribe power to a mental process as such; and I have not been able to find in reports of very backward tribes any case of wish-magic unsupported by magical implements. Dr. Haddon says[121] that, among the eastern islanders of Torres Straits, the power of words and the projection of the will are greatly believed in. A youth who makes love procures a piece of black lava shaped significantly, and anoints it with co-co-nut oil, etc.; he also anoints his own temples, and thinks as intently as possible about the girl, and repeats a spell whenever he sees her, using the names of Sagaro and Pikaro, wife and mistress of the hero Sida. Now, with this complex apparatus of talisman, rite and spell, how much is left to wishing or the projection of the will? He thinks hard about the girl, no doubt; but that needs no voluntary effort: at least, in this climate, voluntary effort is soon exhausted in trying to think of anything else. Mr. Weeks, in his book *Among Congo Cannibals*, describing a people of somewhat higher culture, and much more advanced Animism than the natives of Torres Straits, explains the nervousness in the poison ordeal even of those who are innocent of any nefarious practices, by asking—"For who has not at some time wished another's death?"—and by the admitted doctrine that a man may be full of evil magic without knowing it. From this it seems to be inferable that a mere wish may be effective. But not justly; for a man full of evil magic is an incarnate talisman; and such a man may operate without wishing, as often happens with the evil-eye. At any rate, these casual Congo wishes do not amount to volition; the faintest velleity is enough for the hair-trigger of such explosive personalities. In Japan, too, the angry spirit of a living person may inflict a curse unknown to himself.[122]

Still, with the progress of Magic, deliberate wishes may acquire independent power. A man practising evil Magic, and desiring secrecy, has a strong motive to believe (that is, there is a cause of his believing) that his tacit wish has the power of invisible action at a distance; and the way by which he arrives at that belief is quite clear: for a spell is a magical force; it is also an expressed wish or command; and, if muttered, is more rather than less powerful than when uttered aloud. Why not, then, "sub-muttered," or merely thought?

From this degenerate notion of will-work we must distinguish the personal power of an accomplished wizard in his whole magical activity. Whatever a man does with a talisman or a spell, as it were with a tool or a weapon, may be done with more or less concentration of energy and proficiency in the performance; and one man will be plainly superior to another. Success depends upon doing one's best; therefore upon the will. And Magic often needs courage and resource; but in the development of the art it depends still more upon knowledge; wherein the magician is wont to boast himself. For wizardry is the most reputable faculty of primitive scholarship: to know all spells and rites, the arts of divination and medicine, the ancestry and true name of all dangerous things, which gives control over them: and it is a universal belief that knowledge is power.

------

[121] *Reports of the Cambridge Expedition to Torres Straits*, VI. p. 321.
[122] W. G. Aston, *Shinto*, p. 52.

§ 7. The Evolution of Magic—Direct Magic

§ 7. *The Evolution of Magic—Direct Magic.* —Growth and differentiation; four stages; spells and charms; taboo

From the simple beginnings thus described, Magic, like everything else in the world, proceeds to grow and differentiate. It grows by the lengthening of spells from the briefest wish or command to many verses;[123] by the extension of rites from the waving of a bough to raise the wind to the Australian Intichiuma ceremonies that go on for many days; by the accumulating of charms by the bagful; by the compounding of rites with spells, and by repetition of them three times or some other sacred number. It differentiates by being applied and adapted to more and more purposes: from hunting (if we suppose it to begin there) to war and love; to birth, marriage and death; to the giving of diseases and the curing of them; to the protection of property and to the discovery (or concealment) of theft; to navigation, building, agriculture, the care of flocks and herds, the procuring of rain, renewing the vigour of the sun and binding the influence of the Pleiades. At the same time Magic, originally practised (we may presume) by individuals, comes to engage the concern and co-operation of families, clans and tribes; and a distinction grows up between what we call "white" and "black" Magic: practices that are for the welfare of the tribe, or of some portion of it, and practices designed to gratify private passions without regard to their effect upon the community.

One may notice certain stages (not always serial) in the development of Magic: First, the simple and direct defence of oneself or fellows against other persons or things, storms, diseases, etc.; or, again, direct attack upon such hostile powers—by means of charms, spells or rites. Secondly, indirect or dramatic Magic, operating not upon persons or things themselves, but (expecting the same effect) upon imitations of them, or upon detached parts or appurtenances; as in the well-known device of making a waxen figure of a man and melting it in the fire to his destruction. Thirdly, the alliance of Magic with Animism, leading to sorcery, exorcism and ceremonies associated with Religion—discussed below in the sixth and seventh chapters. Fourthly, the confusion of Magic with Science, as in Astrology and Alchemy—referred to in the seventh and tenth chapters.

Direct magical rites begin in very simple ways, probably with gestures: as to point at a man in threatening; to throw out the open hand in warding off evil; to claw the air behind a man's back, as Australian women do. It becomes more and more elaborate as the result of much study devoted to a matter of supreme interest: especially after the rise of a professional class of medicine-men, with whom inventions accumulate and become traditionary. Similarly, spells are at first merely wishes, or commands, or warnings. An Australian Wind-doctor cries, "Let the west wind be bound."[124] The southern Massim of New Guinea have a spell to open a cave—"O rock, be cleft!" and, again, to shut the cave—"O rock, be closed!"[125] Nothing can be simpler. How spells rise into poetry and are combined with rites

---

[123] One may trace this process in the interesting collection of spells in Skeat's *Malay Magic.*

[124] Howitt, *The Native Tribes of South-East Australia*, p. 397.

[125] Seligman, *Melanesians of British New Guinea*, p. 376.

and charms is shown by a Polynesian example: a man being ill with consumption, which is called *Moomoo*, a medicine-man is sent for. He comes, sits by the patient, and sings—

> "O Moomoo, O Moomoo!
> I'm on the eve of spearing you."

Then, rising, he flourishes his spear over the patient's head, and goes away. No one dares speak or smile.[126]

As to charms, the simplest, and perhaps the earliest, are small pebbles, such as the Australian "bulks," or crystals.[127] In Papua there are quartz charms so powerful that it is not safe for even the owner to touch them. In that country the qualities that make a thing suitable for a charm are: (1) similarity in contour, or in other ways, to the object to be influenced; (2) rarity; (3) unusual shape in not very uncommon objects:[128] in short, whatever arrests attention. Dr. Codrington says: "A stone takes a man's fancy; it is like something, clearly not a common stone; there must be *mana* in it: puts it in his garden; and a good crop proves he was right."[129] Among the Esquimo, strange or curious objects never before seen are sometimes considered to bring success to the finder; and charms are carried shaped like the animals hunted.[130] Such a taste is very ancient, if the same purpose was served by those animal-shaped stones, retouched to increase the resemblance, which have been found in considerable numbers in France and England.[131] In the bag of a West African sorcerer may be seen a bit of leopard skin, of snake's skin, hawk's talons, bone of a dead man, leaves of certain plants, etc.; each having its own virtue, and uniting their powers in the interest of the formidable owner. The *Chanson de Roland* describes a talisman to which the chief of Charlemagne's peers must have owed no small part of his prowess—his famous sword:—

> "Ah! Durendal, most holy, fair indeed!
> Relics enough thy golden hilt conceals:
> Saint Peter's Tooth, the Blood of Saint Basile,
> Some of the Hairs of my lord, Saint Denise,
> Some of the Robe, was worn by Saint Mary."[132]

I cannot call it fair fighting, and wonder that, thus armed, he should ever have been mortally wounded by the miscreant hordes of Mahum and Tervagant, however numerous.

An influential outgrowth of primitive Magic is the taboo. Taboo is the dangerousness of a person, or thing, or action, or word, conceived of as a motive for

[126] Turner, *Samoa*, p. 138. For further development of the spell, see (besides Skeat, op. cit.) the collected examples at the end of Sayce's *Religion of the Ancient Babylonians*.

[127] Parker, *The Euahlayi*, p. 26.

[128] Seligman, *The Melanesians of British New Guinea*, pp. 173-5.

[129] *The Melanesians*, pp. 118-19.

[130] Turner, *Ethnology of the Ungava District*, Am. B. of Ethn., XI. p. 201; and Murdoch, Ethnology of Point Barrow, *Am. B. of Ethn.*, IX. p. 434.

[131] W.M. Newton, On Palæological Figures of Flint, *Journ. of B. Arch. Ass.*, March 1913.

[132] *The Song of Roland*, done into English by C. Scott Moncrieff, CLXXIII.

not touching or uttering or meddling therewith. The dangerousness may either lie in the nature of a person or thing, or be imposed upon it. A chief, for example, and everything belonging to him, is generally taboo by inherent sacredness: he is, like Mr. Weeks's Congolese, full of evil magic. The idea of the talisman has thus been extended to include certain men. In many tribes it includes all women; but since to make them always taboo is too much for human nature, they are treated as such only periodically, or when a man is about to be exposed to some further danger, which will be the more likely to injure him when already contaminated by evil magic.[133] This is very clear in a case reported by Prof. Seligman:[134] at Yam warriors were forbidden to sleep with their wives before battle; else "bow and arrow belong other fellow he smell you, he shoot you, you no got luck." Still, physical consequences (which may explain the superstition) are also considered: a diver for pearl-shell must similarly abstain; because, else, "man he sleepy." The continence required of women to ensure the safety of their husbands when away at war or hunting may be due to a belief in a "sympathy" or "participation," as if husband and wife were in some mysterious *rapport*; but, deeper, there may have been a fetch of policy. When magical taboos are generally recognised and feared, it becomes possible to use them for social purposes: one cannot be sure that every magical observance had its origin in magical belief. Thus the food-rules of Australian tribes consist of taboos upon the enjoyment of certain foods by women and young men, and are plainly devised in the interests of the gerontocracy: so why should not a fiction be founded on Magic in the interest of absent husbands?

The sanctity or dangerousness of the chief is probably due, first, to his being really dangerous; but, secondly, to the biological advantage to a tribe of respecting him, which leads to a selection of those tribes amongst whom respect for the chief arises. As biological adaptation is never more than a moving, oscillating equilibrium, this feeling sometimes becomes excessive, even to the point of insanity. Everything the chief touches becomes taboo; only a few sacred servants can approach him; he may be thus reduced to helplessness. It is one of Nature's checks upon tyranny. Such is the force of taboo, that a Maori tribesman, being hungry, seeing some food by the wayside, and eating it, on learning that it was the remains of the meal of a sacred chief, immediately fell ill, and died. The offence was fatal—as soon as it was known. The dangerousness of women has been referred to their weakness; association with them must be weakening, and is therefore forbidden when exertion is needed.[135] Prof. Westermarck traces it to a "horror of blood";[136] very probably; but other things may co-operate towards it. The life of women separates them from men, and brings them into a freemasonry and community of interests, to which men are not admitted; differentiates their mentality, until the result is mysterious and therefore magical: the sexual orgasm, being more like pain than anything that is not pain, at once attractive and revulsive, acquires the same character. Homicides and mourners, again, are liable to be taboo, either because there clings to them the mysterious quality and taint of death (a magical motive),

[133] T. C. Hodson, *The Naga Tribes of Manipur*, p. 88.
[134] *Reports of the Cambridge Expedition to the Torres Straits*, V. p. 271.
[135] A. E. Crawley, *J.A.I.*, XXIV. p. 123.
[136] *Development of Moral Ideas*, I, c. 26.

or because they are followed by the ghosts of the departed.

There are unlucky words which it is a social offence to utter: words of ill-omen, but especially names of dead people, demons and sometimes gods; for people are apt to come when they are called, and, if the call is conceived of according to Magic, come they certainly will. There are likewise many actions that seem to us entirely innocent, yet in one or another tribe must be avoided by all who desire a prosperous or only a tranquil life. The Papagoe Indians of Mexico forbid a girl at a certain time to scratch her head, or even to touch her hair with her hand; for which there may be an excuse in the sacredness of the head; but her brother comes at the same time under the same restriction.[137] The case seems to be a type of many taboos, as being due wholly to suspicion and anxiety: an anxious mother who sees her boy scratch his head is reminded of his sister who must not do so; her fears are excited, and she prohibits the action that excites her fear: it is taboo. Writing of a Bantu tribe, M. Jounod says, "Most often taboos are inexplicable."[138] So are the penalties that await the breach of them: the punishment rarely fits the crime. Premature baldness, failure in hunting or fishing, boils, lameness, dysentery—may avenge the eating of wild duck or marriage within the forbidden circle. And if any such thing happens to a man, he is liable to be accused of having broken a taboo; and that proves the truth of the belief in taboo.

Besides things that are in their magical nature dangerous, and therefore taboo, things inoffensive in themselves can sometimes be made taboo by merely declaring them to be so, or by setting up a symbolic notice that they are so, or by laying a conditional curse upon anybody who meddles with them. They have then become dangerous. This is the common case of making a talisman by means of a spell, transferring to it invisible power. Such practices, especially common in Melanesia, are often useful as a cheap defence of property (in gardens, for instance), but are also a means of exaction and tyranny. The prevalence of taboo amongst savages, by the way, enables them readily to appreciate our great commandment to do no work on Sunday.[139]

§ 8. Indirect or "Sympathetic" Magic

> § 8. *Indirect or "Sympathetic" Magic.*—Principles of Sympathetic Magic—mimesis and participation; connection with Animism. Exemplary Magic

The use of charms, rites and spells, having been established in one department—say, hunting—may be extended to others by analogy, and is confirmed there in the same way, namely, by still doing one's best. Having obtained the charms and learnt, or invented, the rites and spells, one applies them, but at the same time makes war or love as cunningly as one can, cultivates one's garden, drives a bargain, and so forth, and ascribes all good results to the Magic. At first, I suppose, all such action was direct, discharged at the person or thing to be influ-

[137] Carl Lumholtz, *New Trails in Mexico*, p. 350.

[138] *Life of a South African Tribe*, p. 528.

[139] See the exhaustive treatment of this subject in Frazer's *Taboo and the Perils of the Soul*.

enced. To slay an enemy a bone of a dead man was pointed, or a crocodile's tooth hurled, in his direction (though, probably, not in his sight). To keep off evil Magic a wish was expressed—"Never sharp barn catch me";[140] or to drive away a pest a command was issued, as in Borneo: "O rats, sparrows and noxious insects, go feed on the padi of people down river."[141] But a time came when Magic began also to be carried out by practices indirect and purely dramatic, rites performed and spells recited not at the person or thing to be affected, but upon some substitute, or representative, or symbol; and this must have happened pretty early; for dramatic Magic is met with in Australia. To this sort of Magic belong the widely-diffused methods of operating upon the image of a man or anything assigned to stand for him, or upon hair-clippings, remains of food, or footprints instead of himself; or of tying knots to bind, or untying them to release a curse. With spells the indirect method is less common, but remarkable examples of it occur at a low level of culture. The Yabim of New Guinea, to promote the growth of their taro, tell a story: "Once upon a time, a man labouring in his field complained that he had no taro-shoots. Then came two doves flying from Paum. They had devoured much taro, and they perched upon a tree in the field, and during the night vomited up all the taro. Thus the man got so many shoots that he was even able to sell some of them to other people."[142] Here, then, a mere story of a wish fulfilled is substituted, as a spell, for the wish itself, and expected to have the same effect upon the crop; and as that is, indeed, true, any failure of it is no more liable to be detected. But such practices seem to us sillier and less promising even than direct Magic. What can be the meaning of them?

The indirectness of a rite makes it more mysterious and magical, and that is a recommendation. Moreover, its dramatic character gives an imaginative satisfaction, which must suffice to initiate such pantomime again and again. Amongst ourselves many people are prone to dramatise every situation of their lives; to act in imagination their loves, their revenges, their opportunities of self-display, and to derive satisfaction from such imaginations even to the weakening of their will— satisfaction without effort or danger. But although this impulse may initiate pantomimic magic, it can hardly maintain it in the absence of any deeper satisfaction. The belief in its efficacy, again, once established, the effect of suggestion upon a victim of black Magic (who by some means is acquainted with what has been done against him) may have consequences that seem to verify the rites; but this can only happen when a belief in the efficacy of such practices already prevails. The power of suggestion depends upon the belief; it cannot create the belief. We must fall back upon coincidence. If, indeed, immediate and complete coincidence were requisite, if, when one practised on an enemy's life, nothing less than his speedy death would do, coincidences might be too rare to give the requisite confirmation. But if some less injury will be acceptable, and if it need not follow immediately; if a delay of not merely two or three days, but two or three months will bring the event within the limits of satisfaction; and if the degree of injury may vary from

---

[140] A "barn" is a small spindle-shaped stick, supposed to be thrown in a magical attack by wizards. Howitt, *The Native Tribes of South-East Australia*, p. 377.

[141] Hose and McDougall, *Pagan Tribes of Borneo*, I. p. 110.

[142] Quoted by Frazer, *Spirits of the Corn and of the Wild*, I. p. 105.

death to a bad fall, or some failure in hunting on the victim's part, or a quarrel with his wife; if even (as often happens) a misfortune to any one of his family may suffice—the confirmatory coincidences will be tolerably frequent. There must, of course, be many disappointments; but these count for little, because the particular practice is supported by a general belief in Magic; because men desire to believe and are afraid to disbelieve; because failures are explained by some error in performing the rites, or by the counteraction of superior Magic, or by the intervention of hostile spirits.

Special reasons for practising and believing in indirect operations of black Magic are their greater secrecy and, therefore, greater safety, and greater gratification of the love of cunning: which last (I think) explains much of the elaboration that marks these performances.

In the development of indirect Magic, very many of its practices seem to involve one or other of the assumptions often called the principles of sympathetic Magic, namely, Mimesis and Participation: (1) that to operate upon a likeness or representation, or by analogy, affects the person, or object, or process imitated or represented as if it were directly assailed; and (2) that a part or appurtenance of any one may, in any magical undertaking, be substituted for the whole. Among savages these principles (as has already been said) are only latent forms of procedure, tacitly assumed, not formulated, and cannot have been the source of the practices, but must gradually have been established by them; but when notions of scientific arrangement came into vogue, they were discovered and explicitly stated by the early physicians and alchemists, in whose thoughts Magic and Science were not clearly differentiated.

It has been supposed that these principles are natural consequences of the laws of the association (or reproduction) of ideas. According to the "law of similarity," an idea of one thing often makes us think of another that resembles it: hence the thought of an enemy is supposed to make me think of an image of him, or the sight of his image makes me think of him. According to the law "of contiguity," any two things having been seen or thought of together, thereafter the thought or sight of one of them makes me think of the other: hence the thought of an enemy makes me think of his footprint, or his footprint reminds me of him. Possibly. But must there not have been a long preparation of ideas before the thought of an enemy awakens in me these particular associations rather than many others? And if they should occur to me, how do the laws of association explain my astonishing belief that to put his image in the fire, or to thrust a thorn into his footprint, or to dig it up, carry it home and put it in the oven, will make him lame or afflict him with some wasting disease? There must be some system of ideas to determine these particular judgments.

Some, again, suppose that savages cannot distinguish similarity from identity, part from whole; so that an image appears to them to be in earnest the same thing as a man, or his nail-parings the same as himself. Yet it is certain that in their work-a-day life they do make these distinctions, and that otherwise they could not get on at all. If, then, in certain cases, and in Magic (which is all that concerns us now), they act or speak as if unable to draw such distinctions, it must be from an acquired incapacity in that connection; just as in some cases they suffer from an acquired incapacity to recognise that their beliefs are contradicted by experience; that is to say, some fixed idea or dissociation prevents them from comparing the facts; though sometimes it may be merely that customary forms of speech hinder the expression of distinctions that really exist among their ideas.

It has been suggested that the supposed force of mimetic Magic rests upon the belief that as a man's shadow or reflection implies his presence, so does his image. And we shall see that, in some cases, this explanation is not far from the mark, though it cannot serve for all cases; inasmuch as the image operated upon in any rite need not be a likeness (of course it never is)—a stick will serve, if declared to stand for the victim; and, moreover, his presence is not needed in carrying out rites that act at a distance. What truth there is in this view has been better expressed by Prof. Yrjö Hirn:[143] namely, that a unity or solidarity exists between all persons and things that stand to one another in a relationship of contact or similarity, on account of a certain magical virtue; and that this solidarity is not destroyed by any breach of physical continuity. To take away a man's cloak, or a lock of his hair, or a remnant of his food, does not interrupt the magical continuity which contact has established with the man: something of him, his virtue, remains with it. And in the same way an image of him contains something of his virtue; for to the immature mind, images or pictures are nothing but radiations or decortications of the thing itself, an efflux, like the Epicurean εἴδωλα. Hence the bones of a saint and his picture convey his virtue to a devotee by the same process: both are conductors of some emanation from himself. There is much truth in this theory.

When Animism is called in to explain Magic, this virtue or emanation of a man is apt to be explained as his soul, or part of it. A savage dislikes being photographed, lest you should take away his soul. M. Jounod says the Bantu regard a photograph as "an unsheathing of soul";[144] Mr. Dorsey says no Dakota would have his portrait taken lest one of his souls [out of four] should remain in the picture, instead of going after death to spirit-land;[145] Mr. Carl Lumholtz says the Papagoes refused to be photographed, lest part of themselves should be taken away, and remain behind after death.[146] And it is a trick with some sorcerers to keep a looking-glass, in which they pretend to catch the souls of their dupes; and, of course, shadows and reflections are frequently confounded with the soul. So if the use of an image in Magic does not imply the presence of the man himself, generally it does imply the presence of a very important part of him. And this explanation is strengthened by an apparent exception; for some Malays, when they make an image of an enemy to compass his destruction, think it necessary before operating to coax his soul into it by a potent spell.

> "Hither, Soul, come hither!
> Hither, little one, come hither!
> Hither, bird, come hither!

---

[143] *The Sacred Shrine*, pp. 33-9.
[144] *Life of a South African Tribe*, p. 340.
[145] Sioux Cults, *Am. B. of Ethn.*, XI. p. 484.
[146] *New Trails in Mexico*, p. 61.

Hither, filmy one, come hither!"[147]

Must we not infer that these Malays have in some way lost the common belief, and so are put to this extra trouble?

If it be asked how this account of the matter can justify the use of a stick or stone instead of a man's image, merely assigning it to represent him, the reply (I think) is that the stick is a symbol. Since images are never much like the man, and may be unlike in all degrees, the stick is a sort of limiting case. A symbol is always the remainder, or reminder, of something that once had intrinsic value, as an image, shadow, or reflection has by being or participating in the man's soul. Besides, it is perhaps a tacit assumption of Magic (as in other departments of life—including Philosophy), "that whatever for one's purpose it is necessary to assume, is real or true": the situation demands it.

As to the magical continuity between a man and whatever has been in contact with him, the belief in it may with some confidence be derived from the fact that it retains his odour; and when an animistic explanation is required, it is naturally thought that this odour is his soul or soul-stuff, as the savour of a burnt-offering is its soul-stuff that regales the gods.

Belief in the participation of an image, or part or appurtenance of a man in the man himself, or in his virtue, or in his soul, must give to rites of black Magic a great deal of the subjective satisfaction which is a secret motive of all Magic. The images, or nail-parings, or what not, identify the man to be attacked; they fix the wizard's attention, vivify his imagination, direct the spell whom to strike (as a dog is set upon a trail), and heighten the joy of imaginary revenge.

There are, however, many cases usually classed as "sympathetic Magic" that cannot without great violence be explained in this way; and I complain of the epithet "sympathetic," as applied to all indirect Magic, that it implies this explanation. Consider the Mandan buffalo-dances, the hunting dance and the mating dance; these are imitations or dramatic representations of the hunting of buffaloes and of their mating, which they are designed to prosper: can such dances be interpreted as the efflux or decortications of the future hunt or mating? Or, again, the story of the muræna (quoted above, p. 68) and its resuscitation by the rising tide—is this a radiation of the budding of the taro which it is expected to expedite? Such cases, which are pretty numerous, must be understood upon some other ground than "participation."

Many rites and observances seem to depend upon the notion of favourable or unfavourable currents of invisible power, which may be taken advantage of, or influenced, to obtain one's ends, in hunting, or in obtaining rain, or in fertilisation of animals or crops. It is good to plant seed, or begin any undertaking, when the moon is waxing, or the tide rising; for these events show that the set of the current is favourable to increase or prosperity. Again, one may incite the current or strengthen it, as in bringing on rain by throwing water in the air, or by leaping to help the crops to grow. To instigate or assist in such ways the on-goings of Nature is not the same thing as to cause the event: a rain-wizard does

---

[147] Skeat, *Malay Magic*, p. 48.

not pretend to procure rain in the dry season; the times of ploughing, sowing, reaping (whatever rites may accompany them) are not decided by Magic. Much pantomimic Magic may be best understood as attempting to set up such currents of causation rather than as directly causative. Since instances of cause and effect are observed to repeat themselves, a pantomimic murder, or a hunting dance, or fertility-rites, may be considered as setting an example which Nature is expected to follow: the muræna-spell promotes vitality by merely describing an example of reinvigoration. The Kai of N.E. New Guinea hold that if a man, by falling on a stump of bamboo in the path, wounds himself to death, it is because a sorcerer, having obtained something infected with his victim's soul-stuff, has spread it over a pile stuck in the ground, and pretended to wound himself upon it and to groan with pain.[148] The belief implies that such practices are in vogue; and they seem to rely upon the assumption that "what happens once will happen again"; and that who shall repeat the disaster is determined by the presence, among the conditions, of something belonging to the victim in default of himself. It is not by sympathy or participation that the "something infected with his soul-stuff" acts; but by contributing to reinstate as far as possible all the circumstances of a cause like the cause of the man's death.

In other cases an exemplary cause may be constituted by the substitution of similars that do not imply participation. Dr. Haddon tells us that in the western islands of Torres Straits[149] the Kuman vine breaks up in dry weather, and the segments look like human bones; hence they are employed in Magic. Similarly red ochre or some other stain may be used instead of blood, so that a skeleton may be coloured with it as a means of keeping it alive. In Chinese popular religion, before setting up a new idol, it is first carried to the temple of an older one, who is besought to let a portion of his soul-stuff transmigrate into the new one; then, carried to its own temple and enthroned, its hands, feet, eyes, mouth, nose and ears are smeared with blood, *or with red paint,* to open its senses and bring its soul into relation with the outer world.[150] Such a substitution of similars is true in one sense; red paint is a substitute for blood as colour: Magic requires that it shall also be a substitute in other ways; and, therefore, it is so. Thus, down and feathers thrown into the air in Australian rain-rites are a substitute for clouds; in Mandan hunting-rites, men disguised in buffalo-skins are a substitute for buffaloes; and thus, by substitution, a cause can always be constituted which, once having been set to work, Nature is constrained to repeat the operation.

Ought we not, then, to recognise two kinds of indirect Magic—the sympathetic, and what may be called the exemplary?[151]

---

[148] Quoted by Frazer, *Belief in Immortality*, p. 268.

[149] *Reports of the Cambridge Expedition to the Torres Straits*, V. p. 325.

[150] W. Grube, *Rel. u. K. d. Chinese*, p. 153.

[151] In the *B. of Am. Ethn.*, XIII. p. 374, F. H. Cushing, describing "Zuñi Creation Myths," says the dramaturgic tendency is to suppose that Nature can be made to act by men, if "they do first what they wish the elements to do," according "as these things were done or made to be done by the ancestral gods of creation." The last clause is, perhaps, an animistic gloss of the Zuñis', who were, of course, very far from primitive thought.

The rise of the wizard as a professional authority introduces many changes into magical practice, and decisively alters its social importance. He sometimes experiments in new rites and spells or in new versions of the old ones; he decides some matters arbitrarily, as in imposing taboos on food; generally, he develops the art in the direction of his professional interests, learning to conjure, act, ventriloquise, suggest, hypnotise, and to provide excuses for failure; he begins to train novices, form a school and establish a tradition which influences the whole life of his tribe. How far arbitrary elements enter into rites it is impossible to say, until some one shall discover (as some one may) marks by which to distinguish them. Meanwhile, there may be many rites, or ritual elements, that cannot be explained on any known principles of Magic, because in fact they are arbitrary: still, such things must usually be an imitation of other magical practices. Prof. Leuba suggests, probably enough, that rites may sometimes be adopted to relieve excitement, such as the dancing of women when the men are at war.[152] It was the custom (e. g.) of Araucanian women; and as they danced, they swept the dust away with their fans, and sang: "As we sweep the dust away, so may our husbands scatter the enemy." If this was arbitrarily invented, it was by analogy with much mimetic Magic: they set an example of what should happen and confirmed it with a spell.[153]

§ 9. THE DISSOLUTION OF MAGIC

§ 9. *The Dissolution of Magic*

In spite of the human mind's strong proclivity to Magic, the art, after rising to a maximum power and reputation, in course of time loses its influence, and is to be found festering only in the backwater and stagnant pools of society. Its power is not at the zenith in primitive society, but much later, when there are men in command of great wealth who feel insecure, and turn for confidence to diviners and thaumaturgists, whom they bribe heavily to give what they most desire. But by that time Magic is confused with Animism. As civil order and material civilisation prevail, Magic is no longer invoked to increase one's confidence, because this is ensured by the regularity of ordinary affairs. As positive methods in war, building, commerce are learnt and practised, the magical accompaniments of such undertakings, without being wholly disused, may become less and less important—what we call "survivals," such as the breaking of a bottle of wine on the bows when launching a ship (it is forgotten that the wine must be red). Or they may be lost altogether without injury to industry; whereas in savage economy there is some risk that a most useful craft, such as pottery, weaving, or canoe-building, may be entirely discontinued, if by the extinction of some group of men or women the rites and songs are forgotten with which such labour had always been made good.[154] For who would trust a pot or a canoe unconsecrated?

---

[152] *The Psychological Study of Religion*, p. 165.

[153] Cf. S. H. Ray, "People and Language of Lifu," *J.R.A.I.* (XLVII.), p. 296, who says, a woman whose son or husband was away at war would place a piece of coral to represent him on a mat, move it about with her right hand as he might move in fight, and with her left brush away imaginary evils. This protected him (evidently by exemplary Magic).

[154] W. H. R. Rivers, *The Disappearance of Useful Arts*, also *History of Melanesian Society*, II. p. 445; and in Turner's *Samoa* (p. 145) we are told that the practice of embalming died out

The great systematisations of Oneiromancy, Alchemy, Cheiromancy, Astrology, necessarily come forward late in the day, because they involve the constitution of science; but for that reason they are soon discredited by being confronted with the positive sciences; when, without being forgotten, they are relegated to what may be euphemistically called "select circles."

With the growth of Animism, again, pure Magic becomes comparatively rare; its observances are interpreted according to the fashionable creed, no longer as setting occult, quasi-mechanical forces to work, but as requiring the intervention of a spirit or a god. They become symbolic: ritual now does nothing of itself, but is a sign of what the god does, or is desired to do. Yet Magic often has its revenge upon Animism: enchaining by mysterious uniformities the god himself.

In its own nature Magic comprises qualities that tend to weaken it (at least, to weaken each particular form of it) and to bring about its decline. Magical rites and spells, on whatever scale performed, are things to be repeated, and what is repeated is mechanised and ceases to live. Custom can maintain a practice whilst dispensing with its meaning; slowly the practice (spell or ritual) is slurred and corrupted. Economy, "least effort," is the enemy of all ceremonial. There is also a tendency to the attenuation of rites on the principle (unconscious, of course) that "the sign of a sign is a sign of the thing signified"; whereby a meaning may be disguised in a symbol for the sake of secrecy, or even for politeness. Prof. Westermarck has shown how, in Morocco, the full rite for averting the evil eye is to throw forward the hand with outspread fingers and to exclaim, "Five in your eye." But as this is too insulting for common use, you may instead casually mention the number "five"; or if even that be too plain-spoken, you can refer to "Thursday," which happens to be the fifth day of the week. In this process there is great risk of forgetting the original meaning of the rite or spell; and when this comes to pass, we are left with the empty shells of superstition, such as a dread of "thirteen," "Friday," salt-spilling, walking under a ladder; for hardly a soul knows what they mean.

---

with the family of embalmers.

CHAPTER V

ANIMISM

§ 1. What is Animism?

§ 1. *What is Animism?*—Hyperphysical and psychological Animism.
Not all savages think that every man has a separable soul

IF, when the cohesion of the hunting-pack had weakened, belief in Magic by giving authority to elders became very influential and useful in primitive societies, still greater in subsequent evolution has been the power of Animism. For belief in ghosts led in time to the worship of ancestors, and then especially to the worship of the ancestors of chiefs or heroes, some of whom became gods; and the belief in gods strengthened the authority of chiefs and kings who were descended from them, and helped to maintain the unity of the tribe or nation from generation to generation and from age to age.

In anthropology, the term Animism is usually employed to denote the proneness of savages and barbarians, or people of unscientific culture, to explain natural occurrences, at least the more remarkable or interesting—the weather, the growth of crops, disease and death—as due to the action of spirits: (1) ghosts (that is, spirits that have formerly been incarnate); (2) dream-spirits, that have temporarily quitted some body during sleep or trance; (3) invisible, living, conscious beings that have never been incarnate. This may be called Hyperphysical Animism. Sometimes, however, "Animism" is used to denote a supposed attitude of savages and children toward all things, animate and inanimate, such that they spontaneously and necessarily attribute to everything a consciousness like our own, and regard all the actions and reactions of natural objects as voluntary and purposive. And this may be called Psychological Animism. These two meanings of "Animism" are entirely different: it is one thing to regard an object as moved by its own mind, another to attribute its movement or influence to a separable agent which for the time possesses it; it is one thing to regard an object as having an anthropomorphic consciousness, another to believe that that consciousness is a distinct power capable of quitting it and sometimes returning, or of surviving its destruction, or of existing independently. Even if the doctrine of Animism in the second sense were granted, it would remain to be shown how men came to conceive that the consciousness of a thing can be separated from it, and exist and act by itself, and even with greater powers than it had before—contrary to the opinion of Don Juan,

> "that soul and body, on the whole,
> Were odds against a disembodied soul."

Savages do not always regard a separable spirit as necessarily belonging even to human nature. Dr. Seligman writes that, among the Veddas, a few old men "were by no means confident that all men on their death became *yaku*" (veridical ghosts). Influential men and mediums would do so; but for the rest, at Godatalawa it was determined by experiment. The ordinary man was invoked soon after death, and desired to give good success in hunting; and if much game was then obtained, he had become a *yaka*.[155] Messrs. Spencer and Gillen tell us that, according to the Guanjis, a woman has no *moidna* (spirit part).[156] Major C. H. Stigand says "the Masai have no belief in a future state for any but chiefs"; the common dead are not even buried, but merely thrown out into the bush.[157] Among the Omaha, though each person has a spirit that normally survives the body, still, a suicide ceases to exist.[158] In Tonga the souls of the lowest rank of the people (Tooas) died with their bodies.[159] The human spirit, then, is not necessarily believed to enter upon a life after death; still less is the spirit of an animal. On the other hand, it is held by many tribes that something inherent in weapons, utensils, food and other objects, a "soul" or soul-stuff, may be separable from them and go to Hades or serve as the food of spirits, although the things themselves are not regarded as having a spirit or intelligent life.

§ 2. Psychological Animism

> § 2. *Psychological Animism.* —That everything is animated not an uni-
> versal or primitive illusion. Animatism. Causes of the treatment
> of some inanimate things as living or sentient

Andrew Lang described savages as existing in "a confused frame of mind to which all things, animate and inanimate, ... seem on the same level of life, passion and reason."[160] Children and other immature people are often supposed to be in the same condition. As to children, it is pointed out how deeply concerned they are about dolls and rocking-horses, how passionately they turn to strike a table after knocking their heads against it. But probably it is now admitted that impulsive retaliation, on a table or bramble or shirt-stud (not unknown to civilised men), implies not any belief in the malignity or sensitiveness of those objects. Animals behave in the same way. Th. Roosevelt reports that an elephant was seen to destroy in rage a thorn tree that had pricked its trunk;[161] and that in America he himself saw a bear that was burying a carcass, and lost hold of it and rolled over, strike it a savage whack, like a pettish child.[162] Moreover, in children, such behaviour is in large measure due to suggestion; inasmuch as the setting of them to beat the table, or what not, is an easy way of diverting them from their own pain. And, of course, the dealing with dolls, or rocking-horses, or walking-sticks, as if alive, is

[155] *The Veddas*, pp. 126-7.
[156] *Northern Tribes of Central Australia*, p. 170.
[157] *The Land of Zing*, p. 219.
[158] J. O. Dorsey, *American Bureau of Ethnology*, 1889-90, XI. p. 419.
[159] Mariner's *Tonga*, p. 105.
[160] *Myth, Ritual and Religion*, p. 48.
[161] *African Game Trails*, p. 333.
[162] *Outdoor Pastimes*, p. 77.

play. Such play involves intense imaginative belief, which, at first, is not clearly differentiated from earnest. But this stage corresponds with the play of the young of the higher animals, whilst they are still physically incapable of completing the preluded actions; and the engrossing interest of their play expresses the biological necessity of it as a means of developing their mental and bodily faculties. By the time that children are at all comparable with savages, their play has become a temporary attitude, compatible with brusque transition to matter-of-fact, or even with actions which at the height of play show that the illusion is incomplete.

In savages, likewise, much of the behaviour that is supposed to betray an illusionary animism, even in their simple apprehension of things, is really an acquired way of acting, in a temporary attitude, under the influence of imagination-belief, and is compatible with other actions that show how incomplete is the illusion. Andrew Lang, after the passage above quoted, appears to limit the scope of it by the words "when myth-making": no doubt, when myth-making and in practising many rites, savages speak or act as if they believed in the full sense that the objects dealt with are sensitive intelligent beings; and yet their effective conduct toward them is entirely positive. They may, for example, feed the growing rice-plant with pap; in harvesting it, speak a secret language that the rice may not understand them and be alarmed, and proceed to cut it with knives concealed in their palms: but they do cut it. They carry it home and garner it with honour, and come from time to time to take a portion for food with solemn observances: but then they cook and eat it.[163] Their animistic attitude, therefore, is not primitive, spontaneous, necessary illusion, but an acquired, specialised way of imagining and dealing with certain things. Were it not possible to combine in this way the imaginative with the practical, all wizardry and priestcraft would be nothing but the sheer cheating which it often seems to be to superficial observers. Normally, imagination-beliefs that have only indirect biological utility (say, in maintaining customs in order to ensure the tribe's welfare) are unable to overcome immediate biological needs (say, for food and shelter); but often they do so within certain limits, or in certain directions, as in innumerable taboos of food, customs of destroying a man's property at his death, starving or maiming tribesmen on the war-path. A universal taboo on rice is not inconceivable. For these are social-pathological cases; like the self-destructive beliefs of individuals and sects amongst ourselves, such as the faith-healers, who in sickness call upon their god instead of a physician.

Children, savages and ourselves, in some degree, attribute spontaneously to *some* inanimate things, in our mere apprehension of them (for this has nothing to do with the metaphysics of Pampsychism), something more than external existence: regarding them as force-things and, by empathy, as experiencing effort and quiescence, strain and relief, and sometimes emotion and pain. It is for this attitude toward nature that I adopt Mr. Marett's term "animatism": as not ascribing to inanimate things, or to plants, in general, anything like a human personal consciousness; but merely an obscure, fragmentary, partial consciousness, enough to correspond with our occasional experiences in dealing with them. Perhaps those observers who report in strong terms universal Animism as the tenet of a tribe,

---

[163] Frazer, *Spirits of the Corn and the Wild*, I. p. 183.

mean no more than this; for example, the author above quoted as writing in the *American Bureau of Ethnology*, who says (p. 433) that according to the Dakotas, everything—"the commonest sticks and clays"—has a spirit that may hurt or help and is, therefore, to be propitiated. It would be unjust to the adherents of psychological Animism to accuse them of believing that savages have universally made so much progress in "faculty Psychology" as to distinguish personality, will, passion and reason; especially as they add that savages project these powers into all natural objects through incapacity for discrimination and abstraction; and, at the same time, know very well that in some languages of the most animistic tribes (e. g. Algonquin and Naga) the distinction of animate and inanimate is the ground of grammatical gender.

We find, accordingly, that some explorers explicitly deny that, in their experience, savages regard all things as on the same level of life, passion and reason. Dr. Coddrington says that, in the Banks' Islands, yams and such things are not believed to have any *tarunga* (spirit)—"they do not live with any kind of intelligence";[164] and that Melanesians do not fail to distinguish the animate and the inanimate. Messrs. Skeat and Blagden report that with the Semang of the Malay Peninsula there is very little trace of animistic beliefs; and they relate a folk-tale of how a male elephant tells a female that he has found a live stone (pangolin rolled into a ball): "Swine," said the female, "stones are never alive."[165] Messrs. Hose and McDougall tell us that the Kayans hang garments and weapons on a tomb, and seem to believe that shadowy duplicates of these things are at the service of the ghost, but that such duplicates are inert (relatively) and not to be confused with the principle of intelligence.[166] "Soul" does not imply personality.

To be clear about Animism, it is necessary to bear in mind several modes of belief: (1) Hyperphysical Animism, that certain things have, or are possessed by a conscious spirit, and that this spirit is a separable entity; (2) that things are themselves conscious (or semi-conscious), but their consciousness is not a separable entity; (3) that things are not conscious, but are informed by a separable essence, usually called soul (better, soul-stuff), which may be eaten by spirits, or may go to ghost-land with them; (4) the extension or limitation of these beliefs to more or fewer classes of things. Unless these distinctions are recognised, any report upon savage beliefs can hardly be clear and adequate; but generally we may take it that when a traveller tells us that such and such things are not believed to have souls, and says nothing of any belief as to their consciousness, he means (except with regard to animals) to deny that anything like human consciousness is attributed to them. And when Mr. Torday writes that, according to the Bahuana of the Upper Congo, there are two incorporeal parts—*doshi*, common to man, animals and fetiches, and *bun*, peculiar to man—he seems to leave it as a matter of course that plants and inanimate things have neither of these, and are not conscious beings; though probably some of them have soul-stuff, since clothes, weapons and food are buried with a corpse.[167] The Rev. J. H. Weeks says that the Bakongo of the

[164] *The Melanesians*, pp. 249 and 356.
[165] *Pagan Races of the Malay Peninsula*, II. p. 222.
[166] *Pagan Tribes of Borneo*, II. p. 3.
[167] *Camp and Tramp in African Wilds*, p. 174.

Lower Congo attribute a spirit only to the *nkasa* tree (from whose bark the ordeal poison is derived) amongst plants;[168] and, similarly, the Baloki, further up the river, attribute a spirit only to the *nka* tree.[169] Since many things are buried by these people in a grave, or broken above it, the things may be supposed to have soul-stuff; but from the denying of spirits to plants, and from silence as to psychological Animism, it may be inferred that neither plants nor inanimate things are regarded as conscious beings. Sir E. F. im Thurn tells us that material things of all sorts are believed by the natives of Guiana to have each a body and a spirit—evidently a conscious and malicious spirit; "and that not all inanimate objects have this dual nature avowedly attributed to them, is probably only due to the chance that ... the spirit has not yet been noticed in some cases."[170] Even with these Guiana Indians, then, whose Animism, in every sense, is unusually active and extensive, their attitude is an acquired, specialised way of imagining and dealing with things that draw their attention and excite their suspicions, not a primitive, necessary illusion; else there could be no exceptions.

The reasonable view, therefore, is that savages distinguish between themselves and certain animals, on the one hand, and, on the other, the remaining animals, plants and inanimate things; and raise the second class to the rank of the first, as conscious agents, only when there are special incentives to do so. To find all the causes that excite the animistic attitude toward things would be a difficult task, but some of them may be indicated. Beginning from Animatism, which really is a primitive and necessary illusion, it is reasonable to expect:

(*a*) That any plant or inanimate thing adopted as a Totem should, by that very fact, be endowed with human consciousness; though the savage mind is too inconsistent for us to infer that this must always happen.

(*b*) That whatever seems to move or act spontaneously, like the winds and streams and echoes, the sun, moon, planets, and shooting stars, should be felt as a spiritual agency; especially if it cry out with empathetic reverberation, as winds and cataracts do, trees tormented by the storm, waves, fire, and the ice-floe when it breaks up in spring; or if it excite fear by being extraordinary and dangerous, as thunder and lightning are, whirlwinds and whirlpools, waterspouts and volcanoes. Dr. Speisser writes that at Ambrym, when the volcano is active, the natives climb to the top and bring sacrifices to appease it, throwing coco-nuts and yams into the crater.[171]

(*c*) That whatever has been regarded as having magical force should be treated—after the rise of the ghost-theory (supposing this to be of later origin) has given vogue to a new principle of explanation—as owing its virtue to a spirit, either by immanence or possession (two modes of actuation which may or may not be distinguished), and so become a fetich, instead of being merely an amulet or talisman.

---

[168] *The Primitive Bakongo*, p. 283.

[169] *Among Congo Cannibals*, p. 275.

[170] *Among the Indians of Guiana*, p. 355.

[171] *Two Years with the Natives of the West Pacific*, p. 199. As to waterspouts and shooting stars, see the *Reports of the Cambridge Expedition to Torres Straits*, VI. p. 252.

(*d*) That whatever is much used in ritual, especially if often addressed in spells or incantations, should become an object of reverence, apt to be personified and raised to, or even above, the human level as a conscious agent: for example, padi and rice in Indonesia, the ordeal tree on the Congo, already mentioned. Fire-sticks used in the ritual of sacrifice are often deified. In India, the conch, having for ages been used in religious rites, "the people gradually came to revere the instrument itself and to adore and invoke it."[172] "A strange religious feature [of the *Rigveda*] pointing to a remote antiquity is the occasional deification and worship even of objects fashioned by the hand of man, when regarded as useful to him. These are chiefly sacrificial implements."[173] The practice now extends in India to nearly every tool and utensil. Amongst the very few inanimate gods of the Cherokees are the Stone, invoked by the Shaman when seeking lost goods by means of a pebble suspended by a string; and the Flint, invoked when about to scarify a patient with an arrow-head before rubbing in medicine.[174] By the Apache, heddontin (pollen of the cat-tail rush) is used as the sacrificial powder in nearly all rites, and is personified and prayed to.[175] When spells are addressed to any object, the analogy of address to human beings tends to cause that object to be thought of as humanly conscious.

(*e*) Stocks and stones have been worshipped, as the dwelling-place of spirits in many parts of the world; having superseded in the mind of their devotees the ghost of the men whose burial-place they formerly marked, but who themselves have been forgotten; and probably, on the analogy of these stones, others that no ghost ever haunted.

(*f*) Where Animism is active amongst a timid and suspicious people, whatever injures a man is believed to act of malice: as amongst the Indians of Guiana, who are so timid that rather than go hunting alone they will take a woman or a child along with them.[176]

Under such conditions as these a sort of acquired psychological Animism is very widely though very irregularly diffused; but were it universal and uniform, it could not of itself account for hyperphysical Animism—the doctrine that men (or some men), some animals, plants, things, places, are possessed or informed by spirits that are capable of separate existence.

§ 3. THE GHOST THEORY

§ 3. *The Ghost Theory.*—Originated chiefly by dreams; which are regarded as objective experience

Hyperphysical Animism may be easiest understood as having arisen with the belief in human ghosts. The causes of this belief have been fully set forth by

[172] J. Hernell in the *Quarterly Journal of the Mythical Society* (Bangalore), IV. No. 4, p. 158.

[173] A. A. Macdonell, *Sanskrit Literature*, p. 112.

[174] J. Mooney in *Reports of the American Bureau of Ethnology*, 1885-6, VII. p. 341.

[175] J. E. Bourke in the *Reports of the American Bureau of Ethnology*, 1887-8, IX. pp. 499-507.

[176] E. F. im Thurn, *Among the Indians of Guiana*, pp. 288, 354.

Herbert Spencer[177] and Sir E. B. Tylor[178] in a way that to my mind is convincing. Amongst those causes dreams predominate; wherein the dead are met again as in the flesh. The living body having always been for the savage a conscious force-thing, at death the conscious force leaves the thing or corpse. This might be accepted by him as a fact of the same kind as the loss of its virtue by a talisman or amulet (which is known sometimes to happen), were it not for dreams in which the dead still live. That this conscious force that has left the body is not visible except in dreams need excite little wonder, since many forces natural and magical are invisible.

A dream not being common to two men at the same time, the things that are seen in it cannot be pointed out, nor therefore directly named (in this resembling subjective experiences). It was for ages impossible to narrate a dream as a dream: there was no way of distinguishing it from external events, either for the dreamer himself or (were that possible) in reporting it to another. He was far away and met his father, yet had lain by the fire all night! Hence to find names with which to describe such things men turned to other ways in which they seemed to have a double existence, to shadows and reflections: which in their sudden appearance and disappearance, and sometimes faint, sometimes distorted outlines, bear some resemblance to dream-images; and probably it is felt to be significant that shadows and reflections disappear at night, just when dreams occur. Shadows and reflections are not necessarily identified with the ghost derived from the dream-image, because their names are given to it; but sometimes they certainly are; so that a man who, on looking into water, happens not to see his reflection may believe that his spirit has gone away, and that he himself must be ill, and accordingly he becomes ill; or if at noon near the equator he notices that he has no shadow, he may think his soul is gone, and run to a medicine-man to get it back; and dead bodies may be believed to have no shadows.[179] Inasmuch as a body even lying on the ground casts a shadow, except at tropical noon, the belief that it does not do so at any time implies an acquired inability to see what is before one's eyes; as sometimes happens in hypnosis and other conditions of negative hallucination.

The idea of a separable conscious personal force, or spirit, that leaves the body at death, serves also, as it gathers strength, to explain sleep, fainting, epilepsy; and sometimes every sickness is attributed to the partial detachment or desertion of the spirit; which, therefore, it is the doctor's business to plug in, or to catch and restore; or (if I rightly remember a report of Miss Kingsley's) he may even supply another one from a basketful of souls kept at hand for such exigencies.

That the ghost theory arises not only from dreams, but is also suggested by hallucinations and hypnagogic visions is very probable. In various parts of the world savages have been described as having visions of remarkably coherent and <u>convincing vividness</u> that seem not to have been dreams.[180] But such experienc-

[177] *Principles of Sociology*, Vol. I. chs. viii.-xii.

[178] *Primitive Culture*, chs. xi., xii.

[179] J. H. Weeks, *Among Congo Cannibals*, pp. 262-3. My friend, Mr. Torday, tells me this belief is very common in Africa.

[180] See, e. g., A. W. Howitt, *Native Tribes of South-East Australia*, p. 406; and P. A. Talbot, *In the Shadow of the Bush*, pp. 83-8.

es, even when artificially induced by fasting or drugs (as happens among many tribes), are rare in comparison with dreams; and to the influence of dreams upon these savage beliefs there is abundant testimony. With some tribes dreams are treated as part of their objective experience; so that to be injured by your neighbour in a dream is just ground for avenging yourself as soon as you wake; and to see a dead man in a dream is, therefore, clear proof of his continued existence, and that either he has come to the dreamer or the dreamer has gone to visit him.

Thus Sir Everard im Thurn says of the native of Guiana, his dreams are as real as any events of his waking life; his dream-actions are done by his spirit: in dreams he continues to see the dead—that is, their spirits.[181] Similarly, the Lengua Indians (W. of R. Paragua) have great faith in dreams; wherein the spirit is believed to leave the body and to do in fact what is dreamed.[182] According to the Cherokees, to dream of being bitten by a snake requires the same treatment as actual snake-bite; else (perhaps years later) the same inflammation will appear in the wounded spot, with the same consequences.[183] The Motu hold that *sua* (ghosts or spirits) are seen in dreams, and that when a man sleeps his own *sua* leaves his body.[184] "The Lifuans believe in the reality of what is seen in a dream, and are influenced by it. Their dead ancestors appeared in dreams."[185] And the Polynesians of Manatuki thought that "dreams were occasioned by the spirit going to the places seen in them."[186] Many more of such witnesses might be cited.

It is recognised by psychologists that dreams, as immediate experience, have more the character of perception than of imagination. Children are apt to confuse dreams with reality. It can only have been gradually, with the growing knowledge of continuity and coherence in the course of events, and therewith the demand for corroboration of testimony, that dreams were distinguished from the waking life. When no longer supposed to be all of them real, some are still so regarded: the Dieri, amongst lower savages, distinguish between visions, as revelations made by Kutchi (an evil Spirit), and ordinary dreams, as mere fancies.[187] But so impressive are dreams to many people, in their eagerness to know more than sense and philosophy can tell them, that they persist in hoping, and therefore believing, that dreams, if they give no knowledge of this world, may still be revelations of another, perhaps more real; or if not revelations, adumbrations by way of allegory, which some learned or inspired Daniel may interpret; or, at least, omens of good or evil, which the ancient science of Oneiromancy undertakes to explain. There is now a new and more promising Oneiromancy that interprets dreams as indicating not the future, but one's own past, chiefly a forgotten past, and teaches to know oneself: more promising; for what but experience can possibly be the source of dreams—at least, of dream-elements? Some of the new principles of interpretation, however, may compare for obscurity with the ancient.

[181] *Indians of Guiana*, p. 344.
[182] S. H. C. Hawtrey, "The Lengua Indians," *J.A.I.*, 1901.
[183] J. Mooney, "Sacred Formulas of the Cherokees," *Am. B. of Ethn.*, VII. p. 352.
[184] C. G. Seligman, *Melanesians of British New Guinea*, pp. 190-91.
[185] S. H. Ray, "People and Language of Lifu," *J.R.A.I.*, LXVII. p. 296.
[186] Turner, *Samoa*, p. 277.
[187] A. W. Howitt, op. cit., p. 358.

That the dead are seen alive in dreams is, then, for the savage a fact of observation; and, therefore, the continued existence of the dead is, for him, not in the first place supernatural; although it may be called hyperphysical, because it is experienced only in dreams and not by daylight, and is exempt from ordinary conditions of time and place. But it gradually becomes supernatural, as the capricious incidents of dream-life are felt to be "uncanny," as that which occurs only at night is involved in the fears of the night, and as a great cloud of imaginations accumulates about the dead and obscures the simple facts of dream-perception in which the belief originated. This cloud of imaginations, by its mysterious character and by various alliances with Magic, spreads and deepens until it overshadows the whole of human life; is generally, indeed, dispersed here and there by the forces of biological necessity, often by subterfuges laughable enough; which have, however, the merit of saving mankind from destruction: but sometimes it extinguishes the last ray of common sense, impoverishes the believer, enfeebles him, fills his days and nights with terror, gives him over to practices the most cruel or the most disgusting, leads him to slay his own tribesmen, his own children, his own parents, and to offer up himself in the sure hope of resurrection.

§ 4. EXTENSION OF THE GHOST THEORY TO ANIMALS

§ 4. *Extension of the Ghost Theory to Animals.* — Influence of shadows and reflections. Generally, only things individually interesting have ghosts. Examples

Spirits, having once been conceived of as explaining the actions of men and surviving their bodily death, may by analogy be conceived to explain the action of any other things in circumstances that suggest a motive for the action, and therefore to possess or inhabit such things, and to be capable of separating from them, like ghosts. Other things are already, by Magic and Animatism, force-things, in some degree conscious, whose forces may be capable of acting invisibly at a distance; and at the death of a man it is his conscious force that leaves the body and becomes a ghost. Since, then, there is hardly any natural object whose action may not in some circumstances seem to be interpretable by motives, especially amongst a timid and suspicious people, how can we assign any necessary limits to the spread of Animism? Moreover, the causes most influential in establishing the ghost theory for man directly require its extension to other things. For not human beings only are seen in dreams, but also their clothes, weapons and utensils, and also animals, plants, localities. If, then, the dead, because they are seen in dreams, are inferred still to live under conditions in which they are not visible by daylight to ordinary men, how can the inference be avoided that all sorts of things, artefacts, animals, plants, localities, share in that mode of existence — that all have their doubles? And "Why not?" the savage might ask, since it is literally true of all things, without exception, that they are sometimes visible, sometimes invisible.[188] Similar inferences seem to be justifiable from the alliance of ghosts with shadows and reflections, and the fact that not man only but everything else has a shadow and a reflection, and that their shadows and reflections disappear at night, just

---

[188] Spencer, *Principles of Sociology*, § 53.

when the things themselves sometimes appear in dreams. Moreover, so far as the breath, the pulse, the shining of the eye, which cease in the human corpse, are sometimes identified with the departed spirit, the same processes likewise cease at the death of animals; though, it is true, there is here no analogy with inanimate things, and the breathing and circulation of plants are beyond the savage's observation. Therefore, although Animism is an inferential construction, were the construction entirely due to the logic of analogy, there would be nothing surprising in the discovery that the belief "that everything has a ghost" is just as universal and uniform in the human race as if it had been an innate or primitive belief. That, on the contrary, Animism prevails very irregularly amongst the tribes of men; that, in all directions, inferences that are analogically specious fail to be drawn; that instead of a general system of Animism every tribe has its own Animism; this is surprising and needs to be explained. The extension of the theory is easier to understand than its irregular limitation.

Bearing in mind that we are at present considering Animism as a belief in ghosts, not in spirits generally (to which we shall come in Sec. 6), I venture to think that, although dreams, shadows and reflections certainly suggest a double existence of everything, yet savages never assign a true ghost to anything inanimate, nor to plants, nor even to animals, unless there is a special reason for doing so; because only in the case of human beings is the suggestion interesting enough to take hold of the social imagination. Hence, even though other things appear in the ghost-world, they have no significance there, except in relation to human ghosts (or ghostlike spirits) on whom they attend. Accordingly, human ghosts have a place in the beliefs of every tribe, because human beings excite affection, admiration and fear, have well-marked individuality; are therefore remembered and have stories told of them; and if they are seen after death, it is, of course, reported. The evidence makes it only too plain that the paralysis of attention by fear is the chief (though not the only) emotional factor of belief in ghosts; and what other thing in all nature is to be feared in comparison with one's fellow-man?

The belief in ghosts, escaped and roaming independent of any normally visible body, as a social belief, is involved in the practice of reporting and discussing dreams, which becomes the same thing as telling ghost-stories—the first and most persistent motive of literature. Stories can only be told effectively of things generally interesting; and, at first, such things must have been recognisable by the hearers and must have had some individuality. Hence—

(*a*) Animals that attain to such individuality may have ghosts: (i) An animal that occasions widespread fear, such as a man-eating tiger. We must distinguish from such cases the frequent beliefs that tigers, wolves, sharks, snakes, etc., are, or are possessed by, the spirits or ghosts of men. (ii) An animal that comes to be upon terms of special intimacy with men; such as the very tame dogs and pigs that come when they are called among the Bakongo;[189] or hunting dogs that have been specially doctored among the Baloki.[190]

(*b*) Animals slain at funeral feasts to accompany the dead have ghosts so far as

[189] J. H. Weeks, *The Primitive Bakongo*, p. 238.
[190] J. H. Weeks, *Among Congo Cannibals*, p. 233.

necessary for that purpose; but, wanting individuality and personal interest, they make no further figure in ghost-lore; they do not "walk" or revisit the glimpses of the moon. Thus the Tanghouls say that ghosts, on reaching Kazairam (their Hades), find the gates barred against them by the deity Kokto; so at the burial feast of a rich man a buffalo is killed, that his mighty ghost may burst open the massive gates of that abode. Poor ghosts must wait about outside, till a rich one comes up with his buffalo; when they all rush in behind him.[191] But we hear nothing further of the buffalo. In the Banks' Islands, pigs killed at a funeral feast have no true ghosts to follow the dead to Panoi, but only a sort of wraith; because they only go for show, that their master may be well received there.[192]

(*c*) Animals that are important prey to a hunting tribe are often believed to have ghosts that may be hunted by dead tribesmen; or that must be propitiated when one of them is slain: the ghosts, for example, of seals and bears are bribed by the Esquimo to entice other seals and bears to come and be killed. A seal desires above everything, they say, a drink of fresh water; so as soon as one is brought ashore a dipperful is poured into his mouth; else the other seals will not allow themselves to be caught. The polar bear (male) desires crooked knives and bow-drills, or (female) women's knives and needle-cases. Hence, when a bear is killed, its ghost accompanies its skin into the hunter's hut; and the skin is hung up with the appropriate tools for four or five days. Then the bear-ghost is driven out by a magic formula, takes with it the souls of the tools, and reports well of the hunter in bear-soul land. Whilst in the hut, as an honoured guest, nothing is done that it dislikes in human customs.[193]

(*d*) In the development of mythology, animals and monsters of various kinds may be found inhabiting shadow-land; but these are not true ghosts of any particular things that once died in this world.

This list of the ways in which animals may come to have ghosts is not offered as exhausting all the cases.

§ 5. GHOSTS AND SOUL-STUFF

§ 5. *Ghosts and Soul-stuff.*—Separated spirits need bodies and food,
　　that is, soul-stuff. Abstract ideas of "spirit," "force," etc.

A ghost is a disembodied soul, having a consciousness and power at, or generally (because it is feared) above, the human level; but there may be disembodied souls, or souls capable of disembodiment, that have no consciousness, or none above the level of Animatism. Even if a living thing have a consciousness, its post-mortem apparition may not; like the Banks' Islanders' pig, which, though "a distinguished animal and acknowledged to be intelligent," has no true ghost. Among nearly all tribes, whatever is offered in sacrifice to gods or left in, or at, the tombs of men deceased, is believed to have some sort of soul; because, plainly, spirits do not eat or consume the visible food or utensils; yet it is necessary to the

---

[191] T. C. Hodson, *The Naga Tribes of Manipur*, p. 160.
[192] Coddrington, *The Melanesians*, p. 269.
[193] V. Stefànson, *My Life with the Eskimo*, p. 57.

success of the rites to suppose that the spirits are satisfied; they must, therefore, take the souls of the offerings. And what can be more plausible reasoning than to argue that, as solid men eat solid food, ghosts eat ghostly food? "Soul" thus appears as a sort of ghost-substance, or ghost-body. For, in dreams, the departed are seen as if in the flesh; and moreover analogy requires that the ghost consciousness and ghost-force shall have a body of some sort, and, of course, one that will maintain in ghost-land the same relations to other things that the mortal body did in this world. In ghost-land, or shadow-land, or dream-land, the substance of all things is this soul-stuff. Sometimes the force of analogy requires a tribe to believe that, in order that the souls of things (such as earthen pots or weapons) may be released to accompany a ghost to the underworld, the things themselves must be "killed," that is to say, broken; but other tribes are not such consistent logicians; and in some cases where things left exposed at a grave (not buried) are broken, it may be to prevent their being stolen.

Anything, then, may have "soul" after its kind: relatively inert things have relatively inert souls, but never true ghosts; some animals may have ghosts, especially if they have attained to a certain individuality, but generally only in so far as they are imagined to attend upon human ghosts or spirits. Inasmuch as the word "soul" is often used as equivalent to "ghost," it would be convenient always to speak of the soul which is ghost-food, or ghost-body, "as soul-stuff."[194] Soul-stuff is conceived of as material, though subtle and normally invisible. A man's soul-stuff may be regarded not only as permeating his body, but also as infecting everything he possesses or touches: no doubt by analogy with his odour; for a man's odour is a personal quality, distinguishable by dogs and (I believe) by some savages and hypnotic subjects; and the stench of his putrefying corpse may be supposed to convey his courage and skill to those who inhale it.[195] And the savour of a burnt-offering is food for gods. Indeed, Ellis says explicitly that, in Tahiti, food was put to the mouth of a chieftain's corpse; because, they said, there was a spiritual as well as a material part of food, a part which they could smell.[196]

Savage ideas are generally so little thought out, and are so irregularly thought out by different tribes, that the relation of a thing to its soul-stuff varies widely from one tribe to another. In many cases the extraction by ghost or god of the soul-stuff from an offering may affect it so little, that the devotee or the priest proceeds to feast upon it; and I have nowhere met with the notion (which logic requires) that such metaphysically eviscerated food can only nourish a man's body and not his soul. However, since the eating of the sacrifice may be an act of communion with the ghost, he then naturally extracts the goodness only from his own share. In other cases, the breaking of weapons and utensils buried with a corpse implies an intimate unity between the wholeness of an object and its soul-stuff; and the Rev. J. H. Weeks says of the considerable wealth put into a grave by the Bakongo, that only the shell or semblance of anything is supposed to remain there.[197]

---

[194] Hose and McDougall, *Pagan Tribes of Borneo*, II. p. 3.

[195] J. G. Frazer, *Belief in Immortality*, p. 403.

[196] *Polynesian Researches*, I. p. 523.

[197] *The Primitive Bakongo*, p. 371.

This conception of soul-stuff may have been an important contribution to metaphysics. The doctrine of material substance is reached by abstracting all the qualities of things; but then there would be nothing left, were it not for this venerable idea of something invisible and intangible in things in which qualities may "inhere," or which may serve as a "support" to them; so that, when it is taken away there is only a shell or semblance of anything left. But such a tenet is uncommon. Along another line of speculation this soul-stuff may become the Soul of the World. When by philosophers spirits are no longer conceived to have bodies, but to be the very opposite of bodies, a spiritual substance must be invented to support their qualities, in order to put them upon an equal footing of reality with corporeal things; but as there is no spirit-stuff ready made by the wisdom of our forefathers, this concept remains uncomfortably empty. To appear as ghosts and to have mechanical energy, spirits may be invested with "soul-stuff" as a spiritual body; but this is only subtle matter. Their own substance must be correlative with their proper attributes as pure conscious beings, the very opposite of bodies; and, therefore, immaterial, unextended, simple, self-identical, according to the "paralogisms of Rational Psychology." But such speculations are confined to philosophers and theologians: some of whom, however, maintain (as if reverting to the original savage idea) that spirit is the true substance of material things, at least that material things depend upon a spirit, or spirits, for their existence. Monists, again, say there is one substance of both matter and mind, which is not either of these any more than it is the other. Locke very honestly calls it "a supposed I know not what."

In writing of Magic, I have indicated the origin of the notion of force; and if my view is justifiable, it appears that those celebrated abstractions "force" and "matter," form and substance, spirit and body, may be traced to the savage mind. That savages are incapable of general and abstract ideas we have seen to be an illusion. They are necessary to economy in the organisation of the mind. When a tribe bases its grammatical gender on the distinction of Animate and Inanimate, has it in no sense corresponding ideas? But an abstract idea results from a long process of dissociative growth from its concrete sources, and must exist in some manner at all stages of that growth, before its distinctness is completed by an appropriate name; and it is reasonable to suppose that at every stage of growth it functions and influences the course of thought. Accordingly, it is plain that from very early times thought has been greatly influenced by ideas of force, form, spirit and the rest of them.

§ 6. GHOSTS AND SPIRITS

§ 6. *Ghosts and Spirits.*—Ghosts first imagined, and other spirits on
their model. Some spirits, formerly ghosts, now declared not to
have been; others never incarnate

Whilst of some tribes (for example the Indians of Guiana) it is said that there is nothing to indicate that they "know of any spirits, except such as are, or once were, situated in material bodies,"[198] amongst others we are often told that not

---

[198] E. im Thurn, op. cit., p. 363.

only ghosts are known but also spirits that are declared never to have been incarnate. An extreme form of the ghost-theory maintains that all spirits were once ghosts whose incarnation has been forgotten; but this is needless, and seems not to be true. It is enough that probably the original inhabitants of the spirit-world were ghosts; that some of those now believed not to have been ghosts were once really so; and that those spirits that were never ghosts are later immigrants, who have obtained domicile by having been imagined in analogy with ghosts. The following list indicates more or less probable reasons why (*A*) ghosts have sometimes come to be regarded as non-human spirits, and (*B*) why certain non-human things have come to be regarded as spirits, or as possessed by spirits, more or less resembling the human.

A. Spirits that were formerly ghosts, but are now declared not to have been:

(*a*) Ghosts whose former life has been forgotten by mere lapse of time. The memory of the dead amongst many tribes does not extend beyond three or four generations. If then the ghost of some unusually impressive personality happens to be remembered, when all his relatives and contemporaries have been forgotten, he seems to be separated from the human race. And if his name was that of some natural object, his ghost, according to Spencer's hypothesis, may now be regarded as the spirit of that phenomenon. But as to Spencer's hypothesis,[199] although it gives such a plausible explanation of much nature-worship by real facts as to the working of savage language and thought that it seems to me unreasonable to doubt that it has had some of the effects he traces to it, yet it presses upon me more and more that most cases of nature-worship are to be explained by more particular causes.

(*b*) To dissociate a ghost from mankind is especially easy if his tomb has been forgotten, or if he has no tomb. As the drowned have no tombs, they easily become water-demons. Tombs must often be forgotten in consequence of migrations. In Central Melanesia both ghosts and spirits are recognised; but in the west worship is directed chiefly to ghosts, in the east chiefly to spirits. As migration has been from west to east, the tombs of ancestors can no longer be pointed out by the eastern islanders, and so their ghosts may have become spirits. In Tumloo (northern New Guinea) there are temples of spirits (all female) distinct from ancestral ghosts, and on the banisters of ladders leading up to these temples there are ornamental figures of ape-like animals; the architecture of the temples points to a former superior culture.[200] As there are no apes in New Guinea, these figures and temples may indicate a former residence under better conditions in Java or Borneo; and the spirits with which they are associated may be ancestral ghosts whose tombs and other earthly vestiges have been forgotten in the migration.

(*c*) We may see another way in which a ghost may become a pure spirit, if we suppose that as a ghost he had attained to some measure of worship, but that with the rise of new gods (by conquest, or by the reputation of being more helpful), or by his being himself too good to be worth worshipping, his rites have been neglected and his legend forgotten. Then he is no longer remembered as a ghost,

[199] *Principles of Sociology*, §§ 165-93.
[200] J. G. Frazer, *Belief in Immortality*, p. 220.

or ancestor.

(*d*) It may be thought honourable to a god to deny that he was ever a man.

(*e*) The construction of a world-myth makes it necessary to begin somewhere with some one; and whoever becomes the first being, it is necessary to deny that he was ever begotten. But there may be inconsistent stories: the supreme being of the central Esquimo is a woman, Sedna, who created all things that have life; but other traditions give her a human origin.[201] Similarly, in drawing up the genealogy of ancestral gods, we come at last to one who was never begotten. Such is Unkulunkulu of the Zulus, generally said to have sprung from a bed of reeds.[202]

B. Spirits that were never incarnate, but have been imagined by analogy with ghosts already propitiated:

(*f*) A Totem may become a spirit; whilst, having himself no human antecedents, he can hardly be a ghost as of an ordinary mortal. Nothing can be more irregular than the life of Totemism: with some tribes it seems to die out early, or leaves few and doubtful vestiges; with others traces of it seem to remain even amidst conditions of high culture. Apparently, where it survives, the Totem tends gradually to lose his bestial or vegetal properties, or most of them, and to become an anthropomorphic spirit with his myths, in analogy with heroic or patriarchal ancestors. He has attained to a considerable degree of individuality; yet, by association and tradition, may still confer more or less sacredness upon his animal kindred (cf. chap. ix. § 8).

(*g*) To address any object with a spell, as a man is addressed in summons or command, is (as said above) an approach toward its personification. Hence corn, rice, padi, nkasa, or whatever has been the object of tribal rites and spells—the sun and moon, the earth, fire, wind, clouds and rain—having perhaps long been influenced and reinforced by Magic—are apt, when Animism has gained control of man's imagination, to become first the embodiment and then the possession of spirits; the spells become prayers, and the rites religious ceremonies or mysteries. Such spirits, at first locally honoured, may with the evolution of the tribe or nation, the increasing intercourse of its villages, and the centralisation of its culture in some city, be released from local conditions and generalised into transcendent gods, either each of its own kind—corn or wine—or of still wider sway over agriculture or the weather. The meteorological gods are not impaired in strength by even wide migrations; for they are found to rule everywhere; and this may be a reason of their predominance in the higher religions. Plants from which intoxicants are obtained, such as soma or the vine, bringing men to a condition resembling insanity or the ravings of a sorcerer who is supposed to be possessed, are especially easy to understand as sources of inspiration. A belief in vegetation spirits, having originated in any way, may be extended according to the circumstances and mentality of a tribe, until every wood is populous with dryads.

---

[201] Franz Boas, *American Bureau of Ethnology*, VI. 1884-5, p. 583.

[202] Callaway, *Religious System of the Amazulu*, pp. 1 and 40. Cf. Coddrington, *The Melanesians*, p. 150: Koevasi, a spirit, was never human, yet in some way the originator of the human race.

(*h*) Natural objects that have, at first, been regarded with awe and therefore endowed with magical powers—mountain-tops, ravines, whirlpools, ancient trees—under Animism, become the abode of spirits; and these, again, may, by analogy with others, cease to be conceived as merely local. Among the Moors, "the *jnūn*, which form a special race of beings created before Adam, are generally supposed to be active on occasions or in places which give rise to superstitious fear, and in many cases they are personifications of some mysterious qualities in persons or lifeless objects."[203]

In each of these cases, (*f*), (*g*), (*h*), however, an Euhemerist explanation may be offered. As to (*f*), Spencer, of course, argued that the Totem-ancestor is always a man, who bore the name of an animal, and was confounded with it after death; and Dr. Rivers has suggested that some gods who seem to have been derived from Totems may really represent heroes who had such Totems.[204] As to (*g*), Grant Allen suggested that the spirit of the corn or vine is always at first the spirit of the man upon whose grave the plant grew.[205] And as to (*h*), the spirit of a mountain may be the ghost of a man who was buried on the top of it; and the spirit of a whirlpool the ghost of a man who was drowned in it. Indeed some spirits may have originated in one of these ways, others in another way; and what happened in any particular case can only be determined, if at all, by examination of its particular circumstances.

(*i*) Abstract ideas may, at a very early stage of culture, be personified and treated as spirits. The Semang, according to Messrs. Skeat and Blagden, personify Death, Hunger, Disease;[206] and the Beloki, according to the Rev. J. H. Weeks, attribute all personal qualities to the aid of spirits; so that if one man wrestles better than another, it is because the spirit Embanda is in him.[207] The modern Greeks of Macedonia personify and propitiate Lady Small Pox.[208] In the tenth and latest book of the *Rigveda*, "the deification of purely abstract ideas, such as Wrath and Faith, appears for the first time."[209] At a higher stage of culture we find Fides, Fortuna, Concordia and many others. Such things are conceived of as mysterious powers, and they have names; and so far they resemble demons. Why, then, should they not be personified and propitiated like demons?

(*j*) Various ways have been pointed out in which the grammatical structures of language, metaphors and other figures of speech may influence the growth of mythology.

(*k*) Animism having been generally adopted, spirits may be freely invented in explanatory myths. The Kalinis believe that thunder and lightning are the clang and flash of bracelets on the arms of Kidilumai, a girl who dances in heaven, as

---

[203] E. Westermarck, *Marriage Ceremonies in Morocco*, p. 343.

[204] *J.R.A.I.*, 1909, p. 163.

[205] See his ingenious speculations in *The Evolution of the Idea of God*, ch. xiii.

[206] *Pagan Races of the Malay Peninsula*, II. iii. ch. vi.

[207] *Among Congo Cannibals*, p. 272.

[208] G. F. Abbott, *Macedonian Folklore*, p. 236.

[209] A. A. Macdonell, *Sanskrit Literature*, p. 44.

formerly on earth, for joy of the welcome rain.[210] It would be absurd to suppose that she must once have lived on earth. Some amongst the Ekoi say that Thunder is a giant marching across the sky; others that Thunder is the enemy of Lightning and, on seeing it, growls to drive it away.[211] If free invention may originate myths, it may modify old ones, with results that cannot always be interpreted upon general principles.

Finally, any spirits that have been anthropomorphised in analogy with ancestor-ghosts may be further disguised by giving them mythical family connections with the ancestors and with one another, as happened to Bacchus and Demeter.

§ 7. How Ghosts and Spirits are imagined

§ 7. *How Ghosts and Spirits are imagined.*—Have the same attributes, and not at first immaterial; confused with the corpse. Various conceptions. Number of souls to each body. External souls

Ghosts and spirits have the same qualities and characters, eat the same food, appear in dreams, possess men and animals, help sorcerers, give diseases, determine the success of hunting or agriculture. At first, they are solid things, not truly incorporeal, merely invisible to ordinary people by daylight; though dogs or pigs may see them even then. A ghost is so associated with its corpse, that it is not always clear which it is that escapes from the grave and walks; and one may judge whether a dead man has yet gone to Hades or still haunts the neighbourhood, by observing whether in the morning there are footprints around his grave; and to keep the ghost from walking, one may fill the belly of the corpse with stones, or break its limbs, or bury it deep and pile the earth upon it; or one may burn it. In South-East Australia, ghosts can be heard at night jumping down from the trees or from the sky.[212] They may be heard to speak or sing, usually with thin voices, like bats: as

> "the sheeted dead
> Did squeak and gibber in the streets of Rome."

Spirits may have all the appurtenances of an animal body; for two of them waylaid an Australian, and made a wizard of him by taking out his entrails and filling up the cavity with the entrails of one of themselves.[213] They may marry mortals, as a devil begat Caliban upon a witch; and not long ago the "incubus" was very troublesome throughout Europe. In short, a ghost or spirit can act physically, just as a man can, because he has the same organs; but with greater power, because mysterious and more feared. And such beliefs persist amongst people whose culture is much higher than the Australian, as in Jacob's wrestling with something at the ford Jabbok, and Grettir's slaying of the ghost of Glam at Thorhallstad;[214] and Euthymus, the boxer, having put on his armour, defeated the ghost

---

[210] T. C. Hodson, *The Naga Tribes of Manipur*, p. 126.
[211] P. A. Talbot, *In the Shadow of the Bush*, p. 73.
[212] Howitt, *Native Tribes of South-East Australia*, p. 437.
[213] Spencer and Gillen, *Northern Tribes of Central Australia*, p. 483.
[214] *Grettir Saga*, ch. xxxv.

of Lycas at Temesa.[215] To this day, in Macedonia, there are vampires, or animated corpses (chiefly Turks), that walk, and throttle people and suck their blood.[216] "The Moslem corpse," says R. Burton, "is partly sentient in the tomb."[217] The Karok of California consider it the highest crime to utter the name of the dead; for it makes the mouldering skeleton turn in its grave and groan.[218] In fact, it is difficult to think of one's own future corpse as entirely inanimate, and this adds some discomfort to one's thoughts of death. According to Wundt, the Körperseele, as eine Eigenschaft des lebenden Körpers, is a starting-point of Animism independent of, and probably prior to, the breath and the dream, which suggest the idea of a free separable soul.[219] This confusion of ideas in popular Animism seems to me due to (1) the strong association of the ghost with the corpse, and the performance of rites (which must take place somewhere, if at all) naturally at the grave or in connection with relics; (2) the manifestation of ghosts as visible, speaking, tangible bodies in dreams; (3) the difficulty of imagining spirits to live and act except in the likeness of the body (though non-human forms—usually animal—are sometimes substituted); (4) the convenience of such imaginations to the story-teller; (5) the convenience of them to sorcerers and purveyors of mysteries, who rely upon such imaginations in producing illusion by suggestion. For ages a confusion of ghost with corpse may exist in the popular mind along with the more refined notion of soul-stuff in which a ghost becomes manifest, whilst there is no attempt to reconcile these imaginations; and it is only by metaphysical subtilties about "mind" and "matter," or by mystical aversion to sensuosity, that the notion of pure incorporeal spirit without even spatial limitations is at last freed from these primitive associations, partially and amongst a few people. A tendency to abstract conception of the spirit is set up, indeed, in the ordinary way of "dissociation" by the belief in transmigration. For if a spirit may "possess" all sorts of bodies—men, plants, animals, etc.—it is independent of any particular body; though it may still be thought to need *some* body. Where the idea of pure spirit has been established amongst educated people, it becomes necessary for those who believe in ghosts and have forgotten their soul-stuff to explain how a spirit can manifest itself to eye, ear, nose, hand, without a physical body, by "materialising" itself, as invisible vapour (say one's own breath on a frosty morning) condenses into a cloud or into dew; for the power of analogy as an aid to thought, or as a substitute for it, is not yet exhausted.

The varieties of belief that occur here and there in the world cannot be explained without a much fuller knowledge of local circumstances than is usually available. The Semang say that souls are red, like blood, and no bigger than a grain of maize;[220] the Malays that they are vapoury, shadowy, filmy essences, about as big as one's thumb;[221] in both cases shaped like the owner. Elsewhere in the

[215] *Pausanias,* VI. p. 6.
[216] G. F. Abbott, *Macedonian Folklore,* p. 217.
[217] *First Footsteps in East Africa,* p. 52 note.
[218] *American Bureau of Ethnology,* I. p. 200.
[219] *Mythus und Religion,* 2º ed., p. 78.
[220] *Pagan Races of the Malay Peninsula,* I. p. 194.
[221] *Malay Magic,* p. 47.

Indian Archipelago, "the animating principle is conceived of, not as a tiny being confined to a single part of the body, but as a sort of fluid or ether diffused through every part."[222] The less educated classes in Japan consider the soul as a small, round, black thing that can leave the body during sleep.[223] Amongst the Ekoi, the soul is a small thing dwelling in the breast, whilst a man lives; but at death expands into the body's full stature.[224] The difficulty of finding the soul in the body leads some thinkers to suppose it must be very small, others very attenuated—thin as a shadow and as breath invisible.

Whilst many savages believe, like ourselves, that the body entertains one soul and gives up one ghost, the Ekoi believe in two, one animating a man's body, the other possessing, or changing into, some animal in the bush. Three souls, the vegetative, sensitive and rational, are well known to European philosophy. The Mandans thought that a man has one black, one brown, and one light-coloured soul; but that only the last returned to the Lord of Life.[225] The observer who tells us this also reports (p. 484) that some of the Dakotas assign to each man four spirits: one that dies with the body; one that remains with, or near, it; one that accounts for its deeds and at death goes to the spirit-world; and one that lingers with the small bundle of the deceased's hair, which is kept by relatives until they can throw it into an enemy's country to become a roving, hostile demon. In West Africa, too, Miss Kingsley found four souls: one that survives the body; one that lives with some animal in the bush; one, the body's shadow, that lies down every night in the shadow of the great god, and there recovers its strength; and, finally, the dream-soul. Some natives hold that the three last are functions of the first or true soul; but the witch-doctor treats all four separately.[226] The shadow of a man, his reflection, his name, his totem, his breath, his dream-wraith, his blood, his corpse, supply natural starting-points for such speculations. Some Chinese philosophers held that "each of the five viscera has its own separate male soul."[227] I have found no belief in six souls; but in Siberia the Altaians distinguish six parts or (rather) conditions or stages of the soul; and this probably is only another attempt to convey the same meaning.[228] Mr. Skeat reports that, probably, in the old Animism of the Malays, each man had seven souls; though now they talk of only one; except in using spells, when the souls are addressed separately.[229] In the religion of Osiris there seems to have been a still greater number of souls: as of the name, the shape, the strength, the shadow, etc.: all reuniting with the immortal counterpart of a man's mummy, if justified at the last judgment. Prof. Wiedemann suggests that these beliefs may have been collected from different local sources,

[222] *Spirits of the Corn and the Wild,* I. p. 183.

[223] W. G. Aston, *Shinto,* p. 50.

[224] *In the Shadow of the Bush,* p. 230.

[225] J. O. Dorsey, "Siouan Cults" in the *American Bureau of Ethnology,* 1889-90, XI. p. 512.

[226] *West African Studies,* p. 200.

[227] J. G. Frazer, *Balder the Beautiful,* II. pp. 196-208; where are reported other beliefs in a plurality of souls; in one case thirty, in another thirty-six.

[228] M. A. Czaplicka, *Aboriginal Siberia,* p. 282.

[229] *Malay Magic,* p. 48.

and preserved for fear of losing anything that might be true.[230] Whereas, then, the prescientific mind is often accused of confusing things that are separate, we see here the opposite tendency to reify abstract aspects, and to separate things that are in nature united; and one probable cause of this is the practical interest of treating, and therefore of attending to and addressing, separately, certain aspects of a man in rites of exorcism, lustration, summoning, reinforcing, propitiation.

The belief in an external soul that exists apart from oneself (though identified with oneself for good or evil) in an animal, in the bush, or where not, may have arisen from the connecting of the soul with the shadow or reflection. The shadow is, indeed, attached to a man by the feet (except when he leaps), if the whole is seen; but it goes away at night: it stretches, as the sun declines, far across the plain, and then disappears. The reflection is quite separate, and is seen *within* a pool (as in a mirror), not on the surface, approaching us when we advance, and withdrawing when we retire: whence it is easy to understand that to take a man's photograph may be to take away his soul. If this kind of soul may be some feet distant, why may it not be much further off, if there be any motive (such as the desire of secrecy) to wish or think it so? If it may reside within a pool, why not within anything else? What, in fact, becomes of it when we turn away? That it should be in an animal in the bush is reasonable enough, if one's Totem (even though imperfectly remembered as such) is an animal in the bush, and if oneself is in some sort that animal.

§ 8. Origin and Destiny of Souls

§ 8. *Origin and Destiny of Souls.* — Reincarnation — Transmigration — Liable to second death. Place of the departed. Importance of next life resembling the present

Beliefs as to the origin of souls sometimes bear the character of fanciful explanation myths. The Semang say that souls grow upon a soul-tree in the world of Kari (their chief god); whence they are brought by birds, which are killed and eaten by an expectant mother: souls of fishes and animals are also obtained by the mothers' eating certain fungi and grasses.[231] Here the analogy of the growth of fruits is adopted: being so familiar as to need no further explanation. Leibnitz's suggestion that monads are *fulgurations continuelles de la Divinité*,[232] is at about the same level of thought. In other cases, we see the struggling to birth of ideas that still seem plausible: such is the widespread tenet that every present human soul is the reincarnation of an ancestor, which we find in Australia, Melanesia, Borneo, Manipur, on the Congo, in North America and elsewhere. The Bakongo seem to base their belief in reincarnation partly on personal resemblance; upon which ground a child may be thought to have the soul even of a living man; so that to point out such a resemblance is displeasing, since it implies that, the child having his soul, he must soon die.[233] Another reason they give for their belief is that the child speaks early of things its mother has not taught it, and that this must

[230] *Religion of the Ancient Egyptians*, ch. ix.
[231] *Pagan Races of the Malay Peninsula,* I. p. 194.
[232] *Monadologie*, 47.
[233] *The Primitive Bakongo*, p. 115.

be due to an old soul talking in a new body. But Bakongo albinos are incarnations of water-spirits, and greatly feared. Possibly in some cases people began by naming children after their ancestors, and later inferred that those who bore the same name must be the same persons. Plato thought that, by a sort of law of psychic conservation, there must always be the same number of souls in the world:[234] there must, therefore, be reincarnation. That nothing absolutely begins to be, or perishes, though first explicit in the Ionian philosophy, is generally assumed in savage thinking; so why should it not be true of souls?

As to the destiny of souls there seems to exist amongst the tribes of men even greater variety of belief than as to their origin. They may pass through more than one stage of development: as in the western isles of Torres Straits one becomes at death, first a *mari*, and later a *markai* with a more definite status;[235] or as with the Veddas, one is at first called, without much confidence, "the living one," and only a few days later becomes, after trial of one's virtue, a *yaka*,[236] or authentic ghost. Often the dead will be reincarnated, but the interval between death and rebirth may be passed in an underworld, or in a city in the forest, or indefinitely in a land of ancestors. They may turn into plants; as among the Mafulu old people's ghosts become large funguses growing in the mountains:[237] but more frequently into animals; perhaps their Totems, or (with seeming caprice) into such things as termites or wild pigs; or (because wings seem to suit the spirit) into a butterfly or bee; or into owls or bats that haunt the night and dwell in caves that may be tombs; or into deer or bear-cats, because these are seen in the clearings near tombs; or into snakes, because these are seen to come out of tombs, and often come into huts as if returning to their homes, and, moreover, cast their skins and so typify the renewal of life. They may also become stars, or shooting stars, or mere naked demons, or white men.

It is only after ages of thought concerning the fate of our souls that there arises in any systematic form the doctrine of metempsychosis, which now prevails over great part of southern and eastern Asia, and was formerly known in Egypt and even in Greece. But in the widely diffused doctrines of reincarnation in men or in animals, or even in plants, and in the general belief that a soul may wander and possess any kind of body, we see the sources from which this vast flood of superstition collected its waters. The Buddhist belief that not the soul wanders, but its *karma* (or character) creates a new body, may be considered as a retrogression from Animism to Magic; for what is it but a law of the action of an occult force or virtue?

Though the ghost survive the body, and it may be said (as by the Ekoi) that it cannot perish, and the reason may even be given (as in the Bismarck Archipelago), that it is of different nature from the body,[238] it is by no means always immortal. It may die, as it were a natural death, by oblivion; or, the next world being just like

---

[234] *Republic*, 611*a*.
[235] Haddon, *Cambridge Expedition to the Torres Straits*, Vol. V. p. 355.
[236] C. G. Seligman, *The Veddas*, p. 133.
[237] R. W. Williamson, *The Mafulu*, p. 266.
[238] J. G. Frazer, *Belief in Immortality*, p. 396.

this, ghosts may fight together and kill one another;[239] according to the Tongans a ghost may be killed with a club; amongst the Bakongo it may be destroyed by burning its corpse.[240] It has been thought that to suppress the ghost was the original motive of cremation; but the western Tasmanians cremated their dead, and can hardly have done so to be rid of such mild Animism as seems to have been entertained by the eastern tribes, who buried their dead or abandoned them.[241] However, they seem to have been rid of it; whereas, in general, ghosts survive cremation, because this process cannot put an end to dreams; and it may then come to be believed that burning is necessary in order to set the soul free from its body; and, therefore, the wife of Periander, tyrant of Corinth, complained to him of being cold in the ghost world, because her clothes had been only buried in her tomb and not burnt.[242] According to the Egyptians, the ghost participated in every mutilation of the body, and perished with its dissolution. It may be held that even the gods die if neglected, and depend for their immortality upon the perpetuation of their rites and sacrifices.[243]

Whilst the ghost's life endures, its dwelling may be in the earth or sky, sea or forest, or in the land of the setting sun, or in the land of ancestors whence the tribe remembers to have migrated. Before departing to that undiscovered country, it may haunt the grave or the old home, till burial, or till the flesh decays, or till the funeral feast, or till death has been avenged; or it may roam the country, a resentful demon, if its funeral rites be not duly celebrated. There may be one place for all ghosts, or two, or more, according to their age, or rank, or qualities (as sociable or unsociable), or whether or not their noses were bored; or according to the manner of their death, by violence, or suicide, or sorcery. It is late before our posthumous destiny is thought to depend on moral character (as it does in metempsychosis); and even then varies with the local conception of the good man, as observing custom or religious rites or, finally, the dictates of conscience.[244] I remember how puzzling it was in childhood to make out from sermons how far "going to heaven" depended on being good (conscientious) or on faith. Both seemed very desirable; yet there was a shadow of opposition between them, and to be good was a little dangerous. But faith was indispensable, and apparently the more difficult of the two, needing more elucidation, exhortation and reiteration.

The journey of ghosts to their own world may be short or long, an unadorned migration or rich in details of adventure. They may begin the new life exactly as they finished this one, or the old may be rejuvenated. As to their manner of life there, oftenest it is a repetition of their earthly state, perhaps better, or even much better, perhaps worse. And this conception is historically of the utmost importance: for (1) it seems to give the greatest confidence in a hereafter. Hume ascribes what seemed to him the incredulity of men with regard to a future life "to the faint idea we form of our future condition, derived from its want of resemblance to the

---

[239] C. G. Seligman, *The Melanesians*, p. 658.

[240] J. H. Weeks, *The Primitive Bakongo*, p. 224.

[241] Ling Roth, *The Aborigines of Tasmania*, pp. 57-61.

[242] Herodotus, V. p. 93.

[243] On the mortality of gods, see Frazer, *The Dying God*, ch. i.

[244] *Primitive Culture*, II. pp. 75-96.

present life."[245] And (2) from this conception proceeds the development of ghostly polities: presided over, according to tribes that have no chiefs, by a headman, such as Damarulum, or by the greatest known hunt-leader, like Kande Yaka of the Veddas; under advancing political structures, by chieftains, amongst whom one may be paramount, and so become a king or lord of all. These ghostly politics support the earthly ones they imitate. It is everywhere an edifice built by hope and fear, under the guidance of analogy, and sometimes decorated by caprice, if this find acceptance with the tribe.

§ 9. THE TREATMENT OF GHOSTS

§ 9. *The Treatment of Ghosts.* — Results partly from fear, partly from affection. Funerary rites — extravagance and economy. Simplicity of ghosts. Inconsistent behaviour toward them

The behaviour of men toward the ghosts of their dead is chiefly governed by fear. The human power that has left the corpse is now invisible; that power, rarely quite trustworthy whilst in the body, especially when unobserved, retains its desires, caprices and hatreds that were partially controlled by social influences. What controls them now that the man is exempt from observation? How shall one defend oneself against him, or procure his neutrality, or even (as sometimes in the flesh) his help? The fear of ghosts has peculiar qualities: the invisibility of a spiritual enemy produces a general objectless suspicion and a sense of helplessness; associations with the physical conditions of the corpse and with darkness excite feelings very much like those aroused by snakes and reptiles. This fear explains why savages, such as the Australians, may believe in ghosts for ages without ever venturing to pray even to father or mother deceased; for to pray is to invoke, and they will come, and, on the whole, they are not wanted. Fear may make the survivors quit the neighbourhood of the dead; sometimes makes them adopt means to induce the ghost to leave, and invent stories of how and whither he goes, which are believed by biological necessity; because, unless they can be rid of the ghost and the dread of him, or establish in some way the *pax deorum*, it is impossible to go on living.

The Yerkla-mining never bury their dead, nor in any way dispose of them. On seeing death approaching a tribesman, they make up a good fire for him, and leave the neighbourhood, not to return for a considerable time.[246] The Sakai, having buried the dead affectionately with necklaces, wallets, etc., say to him: "Do not remember any more your father, mother, or relations. Think only of your ancestors gone to another place. Your living friends will find food." They then burn his house and desert the settlement, even abandoning standing crops.[247] Among the Kikuyu, "if a person dies in a village, that village is often burnt, and the people trek off and build elsewhere," though much labour may have been spent on the

[245] *Treatise*, B. I., Part III. § 9.

[246] Howitt, *Native Tribes of South-East Australia*, p. 450.

[247] Skeat and Blagden, *Pagan Races of the Malay Peninsula*, II. pp. 95-9. For similar formulæ of dismission (which, of course, are constraining spells) see W. Ellis, *Polynesian Researches*, I. p. 522; and J. O. Dorsey, "Siouan Cults," *American Bureau of Ethnology*, X. p. 420.

surrounding fields. Sick people are often deserted.[248] Where land is closely settled such flight becomes impossible, and in any case it is very inconvenient; so that if any one can believe it possible to deceive the ghost, or to frighten him away by shouting at him, beating the air with boughs or firebrands, letting off arrows or guns, or to restrain him from walking by breaking the corpse's legs, or by placing loaded "ghost-shooters" (straws filled with gunpowder) around the grave, so much the better. Many such plans are adopted, and they *must* be believed in.[249]

Affection, however, has its part in the treatment of the dead: it is reasonable to attribute to affection the beginnings of the practices of leaving food at the tomb, burying weapons or ornaments with the corpse, celebrating funerary rites with lamentations; though in time this motive may be mixed with, or superseded by, fear of the ghost, or by fear of being suspected of having murdered the deceased by sorcery, should rites be neglected or maimed. It is not uncommon to carry about some bones of the departed, to hang round one's neck the skulls of infants untimely dead. The wild Veddas, though, having covered a corpse with boughs, they avoid the place for a long time for fear of being stoned, nevertheless have a strong feeling of good fellowship for the spirits of their dead.[250] In the eastern isles of Torres Straits, the Miriam perform an eschatological mystery, in which the recently deceased reappear on their way to the other world. The women and children take it for reality: their affections are said to be gratified; and at the same time their fears are allayed by the conviction that the ghosts, having been seen on their way to Hades, will no longer haunt them.[251] The old Norsemen believed that the dead were still united with the living by intense sympathy.[252] As rites begun in affection may become propitiatory through fear, and after prayer has been instituted may be further extended to obtain the aid of spirits or gods in hunting, war, revenge, love, agriculture, trade, or any undertaking for subsistence, riches or power, every passion in turn seeks its gratification through Animism.

Extravagance in funerary rites, often ruinous to the family, may sometimes be checked by considerations of economy or convenience. Thus some tribes of South Australia may burn all the property of the deceased except their stone axes, which are too valuable to be lost to the survivors. The Nagas bury with the body the things most closely associated with the dead; but things of small value, never the gun or the cornelian necklace.[253] The Todas, who burn their dead, lay the body on a bier with many valuable offerings and swing it three times over the fire; they then remove the money and the more valuable ornaments and burn the rest with

---

[248] Stigand, *The Land of Zing*, p. 250.

[249] For the practice of appointing certain seasons at which the whole tribe or nation unites in driving out ghosts or demons by force of arms (sometimes with the help of cannon and elephants), as obtaining at all levels of culture, from Australian savagery to the enlightenment of China and Peru, and with more decorum at Athens and Rome, see Frazer, *The Scapegoat*, ch. iii. § 2.

[250] C. G. Seligman, *The Veddas*, p. 131.

[251] *Cambridge Expedition to Torres Straits*, VI. p. 253.

[252] Vigfussen and Powell, *Corpus Poeticum Boreale*, I. p. 417. For further examples of affectionate interest in ghosts, see *Primitive Culture*, II. pp. 31-3.

[253] Hodson, *The Naga Tribes of Manipur*, p. 100.

the corpse. They say that the dead still have the use of everything that was swung over the fire; and tell a story to explain the ceremony; but Dr. Rivers observes that "this symbolic burning has the great advantage that the objects of value are not consumed, and are available for use another time."[254] The Araucanians buried many things with the dead, and at the grave of a chief slew a horse. But for all valuables—silver spurs and bits and steel lance-heads—they left wooden substitutes. As for the horse, the mourners ate it, and the ghost got nothing but the skin and the soul of it.[255] Economy may also induce the belief that ghosts are easily deceived, or are unaccountably stupid in some special way: as in the widespread practice of carrying a corpse out of its house through a hole in the wall; trusting that, the hole having been immediately repaired, the ghost can never find his way back; so soon does he forget the familiar door. This is cheaper than to burn the house down. Superstitious practices may be carried out with self-destructive infatuation, or restricted at will: in Florida (Melanesia), in a certain stream, a very large eel was taken for a ghost; no one might bathe in, or drink at, the stream—"except at one pool, which for convenience was considered not to be sacred."[256] A conflicting desire creates a limiting belief. Whilst often the most painful or disgusting rites are endured for fear of ghosts, at other times they are assumed to be so dull that we are tempted to say: "Whatever is convenient is credible."

If we desire to know the future, ghosts are so wise that we consult their oracles and pay handsome fees to their inspired priests; but if we dread their presence, it is easy to accept any suggestion that they are obtuse or infatuated. They may (e. g.) be afflicted with what psychiatrists call "arithmomania." Returning from a funeral, strew the ground with millet-seed: then the ghost can never overtake you, for he must stop to count them. Or hang a sieve outside your window: he cannot enter until he has counted all the holes; moreover, his system of numeration does not reach beyond "two." You can always block his path by drawing a line across it and pretending to jump over the line as if it were a stream of water: of course, he cannot pass that. Or blaze through the wood a circular trail, beginning at his grave and returning to it: he must follow it around for ever, always ending at the same cold grave. Alas, poor thin, shivering thing, that would go back to the old hearth and sit close amongst the kinsmen by the fire, and laugh at the old jokes and listen to the old stories—chiefly about ghosts—have you forgotten all the tricks that can be played upon your kind? Such is the homœopathy of superstition: imagination creates the fear of ghosts, and imagination cures it.

Imagination-beliefs, being swayed by moods and passions, are necessarily inconsistent. Natives of the Bismarck Archipelago are cannibals and greatly fear the ghosts of those they devour. Whilst feasting they hang up a slice for the ghost himself, and afterwards make an uproar to scare him away. Nevertheless they keep his skull and jawbone, which the ghost might be supposed especially to haunt; so easily do other passions overcome fear. Of the fear of ghosts sometimes seems true that which Bacon says of the fear of death, that there is no passion in the mind of man so weak but it mates and masters it. Sacrilegious miscreants have always

[254] *The Todas,* p. 363.
[255] E. R. Smith, *The Araucanians,* p. 172.
[256] Coddrington, *The Melanesians,* p. 177.

robbed tombs, even the tombs of Pharaohs who were gods; and timid lovers have kept tryst in graveyards. The Sia Indians of North Mexico had a masterful way of dealing with the ghost of a slain enemy: they annexed him together with his scalp; for this having been brought to the village, a shaman offered a long prayer, and thus addressed the ghost: "You are now no longer an enemy; your scalp is here; you will no more destroy my people."[257] To capture and enslave the ghost of an enemy is said to have been the chief motive of head-hunting in Malaya. Compare the conduct of the Romans in carrying off Juno from Veii and establishing her at Rome. The inconsistency (sometimes met with) of supposing a man's personal qualities to go with his ghost, and yet eating some part of his body to obtain those qualities, may be due to the latter practice having been magical, and having persisted after the rise of Animism. Some of the Esquimo have such control over ghosts by Magic, that they fear them very little. After a death, the ghost remains peaceably in the house four days (if a man) or five (if a woman), and is then dismissed by a ceremony to the grave, to wait there until a child is born in the village, when it is recalled to be the child's tutelary spirit.[258]

§ 10. EVOLUTION AND DISSOLUTION OF ANIMISM

§ 10. *Evolution and Dissolution of Animism.* —Popular and priestly Animism. Different emotions excited by ghosts and by gods

Animism, originating in the belief in ghosts of men, tends to spread as the explanation of whatever had formerly been attributed to Magic (if we take this to have been earlier); although it is far from occupying the whole region that thus lies open to it. We have seen that the extent of its prevalence as an explanatory principle, and consequently as the basis of cults, differs greatly amongst different peoples. But more interesting than the spread of belief as to the agency of spirits so as to include more and more objects, is the gradual differentiation of some of them from common ghosts in power, character and rank, and their integration into families and polities, such as we see in the *Edda* and the *Iliad*. A process, going on for ages and varying with every people, cannot be briefly described: the work of E. B. Tylor, Herbert Spencer, W. Wundt and others in this department is well known. In general it may be said that, allowing for the influences of geographical conditions and tradition and foreign intercourse, the chief cause of the evolution of a spirit-world is the political evolution of those who believe in it; so that the patriarchies, aristocracies, monarchies and despotisms of this world are reflected in heaven. Tribes of the lowest culture—some African Pygmies, Fuegians, Mafulu, Semangs, Veddas—have the least Animism; at successive grades—Australians, Melanesians, Congolese, Amerinds, Polynesians—Animism increases and grows more systematic; and it culminates in the barbaric civilisations of Egypt, Babylonia and India, and of Mexico and Peru. But in civilisations of our modern type it rapidly loses ground.

The cause of such differences in the extension and elaboration of the animistic

[257] Miss M. C. Stevenson, "The Sia" in *American Bureau of Ethnology*, 1889-90, XI. p. 121.

[258] Stefànson, *My Life among the Eskimo*, p. 397.

hypothesis cannot be that some tribes have had more time than others to think it out; since they have all had an equally long past. Animism is known to be very ancient, and there is no reason to think that some races adopted it later than others. That, in the lower grades of culture, men want brains to think it out, is not a satisfactory explanation; because, on contact with superior races, backward peoples show themselves capable of much more than could have been inferred from their original state. Improvement in culture depends upon much besides native brains, namely, opportunities afforded by the resources of their habitat, and communication with other peoples. The most backward peoples are the most isolated peoples. The development of Animism is entirely a matter of operating with ideas; and it seems to me that before men can build with ideas they must build with their hands; there must be occupations that educate, and give advantage to, constructive power, as in the making of boats and the building of houses and temples; for to this day a nation's material edifices are always, in clearness of plan, coherence and serviceableness, much in advance of their systems of theology and philosophy; because they must "work," as the Pragmatists say. If you have ever gone over a battleship, compare her with the *Kritik d. r. Vernunft*. Secondly, a suitable model for the edifice of ideas must be presented in the world of fact; and this, as we have seen, is supplied by the tribe's social and political structure; which, again, is clearly correlated with the improvement of architecture in building the houses of chiefs and gods. Thirdly, a favourable condition of the working out of any theory is to have the means of recording, either in oral literature or (still better) in writing, the advances already made; and, fourthly—a condition historically involved in the foregoing—the growth of a class of men, generally a priestly caste or order, sometimes poets, who have time to think, and the education and vocation to bring the accumulating masses of animistic—now religious—ideas into greater order and consistency. Hence there are two stages in the development of Animism—of course, not sharply separated: first, a long period of irregular growth in the tribal mind; and, secondly, a much shorter period, in which the extension of animistic theory depends more or less upon quasi-philosophical reflection.

With the differentiation of superior beings—heroic, ancestral or other gods—from common ghosts, Religion arises. As to the meaning of the word "religion," indeed, there is no agreement: some lay stress upon the importance of beliefs concerning supernatural beings; others upon prayer, sacrifice and other rites of worship; still others upon the emotions of awe and mystery. To define "religion" (as a tribal institution) by all three of these characters seems to me the most convenient plan, and the most agreeable to common usage. That, on the one hand, pure Buddhism (if it ever was a living faith outside of a coterie of philosophers and saints), and, on the other hand, the spiritual condition of a few savages, may be wanting in one or other mark, is no serious objection. The former case is, in fact, exceptional and aberrant, and the latter rudimentary; not to give them the name of "religion" in a technical sense is no wrong to anybody. Thus understood, then, Religion brings to the development and support of Animism many social utilities and other influences; especially the influence of dynasties supposed to have descended from the gods; and of priesthoods, whose sustentation and authority depend upon the supposed necessity of their intervention in worship. In their hands the free popular development of animistic ideas comes to an end, and gives place to the co-ordination of ideas by reflection, and to the dictation of tenets and rites by policy. The simple motives of hope and fear that actuated popular Animism are now supplemented by dynastic and priestly interests and ambitions; beneath which lies, faintly recognised and ill served, the interest of society in order.

This later sophisticated Animism, so far as it obtains a hold upon the people, is imposed upon them by suggestion, authority and deception; but being super-imposed upon ancient popular traditions that are never obliterated, it still appeals to the sentiments of awe, consolation, hope and enthusiastic devotion. The part of deception in the history of Animism, indeed, begins at the beginning, preceded, perhaps, and prepared for by the devices of Magic-mongers. Amongst the Arunta, women and children are taught that the noise of the bull-roarer during initiation ceremonies is the voice of the spirit Twanyirika.[259] Near Samoa Harbour, at harvest, they offer some of the firstfruits in a bowl to the ghosts; and, whilst the family feasts on the remainder, "the householder will surreptitiously stir the offerings in the bowl with his finger, and then show it to the others in proof that the souls of the dead have really partaken."[260] So early is the end supposed to justify the means. Animism, like Magic, strives to maintain its imaginations by further stimulating the imagination; and, in both cases, such practices are, with many men, compatible with firm belief on the part of the practitioner; who is merely anxious to promote the public good by confirming the weaker brethren: himself weak in the perception of incongruities. But I am concerned chiefly with origins, and will pursue this nauseous topic no further.

Parallel with the development of Religion, a change takes place in the emotions connected with Animism. As the gods emerge from the shadow of night and the grave, and are cleansed from the savour of corruption, and withdraw to the summit of the world, they are no longer regarded with the shuddering fear that ghosts excite; as they acquire the rank of chiefs and kings, the sentiments of attachment, awe, duty, dependence, loyalty, proper to the service of such superiors, are directed to them; and since their power far exceeds that of kings, and implies the total dependence of man and nature upon their support and guidance, these sentiments—often amazingly strong toward earthly rulers—may toward the gods attain to the intensest heat of fanaticism. Extolled by priests and poets, the attributes of the gods are exaggerated, until difficulties occur to a reflective mind as to how any other powers can exist contrary to, or even apart from, them: so that philosophical problems arise as to the existence of evil and responsibility, and the doctors reason high—

> "Of providence, foreknowledge, will and fate,
> Fixed fate, free will, foreknowledge absolute,
> And find no end, in wandering mazes lost."

This is one cause of the dissolution of Animism: the power that comprehends all powers ceases to be an object, and becomes the immanence of all things, good and evil. Another cause is the complexity of theogonies, or of spiritual kingdoms

[259] Spencer and Gillen, *Northern Tribes of Central Australia*, p. 497.
[260] Frazer, *Belief in Immortality*, p. 259.

with their orders and degrees: found too fanciful, when hierarchic despotisms, that furnished the analogues, give place to the simpler social structure of democracies; or, to a certain type of democrat, even insulting, a provocative disparagement of the sovereignty of the people. And Animism has other enemies in the growth of Positivism, and sometimes in the resurgence of Magic.

CHAPTER VI

THE RELATIONS BETWEEN MAGIC AND ANIMISM

§ 1. THE QUESTION OF PRIORITY

§ 1. *The Question of Priority.* —Wundt's theory of Animism and of the
derivation from it of Magic. Reasons for dissenting. Origins of
Magic and of Animism independent

MAGIC and Animism now everywhere flourish side by side, or in confused
association, and, by those who believe in them, are not discriminated as they may
be by a spectator. As to their origin, we have seen that both of them are prehistoric;
it is useless to inquire about it amongst believers (who can only tell you that they
learnt these things from their forefathers), or to look for any sort of direct proof. In
Chapter IV. I mentioned general considerations in favour of the priority of Magic;
but said nothing of the opposite opinion, that Animism is prior and Magic deriva-
tive: an opinion held by many and, amongst them, by Wundt, whose treatment of
the problem claims attention.

Prof. Wundt holds that the idea of the soul is older than Magic and has three
principal sources: (1) the gebundene Seele, or Körperseele (consciousness as an
attribute of the body), is immediately given, without the need of any reflection, as
a result of perception-associations; for thinking, feeling and willing are constant
elements of a living body.[261] The influence of this idea is seen in the practices of
making offerings to the dead at their tombs, of preserving the body itself, of treat-
ing the blood and various parts of the body as vehicles of the soul, the use of hair
and nail-parings in sorcery, and so forth. By contact, this soul can be transfused
into other things. But the freie Seele, a being differing from and opposed to the
body, is suggested (2) by breath and by the cessation of the body's living functions
with the last breath—the Hauchseele; and also (3) by dreams and visions—the
Schattenseele. This third conception gradually subordinates the other two, and
has the chief part in the development of Animism and Mythology.[262] As to sor-
cery (Zauber), it is, at first, always attributed to the human will; inasmuch as this
is the original type of causation. Ordinary events raise no question of causes for
the Naturmensch; but only extraordinary occurrences do so, such as sickness and
death. Even pain or death from wounds is a matter of course, for the antecedents
are visible to him; but pain or death from sickness has no such customary anteced-
ent; so to explain them he imagines an enemy who can operate at a distance by

---

[261] *Mythus und Religion,* pp. 78, 79.
[262] Op. cit., p. 125 et seq.

sorcery. Sorcery he conceives of as an operation of one soul upon another; either directly, or indirectly by various appliances, such as pantomimic injury by means of an image. Pantomime is at first believed to affect the victim's soul, and so to cause sickness in his body; but the oftener such rites are repeated, the more the intervention of the soul is obscured. For in many-linked associations, especially where the first and last links stand as means and end, the middle links are apt to disappear; and since these are, in this case, ideas about the soul, there remains, after their loss, the indefinite idea of some incomprehensible action at a distance by means of the pantomime: it is then no longer Sorcery but Magic. Similarly, a fetich, or a talisman or amulet (which differs from a fetich only in not being the object of a cult), originally owes its power to an indwelling spirit, but may degenerate into a magical object.[263] Magic, therefore, is always derivative and secondary; and Animism is entirely independent of Magic.[264]

This theory is worked out with Prof. Wundt's usual comprehensiveness and methodical clearness; and the exposition abounds with interesting discussions; but it has not convinced me. The Körperseele, as an attribute of the body, is, surely, not a soul at all. Customary perception of other men interpreted by self-consciousness, with the habitual treatment of others (and of ourselves by others) as conscious bodies—making it difficult to conceive that a corpse is really dead—no doubt influences animistic rites; for even though the soul seen in dreams may be believed to live, having the consciousness of its former body in dreamland, yet some consciousness seems to remain with the body in the grave. Many rites performed at a tomb, however, may also be understood in relation to a belief that the soul, though having a separate existence as seen in dreams, still desires to reinhabit its body, or to protect its buried treasures, and therefore, though its new home be far away, frequently returns and haunts the neighbourhood of its tomb, and will certainly return if summoned. But it is not until the soul seen in dreams has become an object of popular belief, that any idea can be formed of a body-soul—or more properly of a soul within the body, and thence of a soul-stuff of the body—which leaves the body at death (and under other conditions) as the vehicle of consciousness. This soul-stuff which leaves the body at death may easily come to be identified with the breath, but not until the discussion of dreams has given rise to the belief in a separable soul. The fact that in cold weather the last breath (or any other!) may appear for a moment as a vapour, and is never seen again, cannot by itself suggest a separate persistent existence like that of the soul; and over a considerable part of the earth such a vapour is seldom formed by the breath. The Körperseele and the Hauchseele, therefore, are not independent sources of Animism, but are entirely dependent for their imaginary existence upon the Schattenseele, upon the growth of a belief in a separable soul as seen in dreams.

As to Sorcery, it may be defined as Magic practised with the aid of spirits; and since its existence implies that a belief in spirits and their influence has already formed itself, it may also be believed to operate, in the first place, on the souls of its victims and so, in the second place, on their bodies. Then, as Prof. Wundt explains, a process of retrogradation sometimes occurs, in the course of which the spirits

[263] Op. cit., p. 202 et seq.
[264] This was also Spencer's opinion, op. cit., § 133.

are forgotten, and only the mechanical rites remain as a residuum of bare Magic. Similarly, a fetich sometimes becomes a merely magical talisman or amulet. This is hardly disputable; but it does not prove that the degeneration of Sorcery is the *only* source of Magic, or that Magic has not (for the most part, indeed,) another, independent origin. The issue is difficult to argue upon the ground of facts, because magical practices are of such high antiquity. If, for example, one should urge that the intichiuma ceremonies of the Arunta are not, so far as we have evidence, designed to operate by spiritual power upon the souls of the emu or the witch-ettygrub, but directly to promote by Magic the fertility of these objects, it might be replied that such, indeed, may be their present character, but that the original intention must have been to promote fertility by first influencing their souls, and that this has been forgotten. Or, again, if one should point to the little stones—tied up in bark and believed by the Kaitish to be stores of evil Magic—as having no mark of the fetich, no character to indicate that their power is due to spirits, so that they seem to be merely magical, the answer would be ready, that by long use and retrogradation they may have ceased to be fetiches, but that a good theory requires them to have been of that nature aforetime. Thus any case of apparently bare Magic may be treated as a residuum of lapsed Animism; or, should its origin be recent and ascertainable, it may still be said to have been constituted by analogy with such residua.

We are driven, therefore, to rest the argument upon the psychological conditions of such beliefs. Is the nature of the human mind, so far as we can interpret it at the savage level, such that the belief in Animism necessarily precedes and (later) gives rise to the belief in Magic; or is it possible to indicate conditions that may independently give rise to Magic? According to Prof. Wundt, as I have said, Sorcery precedes Magic and, at first, is always attributed to human volition, because this is the original type of causation. Contrary to Hume's doctrine (he says), the ordinary course of events does not excite in the savage the idea of causation, or the need of explanation. Customary series of events belong to those matter-of-course properties of things which he, eben wegen ihrer Regelmässigkeit, unmöglich hinweg denken kann.[265] It is the unusual occurrences—accidents, storms, drought (where rain is much desired) and especially sickness and death—that awaken in him the need of causal explanation. He is accustomed to pain from wounds, where he sees the conditions on which they always follow; but the pain of disease has no such antecedents, and he supplies the gap in routine by free associations, imagining that this pain also must be the work of some enemy. For in the regular course of events there is for him only one region in which an effect appears notwendig verknüpft mit dem Vorausgehende: namely, that of his own voluntary actions. The connexion is, indeed, only a matter of fact; but it includes the sensations and feelings of his own power über den Eintritt des Ereignisses. This, as Berkeley saw (says Prof. Wundt), is the true origin of the notion of causality; though the true principle of causality requires the elimination of this subjective ground of its origin.[266]

It is true, of course, that the savage has no definite idea of the principle of <u>causation; but he</u> has obscure ideas of all its chief marks—the need of some an-

[265] Op. cit., p. 263.
[266] Op. cit., p. 267.

tecedent for every event, regularity of connexion, and proportionality; and prob-
ably, in the depths of his mind, the abstract principle has made some progress
toward maturity. (*a*) The ground or source of such ideas, according to Hume, is
customary experience; and that such experience includes its own causation (and,
therefore, needs no explanation) is proved by Prof. Wundt's contention that it is
the unusual which first demands causal explanation; because there the familiar
causation is missing; so that the savage tries to fill up the lacuna, as best he can,
according to the type of what is usual. But (*b*), according to Prof. Wundt, there is in
the regular course of events only one region in which the idea of causation (though
illusory) first arises: namely, our own actions, in which we are aware of our own
power over the beginning of the event. And no one, I suppose, doubts that the no-
tion of power is derived originally from the consciousness of our own exertions[267]:
read, by sympathy, into the actions of other men and animals and, by empathy,
into the movements of trees, stones, winds and waters. All this, however, occurs so
early in the individual and in the race (probably in the higher animals) that, before
the need of causal explanation is felt, the world is seen as if pervaded by forces,
which are manifested in *every* usual course of events and not merely in voluntary
actions. Again (*c*), power is only one character of the primitive belief in causation:
another, not less important, is uniformity; and the study of our own actions is no-
toriously unfavourable for the discovery of uniformity. Without any obvious rea-
son for it, our visceral activities can hardly be controlled at all; compound reflexes
(such as yawning, sneezing, laughing, weeping) are very imperfectly controlled;
our habitual actions, once started, go on of themselves, and often begin without
(or contrary to) our wishes, especially gestures and expressions; in fatigue control
flags, in disease is often lost;[268] we do not always give the same weight to the same
motives, nor fulfil our intentions whether good or bad. But if the relation of will to
action is not apparently uniform, it cannot be seen to be necessary; so that volition
is generally regarded as the peculiar region of caprice. This is very important in
Animism. But, further (*d*), were the connexion between volition and movement
more constant than it is, it would still be most improbable that ideas of causation
should be chiefly drawn from our consciousness of it; for the interest of action lies
not in the mere control of our own movements, or power over the beginning of
events, but in the attainment of our ends; and there is no department of nature in
which the failure of connexion is nearly so impressive. It is because of this failure
that the savage becomes fascinated by ideas of magical and (later) of spiritual aid.
Finally (*e*), no control is exercised by the will over pain—headache, colic, rheuma-
tism, etc.; yet we are told that the savage, when so afflicted, refers his sufferings
at once to the will of some enemy operating at a distance. Such inferences are
not primitive, but the result of a long growth of superstitions. Among Australian
aborigines, disease and natural death are generally believed to be caused by the
magical practices of an enemy, not merely by his will.

We are not, then, obliged to infer that, because volition is the type of necessary
connexion, Sorcery, or any other form of Animism, preceded Magic. On the other
hand, there are conditions that may have given rise independently to a belief in

---

[267] See above, pp. 67 and 80-84.
[268] Hume, *Inquiry*, § vii.

Magic. The savage has frequent experience of regular trains of event which, for want of analytic ability, he does not clearly understand, but which exist in his mind as types determining his apprehension of other sequences. When two interesting events happen about the same time, the later recalls the earlier; because the impression of the earlier, having been deep, perseverates, and is apt to be re-excited by almost any occurrence. An association is then formed between them, and obtains as strong a hold upon the mind as less interesting ones can by many repetitions. The man judges them to be connected; and expects the coincidence to repeat itself as usual occurrences do; and the more vividly the more he desires or fears it. Such expectations, together with the idea of invisible force and the oppression of mystery, by degrees establish the belief in Magic. Probably no traveller amongst wild peoples, or observer of the unsophisticated at home, will think that too much stress is here laid upon the power of coincidence to create general expectations. Even the Chaldean priests (we are told) had grasped but imperfectly the idea of causation. "When two events had been noticed to happen one after another, the first was the cause of the second. Hence their anxiety to record the phenomena of the heavens and the occurrences that took place after each."[269] The Egyptians, says Herodotus, "whenever a prodigy takes place, watch and record the result; then, if anything similar ever happens again, they expect the same consequences."[270] They had merely reduced to a system the universal practice of unanalytic minds.

§ 2. Magic and Religion

§ 2. *Magic and Religion.* — Frazer's hypothesis as to the superseding of
   Magic by Religion. Reasons for dissenting. Alternative hypothe-
   sis. Caprice of spirits the essential distinction of Animism

The origin of Magic, then, is independent of Animism; and in the history of human thought Magic probably preceded Animism as an imaginary agent in the explanation and control of interesting and obscure events. Sir J. G. Frazer, in the *History of the Kingship* and in the *Magic Art*,[271] says that Magic, as a means of gratifying one's desires, is prior to Religion conceived of as a means of attaining one's ends by the propitiation of spirits. This is a much narrower contention than that Magic is prior to Animism (which perhaps he does not maintain), and it is proportionally more defensible. Whilst the priority of Magic to Animism seems to me to have some low degree of probability, the priority of Magic to Religion, as the propitiation of spirits, seems probable in a much higher degree; since we have plain information that both the Australians and the Indians of Guiana practise Magic extensively and also believe in ghosts and spirits without propitiating them.[272]

---

[269] A. H. Sayce, *Religion of the Ancient Babylonians*, p. 398.

[270] Book II. p. 82; Rawlinson's Translation.

[271] Vol. I. ch. iv.

[272] But see the footnote at p. 235 of *The Magic Art*, I.: "faith in magic is probably older than the belief in spirits." In the same note, a passage in Hegel's *Philosophy of Religion* is referred to as anticipating the doctrine of the priority of Magic to Religion. The passage, as translated in an appendix (pp. 423-6), shows, however, no conception of Magic as akin to natural law, as it is described in several passages of *The Golden Bough*, but treats it as a belief in any human being "as the ruling power over nature in virtue of his own will." This

On the other hand, Sir J. G. Frazer's explanation of *how* Religion superseded Magic is questionable. He conjectures "that a tardy recognition of the inherent falsehood and barrenness of magic set the more thoughtful part of mankind to cast about for a truer theory of Nature and a more fruitful method of turning her resources to account. The shrewder intelligences must in time have come to perceive that magical ceremonies and incantations did not really effect the results which they were designed to produce," and the wizard inferred that, "if the great world went on its way without the help of him or his fellows, it must surely be because there were other beings, like himself, but far stronger, who, unseen themselves, directed its course."[273] To these he addressed himself, and sought by prayer what he had formerly hoped to obtain by Magic. Such is Sir J. G. Frazer's suggestion, offered tentatively, and (surely) not agreeing well with the facts which he has set before us. For he has shown that no amount of experience can discredit Magic, generally, in untutored minds; that certain kinds of Magic are sometimes pushed into the background by Religion, but never forgotten; whilst other kinds of Magic become fused with Religion itself and constitute an essential factor in its rites; so that they are indeed few who can be said to have betaken themselves to Religion *instead* of Magic. Besides, the only ground upon which a penetrating mind, that had discarded Magic as discredited by experience, could resort by preference to the worship of spirits must be that experience showed prayer and sacrifice to be more efficacious than Magic in attaining our ends. Is there reason to think that (lucky coincidences apart) this has ever happened? Must we not rather say that, whether one relies on Magic or on Religion, experience of failure counts for almost nothing? So many excuses are at hand.

The matter presents itself to me in this way: at first, belief in Magic arises as a means of obtaining good and averting evil. Grounded, as Sir E. B. Tylor says,[274] in the desire "to discover, to foretell, and to cause events," it is irresistibly attractive by its power of increasing one's confidence, of making sure.

Secondly, at some stage after the rise of Animism, religious practices are added to the magical, to make assurance doubly sure, just as one magical practice may be added to another, a rite to a spell. At this stage, there is no sense of opposition between Magic and Religion. That, in fact, they are opposed in their nature, as an invariable to a capricious force, even if this difference were appreciated by savages, need not prevent their co-operation; for Magic is known to be a tendency that may fail of the effect desired, either by the counteraction of superior Magic, or by imperfection in the rites; and one sees no reason why a spirit should not be supplicated to supplement the imperfect rites, or to frustrate the superior Magic. To supplicate the intervention of spirits, once they are fully believed in, is an act so simple and natural, that we may wonder how it should ever be omitted where Animism prevails. For what can be more spontaneous than to ask the aid of one's

---

is rather an anticipation of Prof. Wundt's doctrine concerning Sorcery; which Hegel seems not to have distinguished from Magic. I need hardly add that a belief in any human being as the ruling power over nature in virtue of his own will has never been discovered in any part of the world.

[273] Op. cit., pp. 237-9.

[274] *Primitive Culture*, I. 116.

father or friend, and why not ask the spirits disembodied as freely as those in the flesh? In Melanesia not every ghost is worshipped (as not having *mana*); but a man in danger may call upon his father, grandfather or uncle: his nearness of kin being sufficient ground for it.[275] Certainly: and that this is not always done where ghosts are rife can only be because it is believed that the less one has to do with them the better! Probably, this consideration restrains for ages the early impulses to pray. Primitive man anticipates the advice of Confucius: "Pay all respect to spiritual beings, but keep them at a distance."[276]

Thirdly, certain forms of Magic come, after a time, to be discountenanced or punished: black Magic, because it is anti-social and criminal; other forms of Magic, when carried on by private practitioners, because they infringe the monopoly of supernatural power that has now been claimed by dynasties and priesthoods; or (in other words) because the public gods are jealous of all competitors. Legitimate Magic has now been incorporated with Religion. And the power of Religion becomes greater than that of Magic without Religion, not only by the support of the influential classes, but also because Religion, whether as worship of the public gods or as sorcery or devil-worship, afflicts the human mind with peculiar terrors; and, again, because Religion, should it clarify morally and æsthetically, appeals more and more to the affections—to the family affections and to loyalty. The impersonality of pure Magic sets it (as it does Science) at a great disadvantage in this competition.

Finally, whilst the failures of Magic always need to be excused,—as by a mistake in the rites or by the opposition of stronger Magic,—Religion brings with it a new excuse for failure, namely, the caprice of the spirits or gods propitiated. At their pleasure they may reject the prayers and sacrifices. Persistence in such conduct on their part is sometimes met by banishment, deprivation of rank, or other punishment—the civilised methods of China; at other times by praying louder and sacrificing more extravagantly, in the style that culminated in Mexico together with the power of barbaric priesthood. Still the gods may be obdurate; and, probably, to excuse the failure of propitiation by the caprice of the gods was, from the first, looked upon as an eligible device:[277] not observing that the caprice of the gods was incompatible with the security of their worshippers; and, therefore, in conflict with that desire of security which is the root of the whole supernatural structure, whether magical or religious. This conflict must have consequences.

Religion, then, very probably, is of later growth than Magic; but whether Animism, as a belief in separable (or separate) spirits, human or other, is later or not than Magic, there is insufficient evidence. At any rate, their origins are independent. Perhaps my own preference for the priority of Magic depends, partly at least, on the convenience of that view in arranging the following considerations.

---

[275] R. H. Coddrington, *The Melanesians*, p. 125.

[276] H. A. Giles, *Chinese Literature*, p. 202.

[277] Animism gave the priest another excuse for the failure of rites (besides those enjoyed by a mere magician), namely, that during, or since, the celebration some fresh offence against the gods had been committed.

§ 3. IDEAS AND PRACTICES OF MAGIC ADOPTED BY ANIMISM

§ 3. *Ideas and Practices of Magic adopted by Animism.*—Invisible force. Power of charms ascribed to spirits. Omens first magical, then spiritual warnings. Spells become prayers. Magical rites become religious ceremonies

(*a*) Fundamental in Magic, wherever practised, is the idea of force, invisible and intangible, which can operate at a distance without any visible or tangible vehicle. The idea may have been formed (as we have seen) by analogy with several natural phenomena, such as the wind, radiant heat, sound, odour, and it is involved in a savage's beliefs concerning the efficacy of charms, rites and spells. When a man dies, he lies speechless and motionless, no longer exerts his accustomed force in any way; but, if seen in a dream, he still speaks and acts, perhaps wrestles with the dreamer. Here, then, is that force which had deserted the body: it is visible and tangible in dreams only, or perhaps sometimes by twilight; or to gifted seers, or to dogs or pigs. The force exerted by the ghost or spirit is the same thing as force magical, except in one character: its action is capricious, depending on the good or ill will of the ghost or spirit; whereas purely magical forces have uniform tendencies. Magic, then, prepares and partially develops this idea of mysterious force, without which the appearance of a dead man in a dream, after his body has been buried or burnt, would have no reality or practical consequences for the living. Comparison with shadows and reflections could not lend reality to dreams; for they require the presence of the body, and themselves have no mechanical significance. Their association with the spirit or ghost probably follows the use of their names to describe the dream-imagery, which cannot at first have a name of its own. The same names being used for shadow or reflection and for spirit or dream-soul, the things are in some measure identified; and then the idea of force may be associated with shadows and reflections; so that the falling of a shadow upon a man may injure or slay him.

Magic-force and spirit-force being the same thing, the question whether *mana* is a magical or animistic notion is misleading. It will be conceived of by different tribes in one way or the other, according to the relative prevalence in one or the other tribe of the animistic or of the magical mode of explanation.

(*b*) It is reasonable to expect that, as the ghost-theory spread, the magical force of things should sometimes be conceived of as spiritual; so that amulets and talismans would come to be regarded as owing their virtue either to a controlling spirit, or to an indwelling spirit peculiar to each: in the latter case the charm is a fetich. When a charm is thus considered, its efficacy is no longer expected to be uniform, but depends on the mood of the indwelling or controlling spirit. The fact that its efficacy, though formerly presumed to be uniform, never was so, favours the new interpretation; and this having been accepted, a cult (or a discipline) of the spirit is apt to follow. Thus the magician becomes a sorcerer or a priest.

In North Central Australia, short sticks or bones are used for pointing at an enemy and directing magical force against him. Only the Guangi and other tribes of the Gulf coast manufacture dead men's bones (femur or fibula) into pointers;

but these are traded southward, and are considered more potent than other point-ers.[278] A stick, then, is the primitive talisman, often "sung" with a spell in Al-cheringa words, which the operator himself does not understand; and it acts by pure magic. The dead man's bone is more potent, at first perhaps only because it is more oppressively gruesome and terrifying; we are not told that it carries the power of its former owner's ghost; but how near the thought must be! In South-East Australia, pointing with the bone (human fibula) is very common; in pointing you name your victim and say how he is to die; but that the efficacy of the rite does not depend upon a spirit is shown by this, that, when pointing, you tie a cord of human hair (attached to the bone) tightly around your upper arm, in order to drive blood into the bone. In other rites, however, in which the fat of a dead man is used, the ghost of the dead is believed to assist the operation; for a man's fat, especially kidney-fat, is the seat of his prowess and other virtues.[279] An easy extension of ideas by analogy would interpret a rite in which a dead man's bone is used, and which is on that account more potent, as owing its superior potency to the assistance of the dead man's ghost. It seems easy; but resistance to the progress of explanation is not peculiar to the civilised mind.

Again, in South-East Australia, a *bulk*—a pebble, usually black and round-ish—is carried by wizards as a powerful talisman. A native dreamt of seeing two ghosts by his camp fire, and, on waking, found a *bulk* where they had stood.[280] How could such an impressive experience fail to raise a belief in a connexion between ghosts and *bulks*: both so attractive to the imagination, and alike mysterious and powerful? Many such situations must strongly indicate an extension of the ghost-theory, once it has been formed, to explain the influence of charms and rites. A time comes with some tribes when the activity and ubiquity of spirits is so much a matter of course that every mysterious power is apt to be ascribed to their presence. If a person or thing was originally taboo, either by inherent virtue or by force of a spell or curse—a talisman dangerous to every one who violated its sanctity—Animism explains the danger by the wrath of a protecting spirit. A boundary having long been taboo, a spirit is imagined to protect the boundary, and becomes the god Terminus. Diseases, at first attributed to Magic, are later explained by Animism; so that whilst an Australian wizard is content to suck a magically implanted stone or splinter from his patient's body, a priest of the Dyaks, having sucked out a similar object, calls it a spirit.[281] The wonder is that at this stage of thought any purely magical power can survive.

(*c*) An Omen is regarded as giving warning of some event, although between event and omen there is no traceable connexion—in this resembling many magical operations; and at first omens may have been always so conceived of, and only by degrees distinguished from charms and spells. But in most parts of the world omens have come to be treated as divine or spiritual premonitions; and the marks which distinguish omens from the rest of Magic are such as to favour a growth of the belief that they are sent by spirits. This subject, however, is so extensive that a

[278] Spencer and Gillen, *Northern Tribes of Central Australia*, pp. 453, 463.

[279] A. W. Howitt, *Native Tribes of South-East Australia*, pp. 359-361-367.

[280] Howitt, op. cit., p. 378.

[281] E. B. Tylor, *Primitive Culture*, II. p. 148.

separate chapter must be given to it.

(*d*) Inasmuch as spells addressed to any object tend to the personification of it, the personified object may, as the ghost-theory gains strength, acquire an indwelling or controlling spirit, and the spell addressed to it may become a prayer. Not that this is the only way in which prayer may originate; for (as remarked above) nothing can be simpler or less in need of explanation than the invoking of the spirit of one's relatives (the ghost-theory having been established) to help one or, at least, not to persecute. Indeed, it is not unreasonable to suppose that this was often attempted, and not persisted in for want of obtaining an answer; so that a long tentative age preceded the settled custom of prayer. Nor is it easy to see how belief in the efficacy of prayer (beginning in this way) could ever have been established, unless it were confirmed by coincidence—just like Magic. However, the earliest form of prayer and of spell (whichever may have been the earlier) being the same—a simple expression of desire—whence prayer and spell have been differentiated, it may be impossible to decide whether a given ejaculation belongs to one class or to the other. Thus Mr. R. W. Williamson tells us that, amongst the Mafulu of New Guinea, when fishing in the river Aduala, the fishers, after forming a weir, but before fixing their net, all join in a sort of prayer or invocation to the river: "Aduala, give us plenty of fish that we may eat well."[282] But he expressly says that, whilst they believe certain parts of the river, such as a waterfall or deep pool, to be haunted by spirits, they do not believe this of the river itself,[283] and that generally their Animism is very backward. The ejaculation, therefore, seems to be a spell. Compare with it the Jakun spell to bring monkeys within shooting distance:

> "Come ye down with souls enchanted,
> Monkeys, by my spells enchanted."[284]

If, then, the original form of prayer and of spell is often the same, the sole difference between them lies in the intention of the speaker. One of the Kurnai, to stop the gales, cried: "Let the West Wind be bound,"[285] and this is evidently a command and a spell; but if he regarded the wind as controlled by a spirit, a change of tone would make it a prayer. Still, whether with the spread of Animism a spell shall become a prayer, must depend upon whether the spirit addressed is believed to be the more easily importuned or coerced.

The taboo that often attaches to the names of the dead and of other spirits may easily have been derived from the magical practice of summoning by name, or of naming the victim of a rite. To call a living man by name draws his attention and often brings him to the spot; a magical naming is (from the temper of Magic) uniformly effective; so that to avoid such control names are kept secret; and when ghosts are believed in, naming has the same power over them and is, therefore, extremely dangerous. Hence, in Sorcery (a dangerous art), to introduce the names of spirits into spells is to secure their presence and assistance: and, in prayer, to use the true name of the spirit or god addressed may be indispensable; the worship-

---

[282] *The Mafulu*, p. 193.
[283] Op. cit., p. 272.
[284] Extract from a spell in Skeat's *Malay Magic*, p. 571.
[285] Howitt, op. cit., p. 397.

per's intention is not enough.

(*e*) With the spread of Animism, magical rites often become religious. This may occur by simply adding the invocation of a spirit to a magical rite (as a spell may be added) in order to strengthen it—the two actions remaining quite distinct; or some degree of fusion may take place, obscuring more or less the original character of the practice. The Kai (Papuans of northern New Guinea) "make rain" by muttering a spell over a stone, and at the same time calling upon Balong and Batu to drive away Yondimi, a woman who holds up the rain; and when rain enough has fallen, they strew hot ashes on the stone, or put it in the fire, to stop the rain.[286] The animistic invocation, being omitted from the process of stopping the rain, seems to be merely adscititious to the making of it. Again, "When rain is badly wanted in the Oraon country, the Oraons of each village fix a day for the rain-making ceremony. On the morning of the appointed day, the women of the village, with the wife of the village priest or Pahan at their head, proceed to the village spring or tank, and there, after ablution, each woman fills her pitcher with water, and all proceed in a body to a sacred pipar-tree.... On their arrival at the sacred tree, all the women simultaneously pour the water in their pitchers over the root of the tree, saying 'May rain fall on the earth like this.' The wife of the village priest now puts marks of vermilion, diluted in oil, on the trunk of the tree. After this the women depart, and the Pahan or village priest proceeds to sacrifice a red cock to the god Baranda at the spot.... In this case, apparently, by direct alliance, sacrifice and the anointing of the tree with vermilion have been superimposed upon what was once, perhaps, purely a ceremony of imitative magic."[287] Mr. Warde Fowler tells us that an ancient Iguvian document contains instructions for the lustration of the people before a campaign: the male population assembled in its military divisions; around the host a procession went three times; at the end of each circuit there was prayer to Mars and to two female associates of his power, to bless the people of Iguvium and to curse their enemies: and he observes that religion has here been imposed upon the original magic-ceremony. For the idea must have been that, by drawing a magic circle around the host, it would be protected in the enemy's country against hostile magic by being rendered holy. "A later and animistic age would think of them (the soldiers) as needing protection against hostile spirits, of whose ways and freaks they were, of course, entirely ignorant." Hence the prayer to Mars.[288]

Similarly, rites connected with seed-time and harvest, originally magical, become religious, as beliefs grow up in spirits of the rice, or corn, or vine, or in gods of agriculture or fertility. Thus, as magical power is the same thing as spiritual power, magical practices may be not merely the antecedents but even the foundations of religious practices. Long after the development of Animism, magical practices are maintained by natural conservatism; if priests exist, they try, of course, to annex such practices to the worship of their god; and if the annexation is accom-

---

[286] J. G. Frazer, *The Belief in Immortality*, p. 288. For similar instances see the same work, pp. 335 and 375.

[287] Sarat Chandra Roy, "Magic and Witchcraft on the Chota Nagpur Plateau," *J.R.A.I.*, XLIV. p. 330. I have slightly altered the last sentence, which seems to have been misprinted.

[288] *Religious Experience of the Roman People*, p. 215.

plished, whether by priestly management or by a popular movement, no incongruity may be felt for a long time between the uniformity of Magic and the caprice of Animism; the whole celebration is called Religion, and becomes suffused with religious feeling.

§ 4. RETROGRADATION

§ 4. *Retrogradation.* — Wundt's theory explains the loss in many cases
of animistic ideas; Fetiches; Omens; Prayers; religious ceremonies

On the other hand, in all these cases, the animistic interpretation of the power of fetiches, omens, prayers, rites, whether original (as Prof. Wundt holds) or acquired, may be lost, and a magical interpretation alone remain. For one's mind becomes so engrossed with objects or practices (such as fetich-things or prayers) that are regarded as necessary to the gratification of any masterful desire, that not only irrelevant ideas, but any ideas not indispensable to the connexion between the objects or practices and the gratifications, may be forgotten; and as objects or practices acquire interest in themselves, even the gratifications formerly desired may be forgotten. Just as such means as money or books, business or study, may become ends to the exclusion of further enjoyments, so images or rites, at first subsidiary to the obtaining of demonic aid in love or revenge, may be cared for with a fervour that excludes the thought of any intervening means to those ends (especially such means as a capricious spirit who may fail one), and may even be employed under a vague fear or discomfort in the omission of them, when no particular purpose is any longer remembered. On the principle of least effort, we attend only to what is necessary.

(*a*) A saint's finger-joint may at first be treasured as a fetich having the power of the saint to save from shipwreck; after a time it may be carried as an amulet without any thought of the saint's interposition; whilst the evil to be averted is more and more vaguely imagined. Seeing that spiritual and magical agencies are the same invisible, unintelligible force, how easy to interchange them!

(*b*) Similarly omens, from being divine messages, each relating to a particular undertaking, may come to be merely occurrences that encourage or discourage a man, or a tribe, at any time; because, by tradition, they are lucky or unlucky. Or practically the same result may be reached by philosophy: as with those Stoics who explained that omens are prophetic not as sent by the gods, but as involved in the same procession of fatal events. Fate, before any laws of nature had been discovered, was nothing but all-comprehensive Magic: which left out or mediatised the gods, because, in a philosophical consideration of the world, they are worse than useless.

(*c*) As to prayers, in any rational conception of them, the form of words conveying them cannot matter to a god, as long as they are piously meant and devoutly meditated. Yet everywhere there has been a tendency to reduce them to strict formulæ, any departure from which may, it is feared, impair their efficacy. So far as this occurs, their operation is magical; they have become spells. Such is the result of custom, with mental inertia too dull to think; of an irreligious temperament, getting quickly through an uncongenial task; of a superstitious unimaginative spirit, afraid to omit any traditionary means of safety and for whom a praying-wheel is the way of peace. To rob prayer of its religious meaning, there is the ever-present example of the magical spells that operate by their own force. A form of words, whether magical or supplicatory, that has been among the antecedents of a time of peace or of gain, seems to be amongst its causes, and is repeated that such a time may continue. Of the countless cases in which prayers have degenerated into spells, none is more instructive than the one recorded by Dr. Rivers in his account of the dairy-ritual of the Todas. The prayers offered during this ritual are uttered in the throat, so that the words are undistinguishable; and they are divided into two parts: first, a list of sacred beings and objects mentioned by sacred names, much of it unintelligible; and, secondly, a petition for the protection and welfare of the buffaloes: the former is now the more important; the latter is apt to be slurred over, or perhaps omitted.[289] Of the Roman public prayers, Mr. Warde Fowler says: "The idea that the spoken formula (derived from an age of Magic) was efficient only if no slip were made, seems to have gained in strength instead of diminishing, as we might have expected it to do with advancing civilisation."[290] To justify the belief in formulæ it may be asserted that the gods themselves prescribed them: an excuse for the superstitious dread of altering what is traditionary, and for the persuasion that the form itself has mysterious virtue.

(*d*) That other religious ceremonies, repeated from age to age, have the same tendency as prayers to become dead forms from which the spirit of communion or devotion has departed—though under favourable conditions it may return from time to time—is too well known; and if in their emptiness they are still believed somehow to serve their purpose, it can only be as magical rites. One may be surprised to find at what an early stage of culture this tendency is fully realised. William Ellis, the celebrated missionary, says of the people of Raiatea: "The efficacy of their [religious] services consisted in the rigid exactness with which sacred days were kept, and religious ceremonies performed, without the least regard to the motives and dispositions of the devotees.... In their idol-worship, however costly the sacrifice, and however near its close the ceremony might be, if the priest omitted or misplaced any word in the prayers, or if his attention was diverted by any means so that the prayer was broken, the whole was rendered unavailing: he must prepare other victims and repeat his prayers over from the commencement."[291] How this concern for details must be a relapse into magical notions may be read in the account of rites to stop the rainfall in Torres Straits; where (we are told) if the wizard omit any detail, the rain continues.[292] Perhaps the notion of the perfect definiteness of causation (though not consistently adhered to in other matters) arose from this meticulous anxiety of superstition: it also, however, furnishes excuses for failure both to priests and wizards.

---

[289] *The Todas*, pp. 30, 213.

[290] *Religious Experience of the Roman People*, p. 286. But whether we should expect the idea to weaken with advancing civilisation must depend upon whether intelligent belief in the gods was increasing. Perhaps this was not the case at Rome.

[291] *Polynesian Researches*, II. pp. 144 and 157 (1st ed.).

[292] *Reports of the Cambridge Expedition to Torres Straits*, VI. p. 199.

(*e*) In Magic there must be something deeply satisfying to the average mind: it precedes Religion, supplies the basis and framework of religious practices, and remains when Religion is in ruins; and when people change their Religion, they retain their Magic. Among the Fijians,[293] those who were Christianised lost their dread of witchcraft last of all the relics of their heathenism. Among the Cherokees, "Gahuni, like several others of their Shamans, combined the professions of Indian conjuror and Methodist preacher."[294] In Norway, after the general acceptance of Christianity, Lapland witchcraft was still valued. The victory of the insurgents at Stiklestad, where St. Olaf fell, was thought to have been due to the magic armour of reindeer-skin that Thore Hund had brought from Lapland; though all St. Olaf's men wore the cross upon helmet and shield.[295]

Since then the spiritualising of Magic and the despiritualising of Religion are both real processes of evolution, it may be difficult, or even impossible, to say of any given magical practice, without particular knowledge of its history, whether it is primitive or residuary. Sir E. B. Tylor writes: "Charm formulas are in very many cases actual prayers, and as such are intelligible. Where they are merely verbal forms, producing their effect on nature and man by some unexplained process, may not they, or the types they were modelled on, have been originally prayers, since dwindled into mystic sentences?"[296] The circumstances of each case must guide our judgment. What shall we say, for example, of the addresses to spirits in Melanesia, where it is difficult to find in any dialect a word for prayer, "so closely does the notion of efficacy cling to the form of words employed"?[297] Are spells there rising into prayers, or prayers sinking back into spells?

§ 5. Spirits know Magic, teach it, and inspire Magicians

§ 5. *Spirits know Magic, teach it, and inspire Magicians.* —Examples of
spirits knowing and teaching Magic. Inspiration and possession

Ghosts know Magic, because they knew it in the flesh; and, by analogy, similar knowledge is likely to be attributed to spirits that are reputed never to have been in the flesh. As fear exalts all the powers of a ghost above his former reach, it may be expected to raise his magical powers, especially if he had already been famous in that way. And, generally, it does so; but, exceptionally, we read that, among the Lengua Indians (west of the Paraguay), whilst any man may attempt Magic, professional "witch-doctors" are numerous and powerful; yet they are not credited with extraordinary powers after death.[298] Elsewhere, however, the dead magician does not forget his art. Where Shamanism prevails and the power of Magic or Sorcery attains its greatest social importance, the spirit of a dead shaman makes some advance toward deification. Among the Buryats, dead shamans are worshipped

[293] Thomas Williams, *Fiji and the Fijians*, p. 209.

[294] J. Mooney, "Sacred Formulas of the Cherokees" in *Am. B. of Ethn.*, VII. p. 314 (1885-6).

[295] *Heimskringla, St. Olaf's Saga*, chs. cciv. and ccxl.

[296] *Primitive Culture*, II. p. 273 (2nd ed.).

[297] Codrington, *The Melanesians*, p. 145.

[298] S. H. C. Hawtrey, "The Lengua Indians," *Journal of the Royal Anthropological Institute*, 1901.

with prayer and sacrifice.[299] According to the *Kalevala*, the famous collection of Finnish poetry, in Tuonela (Hades), whither all dead shamans descend, their wisdom and magical power accumulate, exceeding that of any living adept; so that even Väinämöinen, the wizard hero, goes down to learn there the magical words he does not know.[300]

Spirits, knowing Magic, also teach it, and make magicians and prophets. In South-East Australia, the profession of wizard may be hereditary in the eldest son; or obtained through initiation by another wizard—(a corpse is dug up, its bones pounded for the neophyte to chew; he is plastered with excrement, etc., till he becomes frenzied, his eyes bloodshot, his behaviour maniacal);[301] or a man may become a wizard by meeting a spirit who opens his side and inserts quartz-crystals, etc.; or by deriving power from Daramulun; or by sleeping at a grave, where the deceased opens him, and takes out and replaces his bowels. Here we have a list of the most usual ways in which magical powers can anywhere be acquired—by inheritance, by tuition, by the aid of ghosts or spirits; and it suggests the hypothesis that at first the magic art was inherited, or learnt from a former wizard; and that, with the growth of Animism, it became in some cases preferable, because more impressive (and cheaper), to acquire it from a ghost or spirit. For this is more probable than that, at the early stage in which Animism exists in South-East Australia, retrogradation should have taken place; so that the making of wizards, formerly ascribed only to spirits, should in some cases have been remitted to inheritance or to professional tuition. That in spite of the greater prestige that may attach to a diploma obtained from spirits, the right of practising by inheritance or by tuition often still persists, though, no doubt, due in part to dull conservatism, may also be understood by considering family and professional motives. There are heavy fees for teaching witchcraft, besides the profits made in some tribes by selling the control of familiar spirits; the profession is lucrative, and a wizardy family has an interest in its monopoly; which must be impaired, if any man who loses himself in the bush may come back with some cock-and-bull story about a ghost and his new metaphysical insides, and straightway set himself up with the equivalents of a brass plate and red lantern. Among the Boloki on the Congo, the careers of blacksmith and witch-doctor are open only to the relatives of living adepts. At least, practically (but for a few exceptionally cunning and rascally interlopers who creep and intrude and climb into the fold), the office of witch-doctor is hereditary: a father trains his son, and will train (for a large fee) any youth whose family has already produced a witch-doctor. But a candidate without family connexion is told that he must first kill by witchcraft all the members of his family, as offerings to the fetich of that branch of the profession to which he aspires.[302]

Not only the spirits of primitive Animism, but likewise the gods of maturer

---

[299] "Shamanism," *Journal of the Royal Anthropological Institute,* XXIV. (1894-5).

[300] Comparetti, *The Traditionary Poetry of the Finns,* p. 184.

[301] Howitt, op. cit., p. 404. Is this type of the neophyte's behaviour, which is conformed to on certain occasions by magicians and inspired priests in every age and country, itself conformed to the natural type of insanity or epilepsy; and, if so, consciously or unconsciously?

[302] J. H. Weeks, *Among Congo Cannibals,* pp. 145 and 276.

Religions, know and teach Magic. In the Maori mythology, Tumatauenga, one of the first generation of gods, determined incantations for making all sorts of food abundant and for controlling the winds, as well as prayers to Heaven suited to all the circumstances of human life; and the god Rongotakawin, having shaped the hero Whakatau out of the apron of Apakura, taught him Magic and enchantments of every kind.[303] Prof. Rhys tells us that the Welsh god Mâth ab Mathonwy, or Math Hên (the ancient), was the first of the three great magicians of Welsh Mythology; and he taught Magic to the culture hero, Gwydion ab Dôn, with whose help he created a woman out of flowers.[304] The Teutonic equivalent of Gwydion is Woden, or Othin; and he too was a magician, "the father of spells," who acquired his wisdom by gazing down into the abyss, whilst he hung nine nights on the tree, an offering to himself (and in other ways); and, in turn, he teaches Siegfried the omens.[305] He also taught the northern people shape-changing, and by spells controlled fire and the winds.[306] In Egypt Magic was taught by Thoth, in Babylonia by Merodach, and in Japan by Ohonomachi the earth-god. Indeed, whence, unless from divine beings, could this precious wisdom be obtainable?

Spirits also inspire or possess the magician, so that through him, as their mouthpiece or instrument, prophecies are uttered or wonders wrought. We have seen that in South-East Australia the rites of initiation to wizardry by a wizard, without the aid of spirits, cause a candidate to become frenzied or maniacal. With the growing fashion of animistic interpretation, such behaviour is (along with insanity) put down to possession by a spirit. The common beliefs that a man's soul can slip in and out of him and that a man may reincarnate the spirit of an ancestor, facilitate this idea of possession. Dreams concerning spirits also promote the belief that a miracle-monger owes to them his supernatural powers. The Tunguses of Turnkhausk say that the man destined to be a shaman sees in a dream the devil performing rites, and so learns the secrets of his craft. Among the Trans-Baikal Tunguses, he who wishes to become a shaman declares that such or such a dead shaman appeared to him in a dream, and ordered him to be his successor; and he shows himself crazy, stupefied and timorous. The Yakut shaman is preordained to serve the spirits, whether he wishes it or not: he begins by raging like a madman, gabbles, falls unconscious, runs about the woods, into fire and water, injures himself with weapons. Then an old shaman trains him.[307] On the Congo, a man may become a wizard by claiming to be the medium of a dead man; and a medium falls into a frenzy, shouts, trembles all over, his body undulates, sweat breaks out, foam gathers on his mouth, his eyeballs roll: he speaks an archaic language if he knows one.[308] In Santa Cruz (Melanesia), prophecy is practised by men whose bodies are taken possession of, and their voices used, by ghosts: they foam at the mouth, writhe, are convulsed as if in madness; and the mad, too, are believed to

---

[303] Grey, *Polynesian Mythology*, chs. i. and vii.

[304] *Origin and Growth of Religion as illustrated by Celtic Heathendom*, p. 225.

[305] *Corpus Poeticum Boreale*, pp. 24, 34, 181, 196.

[306] *Heimskringla Saga, Yuglingasaga*, chs. xvii.-xviii.

[307] "Shamanism," *Journal of the Royal Anthropological Institute*, X., XIV. p. 85.

[308] Weeks, *Congo Cannibals*, p. 265.

be possessed.[309] Similarly the Pythoness: the behaviour of the possessed is everywhere the same. But as the same behaviour marks the youth training for a wizard before the theory of possession or inspiration has been adopted, it is plain that the animistic theory does not create the phenomena, but is merely, at a certain stage of thought, the inevitable explanation of them.

Facility of falling into frenzy may be the test of fitness for wizardry; the Bokongo professor who trains a pupil, beats his drum, shakes his rattle, and tries to drive the fetich-power into him; if the pupil remains stolid, he is disqualified; but if he sways to the music of the drum, jumps about like a madman, etc., he passes.[310] These antics at first astonish the beholder, strengthen the faith of patients in the witch-doctor, and of the witch-doctor in himself, and often have a sort of hypnotic fascination for both him and them; and they gain in value under Animism by being also proofs of supernatural assistance or control: and being an essential mark of the adept at certain stages of the art's development, they are sometimes induced by rhythmic drumming, singing and dancing, sometimes by fastings or drugs.

"Black Magic" is, at first, merely the use of Magic for anti-social purposes; very early a distinction is recognised between wizards who cause disease and those who cure it.[311] "Black" and "white" wizards are sometimes at open strife.[312] When tribal gods come to be recognised, "black" wizards are those who are assisted or inspired by inferior gods or demons, who may be opponents and rivals of the high gods. Hence the same god who, whilst paramount, aids or inspires in an honourable way, may, if deposed or superseded, become the abettor of Black Magic—as happened to our own gods, and to others, before and after the coming of Christianity; for the ancient divine sources of power and prophecy became devils and witch-masters. The magicians of our Middle Ages, of whom Faustus is the type, were "black" and, in the spirit of Shamanism, pretended to rule the devils; but, overshadowed by Christianity, they—at least in popular belief—bought their power at a price.

§ 6. Spirits operate by Magic

§ 6. *Spirits operate by Magic.*—Possession; smiting; metamorphosis; charms and spells

Spirits may operate through men whom they possess, or by their naked soul-force, or by words (that is, by spells), or by merely thinking:

(*a*) When a man is possessed by a spirit, it is the soul-force of that spirit which has entered him and taken command of his voice or limbs; and we have seen that this soul-force is the same as force magical. The spirit's action is the same as that of the *bugin* or wizard, who boasted of having entered a horse and galloped off.[313]

[309] The fullest and most dramatic account of such possession may be found in Williams' *Fiji and the Fijians*, p. 190. See below, p. 243.

[310] Weeks, *Primitive Bokongo*, p. 215.

[311] Spencer and Gillen, *Native Tribes of Central Australia*, pp. 480-8.

[312] "Shamanism," *Journal of the Royal Anthropological Institute*, XXIV. p. 130.

[313] Howitt, op. cit., p. 374.

(*b*) By Animism, prior to philosophical reflection, the spirit is not conceived of as strictly incorporeal; its force, which is magical, is quasi-mechanical. Hence, in South-East Australia, spirits can carry off a man in a bag[314] (made, no doubt, of bag-soul-stuff). But spirits may act upon a man very effectually without being mechanically felt; as among the Ekoi, where ghosts are either good or bad, and generally a good goes with a bad one to counteract his malevolence; but should a bad one wander forth alone, and should a man without the gift of seeing ghosts (which depends upon his having four eyes) run against it in the street, the ghost will not step aside, but strikes the man in the face; who then has lock-jaw, and dies.[315] As we have reason to believe that this is not the natural ætiology of lock-jaw, the ghost's action is plainly magical: like that of the corpse-candle which, not long ago, on a slope of Plinlimmon one rainy night, a man inadvertently ran against, and was "struck down dead as a horse."[316] The mere apparition of a ghost (at least, to any one who has not four eyes) is magical. The sending of a bird as an omen is magical.

This immediate power of the gods is nowhere shown more emphatically than in their metamorphoses: that these are sometimes wrought by spells or other enchantments proves that the operation is magical. Australian wizards transform themselves into kangaroos and other animals; and, in Arunta mythology, in the earliest Alcheringa (period of mythical ancestors), the Ungambikula—so called from having arisen out of nothing—with stone knives cut men out of rudimentary masses of unorganised matter (inapertua), and then transformed themselves into little lizards.[317] So this sort of self-conjuring may be said to begin at the beginning; and it cannot be necessary to accumulate examples of metamorphosis.

Several explanations of this belief in the possibility of changing the form of one's body, or of having it changed by others, have been offered: none perhaps entirely satisfactory. We are not here concerned with the passing of a soul from one body to another—from a man into a wolf or into a serpent, or conversely: given the conception of a separable soul, that is easy to understand. What has to be explained is the belief in a magical change of the body itself, as in the common European superstition that a man may turn into a wolf, and back again, like Sigmund and his son in the *Volsung Saga*. It has been pointed out (i) that the savage may observe striking changes in nature: as in the shape of clouds and smoke, the burning of wood into flame, smoke and ashes, the evaporation of water; the turning of eggs into caterpillars, reptiles, birds, or of a chrysalis into an imago; the appearance of worms in putrefying bodies, and so forth.[318] With such facts before him, why should not the savage imagine himself also capable of transformation? (ii) Dream-images, too, pass one into another in a marvellous way. (iii) Since men are often called by the names of animals, how easy to suppose that, at times, they may really be those animals. How easy to confound a man with his Totem. In many savage dances, animals are imitated, and the imagination-belief in the reali-

[314] Ibid., p. 437.
[315] P. A. Talbot, *In the Shadow of the Bush*, p. 230.
[316] G. Borrow, *Wild Wales*, ch. lxxxviii.
[317] Spencer and Gillen, op. cit., p. 388.
[318] H. Spencer, *Principles of Sociology*, § 55.

ty of the pantomime grows very strong. (iv) The savage, when his imagination has been excited, is not clever at penetrating conjuring tricks and disguises; and some men, at first for their own ends, may have disguised themselves as animals and passed as animals; and in support of this explanation it may be observed that the animal into which men transform themselves is oftenest the most feared in their neighbourhood—the wolf, leopard, or tiger; and, of course, one case believed in, others follow by analogy. The mere report of such an happening might generate belief by force of fear. (v) In a wild country, a man (say one who is pursued) often disappears and is indiscoverable; so that he may seem to have turned into a kangaroo, or a stone, or a tree that appears in his place, as Daphne hid successfully in a laurel-thicket: or if such an occurrence did not originate the belief in metamorphosis, it may have helped to confirm it. (vi) In mental disease, the patient sometimes believes himself to be some kind of animal, and acts accordingly: perhaps as a result of the popular belief, but doubtless also confirming it.[319] Weighing all these hypotheses, I lean to the view that, starting from the fact (as ground of analogy) that astonishing changes are observed in nature and in dreams, the belief in metamorphosis as a magical operation rests chiefly upon the deceptions and confident assertions of wizards that they can, and do, change their form, supported by their reputation for wonder-working and by the fears of their neighbours. Now, if wizards can change their shapes, of course the gods can.[320]

(*c*) Spirits and gods are known to use amulets and talismans, not invented by poets as symbols, but prized as the instruments of their power, as an enchanter values his wand. Such are the caduceus of Hermes, the cestus of Aphrodite, Thor's hammer Mjölnir, Woden's spear Gunguir and his wishing staff. The gods of Egypt and Babylon also wore charms. Since chieftains are frequently magicians, and also become gods, it follows that the gods are magicians; though, indeed, as Grimm observes, their power is to be called miraculous rather than magical. But Magic, being the highest power known to men, and the most desired, is of course attribut-

---

[319] E. B. Tylor, *Primitive Culture*, I. 308 et seq.

[320] In a paper on *Leopard Men of the Naga Hills*, read at a meeting of the R.A.I. (December 9, 1919), Mr. J. J. H. Hutton reported that such men do not change into leopards; but sometimes their souls involuntarily pass into them. If the leopard be injured or killed he whose soul was in it suffers or dies—when he hears of it. Such men are not feared, because their leopards do very little harm.

For this reason (I suppose) the belief is not exploited by wizards, who have no use for innocent superstition, and it remains pure folklore. There may not be any connexion between this animistic doctrine of human souls possessing animals and the magical doctrine of shape-changing. If they are connected, it is easy to see that in a certain atmosphere of popular philosophy, if shape-changing were believed in, the possession theory might be accepted as the true explanation upon merely being proposed. Indeed, it would make intelligible such a case as this: a man's leopard is seen on the skirts of the village; but he himself is known to be in his hut.

Animistic explanation does not always follow culture: Europe adheres to shape-changing. Yet in the *Volsung Saga* the superstition is already degenerate: Sigmund and his son change into wolves by putting on wolf-skins belonging to two were-wolves whom they find asleep. This is a rationalisation—disguise as a step toward change. An earlier step is to say a man who would change must put on a belt of wolf-skin.

ed to spirits and to gods.

The most extensive powers of spirits, however, depend on the use of words or spells. The hero of the Western Isles of Torres Straits, Kwoiam, employed magical formulæ.[321] The gods and demigods of the Maories carried out their extraordinary adventures by the power of incantations. Maui, by incantations, fishes up dry land from the bottom of the sea, and turns his brother-in-law into a dog; Tawhaki and his brother Karahi, by incantations, make themselves invisible, and avenge their father Hema upon his enemies; and so forth.[322] Celtic and Teutonic deities worked wonders by songs and spells. Isis was the greatest enchantress that ever lived. She made from the spittle of Ra a serpent that bit and poisoned him; and then she healed him by an incantation, having first compelled him to reveal to her his name, to the knowledge of which the god himself owed his power over gods and men; so that she obtained the mastery over all the gods.[323]

As spells, when used by men, may be more efficacious when muttered and whispered than when spoken aloud, so they may retain their power when silently wished or thought; and it is the same with spirits: to control events it may be enough for them to think. And this belief emerges at no very high level of Animism; it needs no philosophical instruction in the mysterious energy of ideas. The Sia Indians (North Mexico) have a Cougar Society, which meets for a two days' ceremonial, before a hunting expedition, to propitiate the cougar (puma), because he is the great father and master of all game. He is believed to draw all kinds of game to him by sitting still with folded arms and mentally demanding their presence; and by the same means he sends game to whomsoever he favours.[324]

Apparently, then, Magic is an art antecedent to the existence of spirits and ready for their use; and they stand in the same relations to it as men do. Animistic usages are originally magical—spells, rites, metamorphoses; and all animistic ideas are magical, except one—the capriciousness of spiritual agency.

§ 7. Spirits are controlled by Magic

> § 7. *Spirits are controlled by Magic.*—Biological necessity of controlling spirits—by fear—or by Magic. Analogy with politics. The higher barbaric religions. Magico-legal control of gods. Idea of Fate. Free-will and uniformity

The savage imagination having created out of dreams and other strange experiences a world of invisible and powerful beings who may be friendly or hostile,—so human that they must be accessible to prayers, but often turn a deaf ear to them—must desire sacrifices, yet often reject them—capricious and inscrutable—it became necessary, in order to restore confidence in all the relations of life, that their caprice should somehow be overcome; and to accomplish this three ways were open: first, to increase the prayers and sacrifices until their importunity and costliness should prove irresistible—and this way led to all the magnificence and

[321] Haddon, *Reports of the Cambridge Expedition to Torres Straits*, V. p. 329.
[322] Grey, op. cit., "Legends of Maui and Tawhaki."
[323] Wiedemann, *Religion of the Ancient Egyptians*, pp. 54-8.
[324] M. C. Stevenson, "The Sia," *Am. B. of Ethn.*, XI. p. 118.

to all the horrors of religious rites; secondly, to work upon the fears or vulnerability of spirits by beating, starving, slaying, banishing or degrading them; or, thirdly, to constrain them, as men are often constrained, by magical rites and formulæ. From the beginning this necessity is felt.

The constraint of spirits by fear or violence is characteristic of Fetichism. The wizards of the Congo catch spirits in traps; or drive them into animals, which they behead; or spear them in some dark corner, and then exhibit their blood upon the spear-head. Passing from the Congo through many ages of progress, we arrive in China, and find that in time of drought, if the city-god neglects to put an end to it, he is first of all entreated; but that failing, his idol is stripped naked and put to stand in the sun; or an iron chain is hung round his neck—the mark of a criminal—till rain falls; or he may be dethroned altogether.[325] With such crude practices, however, we are not now concerned.

The control of spirits by Magic, especially by spells—or by other spirits who, in turn, are controlled by spells—is in its earlier form characteristic of Shamanism: indeed, it is the essence of Shamanism; though, of course, in many shamanistic tribes, having intercourse with peoples of different culture, other beliefs, ascribing independent or even superior power to spirits, are often found. Spirits may be so completely subdued by spells as to excite little fear. Among the Yurats and Ostyaks, the shamans treat their spirits without ceremony, and even buy and sell them.[326] So do the Esquimo angekoqs. In Greenland, "all phenomena are controlled by spirits, and these spirits are controlled by formulæ or charms, which are mainly in possession of the medicine-men, although certain simple charms may be owned and used by any one." Hence, "nothing like prayer or worship is possible";[327] for why supplicate spirits whom you can command? "The rule of man—not of all men, but of one specially gifted (the shaman), over Nature, or over the superior beings who direct her, is the fundamental idea of Shamanism."[328] The shaman's power depends on knowledge of the names, natures and origins of all things and spirits, and of the words that control them; but also on his own extraordinary personality, as manifested in orgiastic frenzy. Megalomania, the vain imagination of being a "superman," is generally characteristic of magicians. Nothing can be more contrary than this attitude to what most of us understand by Religion.

One condition of the prevalence of Shamanism among any people, or group of peoples, seems to be the absence from among them of chieftains who have attained to any high degree of political power, and the consequent non-existence of authoritative gods. Hence it spreads throughout the tribes of Northern Europe and Asia, from Finland to Kamtchatka, and with a less intensive sway amongst the Indians of North and South America. Under such conditions the shaman is subordinate to no one in this world; nor, therefore, in the spirit-world. But where there are authoritative chiefs, authoritative gods correlative with them are approached by an order of men who are priests rather than magicians—that is to say, are regard-

---

[325] W. Grube, *Rel. u. K. d. Chinese*, p. 132.

[326] "Shamanism," *Journal of the Royal Anthropological Institute*, ch. xxiv. p. 133.

[327] Stephánsen, *My Life with the Eskimo*, p. 391.

[328] D. Comparetti, *The Traditional Poetry of the Finns*, p. 26.

ed as dealing less in magic than in prayer and sacrifice. And this state of affairs is apt to give rise to increasing pomp and extravagance of rites, to which there is no visible limit; so that in some cases, as in Ashanti and Mexico, worship became homicide, and a sort of national insanity was established. For from such practices there results no security in the satisfaction of desire; the caprice of the gods cannot by such means be overcome; their appetite grows by what it feeds on, and so does the fanaticism of the priesthood.

Now, in political affairs something similar happens: the caprice of despotic rulers becomes intolerable; and, in some countries, submission to their tyranny has amounted to a sort of national insanity. Elsewhere devices have been adopted to limit the power of rulers. Avoiding assassination or revolution, it has been found possible to impose upon a king restraints derived from his own sanctity and divine power. One such device has been to surround him with innumerable taboos which, at length, prevent him from doing anything. It is true that the ostensive reason for this was not the limitation of his power, but the preservation of his vitality, upon which hung the welfare of the whole world; and probably this was, at first, the conscious purpose; but one effect of it was to limit his power, and the utility of this was its natural sanction. There are many cases in human life in which a great advantage has been gained for the race by means which were intended by the conscious agents to have an entirely different result.[329] In several countries, where the king has been bound by taboos, another man has by some pretext usurped his power; so that this way of restraining despotism is not a good one. But in Japan, where it had been adopted by a political people, the Tycoon, who succeeded to the power of the taboo-burdened Mikado, himself fell at last under equivalent restrictions, whilst affairs were directed by his ministers. Such is the natural tendency of this device amongst positivists, like the Japanese; elsewhere it may transfer the regal power to warriors or to priests.[330] Another way of restraining the king is to establish the principle that he rules by the laws, and that laws, though made by himself, cannot be altered. And this may have been the purpose of the unchangeableness of the laws of the Medes and Persians; and according to the *Book of Daniel*[331] it was used in this way; though, certainly, the older authority of Herodotus[332] shows that, in some cases, the king's advisers could find a way out for their master. Our own forefathers were no doubt the wisest people that ever lived; and their plan was to acknowledge fully the divinity that doth hedge a king, to declare that, in fact, he could do no wrong, and then to visit all the iniquities of government upon his ministers.

If kings need restraint, much more do invisible gods: and many nations have sought to limit their prerogative, either by Magic or by legal fictions which, in relation to gods, can have only a magical operation. Whilst the tone of the *Rigveda* is truly religious (though even there "the idea is often expressed that the might and valour of the gods is produced by hymns, sacrifices and especially offerings of soma"), "in the Yajurveda the sacrifice itself has become the centre of thought

[329] *Natural and Social Morals*, ch. ii. § 4.
[330] See many examples in J. G. Frazer's *Taboo and the Perils of the Soul*, ch. i.
[331] Ch. vi.
[332] III. p. 31.

and desire, its correct performance in every detail being all-important. Its power is now so great that it not only influences but compels the gods to do the will of the officiating priest."[333] In Egyptian rites of sacrifice and prayer, the kind of victim and the manner of slaying and cutting it up were minutely and unchangeably decreed. "The formulas accompanying each act of the sacrificial priest contained a certain number of words, whose due sequence and harmonies might not suffer the slightest modification even by the god himself, under penalty of losing their efficacy. They were always recited with the same rhythm, according to a system of melody in which every tone had its virtue, combined with movements that confirmed the sense and worked with irresistible effect; one false note, a single discord between the succession of gestures and the utterance of the sacramental words, any hesitation, any awkwardness in the accomplishment of a rite, and the sacrifice was vain."[334] But if all was in order, the god was bound to grant the petition. Babylonian religious ceremonies "had for the most part the same end and object as the magical text used with them; they were not so much a communion with the deities of heaven, as an attempt to compel them by particular words to relieve the worshipper from trouble, or to bestow upon him some benefit." Ceremonies, therefore, were useless unless accurately performed in word and deed; "ritual was a sort of acted magic."[335] These accounts of the religious ceremonies of the highest barbaric civilisations are almost in the same words as William Ellis uses in his account of worship at Raiatea about the beginning of the nineteenth century; except that Ellis does not say that the Polynesian gods were bound to grant the requests so presented. Accordingly, I have treated the Raiatean example under Retrogradation, and those of Egypt and Babylon as cases of half-conscious policy. No doubt both retrogradation and policy were present in all cases; but it seems reasonable to suppose that the latter predominated where order was more settled (an analogue of the order required in heaven) and thought was better trained.

One may wonder why a magical ritual should be preferred and trusted rather than genuinely devotional worship; since it must, in fact, just as often result in disappointment. But, first, as to the priesthood, an elaborate ritual, difficult to carry out, is favourable to their power, because only professionals can execute it; so that they must necessarily be employed; and the more elaborate and exigent it is, the more necessary they are. But, then, the more attention the ritual demands, the less there is to spare for thinking of the gods. Secondly, as to the people, since the failure of worship in attaining our ends may be due either (animistically) to the caprice of the gods or (magically) to an error of the priest, it is not surprising that men should trust the specialist whose education is well attested rather than the god whose character is inscrutable. Thirdly, a magical ritual appeals to the expectation of uniformity, the sole ground of confidence concerning the future, and therefore what men most desire. Nevertheless, the religious form of the rites (though empty of religious feeling) is maintained; partly, because the whole political and ecclesiastical fabric rests upon the animistic tradition; partly, because Animism has such hold upon men's minds that a few remain devout; whilst even

[333] Macdonell, *Sanskrit Literature*, pp. 73 and 183.

[334] Maspero, *The Dawn of Civilization*, p. 124.

[335] A. H. Sayce, *Religion of the Ancient Babylonians*, p. 319.

those who regard the rites as magical do not perceive that magic is the antithesis of religion and rigidly excludes it. Only a few natural positivists and philosophers regard public worship as merely a political institution.

The idea of a transaction by which the gods are legally bound—so much help for so much worship—may be present in all magical ritual; but in some religions the analogy of human relations according to law is explicitly extended to the relations of men with gods. The Jewish religion was based on a covenant; and, according to some theologians, so is the Christian. It has often been said that Roman religion implied a belief in legal obligation imposed upon the gods by rites duly performed; and Mr. Warde Fowler, who thinks more highly than some have done of the genuineness of religious feeling amongst the Romans, at least in private worship, yet says that in the *vota publica* we find something like a bargain or covenant with the deity in the name of the State.[336] Legal obligation implies effectual sanctions that may be brought to bear upon transgressors, gods or men; and at a low stage of Animism, when no spirit exceeds the rank of demon, there may be no incongruity in bringing to reason a recalcitrant spirit by stopping his rations or maltreating his image; but when high gods have obtained the homage of men, to punish *them* calls for great audacity or very subtle management. The Chinese have managed the matter to admiration. The Emperor of China acknowledged himself subject to the spirits of Earth and Heaven; but he himself was the son of Heaven, and all other spirits were subject to him. He ruled alike over the dead and the living. He made deities and appointed them their functions; promoted them and distributed amongst them titles of honour, if they did good works; or, if they failed in their duties, degraded them. In the *Pekin Gazette* one finds "the deities figuring, not occasionally but very frequently, in every department of official business, and treated much as if they were highly respectable functionaries of a superior order, promoted to some kind of upper house, whose abilities and influence were nevertheless still at the service of the State."[337] Nowhere has the unity of Church and State been so completely realised, and the *pax deorum* so conclusively established. One may interpret the facts at discretion: an animist may accept them literally and seriously; a devotee of Magic may regard decrees in the *Pekin Gazette* as spells that have coercive power in the spirit-world; a Confucian mandarin will think that an excellent plan has been devised for enlisting the superstitions of the simple-minded in support of law and order. We may suppose that for him Animism is but an episode in the history of human thought.

Another way of excluding spiritual caprice, which we might suppose to have been discovered by philosophers, but which appears to be older than what we usually call "Philosophy," is to subordinate the gods to Fate. The idea has been attributed to the astronomers or astrologers of Babylon that Fate must be above the gods as the constant heaven of the fixed stars is above the planets:[338] an analogy characteristic of magical thought. But the roots of the idea of Fate are much older and wider spread in the slow, steady growth of the belief in uniformity, which is

[336] *Religious Experience of the Roman People*, p. 202.

[337] Alfred Lyall, *Asiatic Studies*, essays on *The State and Religion in China*. In a milder form this system has been adopted by Japan; W. E. Aston, *Shinto*, p. 237.

[338] Franz Cumont, *Astrology and Religion*.

the common ground of Magic and Science; and (as I have said) before laws of nature had been discovered, Fate was an all-comprehensive Magic. Fate reduces the gods to the status of wheels in a machine; omens and oracles, instead of being sent or inspired by the gods, are also part of the machinery, and may point to their destruction; prayers and sacrifices are other parts of the machinery and, at most, may be a means of assuaging the anxiety of one's own heart. A stern way of envisaging the world: but it gives not only security against the gods, but also resignation and tranquillity.

Philosophical Christianity regards the actions of God as always manifested, in the physical order, through "second causes," or, in other words, in "the laws of nature"; and, in the spiritual order, as always observing the moral laws that are the principles of divine Reason; in either case there can be no variableness nor shadow of turning.

Magic, like Science, believes in uniformities of nature, and seeks by a knowledge of them to control events; but Magic is so eager to control events that it cannot wait to learn the true uniformities; it is not moved, like Science, by curiosity as to the truth, but by blind desire for present results. The cult of spirits seeks to control events not by knowledge of their natural causes, but by appealing to hyperphysical causes, and it resembles the belief in Free Will, by which men hope, through the influx of some unknown energy, to escape the bondage of their own vices: for Kant rightly treated "Freedom" as a cosmological problem, the supposed intervention of a cause that is transcendent and not in the course of nature. The intervention of Free Will (whether divine or human) is sought in order to avert injurious fortune, to realise our personal or social schemes more quickly and cheaply than our own efforts can, to avoid the consequences of our own actions, amongst which is bondage to our own vices: for all these, give us variability, miracle, caprice. But to foresee and control events physical or social, including the conduct of others, to be confident in the effects of our own actions according to our purposes, and in the stability of our own character: for all these, there must be uniformity. In the long run the latter considerations determine our thoughts; and the necessity of uniformity to a rational life may be one cause of our belief (so far out-running the evidence) in uniformities of causation and of space-relations and of all that we mean by natural law.

CHAPTER VII

OMENS

§ 1. The Prevalence of Omens

§ 1. *The Prevalence of Omens* everywhere, in all ages. Examples

"WHEN great disasters are about to befall a state or nation it often happens that there is some warning," says Herodotus.[339] It happens, indeed, not only to states and nations, but to eminent men, or even to common men, children and old women. An old woman who in England sees the new moon for the first time through glass, will not be surprised when, next morning, the market-basket drops from her arm in the middle of the street. In Fiji, if a woman putting bananas into a pot let one fall on the outside, or if the bread-fruit burst in roasting, she wrung her hands in dismay and cried aloud.[340] The whole world is full of such portents, and has been many thousands of years; and there is no clearer disproof of the vulgar error that age is the mother of wisdom than this, that the older the race grows the less it attends to them: or rather, whilst it attends to them more and more sedulously up to a certain critical hour — reached by the Greeks (say) 400 B.C., and by Western Europe (say) A.D. 1600 — it then begins to disregard, rapidly neglects them, till in a comparatively short time what is called the "enlightened" part of mankind forgets to take account of them at all; although it is well known that an eclipse of the moon a little before sunrise in the sign of Leo was a token that Darius should be defeated at Arbela; that on the first day that Julius Cæsar sat on the golden throne and wore the purple robe, an ox, having been sacrificed, was found to have no heart — at which Cæsar himself was surprised, and soon after he was assassinated; and that many signs and wonders announced quite recently the coming of the Spaniards into Mexico; Montezuma had visions and grew melancholy; the idol of Quetzalchoatl declared that a strange people approached to possess his kingdom, and so did witches and sorcerers; a stone spoke and warned him; a lake overflowed its banks; a pyramid of fire was seen in the sky; monsters were born with two heads, and there were other portents, all to no purpose.[341]

Omens, enjoyed with fear and trembling by all men in all ages, have sometimes been conceived of as due to magical power, but much more generally as the sendings of demons or gods; although the fact that they are rarely of any use to the recipient, or even intelligible to him until after the event, makes it very improb-

---

[339] VI. c. 27 (Rawlinson's Translation).
[340] Williams, *Fiji and the Fijians*, p. 152.
[341] De Acosta, *History of the Indies*, VII. c. 23 (translated by C. R. Markham).

able that they involve the intervention of any intelligent cause. And what are we to think of the intelligence of mankind, who in spite of their experience of omens during so many ages, were still eager to observe them?

§ 2. Omens and Natural Signs

§ 2. *Omens and Natural Signs.* — Natural signs all-important to hunters; and Omens are imaginary signs

For the wild man seeking game or on the alert for enemies it is necessary to read every sign of the presence of enemies or of game in the neighbourhood: footprints, broken twigs and bent grass, droppings of feathers, hair or dung, remnants of food or marks of habitation instantly catch his eye; noises or odours arrest his other senses. His world is full of these signs, and he must always be on the watch for them: the birds being suddenly silent, on looking up he sees a hawk; a change of wind, or the aspect of clouds, announces rain or fair weather; the coming and departure of certain birds — as with us the swallow and the cuckoo — portend the change of seasons. In all these cases causation is active and sometimes obvious, but often very obscure: the apparent may be the reverse of the real order: for the coming of swallows is the antecedent of our enjoying the summer; but in the order of nature the course of the seasons determines the migration of birds. That the true relation may be misunderstood is shown by the behaviour of certain Australian natives who, noticing that plovers cry before the coming of rain, take their cry to be a cause of rain, and therefore imitate it when performing their rain-rites.[342] We may observe how obscure is the distinction between sign and cause even amongst ourselves, in the general belief that "a change of the moon" is connected somehow with a change of weather; for what the relation is no one seems clearly to conceive.

The relation between natural signs and the events signified, being obscure, may be mysterious; and accordingly its obscurity has been made use of to defend the belief in Omens. In the *De Divinatione*[343] Quintus, who is unkindly given by his brother the post of apologist for all that nonsense, (following, I suppose, the sophistry of some Stoic) quotes Aratus' description of how certain movements of the sea presage a coming storm; the gull, too, and the crow by their behaviour: and the croaking of frogs and the snuffing of cattle foretell rain. I cannot explain, he says, how animals have such knowledge any more than I can explain the divinations of augurs; nor is it necessary to do so: in both cases there are the facts.

No wonder, then, that the savage, depending for his life upon a knowledge of signs, driven by eagerness and anxiety to observe them, and unable to distinguish coincidence from causation and the entanglements of causation, should imagine himself to have discovered many more signs than are comprised in the order of nature. Thus in Torres Straits, the biro-biro announces by its arrival that yams are ready for eating (which seems needless), and the cry of the koko predicts fine weather (which is credible); but, further, the sunbird can foretell the coming of a boat,[344] and that must be imagination.

[342] Spencer and Gillen, *Across Australia*, p. 220.
[343] Book I. cc. 7-10.
[344] *Reports of the Cambridge Expedition to Torres Straits*, VI. p. 260.

§ 3. Some Signs Conceived of as Magical

§ 3. *Some Signs Conceived of as Magical.*—By coincidence some events become signs of others by a mysterious and infallible tie. Moods of elation or depression favour belief in Omens; their validity may depend upon acceptance. Antiquity of subjective Omens. Whatever causes elation or depression is ominous. Coincidence and analogy

Very gradually, we may suppose, a difference came to be felt between two classes of signs: (1) those that are of a usual kind, such as the tracks of game, the return of the swallows, the croaking of frogs, which are almost constantly the antecedents of interesting events, such as the getting of food, the coming of spring, or of rain; sequences that recur again and again, some of them being, like the tracks of game, easily intelligible; all which, accordingly, are accepted as a matter of course and incorporated with common sense. (2) Less usual events, such as strange animals, lightning, eclipses, shooting-stars; which come to be considered as signs by being connected in imagination with interesting events which happen soon after them, such as a failure in hunting, an attack by enemies, a death in the tribe, the wreck of a canoe; though the connexions are irregular and never intelligible, and are accepted not as a matter of course, but as mysterious, magical and portentous: they are Omens. They acquire the hold upon men that belongs to the growing body of superstition. Although irregular, they are classed with the connexions that are believed to be most regular, and failures are overlooked. To these are added and accumulated in tradition, by analogy or caprice, innumerable other signs and warnings.

That Omens obtain an inextricable hold in the tangle of superstitious beliefs results from men's strong desire to foresee the future, especially in social conditions full of dangers and uncertainties, without the settled organisation which, with us in ordinary times, makes one year so much like another. Upon many people, indeed, this desire has the same effect to this day, and becomes more active in troubled times like the present. Anxious to know whether they are to marry, or to hear of a death, or to come into money or some other advancement, they hope to find out by visiting Mrs. Sludge in a stuffy chamber, or (as you may see in London) by consulting a canary at the street-corner. When a fixed idea of love or ambition or anxiety possesses the mind and leaves it no peace, we are ready to try any device that promises to relieve the strain, and we do things sillier than could have been predicted even by those who knew us best.

Belief in Omens and the practice of observing them having been established, the list of portentous events grows ever larger. (*a*) In a depressed frame of mind the future looks gloomy; in exhilaration, cheerful. A sensation, such as shivering, or sweating, that accompanies fear is apt to excite fear. In fear or depression one acts feebly and fails; in hope and confidence one acts vigorously and wins: the expectations produced by such moods fulfil themselves, and therefore the moods are ominous. This may be the reason why, when men are at strife and some ambiguous Omen occurs, he who first claims its favour or denounces its menace upon his enemy, gains an advantage;[345] for the other may be daunted and unable to rally his forces. But that depends on character.

This subjective value of an Omen, making its virtue a function of the recipient's disposition, sometimes became so prominent as to obscure its truly magical character; according to which it must be indissolubly connected in some way with the event and can have nothing to do with the recipient's attitude. Thus it might be held that an Omen, if it deeply affected a man's imagination, would be fulfilled; but, if neglected, it might not be. Pliny says[346] that, according to the augurs, auspices had no import for one who in any enterprise declared that he would not regard them. Or, again, the bearing of an Omen may be determined by the way in which it is accepted: Julius Cæsar, landing in Africa, fell; and that must have seemed a very bad Omen; but he, having the presence of mind (though not exempt from superstition) to exclaim: "Africa, I lay hold of thee!" changed its significance;[347] and, doubtless, greatly altered its effect upon the minds of his officers and soldiers and of all who heard of it; and that was the important matter. Hope and desire and anxiety created Omens, and they had also the power to direct the incidence and corrupt the interpretation of Omens. In fact, there were conventional formulæ for accepting good Omens and rejecting bad ones: *Accipio omen, Absit omen, Tibi in caput redeat;* which were counteractive spells; and it is agreed that Magic may be overcome by stronger Magic.

This attitude of mind that makes an Omen subject to its acceptance, may explain the otherwise absurd practice of taking the Omens again and again, when the earlier have been unfavourable, until one is obtained that flatters the inquirer's hopes. Not only amongst sophisticated peoples, who might be supposed to treat Omens in a formal and perfunctory way, but even in the lower barbarism Omens are thus garbled. The Karens of Borneo, consulting the liver of a pig to authorise an expedition, if with one pig the appearance is forbidding, sacrifice a second, third, or fourth; though without a satisfactory forecast they will not set out. Then, having set out, they try to avoid hearing the cry of the woodpecker (which has two notes, the one of good, the other of evil augury), lest it should be against their plans. And the same simple-minded people believe in the magical efficacy of the sign, no matter how obtained. Vaticinating by the flight of a hawk, a man will try, by shouting and by waving to it, to turn its flight toward the left, that being with them the prosperous direction.[348] Imagination-beliefs are saturated with insincerity; their unconscious maxim is, "Believe as you list."

Although it may be a general principle that savages are more impressed by external than by internal experiences, yet the suggestion of the foregoing paragraphs, that the finding of Omens in one's own sensations is secondary to, and dependent on, the growth of a belief in Omens presented by physical events, is not one upon which I much rely. Possibly sensations and moods are a distinct and primitive source of this superstition: for it has been noticed in Australia, where the

[345] W. R. Halliday, *Greek Divination*, p. 15.

[346] *Historia Naturalis*, XXVII. p. 4.

[347] Suetonius: *Julius*, c. 59.

[348] Hose and McDougall, *Pagan Tribes of Borneo*, II. pp. 56-64.

lore of Omens in general has made but little progress. Whilst performing tribal ceremonies under strong emotion, the aborigines think that their entrails sometimes acquire "sight"; so that they know whether their wives have been unfaithful, or they feel the approach of danger.[349] In the Western Isles of Torres Straits shivering and uneasy feelings are presentiments; and in the Eastern Isles, a dryness of one's skin or sneezing:[350] in New Guinea, if the right shoulder ache, expect good news; if the left, bad.[351] And these simplest of all whims are the longest lived; for amongst ourselves many a woman suddenly has a presentiment, "as if some one were walking over her grave."

(*b*) As a mood of elation or depression is itself ominous, so is whatever excites such a mood. Depressing objects are cripples, old women, sick people, timid hares, loathsome toads, a snake coming to meet a war-party, discouraging words, ugly dreams; whereas pleasant dreams, encouraging words, a snake going before us as against the enemy, hawks, wolves and blooming youth are all exhilarating: the list varies from tribe to tribe. Many ominous things promise good or evil according as they appear on the right hand or on the left: the left being generally held inauspicious, because (it is said) the left hand is the clumsier and weaker; and this may be true. But we have seen that in Borneo the left is preferred; and whereas the Greeks followed the general rule, assigning evil to the left hand, the Romans thought the right hand was the direction of danger. And this contrariety has been explained as due to a difference of orientation in the formal taking of Omens; for the Greek then faced northward, and had the place of sunrise upon his right hand; whilst the Roman faced southward and had on his right hand the place of sunset: so that it was not anything to do with his own body, but the direction whence the sun appeared and advanced with growing power and splendour which each of them judged of good hope, in contrast with that whither the sun declined and weakened to his death. To illustrate these fancies would be an endless task, and a superfluous labour, since nothing is better known.

(*c*) Coincidence, the occurrence near together of two interesting events, is sure to make people think there must be some connexion between them; and the earlier event will be classed, according to circumstances, as either a cause or a sign of the later; and if the connexion is mysterious, it must be either a magical power like that of a talisman, or that special kind of Magic which is an Omen. What circumstances determine this distinction, I will presently try to show. Possibly all Omens that are not derived from subjective moods and sensations, or from things or events that excite such moods, were originally founded upon coincidence. Upon this, apparently, the Egyptians relied in the records they kept (according to Herodotus) of Omens and their fulfilment; and Quintus Cicero is represented[352] as believing that the Babylonians kept such records for 470,000 years: so that it was, in their view, an inductive science; but we never hear of their having kept a record of failures and disappointments.

[349] *Northern Tribes of Central Australia*, p. 266.
[350] *Reports of the Cambridge Expedition to Torres Straits*, V. p. 361; VI. p. 259.
[351] Seligman, *Mel. of B. N. G.*, p. 309.
[352] *De Divinatione*, I. c. 19.

Some Omens having been established by subjective prognostication or by co-incidence, many more may be added by analogy, or by a sort of reasoning. An analogy with the contrast of right and left hand may be noticed in all opposites: the woodpecker in Borneo, for example, having two cries, and one of them a warn-ing, must not the other be an encouragement? The belief in Omens having taken hold of the public mind, everybody is on the look-out for signs and wonders; and anything unusual seen, or heard, or rumoured, becomes a possible Omen of any-thing else, and men ask one another what it portends. The superstitious imagina-tion is greedy of its accustomed food. Under such conditions, too, Omens are dis-covered by retrospection: a public calamity, such as the death of a king, the defeat of an army, or a pestilence (or in private life some private misfortune), makes us remember some foregoing event or events, which must have forewarned us, had we had the skill to interpret the significance of Time's progression.

§ 4. Differentiation of Omens from General Magic

§ 4. *Differentiation of Omens from General Magic.*—Omens are classed
with charms, rites and spells, but distinguished by being signs
only, not causes. Other differences

The savage mind, sensitive to the resemblance of relations, cannot overlook the analogy between signs and warning cries; many Omens are cries; and with the spread of animistic explanation, they came to be considered as the sendings of spirits or gods. But, at first, by mere magical thinking, under the stress of anx-iety to know the future, and the helplessness of common sense to predict any-thing outside the everyday routine, Omens are gradually separated from ordi-nary probable signs (such as the tracks of game) as necessary infallible signs (or tendencies) if cunning can find them out, connected by some supernatural law with the unknown future that certainly awaits us, and as a kind of Magic. The magical habit of mind may be supposed to have resulted from the coalescence of beliefs concerning several imaginary operations—by charms, spells, rites—each class of beliefs having its own occasions, causes, or fallacious grounds. Those op-erations had in common the marks of being connexions of events due to imagined forces of a mysterious kind, and therefore grouped themselves together in men's minds as the Magic apperception-mass. Omens had these marks and, therefore, were assimilated to Magic. An Omen is an event regarded as a magical sign of the good or ill success of some undertaking, or of the approach of good fortune, or of calamity. And on the principle that ideas are differentiated from a confused matrix, it is probable that Omens, having at first been confused with other magical antecedents of events, were only gradually again distinguished from them. But an important distinction existed and at last came to light: charms, rites and spells are causes of events; whereas Omens are signs only, not causes. The difference is that whereas charms, rites and spells directly exert their powers upon the course of things, Omens themselves exert no power, but show only that there is some power at work, which will have such or such results.[353]

[353] An infallible sign is, in Formal Logic, the same as a cause, according to the scheme *If A, then B*; and it is conceivable that, with strict thinking, a belief in an Omen may give rise to a magical practice. "For," says Lord Avebury, "granted that the fall of a stick certainly

Comparing Omens with other modes of Magic, several peculiarities may be noticed: (*a*) Omens themselves (apart from the preparation of victims, etc.) imply no human intervention, whereas rites and spells must be performed or recited by some one, and even charms are carried about one, or used in rites, or solemnly affixed to doors, animals or other possessions. (*b*) Partly as a consequence of this, Omens, considered in themselves, generally (as I have said) convey no suggestion of force. This cannot, indeed, be said of eclipses and thunderstorms; but the note of a bird, the appearance of entrails, a mere shivering or other change of feeling, though ominous, suggests no energetic operation; whilst rites and spells are often carried out with much expenditure of energy, and even charms, though not obviously active, are necessarily believed to be powerful in some obscure way of their own. (*c*) Omens are often so remote in time, as well as in place, from the events indicated that any quasi-mechanical determination of the issue by them can hardly be thought of; but with rites and spells, though they may not operate openly in the hour of their setting to work, yet the delay is not expected to be great, and (as said) their impulsion or *nisus* is often very impressive; and charms are incessantly and immediately active. (*d*) Omens in general do not foretell precisely what is to happen, but only the success or failure of some enterprise (not the "how" of it), happiness or misfortune; whereas rites and spells have some definite object, and most charms inflict, or guard against, some one kind of evil, disease or shipwreck; though others (it is true) bring luck or loss at large. Thus Omens are very different from other magical conditions; and although it is not likely that the ordinary savage or even the wizard ever consciously draws these distinctions or sums them up, still they have an effect upon his mind, and the observation of Omens and the reading of them becomes at last a special branch of the Magic Art—Divination.

§ 5. OMENS INTERPRETED BY ANIMISM

§ 5. *Omens Interpreted by Animism.*—Omens resemble warnings—at
first given by friendly animals, then by spirits, hence connected
with Oracles and Dreams

Omens, then, being only signs and not causes of future events, having no power in themselves, must be connected with some efficient power, or else the events prognosticated could not happen. How is that power to be understood? For a long time, probably, there is no clear conception of it: the connexion is mysterious. But there are two ways in which it may be interpreted: (*a*) Following the impersonal magical way of thinking, we are led to the idea of currents of force in which both Omen and event are borne along; and, at last, to the conception of a fatal order of the world in which all events have their necessary places. There A is always followed by B; so that, although A exerts no power over B, yet (if we know the law of the sequence) when the former appears it is an infallible portent of the latter. The

preludes that of the person it represents, it follows that by upsetting the stick his death can be caused" (*Origin of Civilisation*, p. 166). I do not see why such an inference should not be drawn, but can give no example of it. The possibility shows how much community there is between Magic and the lore of Omens; but as to this particular case, the magical cast of mind is already implied in the original setting up of the stick whose fall should prelude that of a given individual.

power at work is Fate; and to this idea I must return; for in its full development it comes late in history.

(*b*) The other and much simpler way of explaining Omens is to attribute them to the intervention of spirits who, whether they control events or not, at least foresee them, and send messages of warning to mankind. With the spread of Animism this is a matter of course. A sophisticated age may ask how a spirit should be able to see the future; and may answer that spirits, having greater knowledge than we of the present state of the world and its laws of causation, are able to calculate the outcome, just as an astronomer foretells an eclipse of the sun. A precious rationalisation! To the untutored savage there is no difficulty. To foresee the future is a very common performance: whenever we form an expectation which is fulfilled (and that happens many times a day) we accomplish this feat; and for the most part we are unconscious of the grounds upon which we formed the expectation. The savage is always in this position: he has not analysed the relation of "ground and consequence" nor examined the mental conditions that precede an inference. To him, therefore, foreknowledge, within a certain range, is not even mysterious; and, of course, spirits have the gift in a much higher degree. In Melanesia a *vui* (spirit) knows secret things without seeing;[354] and here begins the rôle of intuition in Philosophy. Later, a high god may give warnings, not merely of what he foresees in the course of the world, but of what he of his own volition will bring to pass; or a lesser god may announce what he knows to be the will of the higher; or, later still, all spiritual warnings may sink back into helpless incidents in the course of Fate.

Omens (as has been mentioned) resemble warnings: (*a*) Like warnings, they precede events, but do not cause them. (*b*) They sometimes precede an event by a considerable interval, as if to give time for precaution. (*c*) They do not announce the details of any event (which a friendly counsellor may not know), but only its character as good or evil. Then, if they are warnings (implying foreknowledge), since they are not the act of any man, they must be given by some spirit or other intelligence. So that once a belief in the intervention of spirits in mundane affairs has become prevalent in any tribe, nothing can be more natural than to regard Omens as spiritual messages. Still, this way of thinking may have been preceded by a disposition to attribute Omens to the good will of animals, especially Totems; for animals are often wiser than we are. In Australia the Turbal tribe held that the chirping of insects foretold the coming of blacks; a Wakelbwa who dreamed of a kangaroo would expect one of the Banbe subclass next day; to dream of old-man kangaroos sitting round the fire presaged danger.[355] Among the Yuin (Western Australia) a Black-Duck clansman thought that black ducks warned him against enemies; and men of the Kurnai, who had personal Totems, thought they gave protection by warnings.[356] Very early, however, ghosts or spirits sometimes come themselves to instruct us; as amongst the Kurnai, the Biraark (wizards) hold *séances* at night, when ghosts attend, and give news of enemies or of absent friends.[357] In New Guinea, the ghosts of dead tribesmen send their surviving relatives Omens

[354] Coddrington, *The Melanesians*, p. 123.

[355] A. W. Howitt, *Native Tribes of South-East Australia*, p. 401.

[356] Quoted by Frazer, *Totemism and Exogamy*, I. pp. 489 and 495.

[357] A. W. Howitt, op. cit., p. 389.

by fishes or birds.[358]

By this animistic theory Omens are intimately connected with Oracles and Dreams; for these, too, are messages from the spirit-world. Dreams are the chief causes of belief in spirits, and with many people have not yet lost the character of supernatural visitations. Probably for ages past there have been in each generation a few rationalists, who treated dreams in the manner of Artabanes (as reported by Herodotus[359]—who, however, will show that the event refuted him), holding that "whatever a man has been thinking of during the day is wont to hover round him in the visions of his dreams at night." Incensed against the diviners, rationalists have, in fact, too much despised and neglected dreams.

Oracles and Dreams are amongst the phenomena of "possession." Spirits, demons, gods, roaming the world and indwelling or haunting various bodies or localities, sometimes take up their abode in stones or bags of charms, which then become fetiches; or attain greater dignity in images and temples; or enter into men and women, afflicting them with diseases, or else with dreams, or drunkenness, or madness, or prophecy, or poetry;[360] for these things are hard to distinguish. And sometimes the people thus afflicted wander at large, sometimes are to be found only by some tree, or spring, or cave, or temple, where the spirit that makes them wise above others has chosen to reside, perhaps because his body was buried there.

Omens, Oracles and Dreams have, besides their dependence on spirits, another trait in common, namely, obscurity of meaning. When you have been favoured with one of these communications, what does it promise or threaten? To answer this question passes the wit of ordinary men; and, therefore, certain superior minds assume the important function of Diviners and, to guide their judgment, work out in course of ages with infinite ingenuity the Art of Divination.

§ 6. Natural and Artificial Omens

§ 6. *Natural and Artificial Omens*—Natural Omens not being always at
    hand, means are discovered for obtaining them at any time; e. g.
    Dice, Hepatomancy, Astrology

Before discussing Divination we had better remind ourselves of the immense extension that the lore of Omens undergoes beyond the early recognition of mysterious natural signs (thunder or the behaviour of birds, etc.), by the preparation in various ways of conditions under which Omens may be obtained at will (throwing

---

[358] C. G. Seligman, op. cit., p. 188.

[359] VII. c. 16.

[360] The poet is closely allied at first to the wizard; for (besides that the greatest spells and oracles are versified) the poet is inspired. In Australia poets are sometimes carried by ghosts into skyland, where they learn songs and dances. Some compose awake; but the belief prevails that they are inspired in dreams by dead and kindred spirits. Their songs travel far amongst tribes that no longer understand the language. (Howitt, *Native Tribes of South-East Australia*, pp. 389 and 413.) Similarly in Fiji (*Fiji and the Fijians*, p. 98). "The poem is too wonderful for me"—such is the poet's humility; "it was made by the gods"—such is his arrogance.

dice, roasting shoulder-blades, sacrificing pigs, etc.). Men are eager to know the future, at least the general complexion of it as happy or unhappy; and for this purpose they desire Omens. But natural Omens do not always appear when wanted, though probably the mere desire of them has multiplied them greatly; it is, therefore, very convenient to discover devices by which Omens can always be obtained by any one for any purpose. A common practice is to toss a halfpenny, and decide a doubtful choice of action by head or tail: reinforcing imbecility with superstition. It is impossible we should ever learn how such conventions originated, but may assume that the earlier were suggested by some accident, and many of the later by analogy. The Warramunga have a very simple plan, when a man dies, for discovering who it was that by evil magic slew him. They smooth the ground about the spot where the death occurred, and next morning come to examine it; and if they find there the trail of a snake, they know that the murderer was a man of the Snake-totem.[361] It is reasonable to suppose that in the first instance they found such a trail of snake or other animal upon unprepared ground, and thereafter smoothed the ground to make such signs plainer: thus they began the preparation of conditions for the taking of Omens. A New Zealand wizard had a simple construction for discovering beforehand who would have the better of a battle: he set up two sticks near together, one for his own party, the other for the enemy, and let them fall: whichever stick fell on the top of the other the party it had stood for was to conquer in the fight.[362] As ages go by and more and more intellect is concentrated upon the problem of foreknowledge, more and more ways are discovered of preparing the conditions of taking Omens, more and more expensive and complicated ones; for the more difficult the preparation and interpretation, the more necessary it is to employ a professional augur. The casting of dice, the drawing of lots, the taking of one's chance with verses of Virgil or of the Bible, may seem easy, but even such devices may be made difficult by accumulating rules of interpretation. The sacred chicken, whose vagaries in feeding occasionally relieve with grateful diversion the strenuous page of Roman History, cannot have required highly skilled manipulation, but to watch them a professional eye was necessary; and when sacrifices are employed as opportunities of taking Omens from the behaviour of the victims, the manner of their dying and the condition of their entrails, a technical specialist of high training becomes indispensable. This led to the intensive study of entrails, especially of livers (Hepatoscopy, Hepatomancy), with some gain of knowledge in Anatomy. The study was widely diffused; but still more widely, perhaps, the art of prophesying by the lines to be observed in shoulder-blades cracked by roasting over a fire (Scapulomancy).

Where nothing is or can be done to alter the physical conditions of premonitory signs, yet a painstaking analysis has been made of those conditions in order to interpret them in a methodical way; and this study may demand far greater skill than augury. In Cheiromancy the lines and eminences of the hand have been exactly mapped and defined, and have had their several values and meanings assigned. It is really a perplexing study, not to be entered upon with a light heart, yet simple and obvious in comparison with Astrology. The Astrologer who would un-

---

[361] Spencer and Gillen, *Native Tribes of Central Australia*, p. 526.
[362] Tylor, *Primitive Culture*, I. p. 125.

dertake to forecast the future fate of men or nations, or to recover forgotten facts of antiquity, such as the date of a hero's birth (for it was understood that a difference of forward or backward in time should not hinder scientific calculations), had to take account of all the visible furniture of heaven, the stars in their constellations, especially the signs of the Zodiac; the seven planets, each with its own qualities and powers assumed arbitrarily or by fanciful analogies, all unquantified and all varying in the Twelve Houses of Heaven. What learning, what stupendous abilities were demanded for such a task! In fact, any one who now hears of it, immediately knows it to be impossible. But until many problems had been solved and the method of them appreciated, no one could understand what kind of problems are insoluble. Meanwhile, in this study, for ages so honoured, a mixture of genuine Astronomy and a parade of systematic procedure (of which philosophers well know the force) made fatuity plausible.

§ 7. Divination and Oracles

§ 7. *Divination and Oracles.*—Diviners and the art of Divination. Power
of Diviners and Oracles. Ways of obtaining oracles and of being
inspired derived from low savagery

Omens and Oracles are, no doubt, infallible premonitions of something, if one can find it out; but they are often so obscure or ambiguous that one gets no guidance from them, and indeed it is sometimes impossible to judge whether they are ever fulfilled, or not. It is, therefore, most important that some one should be able to expound them; and here, as in every department of human effort, we may be sure that, of the many who attempt interpretation, one will be more successful than others; and then to him all men flock for enlightenment, especially if he make one good guess about some Omen or Oracle of general interest. Such a man was thereby constituted a Diviner, and became the founder of a profession, or (at least) of a branch or function of the great wizardly profession. It happened long ago; for in savagery most wizards are already Diviners.

In course of time the profession can no longer be satisfied with interpretation by guesswork, but elaborates the principles of the subject, the Art of Divination, upon which, perhaps, as much painstaking and ingenuity have been expended as upon industry and science put together. The *savants* who carried out such work were probably (many of them) as honest as fanatics can be; but the result always was to raise the reputation of the profession for occult knowledge and mysterious insight.

Diviners are either free and independent seers, soothsayers, fortune-tellers, mostly poverty-stricken and disreputable, though sometimes eminent and influential, like Tiresias and Epimenides; or else officials (a much smaller party) attached to some temple or government. Official soothsayers have often exercised immense power in society and politics. They are not found, of course, at the bottom of the scale of culture, where there is no government in Church or State; but in the lower barbarism, among the Bantu tribes (for example), Diviners have a highly influential station. The chief of a tribe usually has a specially trusted Diviner, and also consults others in discovering sorcerers and in forecasting the future.[363] In the Mazwaya clan of the Thonga there is an official Diviner who alone knows the exact composition of the royal "medicine," on which the welfare of the whole tribe depends. He is very much feared: no one dares dispute with him; and he has the right of cursing even the chief himself.[364] Such a powerful subject naturally excites the jealousy of the chief, who sometimes endeavours to get into his own hands all the medicines and occult virtues possessed by any of his tribesmen.[365] The danger of opposition between Church and State was also felt in Melanesia and Polynesia; and in Hawaii it was decisively overcome; for when the oracle was to be consulted, the king, concealed in a frame of wickerwork, gave the responses himself.[366]

In Greece (sixth and fifth centuries B.C.) oracles were still more powerful: the record may be read in Herodotus. The most flourishing States observed the Omens, and never ventured to go to war without consulting the Oracles; and the Oracles undertook to advise on war and peace and alliances, to settle disputed claims to sovereignty and the constitution of States, to sanction new laws and the foundation of colonies, to order the erection of new temples and even the worship of new deities—some of them of very dubious reputation: to say nothing of the infinite extent of their private practice. Their utterances were often unintelligible; they were sometimes known to have accepted bribes; yet the most enlightened people in the world continued to consult them: whether in good faith, or for their effect upon the vulgar both friends and enemies, or perhaps to share responsibility for an action with the gods, or even because one then felt more comfortable than in leaving them alone. But the diffusion of philosophy was too much for them; and, as Cicero says,[367] even the Delphic Oracle declined in reputation, not because with lapse of time the divine virtue failed of those exhalations that inspired the priestess, but when men became less credulous. Perhaps it was also because social life had become, under Roman government, safer and more settled and regular; so that a reasonable amount of foresight could be exercised without supernatural aid. Still, after the Oracles seemed to have been struck dumb, they revived from time to time for two or three centuries; Plutarch was far from incredulous; and the equivalent of them will (I suppose) continue to revive now and then, unless insane desire, and anxiety, and pusillanimity, and wonder and confusion of mind shall one day be extinguished.

In the great empires of the higher barbarism, the Magi amongst the Medes and Persians, and in Egypt, Babylonia and India the priesthood who practised sooth-saying and vaticination with their other functions, obtained still greater control over national life. The development of Astrology has always been imputed to the Chaldeans; and the importance of dreams and their interpretation in Egypt and Babylon is reflected in the stories of Joseph and Daniel as well as in the profaner

---

[363] Casalis, *Les Bassoutos*, pp. 299 and 340.

[364] Jounod, *Life of a South African Tribe*, I. 361. This "medicine" is the chief's great store of magical force: its principal ingredients are the nails and hair of chiefs deceased, fixed together by a kind of wax.

[365] Callaway, *Religion of the Amazulu*, p. 417.

[366] W. Ellis, *Polynesian Researches*, II. p. 235.

[367] *De Div.*, II. c. 57.

pages of Herodotus.

The character of Omens and the way of obtaining Oracles and of being inspired in Greece were merely modifications of those that have been in vogue amongst savages. Imagination-beliefs, in spite of their extravagance, have, in fact, a short tether and move in narrow circles, perpetually renewing the same themes. The ravings of the Pythoness possessed, which are said to have sometimes frightened the priests, might have been studied in Fiji. This was what happened when a priest was inspired: he "becomes absorbed in thought ... in a few minutes he trembles; slight distortions are seen in his face, and twitching movements in his limbs. These increase to a violent muscular action, which spreads until the whole frame is violently convulsed, and the man shivers as with a strong ague-fit. In some instances this is accompanied by murmurs and sobs; the veins are greatly enlarged, and the circulation of the blood quickened. The priest is now possessed by his god, and all his words and actions are considered as no longer his own, but those of the deity who has entered him. Shrill cries of Koi au! Koi au! 'It is I! It is I!' fill the air, and the god is supposed thus to notify his approach. While giving the answer the priest's eyes stand out and roll as in a frenzy; his voice is unnatural, his face pale, his lips livid, his breathing depressed and his entire appearance that of a furious madman. The sweat runs from every pore, the tears start from his strained eyes; after which the symptoms gradually disappear. The priest looks round with a vacant stare, and as the god says 'I depart,' announces his actual departure by violently flinging himself down on the mat, or by suddenly striking the ground with a club.... The convulsive movements do not entirely disappear for some time."[368]

To become inspired by means of visions or dreams, or endowed with the powers of a prophet or diviner, the obvious plan is to go to places frequented by spirits, namely, tombs, caves and temples. The Oracle of Trophonius in Bœotia was situated in a cave into which the consultant descended, and there saw visions or heard strange noises, and lost his senses: on returning to the upper air, he sat in the Chair of Memory and reported to the priests what had happened; and they delivered him to his friends "overpowered with fear, and quite unconscious of himself and his surroundings."[369] Afterwards he recovered his wits. At Oropus was a sanctuary of Amphiaraus, who (against his better judgment) had joined the expedition of Adrastus against Thebes and, amidst the general defeat of the army, fled and was swallowed up in the earth. His death ought to have occurred where his sanctuary stood; for it was a famous Oracle, and to consult it you purified yourself and sacrificed a ram and, spreading the skin under you, went asleep there, awaiting a revelation in a dream.[370] In the temple of Pasiphæ, too, near Sparta, one might hope for a divine message in a dream; and a shepherd, sleeping by the grave of Orpheus at Libethra, was moved to sing the verses of Orpheus.[371]

To lose one's memory and afterwards recover one's wits is incidental to many initiation ceremonies, and the darkness and secrecy of caves—which, moreover,

---

[368] Thomas Williams, *Fiji and the Fijians*, p. 190.
[369] Pausanias, IX. c. 10 (Frazer's Translation).
[370] Pausanias, I. p. 34.
[371] Ibid., IX. p. 30.

are often burial-places—have always deeply impressed our imagination. Amongst the Arunta there is a way of obtaining powers of Magic and Divination by going to sleep at the mouth of a cave; when the Iruntarinia (a kind of spirits), who live there, pierce the sleeper's head with lances, drag him into the cave, disembowel him and give him new entrails. He awakes dazed and silly; and the spirits lead him home, where gradually he recovers his right mind.[372] Amongst the Kurnai, again, one may become a wizard and diviner by sleeping at a grave; for in the night the dead man disembowels one, and provides new visceral organs.[373] Elsewhere in Australia a candidate for the wizardly profession is tied down at night in the tribal burial-ground and visited by spirits who force a stone into his head—apparently a kind of crystal, by gazing into which a wizard is able to see the past, the distant and the future.[374]

The seeking of enlightenment where spirits dwell in caves or graves, loss of wits by contact with them and subsequent recovery—all this may remind us of stories in Pausanias; but what of the disembowelling and renewing of the viscera? We are told by Spencer and Gillen that during the performance of certain traditionary ceremonies, an Australian's emotion is very great, so that he says his inward parts get "tied up in knots," and sometimes acquire "sight" and give omens;[375] and Howitt tells us that fat of the kidneys is believed to be the seat of a man's prowess and other virtues.[376] To extract and renew a man's entrails, therefore, is to renew his spirit, just as we speak metaphorically of a "change of heart," so that he has more vivid emotions, firmer courage, clearer insight. In fact, it is the magical equivalent of inspiration; the crystal, too, of the Euahlayi is a magic source; and this is as far as the Australians have got:[377] gross materialism, which the progress or (at least) the movement of animistic thought has happily superseded by conceptions more refined, if not more truthful.

§ 8. Apparent Failure of Omens

§ 8. *Apparent Failure of Omens*—ascribed to faulty observation or interpretation; frustration by spirits, or by superior Magic; or by having been symbolically fulfilled

Though in their nature infallible, Omens are not always fulfilled—at least, their fulfilment is not always ascertainable. But this is easily explained; for whatever an Omen may be in itself, our knowledge of it depends on observation, which may be superficial and incomplete, so that we may not know what it was. What

[372] Spencer and Gillen, *Native Tribes of Central Australia*, p. 523.

[373] A. W. Howitt, op. cit., p. 404.

[374] Langloh Parker, *The Euahlayi*, p. 25.

[375] *Northern Tribes of Central Australia*, p. 181.

[376] *Native Tribes of South-East Australia*, p. 367.

[377] This is unjust to the Australians. Amongst the Dieri (L. Eyre) wizards with renewed entrails communicate with supernatural beings, interpret dreams and discover murderers; but they also recognise spiritual communication with ordinary men in visions; not ordinary dreams, which are mere fancies, but those that are repeated; and these come from Kutchi, an evil spirit (Howitt, op. cit., p. 358). We may be sure the Greeks were mistaken in supposing that it was Amphiaraus who instituted divination by dreams.

kind of bird was it? Which way did it fly? How many cries did it utter? These questions go to the heart of the matter; yet each of them points out an opportunity of error. But granting the observations perfect, we have still to learn what the Omen portends; and although a simple mind, trusting to simple rules, may be ready offhand with an answer, it becomes, with the development of the art of Divination, more and more complicated and difficult, demanding long experience and profound erudition—something worth paying for. It is popularly known that dreams are perplexing as the guide of life. Are they to be accepted at face value, or do they go by contraries? What difference does it make whether they happen early in the night, or in the morning, or whether we sleep in white or in coloured night-clothes? There is an extensive casuistry of this matter. Interpretations of Omens proceeded generally by analogy: the length and direction of the cracks in a shoulder-blade indicate the length and tenor of a man's life. Oracles, again, were often distractingly obscure; from Delphi much like riddles; but those of Zeus at Dodona are said to have been sometimes taken to Apollo at Delphi to ask what they meant. Clearly, then, besides possible errors of observation, there were further pitfalls of interpretation; if a physician or a pilot is sometimes out in his reckoning, why not also a diviner? So that an Omen might very well be fulfilled without our knowing exactly what it was or what it indicated.

But that is not all; for we have seen that any kind of magical force is only infallible as a tendency; it may be counteracted, and this is generally thought to be the case with Omens. Just as the rites of one magician may be frustrated by the more powerful operations of another, so an Omen indicates a course of events which may, perhaps, be turned aside. That which is foreseen by one spirit may be prevented by another, whose intervention was not foreseen; for spirits are by no means infallible. Hence, however well observed and interpreted, the tendency of an Omen, or of the force it manifests, may be diverted or reversed by some unknown cause. Moreover, we ourselves are loth to relinquish all control over affairs. We have seen that the efficacy of Omens depended (not without reason) on the way they were received; and that we may meet them with our own magical influence, accepting them, or rejecting with a spell.

And further, we have seen that Magic often works by symbols, and that a symbolic action will cause or incite a real event; and similarly it is believed that the event foreshown by an Omen may be symbolically fulfilled; that some harmless semblance of the event may be substituted for it, absorb (as it were) the poison of the menace and let the threatened man go free. Astyages dreamed a dream which the Magi interpreted to mean that the child of his daughter (married to a Persian) should reign over Asia in his stead—implying that the kingdom must pass from the Medes. He therefore took measures to have the child destroyed; but by a series of happy chances Cyrus, the child, escaped and grew up; and in his boyhood Astyages discovered who he was, and was greatly alarmed. So he sent again for the Magi; but they, on learning that the boys in the village where Cyrus had been reared had in games appointed him their king, decided that this fulfilled the dream; for, said they, "he will not reign a second time."[378] So Cyrus lived, and the

____

[378] Herodotus, I. cc. 107, 28.

lordship of Asia passed to the Persians; for the Magi in this case overestimated the value of symbols. But all these ways of frustrating an Omen are incompatible with the interpretation of them by the course of Fate, and are only fit to be believed in by the weaker brethren.

§ 9. APOLOGY FOR OMENS

§ 9. *Apology for Omens.* — The Diviner or oracular person tries to be well-informed. The Stoics and Divination. Omens involved in Fate. Conditional and unconditional Omens

It may be some excuse for Omens that the interpretation of them was a sort of gymnastic for ingenuity, and was a means by which the quick-witted maintained themselves in a world of violence. It is, moreover, the business of those who undertake such work to study social and political conditions, just as rain-doctors study the weather. Their judgment, therefore, may often be better than that of men immersed in affairs and biassed by particular interests. Even in the lower savagery diviners manage to know more than others. In Queensland, when a big mob has assembled at a camp, diviners are believed to keep their eyes and ears open, sleepless — to learn who have death-bones, who has operated with one, who has been pointed at, etc.;[379] and in South Africa (two or three steps higher in culture) diviners take pains to obtain information as a means of "opening the gates of distance."[380] At Delphi, also, news was welcome from all parts, and men of capacity kept a steady eye upon the affairs of Greece and Asia. Of course, Divination, like every other superstition, was exploited by politicians. The Roman Government, according to Cicero, maintained the College of Augurs for the advantage of the State in civil affairs, although in his time the leaders of armies had ceased to consult the Omens:[381] and Polybius thought that religion was Rome's most useful institution.[382] A law that the comitia should not be held when Jupiter thundered and lightened was especially convenient when that assembly was inconvenient; for the official whose function it was had only to declare that he saw lightning, and thereupon the comitia broke up. Probably even those who thus abused a superstition, yet believed (at least in times of danger) "there was something in it." Omens and Oracles were sought after to allay fear and to gain confidence, and often they gave confidence and the strength that goes with confidence; or perhaps the rashness and folly that go with confidence, and so betrayed the devotee; or, again, they dashed the courage of brave men, and spread dismay, distrust and weakness.

No superiority of mere intellect seems to ensure men against participating in these delusions. Many Stoics, though highly disciplined in Logic, upheld the practices of Divination and Astrology. Panætius, indeed, rejected them; and Epictetus on moral grounds discouraged Divination. "For," said he, "what the diviner foresees is not what really concerns us. We have within us a diviner who tells us what good and evil are, and what are the signs of them. Does the diviner under-

---

[379] W. E. Roth, *Ethnological Studies*, p. 154.
[380] Kidd, *The Essential Kafir*, p. 193.
[381] *De Div.*, II. cc. 33, 35.
[382] Polybius, VI. c. 2.

stand that—after all his studies of the viscera? Not what is to happen in the future, but to do as we ought whatever happens is our true concern."[383] But this genuine expression of Stoic thought was abandoned by most of the sect in their desire to defend as much as possible the popular religion. They even staked the existence of the gods upon the genuineness of Divination: arguing that if Divination exists there must be gods who send Omens; and that if Divination does not exist there can be no gods—since if there are gods who know the future, and have a regard for mankind, and are able to give warnings, they will certainly do so. Therefore, no Divination, no gods.[384] There is, indeed, a widespread pitiful persuasion that some provision must have been made whereby a man may foresee his future; and so, in a sense, there is; for the existence of order in nature implies the possibility of foresight; and a fanciful mind might regard Divination as the anticipatory manifestation of an instinct in play before the faculties became capable of serious exercise. But the play was taken too seriously; and the worst of it was that its inane methods diverted attention from the only possible method—if not always on the part of the diviner, at least on the part of the great multitude, his dupes. M. H. A. Jounod says of the Bantu tribes, "Divination kills any attempt to use reason or experience in practical life."[385] And, clearly, this is everywhere its tendency, be it a question of consulting a canary at the street-corner, whether or not we should marry, or an augur rather than an experienced general whether or not now to engage the enemy.

Seneca[386] treated Omens as a necessary consequence of universal Fate: for if all events are factors of one predetermined order, everything in the present is a sign or omen of everything to occur in the future; and some events, such as the flight of birds, have been selected as Omens, merely because the meaning or consequents of these happen to have been observed; and whether Omens are respected or despised, Fate determines the whole course of events. By this way of thinking, as it was fated that the Romans should be defeated at Lake Trasimenus, it was also fated that the Omens should be declared unfavourable and that the warning should not be taken; and if it was fated that the Romans should be defeated at Cannæ, it was also fated that the Omens should be declared favourable and that they should be accepted. A belief in Fate makes Omens useless.

If, however, instead of Fate (all-comprehensive Magic) or predestination (by a supreme God), we regard the course of the world as determined by natural causation, whether Omens or Oracles may be useful or not (supposing them possible) depends on the nature of the event foretold—on whether it involves ourselves conditionally only or unconditionally. Omens that warn us against events conditionally may be useful enough, and few will think it a serious fault that they discourage the use of reason. King Deiotarus, having set out on a journey, was warned by an eagle not to go forward with it, and he turned back; and that same night the house at which he was to have slept fell down; so he escaped.[387] The dan-

---

[383] *Discourses*, II. c. 7.
[384] *De Div.*, II. c. 17; cf. c. 49.
[385] *Life of a South African Tribe*, p. 521.
[386] *Questiones Naturales*, II. c. 32.
[387] *De Div.*, I. c. 15.

ger was conditional on his continuing the journey; and, in the course of causation, a warning of danger, whether announced by an augur or by our own sagacity, may often enable us to avoid it. The causes of the future are present, and (within certain limits) are in our power. If I have reason to believe that there will be a fire at the Opera to-night, or have a presentiment of some calamity there, I need not go; and, then, I shall not be burnt alive. Whether the presage come to me by an Omen, or by a message from a god, or in an anonymous letter from one of the incendiaries who happens to be a friend of mine, cannot matter. No, if there were gods with intuitions of futurity, or with better knowledge than we have of present fact and greater power of calculating the consequences, they might make themselves useful. On this hypothesis there is not *a priori* any absurdity in the doctrine of Omens.

But with Omens or Oracles of magical or divine authority, that foreshadow our own fate unconditionally, the case is different. If, for example, they tell a man that he will die by the fall of the roof of his own house, that must be his end; and any one who examines his career afterwards will find that all his efforts to escape, all his pusillanimous crouchings and windings, were just so many steps of causation upon the road to inevitable doom. To convey such a presage serves no purpose but to fill the victim's last days with anxiety and dread: it is as bad as cruelty to animals.

The defence of Omens is mere rationalisation. They took possession of men's minds not in an age of reason, but when beliefs were freely born of hope and fear, were entirely practical, were never thought out and never verified. Whether the connection of Omen with event was conceived of magically or animistically, it was always mysterious, and on that account was the more impressive and acceptable. The uniformity of such connexions was, indeed, assumed—otherwise they were useless; the same bird's call on this hand or on that had always the same significance; but each case at first stood by itself; it was what we call "a miracle." Even such assumption of causation in ordinary cases as common sense implies did not compel the reflection that each cause must itself be an effect of other causes, and so again, and so on for ever. Nor did the assumption that spirits could foresee the future require that they should foresee the whole future, so as to imply an inviolable order of the world. Such considerations were left to amuse or perplex a later age. A great advance is marked by the saying of the Bechuana prince to Casalis, that "one event is the son of another, and we must never forget the genealogy."[388] But quite recently amongst ourselves causation was so feebly appreciated, even by the most educated, that testimony concerning miracles could still be appealed to as a ground for believing something further. One reviews all these wonderful fossils of the soul which are dead and yet alive, not without sympathy. For myself, I am free to confess, as they used to say in Parliament, that Omens and presentiments still haunt the shadowy precincts of imagination with vague shapes and mutterings of evils to come; which when they approach will be (I suppose) as hard and definite as daylight.

---

[388] *Les Bassoutos*, p. 248.

CHAPTER VIII

THE MIND OF THE WIZARD

§ 1. THE RISE AND FALL OF WIZARDRY

§ 1. *The Rise and Fall of Wizardry.* —At first no professionals. Early professionals unpaid; except by influence; which enables them to maintain order. Animism gives rise to sorcerers and priests. Priests suppress sorcery and black Magic, and absorb white Magic in religious rites. Societies of wizards

In describing the occult arts and those who practise them, terms are so loosely used that it may be convenient to premise that by "Wizard" (or Medicine-man) is here meant either a magician or a sorcerer; that is, either one who puts into operation impersonal magical forces (or so far as he does so), or one who relies upon the aid (or so far as he does so) of ghosts or spirits under magical control. It is an objection to this use of the word "sorcerer," that it is often applied to those chiefly whose practice is maleficent: but there seems to be no word used only in the more general sense; and the difference between maleficent and beneficent wizards, whether magicians or sorcerers, will here be marked, when necessary, by the familiar epithets "black" and "white."

In backward societies, wizardry is, or may be, practised by every man or woman; and, indeed, in its simpler operations or observances this is true at every stage of culture. But in every kind of task it appears that some men can do it better than others, and they attract the attention of the rest; and probably this is the beginning of the differentiation of the professional wizard: he is at first merely one whom others ask to help them in certain matters, because they believe that he, more than themselves, has the knack of it. As the occult arts become complicated and dangerous the superiority of the master-mind is more manifest. We are told that amongst the Tasmanians there were no professional wizards or medicine-men, but that some people practised more than others. From the beginning the art excites wonder, and wonder credulity; and an old fellow, who was subject to fits of contraction in the muscles of one breast, used this mysterious affection to impose upon his neighbours.[389] Wonder and the deference it brings with it, with the self-delusion of power it generates, are at first the wizard's sole recompense; and to the end they remain his chief recompense. In Australia a wizard is initiated (in fact or by repute), and is in some ways a man apart from others; yet in several cases it is reported that he receives no fees. For magical services amongst the Arun-

---

[389] Ling Roth, *The Aborigines of Tasmania*, p. 65.

ta "no reward of any kind is given or expected."[390] Sometimes a wizard expects no fee unless he is successful, as among the Tungus, Yakut and Buryats.[391] Generally, the wizard earns his living like other men, and merely supplements it by fees and presents. He rarely attains the professional dignity of living solely by his art and mystery.

Nevertheless in simple societies the wizard is a leader or a chief. The predominance of old men in council depends upon their occult powers rather than upon their worldly wisdom: even hereditary chiefs may have greater prestige through Magic than through royal descent.[392] I conceive that after the organisation of the primitive hunting-pack had, by various causes, been weakened or destroyed, it was through belief in Magic that some sort of leadership and subordination were re-established: perhaps in many experimental social forms, of which some specimens may be found in Australia and survivals of others in all parts of the world. Among the Massim of the Trobriand Islands, hereditary chieftainship is better developed than anywhere to the south or west; yet "at the back of every chief's power over his people is the dread of sorcery, without which I feel sure he is little more than a cypher."[393] Or the medicine-man may appear as the chief's rival, as among the Indians of the upper Amazons described by Capt. Whiffen, who observes that in a contest between the medicine-man and the chief the odds are in favour of the former, since to his opponents death comes speedily (by poison). He has great influence over international policy: war is never made without his advice. Here we see the beginning of that struggle between the temporal and spiritual powers which continues with alternate victory and defeat through the whole course of history. Callaway[394] describes a Bantu chief as inducted to his office by diviners that he may be "really a chief" not merely by descent. A dangerous concession! But other Bantu chiefs are themselves wizards, and strive to collect all the medicine of the tribe in their own hands; and Chaka declared he was the only diviner in the country.[395] The rise and spread of the political power of wizards, however, has been fully illustrated by Sir J. G. Frazer in the sixth chapter of *The Magic Art*.

As animistic interpretation prevails in any society, so that the marvels of Magic come to be attributed to spiritual causes, magicians tend to become sorcerers, and, being thus associated with spirits, may not be easily distinguishable from priests. Among the Buryat a shaman was a priest, as knowing the will of the gods and directing sacrifices, but he was also an exorcist and diviner.[396] The great majority of those who deal with spirits rely, more or less openly, upon both coercion and propitiation: but we may say generally that an officiant is a sorcerer so far as he depends upon coercing spirits by Magic; a priest so far as he relies upon propitiating them by prayer and sacrifice. The sorcerer is aggressive and domineering

[390] Spencer and Gillen, *Across Australia*, p. 336.
[391] Czaplicka, *Aboriginal Siberia*, p. 177.
[392] The political importance of the wizard seems to have been first noticed by Spencer, *Principles of Sociology*, II. p. 178 (§ 474).
[393] Bellamy, quoted by Seligman, *Melanesians of British North Guinea*, p. 694.
[394] *Religion of the Amazulu*, p. 40.
[395] Dudley Kidd, *The Essential Kafir*, p. 114.
[396] Czaplicka, *Aboriginal Siberia*, p. 191.

toward supernatural powers; the priest professes humility. In any case the character of a cult is liable, in course of time, to change from one side to the other; and at the same time, two men may officiate in the same rites and, at heart, one of them may be a priest and the other a sorcerer. Custom gives the name of priest to him who, when a certain stage has been reached in the development of Animism, when gods are recognised, serves and sacrifices to the more public and reputable spirits. A conflict then breaks out between him and the sorcerer.

Whilst magic-beliefs greatly strengthen chieftainship, religion, without impairing the magical sanction, reinforces it with other ideas, and therefore has a political advantage. A god is often the ancestor of the king and the ground of his sovereignty; and the king himself, or his brother, may be high-priest. The priesthood acquires commanding dignity; it shares the culture of the highest social rank, and may become almost the sole repository of learning and art. Wizards then lose their place in the sun. The beneficent practice of wizardry (or White Magic) is more or less incorporated with religious rites; the maleficent practice (or Black Magic) is forbidden and punished: under polytheism because "it is destructive to human life or welfare"; under monotheism, as offensive to God.[397] The sorcerer is outlawed, and betakes himself to the secret performance of unholy rites in dark and unwholesome circumstances. He may be in full antagonism to the official gods, invoking demons or old down-trodden gods not yet forgotten by the people, and, in the service of demons, inverting and profaning the rites of public worship. But to forbid and punish the black art is to punish crime, not to persecute Magic as such; whose beneficent practices still flourish under another name. Prof. Yrjö Hirn has shown that, during all the ignorant and superstitious prosecutions of witches in Europe, the public religious ceremonies and observances were permeated by magical ideas.[398] In spite of the antagonism between priest and sorcerer, there is not the full opposition between Religion and Sorcery that exists between Animism and Magic—between the recognition of caprice and the belief in uniformity—since the gods themselves work by Magic and may be subject to its powers. It is not an antagonism of principle, but partly of allegiance and partly of ambition.

The influence of wizards is generally extended by means of clubs and secret societies: wizards form a marked class, are well aware of it, and are naturally drawn into mutual understanding. In Australia no regular societies seem to have existed, but the medicine-men recognised one another, initiated and trained new-comers into the profession, had an esoteric tradition of rites and methods and fictions, and sometimes met for consultation. Among the savages of Torres Straits, the *maidelaig* meet together in the bush at night, in order to perform their sorcery, and the body of sorcerers can control an individual *maidelaig*; but they appear not to have a definitely organised society.[399] In Melanesia, however, many regular societies exist;[400] and among the Northern Amerinds they were numerous and powerful. The Midewinian society of the Ojibways is typical of these institutions. It was the club of the legitimate professionals, in contrast with private practitioners, who were

[397] E. Westermarck, *The Origin and Development of Moral Ideas*, ch. xlix.
[398] *The Sacred Shrine.*
[399] *Report of the Cambridge Expedition to Torres Straits*, V. pp. 322-3.
[400] Rivers, *History of Melanesian Sociology.*

said (of course) to be favoured by evil *manidos*. To join the society one must undergo instruction, paying fees and making presents to its members. It comprised about one-tenth of the tribe, and what with influence, what with perquisites, did very well.[401] In Africa also such societies flourish.

Every profession, organised or unorganised, provided there be an understanding amongst its members, is prone to acquire anti-social interests and to establish a secret tradition; and as long as moral sense is very imperfect, the antagonism of the profession to the public may be a virulent evil, as we see in the history of wizardry and priestcraft. Both the profession and its tradition begin with practices common to all members of a tribe; and the tradition grows by accumulating the discoveries and inventions of the professionals. Experiment and observation are employed by them (according to their lights) probably from the first. Dr. Haddon says that, in controlling the wind and rain, the procedure of wizards in the eastern islands of Torres Straits was subject to variation, and so doubtless were the spells, and experts relied on their own variants;[402] and Prof. Seligman[403] observes that, in British New Guinea, the knowledge of "the departmental expert" (wizard controlling rain, or fertility of garden, or what not) is traditionary from father to son, consisting partly of magical processes or formulæ, partly of the results of years of observation and thought. All improvements in science, art, industry and humbug are made by individuals. The cumulative tradition becomes more voluminous, the spells more intricate, the rites more elaborate; because the possible membership of the profession is thereby narrowed, the self-valuation of the initiated is heightened, the wonder and credulity of the laity is enhanced: so much of the doctrine and discipline being allowed to transpire as to make this last effect a maximum. Whilst tribal belief in Magic is the necessary ground of the wizard's existence, he — being once recognised — thenceforth confirms, sways and guides the tribal belief.

§ 2. The Wizard's Pretensions

§ 2. *The Wizard's Pretensions.* — Control of Nature; shape-changing and flying; the causing and curing of diseases; Divination; control of ghosts and spirits. General trust in them

Whilst societies are formed to promote the common interests of wizards, too severe competition amongst themselves is in some measure avoided by the specialisation of individuals in different branches of their mystery. In pure Magic there is some room for the division of labour to deal with the weather, or fertility, or disease, but the spread of Animism and the multiplication of fetiches and demons open to the sorcerers a wide field for the multiplication of specialists. Amongst the Beloki, says Mr. Weeks,[404] there are eighteen classes of specialists; on the lower Congo, fifty.

---

[401] *Am. B. of Ethn.*, VII., "Ojibway Medicine," by W. J. Hoffman; XI., "The Sia," by M. C. Stevenson; XIV., "The Menomini Indians," by W. Hoffman. For a collection of the facts see Frazer, *Totemism and Exogamy*, IV. ch. xix; and Hutton Webster, *Primitive Secret Societies*.

[402] *Report of the Cambridge Expedition to Torres Straits*, VI. p. 200.

[403] Op. cit., p. 278.

[404] *Among Congo Cannibals*, p. 251.

By spells and rites and charms wizards undertake the general control of Nature. They cause rain or drought, determine the rising of the sun and, for this purpose, may go every morning to a hill-top to summon him. An Australian wizard claimed to have driven away a comet by means of his sacred stones.[405] The adept procures a favourable wind for his friends, or for his enemies an adverse; prospers the crops or blights them; controls the game of the hunter, and the cattle of the herdsman. The height of such claims may be read in Medea's boast in the *Metamorphoses*.[406]

In his own person the wizard may have the power of shape-changing into some animal, or into any animal. He can fly through the air to skyland to visit Daramulun; or to help dull imaginations, he throws up a rope and climbs up by it, or throws up a thread (like a spider's) and climbs up by that.[407] Or he may fly to the moon to be the guest of the man whom we see there;[408] or to the region of death to visit Erlik Khan.[409] By daylight he only flies in the spirit, during a trance; but when it is quite dark he can go bodily. And probably this points to the origin of such beliefs: for to dream that one flies is not uncommon; and as in dreams we visit distant places, and on waking seem suddenly to have returned by no known means, the analogy of flight offers the easiest explanation of such experiences. To fly is one of the most ancient and persistent exploits of the profession: European witches flew upon broomsticks (degenerate from Siberian horse-staves); Dr. Faustus upon his magical cloak; and "levitation" has been exhibited by recent "mediums."

Wizards cause and cure love and other forms of sickness; slay, or recall the soul to its accustomed habitation; sometimes the same man kills and cures; sometimes he works only evil, or only against evil; the Black and the White Magicians may become well-recognised hostile sects. Wizards discover thieves and murderers, or sell a fetich by whose power an evil-doer walks invisible, if he takes care not to be seen. They administer the ordeal and have in their power the life of every one who undergoes it. They interpret dreams, and prophesy by the flight of birds, the fall of dice, the making of shoulder-blades and the aspect of the stars.

The sorcerer communicates with the ghosts of the dead or with the spirits of nature and, by their aid, accomplishes whatever can be done by Magic. He is possessed by them, and operates or speaks by their power or inspiration; he drives them out of others whom they possess, or sends them on errands, controlling them either by the help of stronger spirits or by his profound knowledge of enchantments. Many of these things he is believed to do best during fits or ecstasy; which he produces in himself by rhythmic drumming and dancing, or by drugs, or by voluntary control of a disciplined temperament, to the astonishment and conviction of all beholders.

Such are the wizard's pretensions, so well known that a brief recital of them

[405] Spencer and Gillen, *Across Australia*, p. 326.
[406] Book VII. The witch, imitated from Circe and Medea by Ariosto, Tasso, Spenser, became a traditionary, romantic motive.
[407] Howitt, *Native Tribes of South-East Australia*, p. 388.
[408] Stefánson, op. cit., p. 403.
[409] Czaplicka, op. cit., p. 240.

suffices; and whilst they seem to us too absurd for any one to believe, least of all the wizard himself, yet observers assure us that he often does believe in them, and they are certainly taken to be genuine by the majority of his tribesmen. For them his performances are so wonderful as to put to shame the achievements of scientific invention; and probably this partly explains the frequent reports that savages are deficient in wonder. "It takes a good deal to astonish a savage," say Spencer and Gillen; "he is brought up on Magic, and things that strike us with astonishment he regards as simply the exhibition of Magic more powerful than any possessed by himself."[410] Still the blacks were astonished by the phonograph. Similarly we are told by Stefánson[411] that things unusual but of an understood kind—a bow that shoots fifty yards further than any other—may excite endless marvelling amongst the Esquimo; but what seems miraculous—a rifle-shot, or a binocular—is compared with the supposed powers of the shaman, who can kill an animal on the other side of a mountain, or see things that are to happen to-morrow. Our surgery, too, is very inferior to the shaman's, who can take out a diseased heart or vertebral column and replace it with a sound one.

§ 3. CHARACTERISTICS OF THE WIZARD

§ 3. *Characteristics of the Wizard*—Intelligence and knowledge; force of will and daring (initiation); motives—attraction of mystery, reputation, power; distinctive costume and demeanour of a "superman"; jealousy of rivals; histrionic temperament; hysterical diathesis. Suggestibility of his clients

(1) Observers generally agree that the wizard, or medicine-man, is distinguished in his tribe for intelligence and penetration, or at least for cunning. He is apt to impress an unsympathetic witness as "some fellow with more brains and less industry than his fellows." The wizard amongst the Fuegians, says Fitzroy, is the most cunning and deceitful of his tribe, and has great influence over his companions.[412] Amongst the Bakongo, the witch-doctors, according to Mr. Weeks, have sharp eyes, acute knowledge of human nature, and tact.[413] The Samoyed shamans "are, as a rule, the most intelligent and cunning of the whole race."[414] Cunning is plainly necessary to the wizard's life, and, for some of his functions, much more than cunning. In many tribes his advice is asked in every difficulty and upon every undertaking. Sir E. im Thurn reports that the *peaiman* of the Arawaks learns and hands down the traditions of his tribe and is the depository of its medical and hunting lore.[415] The surgical skill of Cherokee medicine-men in the treatment of wounds was considerable.[416] Still greater seems to have been that of the Fijians, with no mean knowledge of anatomy learnt during their incessant wars.[417]

[410] *Across Australia*, p. 51.

[411] Op. cit., p. 184.

[412] *Voyages of the Adventure and Beagle*, II. p. 178.

[413] *The Primitive Bakongo*, p. 216.

[414] *Journal of the Anthropological Institute*, XXIV., "Shamanism," p. 144.

[415] *Among the Indians of Guiana*, p. 335.

[416] *Am. B. of Ethn.*, "Sacred Formulas of the Cherokees," by J. Mooney, p. 323.

[417] W. Mariner's *Account of the Tonga Islands*, ch. xxi.

Medicine-men of the Amerinds discovered the virtues of coca, jalap, sarsaparilla, chinchona, and guiacum,[418] implying on their part superior curiosity and observation. The Bantu doctors of S. Africa employ aloes, nux vomica, castor-oil, fern, rhubarb and other drugs.[419] Livingstone says[420] that the doctors, who inherit their profession, have "valuable knowledge, the result of long and close observation," and that they thankfully learnt from him—when their patients were not present. In all parts of the world some knowledge of drugs and of certain methods of treatment, such as sweat-baths and massage, ligatures, cauterisation and fomentation, seems to have been possessed by the magical profession. As weather-doctors and crop-guardians, they laid out the first rudiments of astronomy and meteorology. All their knowledge of this sort is, of course, no Magic, but experience and common sense; though science is not derived from Magic, the scientist does descend from the magician: not, however, in so far as the magician operates by Magic, but in so far as he operates by common sense. Among the Lushai tribes the name for sorcerer, *puithiam*, means "great knower,"[421] the equivalent of our "wizard." But sorcery degrades the magic art of medicine by discouraging with its theory of "possession" every impulse of rational curiosity, and by substituting for empirical treatment (however crude) its rites of exorcism and propitiation.

In parts of the world so widely separated as Siberia, Greenland, the remote back-woods of Brazil and S. Africa, wizards have discovered the secret of ventriloquism. Everywhere they have learned the art of conjuring, without which (especially the trick of "palming") many of their performances, and notably the sucking-cure, could not be accomplished. Their practice is generally clumsy and easily detected by sophisticated whites, but imposes upon their patients and the native bystanders.[422] In India it is carried to a much higher degree of illusion. Wizards often have a practical knowledge of some obscure regions of psychology; such as the force of suggestion and various means of conveying it, and the effect of continuous rhythmic movements and noises in inducing a state of exaltation or of dissociation.

A wizard's tribesmen, of course, believe him to possess knowledge absurdly in excess of the reality. He boasts of it as the foundation of his power over nature or over spirits; often as a supernatural gift of spirits whom he has visited, or who have visited him, and who have initiated him; or else as secret traditionary lore. It is by knowledge of human nature that he rules his fellows; and he asserts that knowledge of the names and origins of things and of spirits gives him the same control over them. In Mr. Skeat's *Malay Magic*, incantations addressed by a miner to spirits or to metals, adjuring the spirits to withdraw from his "claim," or the grains of metal to assemble there, contain the intimidating and subduing verse:

"I know the origin from which you sprang!"

---

[418] *Am. B. of Ethn.*, IX., "Medicine Men of the Apache," by J. E. Bourke, p. 471.

[419] Dudley Kidd, *The Essential Kafir*, p. 135.

[420] *Travels and Researches in South Africa*, ch. i.

[421] J. Shakespeare, *The Lushai Kuki Clans*, p. 80.

[422] Hose and McDougall, *Pagan Tribes of Borneo*, p. 120, and *Am. B. of Ethn.*, XI. p. 417; XIV. pp. 97, 148.

The same compelling power was employed—if we may trust the *Kalevala*—by Finnish wizards; for "every thing or being loses its ability for evil, as soon as some one is found who knows, who proclaims its essence, its origin, its genealogy." "Tietaja, which etymologically signifies wise, or learned, is ordinarily used for magician."[423] It was by profound science that mediæval magicians were believed to control demons; and anybody celebrated for science was suspected of sorcery: such as Grosseteste, Albertus Magnus, Roger Bacon, Aquinas, and Raymond Lulli; whose reputation supported the credit of such men as Paracelsus and John Dee.

The fine arts in their rudiments owe much to the wizards. Incantations in verse often reach a high pitch of lyric fervour. The words *rune, carmen, laulaa* bear witness to the magic of poetry. Virgil and Taliessin have been famous for more than natural gifts; that one by superstitious repute, and this by his own vaunting.[424] Dancing and pantomime were cultivated for their magical virtues. Primitive carving and painting are in many cases undertaken in order to influence the spirits, or the animals, or the natural powers they represent; and if Magic was the motive of the recently discovered animal paintings dating from the old Stone Age, its efficacy in encouraging art at that remote period rivalled that of religious patronage in some later ages.

(2) In most tribes the wizard needs great force of will and persistency of purpose—whether from deliberate choice or from infatuation with the profession—to carry him through the severe training that is often exacted from candidates for the office; great audacity and courage to impel and sustain him in the practice of his art, pestered by taboos and (the sorcerer especially) always beset by supernatural terrors and often by more real dangers; and unusual presence of mind to extricate himself from very embarrassing situations. It is true that, in some cases, where the office of wizard is hereditary, or may be assumed by alleging the favour of spirits, or some other underhand device—perhaps upon the evidence of visions, or by mere fraud, or by a mixture of both—we hear little of really serious initiatory rites; but often these formalities are very painful or very expensive. Among the Arunta, there are three classes of wizards: the first and second, made by spirits, undergo no severe trial—except the boring of a hole in their own tongues and the keeping of it open, as evidence of a professional story about spirits who slew them with spears, cut out their entrails and replaced them with a new set and certain magic stones. But the third class are initiated by two wizards of the first and second class, who pretend to force crystal stones[425] into their bleeding bodies from the

[423] D. Comparetti, *The Traditional Poetry of the Finns*, pp. 27 and 25.

[424] Rhys, *Celtic Heathendom*, pp. 548-50.

[425] The crystals forced into a wizard's body, whether by spirits or by other wizards, are essential to his profession, and if they leave him his power is lost. "It is the possession of these stones which gives his virtue to the medicine-man" (Spencer and Gillen, *Northern Tribes of Central Australia*, p. 480 note). John Mathew says that, according to the belief of the Kabi (Queensland): "A man's power in the occult art would appear to be proportioned to his vitality, and the degree of vitality which he possessed depended upon the number of sacred pebbles and the quantity of *yurru* (rope) which he carried within him" (*Eagle-hawk and Crow*, p. 143). "Rope" was the property of the higher grade of medicine-men (substitute for snakes?), who had obtained it from the Rainbow in exchange for some of their pebbles. Certain pebbles, especially crystals, are independent magic-powers throughout Australasia

front of the leg up to the breast bone, into the crown of their heads and under the nail of the right forefinger. This they must suffer in perfect silence, three times a day on three consecutive days, with other tortures, followed by various taboos; and, after all, they do not stand as well with the tribe as those whom the spirits have initiated.[426] Can there be any doubt that the initiatory rites of the third class represent the older magical custom, and that the fabulous initiation by spirits is an overgrowth of Animism? There are clear motives for the change; since the latter method is easily carried out by oneself, is far less painful, and is more stimulating to the imaginative belief of the laity, and therefore more imposing. For the inverse change there are no motives. And therefore, probably, wizards of the third class are really less competent than the others; for the man who, after the new spirit-path has been opened up, still prefers the old road through pain and privation must be (comparatively) an unimaginative, dull, honest, inferior fellow.

Old wizards of the Warramunga, receiving a new candidate for the profession, allow him during the process no rest; he must stand or walk until quite worn out, when he scarcely knows what is happening to him; deprived for a long time of water and food, he becomes dazed and stupefied.[427] In the western islands of Torres Straits, a novice was taken into the bush by his instructor, who defæcated into a shell full of water and made him drink it with his eyes open; next he must chew certain fruits and plants, which made his inside bad and his skin itch; then shark's flesh, and, finally, the decomposing flesh of a dead man full of maggots. He became very ill and half frantic. Few cared to undergo these rites; some gave up the undertaking; some died of it.[428] In British Guiana, an aspirant to wizardry undergoes long fasts, wanders alone in the bush (full of terrors to the timid Indian), and accustoms himself to take large draughts of tobacco-juice mixed with water, which cause temporary insanity.[429] Across the watershed to the S.W., the office of medicine-man is hereditary; yet Waterton reports that probationers have to endure exhausting ordeals and tortures.[430] The severe training of the Bantu witch-doctor kills many novices.[431] Under such conditions, only men of unusual force of will, or constancy of infatuation (qualities not always easy to discriminate), can become wizards. Preparatory ritual for the office of shaman among the Buryats of Siberia is elaborate, expensive and intimidating: a candidate of poor family is helped by the community to get animals for sacrifice and objects necessary for the rites; but many shrink from the trial, "dreading the vast responsibility it brings; for the gods deal severely with those who have undergone consecration, and punish with death any serious mistake." There are nine degrees in the profession, each

and elsewhere, probably of much older repute than the profession of wizardry; and the wizard gets his personal power by having them inside him. Similarly, Jounod describes Bantu wizards as "endowed with magical power, or rather possessing enchanted drugs" (*Life of a South African Tribe*, p. 293): whereas we are often told that the occult art begins with the extraordinary personality of the wizard.

[426] *Native Tribes of Central Australia*, pp. 522-9.

[427] Spencer and Gillen, *Northern Tribes of Central Australia*, p. 485.

[428] Haddon, *Reports of the Cambridge Expedition to Torres Straits*, V. p. 321.

[429] E. im Thurn, *The Indians of Guiana*, p. 334.

[430] Thomas Whiffen, *The North-West Amazons*, p. 181.

[431] Dudley Kidd, *The Essential Kafir*, p. 156.

requiring a special initiation.[432] Thus, in many cases, the ordeal of initiation turns away the weak and incompetent, and keeps up the wizardly profession at a high level of resolution and endurance. In more sophisticated societies a similar result is obtained by the belief that the attainment of magical powers depends upon the undergoing of prolonged austerity in study, or in privations and tortures, which give a mystical right to supernatural power: the superstition upon which Southey raised *The Curse of Kehama*—least unreadable of his romances.

As for the courage that may be requisite for carrying on the wizard's practices, when he is the terror of his neighbours, their attitude towards him varies, in different tribes, from the tamest toleration to murderous antagonism. Thus, in the western islands of Torres Straits, Professor Haddon never knew the sorcerers mobbed or violently put to death on account of their magical practices.[433] In New Caledonia, when a sorcerer causes a general famine, the people merely make him presents to procure a return of plenty.[434] Among the Todas, a man who is the victim of a sorcerer pays him to have the curse removed.[435] In such cases, effrontery is all the sorcerer needs. On the other hand, near Finsch Harbour in New Guinea, a dangerous sorcerer is often put to death; and so he is amongst the neighbouring Kais.[436] Such in fact is the more general practice;[437] and the wizard, carrying on his profession at the risk of his life, must be supported by the sort of fearlessness that criminals often show.

Confronted with supernatural dangers, the sorcerer's need of courage must depend upon the sincerity of his own belief in them: a matter to be discussed in the fourth section of this chapter. If his professions are veracious, the attitude of such a man toward spiritual powers cannot be sustained by any ordinary daring. In the N.W. Amazons the shaman is the only one of his tribe who dares go alone into the haunted forest. Zulu doctors, who specialise as "heaven-herds," fight the Thunderstorm with spear and shield until he flees away.[438] Everywhere the sorcerer fights the demons of disease with reckless valour. On the Congo he drives them into some animal, and then cuts its head off. In North America he intimidates, quells and exorcises them with furious boasting. In Siberia, to capture the fleeting soul of a patient, he follows it over land and sea and into the regions of the dead. The Innuit of Greenland acknowledge Sedna as the supreme Being and the creatress of all living things; yet their angakoq subdue even her: one lures her from Adlivun with a magic song; whilst another, as she emerges, harpoons her with a seal-spear, which is then found to be smeared with blood.[439] To obtain assistance

[432] *Journal of the Anthropological Institute*, XXIV., "Shamanism," pp. 87-90.

[433] *Reports of the Cambridge Expedition to Torres Straits*, V. p. 322.

[434] J. G. Frazer, *Belief in Immortality*, p. 334.

[435] W. H. R. Rivers, *The Todas*, pp. 256-7.

[436] *Belief in Immortality*, pp. 249, 269.

[437] For examples see Weeks, *The Primitive Bakongo*, p. 204; Dudley Kidd, *The Essential Kafir*, p. 149; Callaway, *Religion of the Amazulu*, p. 391; Hose and McDougall, *The Pagan Tribes of Borneo*, II. p. 115; Turner, *Samoa*, p. 342; *Shamanism*, p. 130; Carl Lumholtz, *New Trails in Mexico*, p. 24; T. A. Joyce, *South American Archæology*, p. 245; E. Westermarck, *Origin and Development of Moral Ideas*, II. pp. 650-2.

[438] Callaway, *Religion of the Amazulu*, pp. 384-6 and 404.

[439] Franz Boas, "The Central Esquimo," *Am. B. of Ethn.*, VI. (1884-5), p. 603.

from even the highest spirits the wizard deceives them; or to slay an enemy he usurps their powers. The Malay avenges himself by making an image of his victim in a shroud, and praying over it as over the dead; then he buries it in the path to his victim's house, and says:

> "Peace be to you, ho prophet Tap, in whose charge the earth is!
> Lo I am burying the corpse of (name of victim)
> I am bidden by the prophet Mohammed,
> Because he (the victim) was a rebel against God.
> Do you assist in killing him.
> If you do not kill him,
> You shall be a rebel against God,
> A rebel against Mohammed.
> It is not I who am burying him.
> It is Gabriel who is burying him.
> Do you grant my prayer this day:
> Grant it by the grace of my petition within the fold of the creed
> La ilaha, etc."[440]

One might suppose that the audacity of blaspheming could rise no higher than this; but an Egyptian woman, when in labour, was taught to declare herself to be Isis, and to summon the gods to her help. "Should they refuse to come, 'Then shall ye be destroyed, ye nine gods; the heaven shall no longer exist, the earth shall no longer exist, the five days over and above the year shall cease to be; offerings shall no more be made to the gods, the lords of Heliopolis, etc.'"[441] If the facts were not before us, it would be incredible that a fixed purpose of obtaining supernatural aid should thus exclude from the mind all thoughts of the divine attributes and of one's own insignificance.

(3) What motives impel a man to adopt this strange and hazardous profession, or sustain him amidst all the dangers and disappointments of exercising it? In the first place, some men are oppressed by a vocation toward wizardry; just as amongst ourselves some men have an irresistible vocation to be poets, though that way poverty stares them in the face. To ordinary people these seem to be cases for the asylum. Yet we may understand the "votary of the Muses" by considering that the poet, as the master of rhythm, the treasurer of tradition, the arbiter of fame, has had a necessary place in the ancient culture of the tribes, and greatest in the noblest tribes. A tribe that produces poets has an advantage in the struggle of life; and, accordingly, a strain of poet-blood is bred in the tribe, and shows itself in a certain number of youths in each generation. I think the same must be true of wizards. They are often "called"; the Altaians believe that no man of his free will becomes a shaman.[442] Like poets, they are sacred and possessed. They are also very useful: their functions in several ways overlap those of the poet, as in cherishing traditions; and often they themselves are poets. They give confidence to their fellows amidst the awful imaginary dangers of savage life. Their nervous temper-

[440] W. W. Skeat, *Malay Magic*, p. 571.

[441] A. Wiedemann, *The Religion of the Egyptians*, pp. 273-4.

[442] A. M. Czaplicka, *Aboriginal Siberia*, p. 178.

ament may raise the vital level of a tribe. They keep alive the beliefs in taboo and the like mysterious dangers, on which savage order and morality depend; and in many cases they become leaders and chieftains. In this way, belief in Magic and Animism seems to have been the necessary scaffolding of social life.[443] And were this all, the utility of wizards would be clear. But they often do so much and such horrible mischief, prohibiting every improvement and spreading general terror, that it is difficult to judge, in such cases, whether their activities leave a balance of good or of evil. Perhaps sometimes the evil may exceed, and a tribe may degenerate and perish of it. On the whole, however, there is certainly a balance of good, especially by leadership at early stages of social development; and this accounts for the flourishing from age to age of the wizardly profession, and for the attraction it has for those of wizardly blood who enter it, because it promises to satisfy an innate disposition. Even in a civilised country, this disposition still, in a few people, manifests itself in the old way; but for the most part has been "sublimated" into other professions. Of course that which attracts the neophyte of wizardry is not the utility of the profession, any more than the youthful poet is allured by the utility of poetry. That which appeals to the wizard of inbred genius is (besides the indulgence of his personal powers) the mystery of wizardry; which excites in his soul a complex, consisting chiefly of curiosity as to the unknown powers that control nature and spirit, the fascination of fear in approaching them and an exaltation of self-consciousness at the prospect of attaining superhuman wisdom and authority. The article on Shamanism,[444] which I have cited so often, describes the shaman as sometimes profoundly convinced that he was chosen for the service of the spirits; and says that some feel a compulsive vocation, and endure persecution for their faith; they cannot help shamanising. One is mentioned as having been gifted with a sensitive nature and an ardent imagination, he had a strong belief in the spirits and in his own mysterious intercourse with them.

Men of such a temperament, I take it, distinguishing themselves above others when every man practised magic or sorcery, founded the profession, and are always its vital nucleus, though in time they may become but a small proportion of its members. Under sincere infatuation they established its observances—the fastings, sufferings, austerities, visions and frenzies of initiation, whether into magical knowledge or spiritual possession; the working of themselves up, whilst officiating, into the orgiastic intoxication in which they felt their own greatness and dominated their audience; and they discovered some of the modes of operating by drugs and suggestion and some real remedies. But the profession, once formed, soon had attractions for a very different sort of man, impelled by very different motives; who saw in it the road sometimes to wealth, always to reputation and power. Since, amongst very primitive people there is little wealth to collect, and sometimes (as we have seen) remuneration of magical services is neither given nor expected, the earlier of these motives must have been the love of causing wonder and fear, of the power which their fellows' fears conferred and of the reputation which consequently spread far and wide. In Mota (Melanesia) a man in control of magical virtue will render services without reward, merely to add to his reputa-

[443] J. G. Frazer, *Psyche's Task*.
[444] Pp. 138-9.

tion for the possession of *mana*.[445] At first they seem to have had no privileges, but power acquires privilege: so that, among the Warramunga, wizards are free from sexual taboos;[446] in Guiana no tribesman dares refuse the sorcerer anything, not even his wife;[447] among the Boloki, the sorcerer is never charged with injurious witchcraft and, therefore, is never in danger of the ordeal.[448]

Sometimes, indeed, the wizard may not be respected in private life, but only in the exercise of his office. Fear and wonder, in fact, do not always entirely blind the eyes of neighbours to his shortcomings. Spencer and Gillen tell us that the Magic of distant places, being the less known, is the more feared.[449] The Rev. J. H. Weeks even says that on the Congo the village medicine-man is seldom engaged at home; for the people know that his fetich cannot protect him or his from harm and, therefore, hire some one from another village of whom they know less.[450] Similarly, a tribe is apt to fear its own adepts less than those of another tribe of lower culture, whose ways are less known and more mysterious: as Malays fear especially the Jakuns;[451] formerly the Swedes the Finns, and the Finns the Lapps; the Todas the Kurumba;[452] and in Macedonia Mohammedan monks enjoy a far higher reputation for Magic than the Christian.[453]

Still, the wizard, whether of home or foreign growth, becomes necessary in every crisis of life, at birth and marriage, in misfortune, sickness and death; in every undertaking—hunting, agriculture or commerce; and by his omens and auguries may determine war and peace. After his own death, he may sometimes look forward to being deified. With such powers, surrounded by intimidated and dependent crowds, and often enjoying a long career of conscious or unconscious imposture, he seems to himself, as to others, a "superman"; his *Selbstgefühl* rises to megalomania, and his boasting becomes monstrous and stupefying.

(4) The more to impress the imagination of all spectators and enhance his reputation, the wizard usually affects a costume, or behaviour, or strange companionship of animals, that distinguishes him from the rest of his tribe. Not always; for Miss Czaplicka[454] says that in Siberia the shaman is in everyday life not distinguished from others, except occasionally by a haughty demeanour; but the rule is otherwise. A. W. Howitt[455] relates that one Australian medicine-man obtained influence by always carrying about with him a lace-lizard four feet long; another cherished a tame brown snake; and an old woman kept a native cat (*Daysurus*): "familiars" that correspond to the black cats and goats of our own witches. The Arunta medicine-man bores a hole in his tongue, appears with a broad band of

[445] Rivers, *History of Melanesian Sociology*, II. p. 156.
[446] Spencer and Gillen, *Northern Tribes of Central Australia*.
[447] im Thurn, op. cit., p. 339.
[448] J. H. Weeks, *Among Congo Cannibals*, p. 145.
[449] *Across Australia*, p. 350.
[450] *Primitive Bakongo*, p. 285.
[451] Skeat, *Pagan Races of the Malay Peninsula*, I. p. 563.
[452] Rivers, *The Todas*, p. 263.
[453] Abbot, *Macedonian Folk-Lore*, p. 225.
[454] Op. cit., p. 203.
[455] *Native Tribes of South-East Australia*, pp. 387-8.

powdered charcoal and fat across the bridge of his nose and learns to look preternaturally solemn, as one possessing knowledge hidden from ordinary men.[456] In the forest of the upper Amazons, the medicine-man does not depilate, though the rest of his tribe do so to distinguish themselves from monkeys; and he attempts to present in his costume something original and striking.[457] In S. Africa, too, the witch-doctor's dress is often very conspicuous. So it is throughout history: the thaumaturgist, by his wand, robes, austerities, demeanour, advertises himself as a man apart from the crowd. Rites of initiation mark this superiority: as tribal initiation separates a man from women and boys, so the wizard's initiation makes him a "superman."

(5) Such a temper cannot endure opposition, and is jealous of rivalry; the man whom it actuates lives in constant fear of failure and discredit and is, therefore, full of suspicion and cruelty. In S. Africa, professional hatred is pushed to its last limits amongst magicians. They test their colleagues, steal each other's drugs, or pray to the gods to make their rival's art inefficient.[458] The savage sorcerer looks with no kindly eye upon the European; who, too plainly, possesses extraordinary Magic. Captain Whiffen says[459] of the sorcerer amongst the South Amerinds, who has much knowledge of poisons, that to maintain his reputation, if he has declared that he cannot cure a patient, he poisons him. Of the sorcerer of the Lower Congo, Mr. Weeks says, that "his face becomes ugly, repulsive, the canvas on which cruelty, chicanery, hatred and all devilish passions are portrayed with repellent accuracy."[460] An extreme case perhaps; but, leading up to it, there are all degrees of rancour and malignity toward those who hinder our ambitions; and it can only be in exceptional magicians that megalomania is reconcilable with considerateness and magnanimity.

(6) Since the greater part of the wizard's practice is imposture (whether he believes in himself or not), he must be an actor; and his success must greatly depend on the degree in which he possesses the actor's special gifts and temperament: an audience must be a stimulus to him and not a check; he exhibits himself not unwillingly. To the shaman, Miss Czaplicka tells us,[461] an audience is useful: though the presence of an European is depressing. A Chuckchee shaman without a sort of chorus considers himself unable to discharge his office: novices in training usually get a brother or sister to respond to their exercises. And, indeed, a wizard's exhibitions often provide without design the same sort of social entertainment as those of an actor. One cannot read of the shaman's performance of a pantomimic journey on horseback to the South, over frozen mountains, burning deserts, and along the bridge of a single hair, stretched across a chasm over foaming whirlpools, to Erlik Khan's abode, and then home again on the back of a flying goose, without perceiving that in the wilds of Siberia such an entertainment, whatever other virtues it may have, supplies the want of theatres and music-halls, and that in such

[456] Spencer and Gillen, *Across Australia,* pp. 334-5.
[457] Whiffen, op. cit., pp. 182-3.
[458] Jounod, *Life of a South African Tribe,* II. p. 456.
[459] Whiffen, op. cit., pp. 64 and 168.
[460] *Primitive Bakongo,* p. 216.
[461] *Aboriginal Siberia,* pp. 230, 240.

displays a dramatic profession might originate.

But there are two kinds of actors; and they correspond well enough with the two kinds of wizards already described — the vocational and the exploitative. Some actors are said to identify themselves with their assumed character and situation so profoundly as to substantiate the fiction: concentration of imagination, amounting to dissociation, makes the part they play, whilst it lasts, more real than anything else; and raises them, for that time, in energy of thought, feeling and action, much above their ordinary powers; so that they compel the attention, sympathy and belief of the audience. But others study their part and determine beforehand exactly what tones, gestures, expressions are the most effective reinforcement of every word, and thereafter carry out upon the stage in cold blood the whole dramatic lesson which they have taught themselves. Perhaps more common than either of these extreme types is the actor who begins by studying under a sort of inspiration, and after experimenting for a few nights, repeats what he has found to answer best. We need not consider those who can do nothing but what they have been taught by others. Well, the wizard by vocation probably behaves like the first kind of actor: enters upon any office to which he may be called in exclusive devotion to his task; works himself into a frenzy, groans, writhes and sweats under the possession of his demon; chants incantations in an archaic tongue; drums and dances by the hour, and falls into speechless trance — according to the professional pattern — all in what may be described as dramatic good faith. By native disposition and by practised self-suggestion he obtains a temporary dissociation. The opposite sort of wizard, exploiting the profession, sees all this, and imitates it with such improvements as he may be able to devise. Of the intervening crowd of charlatans, who mingle self-delusion with deceit in all possible proportions, no definite account can be given.

According to Diderot,[462] the greatest actors belong to the second class, to the deliberate and disciplined artists. We may be sure the gods in the gallery, if they understood what was going on under their eyes, would always prefer the inspired performers. Probably these are, in fact, the greatest in their best hours, but less to be depended on, less sure of being always equal to themselves. And the same may be true of the corresponding sorts of wizards. The lucid impostor, at any rate, is less likely to be abashed by unforeseen difficulties and by the awkwardness of failure, less likely to be mobbed and murdered and pegged down in his grave with aspen stakes.

(7) Wizards are very often people who manifest an hysterical or epileptoid diathesis; and candidates for the profession who show signs of it are often preferred by the doctors. According to Miss Czaplicka, hysteria (common in Siberia) is at the bottom of the shaman's vocation: but it is not merely a matter of climate; for the Rev. E. T. Bryant writes of the Zulus — "the great majority of diviners being clearly of neurotic type";[463] and on all sides we obtain from descriptions of wizards the

[462] *Paradoxe sur le comédien*. Mr. William Archer, some years ago, published *Masks and Faces*, an entertaining and very instructive book, in which he (as a genuine though unprofessional psychologist) discusses this paradox in the light of evidence obtained, by *questionnaire* and otherwise, from actors then living.

[463] *Man*, September 1817, p. 144.

same impression. The word "shaman" comes not, as usually supposed, from the Sanskrit (*śramana* = work, a religious mendicant), but from *saman*, which is Manchu for "one who is excited, moved, raised."[464] The effect on the audience of shamanising depends in great measure upon the fits, ecstasy, convulsions introduced at some stage of the performance and attributed to possession by the spirits. Similar exhibitions have been reported by all observers of wizardry. Professor Otto Stoll of Zurich has described[465] the phenomena as they occur in all countries and all ages; and he attributes them, as well as hallucinations and analgesia (as in the fire-walk), which wizards also have at command, to the power of self-suggestion acquired by practice and training, on the basis (of course) of a natural disposition. Cagliostro declared that he could smell atheists and blasphemers; "the vapour from such throws him into epileptic fits; into which sacred disorder he, like a true juggler, has the art of falling when he likes."[466] The wizard's fits are voluntarily induced; but from the moment the attack takes place the development of its symptoms becomes automatic. Between the fits, however, says Miss Czaplicka, he must be able to master himself, or else he becomes incapable of his profession: nervous and excitable often to the verge of insanity, if he passes that verge he must retire.[467] In short, his ecstasy is the climacterical scene of his dramatic performance, the whole of which must be rendered with the disciplined accuracy of an artist. We are not to think of the shaman as an hysterical patient: if he were, there would be greater, not less, reason to suspect him of deceit. No doubt the training which gives control of the nervous attack protects the subject from its unwholesome consequences; there seems to be no special liability to disease or to a shortening of life. Formerly in Siberia, before the power of the profession was broken by immigrant beliefs and practices, it was necessary that the shaman should be well-developed mentally and physically (as has often been required of priests); and such a constitution is by no means incompatible with an intense histrionic temperament.

A necessary complement to the suggestive devices of a wizard is the suggestibility of his clients. There is such a thing as an assenting or a dissenting disposition—suggestibility or contrasuggestibility; but the latter is, like the former, a tendency to react without reflection, and may be as well controlled by appropriate suggestions. The power of any given suggestion to control the course of a man's thought and action depends upon the resistance (apart from contra-suggestibility) which it meets with in his mind; and this depends upon the extent, quality and integration of his apperceptive masses, and upon the facility with which they come into action. Upon the perceptual plane a savage's mind is well organised, and accordingly his suggestibility is low; but upon the ideational plane it is in most cases ill organised, poor in analysis, classification, generalisation, poor in knowledge, abounding in imagination-beliefs about Magic and Animism; so that, except in natural sceptics (who, as we shall see, exist among savages), the suggestions of the wizard meet with little resistance from common sense and with ready acceptance by magical and animistic prejudice. But even with a man of common

---

[464] *Aboriginal Siberia*, p. 197.
[465] *Suggestion und Hypnotismus in der Völkerpsychologie.*
[466] Meiners, *Briefe über die Schweiz* (quoted by Carlyle in essay on *Count Cagliostro*).
[467] *Aboriginal Siberia*, pp. 169, 172.

sense, a suggestion, however absurd, may for a time prevail, if his mental reaction is slow; although, with time for reflection, he will certainly reject it. The art of the wizard consists in getting such hold of his client's attention that, as in hypnosis, the power of reflective comparison is suspended and criticism abolished. There are many masters of this art. The client's state of mind is very common in the effects of oratory, the theatre, ghost-stories and generally in the propagation of opinion, suspicion and prejudice.

§ 4. The Wizard and the Sceptic

§ 4. *The Wizard and the Sceptic.* —Social delusion and imposture. Scepticism frequent amongst chiefs and the higher social ranks, and also amongst the people, because of common sense. Still more difficult for Wizards to maintain self-delusion

Inasmuch as the wizard's boasting, conjuring, ventriloquising, dramatising and practising of all the arts of suggestion, seem incompatible with sincerity, whilst nevertheless he is devoted to his calling, some observers have declared him a calculating impostor, whilst others maintain that he, in various degrees, believes in himself and shares the delusions which he propagates. Examples may be found in support of either position.

Some say that the wizard believes in himself because all others believe in him; that at a certain level of culture, there is an universal social obsession by certain ideas, from which the individual cannot escape, and for whose consequences, therefore, he is not responsible. According to this theory, a sort of tribal insanity prevails. Dr. Mercier says that, in the individual, paranoia is characterised by systematised delusion: "there is an organised body of (false) knowledge, and it differs from other delusions in the fact that it colours the whole life of the patient; it regulates his daily conduct; it provides him with an explanation of all his experiences; it is his theory of the cosmos." And, again, "as long as the highest level of thought is intact, so that we can and do recognise that our mistakes are mistakes and our disorders, whether of mind or conduct, are disorders, so long sanity is unaffected, and our mistakes and disorders are sane. As soon, however, as we become incompetent to make this adjustment ... insanity is established."[468] These passages exactly describe the condition of a wizard and his tribe afflicted with social paranoia: their theories of Magic and Animism and of the wizard's relations with invisible powers, may truly be said to form an organised body of (false) knowledge, to colour all their lives, to explain everything that happens to them; and their mistakes and disorders to be incorrigible by reflection or experience. Such conditions of the social mind have, I believe, existed (and may still exist), tending toward, and sometimes ending in, a tribe's destruction. That, in such a case, there should be unanimity is not necessary; it is enough that the current of belief, in certain directions, be overwhelming. But such extreme cases are rare. Normally there may be found, even in backward tribes, a good deal of incredulity and of what may be called primitive rationalism or positivism.

Considerable sections of a tribe sometimes co-operate in imposture, the men

[468] *Text-book of Insanity*, pp. 281 and 79.

against the women and children, or the old against the young; and it cannot be supposed that, where this occurs, anything like universal delusion prevails. The Arunta, who teach their women and children that Twanyiriki is a spirit living in wild regions, who attends initiations, and that the noise of the bull-roarer is his voice; whilst they reveal to the youths when initiated that the bundle of churinga is the true Twanyiriki,[469] cannot be blind to the existence of social fictions. The discovery by initiated youths in some parts of New Guinea, that Balum, the monster that is believed to swallow them during initiation, is nothing but a bug-a-boo, and that his growl is only the bull-roarer, must be a shock to their credulity.[470] Indeed, disillusionment as to some popular superstition is a common characteristic of initiation ceremonies.[471] On the mainland of New Caledonia, a spirit-night is held every five months; when the people assemble around a cave and call upon the ghosts, supposed to be inside it, to sing; and they do sing—the nasal squeak of old men and women predominating.[472] There is not in such cases any natural growth of social delusion, subduing the individual mind, but prearranged cozenage; and a wizard with such surroundings, instead of being confirmed in the genuineness of his art, only reads there the method of his own imposture in large type.[473]

Home-bred wizards, who are less trusted than those who live further off, or than those of an inferior tribe, do not derive self-confidence from the unanimous approval of their neighbours.

Again, the general prevalence of delusions in a tribe does not suppress the scepticism of individuals. It is reasonable to expect such scepticism to be most prevalent amongst men of rank, who are comparatively exempt from the oppression of popular sanctions; and probably this is the fact. Such exemption, by preserving a nucleus of relatively sane people, is one of the great social utilities of rank. The Basuto chief, Mokatchané, surrounded by people grossly superstitious, lent himself to their practices; but in paying his diviners he did not hesitate so say "that he regarded them as the biggest impostors in the world."[474] In Fiji, it is doubtful whether the high chiefs believed in the inspiration of the priests, though it suited their policy to appear to do so. There was an understanding between the two orders: one got sacrifices (food), the other good oracles. A chieftain, on receiving an unfavourable oracle, said to the priest: "Who are you? Who is your god? If you make a stir, I will eat you"[475]—not metaphorically. In Tonga, "even seventeen years before the arrival of the first missionaries, the chiefs did not care to conceal their scepticism." In Vavou, Taufaahan, having long been sceptical of his ancestral faith, on learning of Christianity, hanged five idols by the neck, beat the priestess, and burned the spirit-houses.[476] The Vikings, like the Homeric heroes,

---

[469] Spencer and Gillen, *Northern Tribes of Central Australia*, p. 497.

[470] J. G. Frazer, *Belief in Immortality*, pp. 250-60.

[471] For another example see Rivers, *History of Melanesian Sociology*, II. p. 411.

[472] G. Turner, *Samoa*, p. 346.

[473] For the most elaborate of all such performances, see the initiation into the Ghost Society of the Kwakintle Indians, in Frazer's *Totemism and Exogamy*, III. p. 538.

[474] Casalis, *My Life in Basuto Land*, p. 185.

[475] Basil Thompson, *The Fijians*, p. 158.

[476] Basil Thompson, *Diversions of a Prime Minister*, pp. 201 and 346.

are said to have fought their gods; and at other times to have declared entire disbelief in them. Hence the easy conversion of the North to Christianity. Scepticism may have been fashionable at court much earlier: "It is scarcely possible to doubt," says Mr. Chadwick, "that familiarity, not to say levity, in the treatment of the gods characterised the Heroic Age [Teutonic—A.D. 350-550] just as much as that of the Vikings."[477] The burlesque representations of the gods in some passages of the *Iliad* are a sort of atheism: in astonishing contrast with the sublime piety elsewhere expressed. And the inadequacy of such a literary religion (like that of Valhalla) may explain the facile reception (or revival) of the Mysteries in the sixth century B.C. History abounds with examples of rulers and priests who, in collusion, have used religion for political convenience, in a way that implied their own disbelief and opened unintentionally the doors of disbelief to others.

But it is not only chiefs and heroes whose minds are sometimes emancipated from popular superstitions. An old Australian whose duty it was to watch the bones of a dead man and to keep alight a fire near them, sold them for some tobacco and a tomahawk, in great fear lest it should be known to his tribesmen; but he "evidently suffered from no qualms of conscience":[478] that is to say, he feared the living, but not the dead. W. Stanbridge says of the aborigines of Victoria that "there are doctors or priests of several vocations; of the rain, of rivers and of human diseases ... but there are natives who refuse to become doctors and disbelieve altogether the pretensions of those persons."[479] John Matthew writes of the tribe with which he was best acquainted—"whilst the blacks had a term for ghosts and behind these were departed spirits, ... individual men would tell you upon inquiry that they believed that death was the last of them."[480] Near Cape King William in New Guinea, there is a general belief in spirits and ghosts and also in one Mate; but some whisper that there is no such being.[481] The Bakongo villagers do not believe in all witchcraft; but respect some sorcerers, and regard others with more or less contempt: every man, however, must profess belief, or else "his life will be made wretched by accusations of witchcraft."[482] Before missionaries came amongst the Baloki, many people had no faith in the medicine-men, but would not oppose them for fear of being charged with witchcraft.[483] The religious convictions of the Zulus were very shallow; belief in the spirit-world depended on prosperity: "fullness declares the Itongo exists; affliction says it does not exist." ... "For my part, I say the Amadhlozi of our house died forever."[484] Capt. Whiffen reports of the tribes of S. Amerinds whom he visited that, "among individuals there are sceptics of every grade."[485] Whilst all Dakotas reverence the great, intangible, mysterious power Takoo-Wahkon, as to particular divinities, any man

[477] *The Heroic Age*, p. 413.

[478] Spencer and Gillen, *Across Australia*, pp. 374-5.

[479] "Aborigines of Victoria," *Transactions of the Ethnological Society*, New Series, I. p. 300.

[480] *Eagle-hawk and Crow*, p. 146.

[481] J. G. Frazer, *Belief in Immortality*, p. 239.

[482] J. H. Weeks, *The Primitive Bakongo*, pp. 284 and 285.

[483] J. H. Weeks, *Among Congo Cannibals*, p. 293.

[484] Callaway, op. cit., pp. 29-30.

[485] *The North-West Amazons*, p. 218.

may worship some and despise others. "One speaks of the medicine-dance with respect; another smiles at the name." The Assiniboin generally believe that good ghosts migrate to the south where game is abundant; whilst the wicked go northward; but some think that death ends all.[486] At Ureparapara (Banks Islands) food is buried with a corpse; and "if there be too much, some is hung above the grave, whence the bolder people take it secretly and eat it."[487] Disbelief is expressed in actions more emphatically than in words; the plundering of tombs has been universal. An idol-maker of Maeva assured Ellis that, "although at times he thought it was all deception and only practised his trade for gain, yet at other times he really thought the gods he himself had made were powerful beings."[488] In Tonga it was orthodox that chiefs and their retainers were immortal, doubtful whether men of the third rank were so, certain that those of the lowest rank, Tooas, were not; their souls died with the body; yet some of these Tooas ventured to think that they too would live again.[489] A sceptical Kayan could hardly believe that men continue to exist after death; for then they would return to visit those they love. "But," he concluded, "who knows?" The traditionary lore of the Kayans answers many deep questions; but the keener intelligences inquire further—"why do the dead become visible only in dreams?" etc.[490] A Tanghul told me, says Mr. T. C. Hodson, that no one had ever seen a Lai (deity): when things happened men said a Lai had done it. "In his view clearly a Lai was a mere hypothesis."[491]

Of such examples of the occurrence of "free-thought" in all parts of the world, no doubt, a little investigation would discover many more. Everywhere some savages think for themselves; though, like civilised folk, they cannot always venture to avow their conclusions. We must not suppose that belief is as uniform as custom or conventional doctrine: custom and convention hinder thought in dull people, but do not enslave it in the "keener intelligence." Without the enviable advantage of personal intimacy with savages, I have, by reading about them, gained the impression that they enjoy a considerable measure of individuality—as much as the less educated Europeans—and are not mere creatures of a social environment.

The most backward savages have a large stock of common sense concerning the properties of bodies, of wind and water and fire, of plants and animals and human nature; for this is the necessary ground of their life. This common sense has certain characters which are in conflict with their superstitions; the facts known to common sense are regular, proportional, the same for all; not often failing and needing excuses, not extravagant and disconnected, not depending on the presence of some fantastic mountebank. Savages do not draw explicitly the comparisons that make this conflict apparent; but it may be felt without being defined. Some of them, especially, are (as amongst ourselves) naturally inclined to a positive way of thinking; their common sense predominates over the suggestions of Magic and Animism, and they, more than others aware of the conflict, become the

[486] J. O. Dorsey, "Siouan Cults," pp. 431-2 and 485, *Am. B. of Ethn.*, XI.
[487] Coddrington, *The Melanesians*, p. 270.
[488] *Polynesian Researches*, II. p. 204.
[489] John Martin, *W. Mariner's Account of the Tonga Islands*, II. pp. 105 and 137.
[490] Hose and McDougall, *The Pagan Tribes of Borneo*, II. pp. 48 and 214.
[491] *The Naga Tribes of Manipur*, p. 126.

proto-sceptics or rationalists. Lecky observes that beliefs and changes of belief depend not upon definite arguments, but upon habits of thought. In the seventeenth century a new habit of thought overcame the belief in witchcraft and miracles;[492] and in many other centuries it has everywhere done the same for those in whom the "apperceptive mass" of common sense became more or less clearly and steadily a standard of belief, repelling the apperceptive masses of Magic and Animism with all their contents and alliances. They had more definite ideas than others, little love of the marvellous, little subjection to fear, desire, imagination.

Sometimes the dictates of common sense are imposed by necessity. The Motu (Papuasian) were accustomed to rub spears with ginger to make them fly straight. It had, however, been discovered that no amount of Magic would turn a poor spearman into an accurate thrower.[493] Spear-throwing is too serious a concern not to be judged of upon its merits, however interesting the properties of ginger. A whole tribe may in some vital matter, whilst practising a superstitious rite, disregard its significance: like the Kalims, who hold a crop-festival in January, and afterwards take the omens as to what ground shall be cultivated for next harvest; "but this seems a relic of old times, for the circle of cultivation is never broken, let the omens be what they may."[494] That is a tacit triumph of common sense.

The bearing of all this on the character of the wizard is as follows: since everywhere sceptics occur, and some individuals go further than others in openly or secretly rejecting superstitions, why should not the wizard or sorcerer, who is amongst the most intelligent and daring of his tribe, be himself a rationalist and, therefore, a conscious impostor? That much of his art is imposture no one disputes; and so far as it is so, he sees it as part of the ordinary course of experience. The sorcerer on the Congo who drove a spirit into the dark corner of a hut, stabbed it there, and showed the blood upon his spear, having produced the blood (as his son confessed to Mr. Weeks) by scratching his own gums, was by that action himself instructed in common sense.[495] He saw in it quite plainly an ordinary course of events, the "routine of experience"; whilst the spectators were mystified. Must he not, then, have more common sense than other people?

In fact, he recognises the course of nature and his own impotence, whenever an attempt to conjure would endanger his reputation. The Arunta medicine-men exhibit great dramatic action in curing various diseases; but waste no antics on recognisable senile decay.[496] The medicine-man of Torres Straits admits that he cannot make a "big wind" from the south-east during the north-west season.[497] The Polynesian sorcerers confessed their practices harmless to Europeans;[498]—who were not suggestible on that plane of ideas. Shamans amongst the Yakuts would not try to cure diarrhœa, small-pox, syphilis, scrofula or leprosy, and would not

[492] Introduction to *The Rise of the Spirit of Rationalism in Europe*.

[493] C. G. Seligman, *Melanesians of British New Guinea*, p. 179.

[494] T. C. Hodson, op. cit., p. 171.

[495] *Among Congo Cannibals*, p. 284.

[496] Spencer and Gillen, *Native Tribes of Central Australia*, pp. 531-2.

[497] Haddon, *Reports of the Cambridge Expedition to Torres Straits*, VI. p. 201.

[498] Ellis, op. cit., II. p. 232.

shamanise in a house where small-pox had been.[499] These miracle-mongers some-times know a hawk from a handsaw. It seems reasonable, then, to assume that wizards have more common sense than other people; since, besides the instruction of common experience, they know in their professional practice (at least in a su-perficial way) the real course of events, which is concealed from the laity. And, no doubt, of those whose art is deliberate imposture, this is true. But the infatuation of those who are wizards by vocation may be incorrigible by any kind of evidence: especially as to the genuineness of another's performance. Dr. Rivers speaks of the blindness of the man of rude culture to deceitful proceedings on the part of others with which he is familiar in his own actions.[500] For the wizard there are estab-lished prejudices, professional and personal interest, fear of trusting his own judg-ment, supernatural responsibility, desire of superhuman power, sometimes even a passionate desire to alleviate the sufferings of his tribesmen, and everything else that confirms the will to believe.

§ 5. The Wizard's Persuasion

§ 5. *The Wizard's Persuasion.* — Honesty and fraud. The Wizard by vo-
cation. Fascination of Black Wizardry. Artifices professionally
necessary seem justified by social utility. His belief strengthened
by effects of natural causes set going by himself or by his clients,
and by coincidences

Many practices of wizards involve a representation of the course of events as something very different from the reality; and there is no doubt that frequently, or even in most cases, wizards are aware of this, as in performing the sucking cure or visiting the man in the moon. But some anthropologists dislike to hear such practices described as "fraud," "imposture" or "deceit"; and for certain classes of wizards it seems (as I shall show) unjust to speak in these terms of their profession. Still, taking the profession and its actions on the whole, it is difficult to find in pop-ular language terms more fairly descriptive. We meet here the inconvenience that other social or moral sciences find when they try to use common words in a spe-cially restricted sense. In Economics, e. g., "rent," "wages," "profits" have definite meanings very different from their popular acceptance. In Ethics, what controver-sy, what confusion in the defining of "virtue" and "the good"! In Metaphysics, what is the meaning of "cause"; what is the meaning of "intuition"? The terms must be defined in each system. If then, in these pages, the conduct of a man who, on his way to cure a sufferer of "stitch in the side," conceals in his mouth a piece of bone or pebble, and after dancing, and sucking hard enough at the patient's belly, produces that bone or pebble as the cause of pain — is described as "fraud," or "imposture," or "deceit," the words are used to describe the fact only, without any such imputation upon the man's character as they convey in popular usage. Scientifically considered, the man and his circumstances being such as they are, his actions are a necessary consequence; in this limited region of thought moral censure is irrelevant.

[499] *Shamanism*, p. 92.
[500] *History of Melanesian Society*, II. p. 107.

There are some wizards, as it were in minor orders, such as Professor Seligman calls "departmental experts," especially the man who blesses gardens, so earnest and harmless that no one will abuse them. They visit the garden at the owner's request, practise a little hocus-pocus, mutter a few spells, take a small fee and go peaceably home. The owner indeed supposes himself to buy fertility, and obtains only peace of mind—a greater good say the moralists. The wizard has done what he learnt of his father, what respectable neighbours approve of; there is always some crop to justify his ministry, and many an evil power to excuse occasional blight or drought. If he is convinced of being a really indispensable man, it is easily intelligible.

As to the profession in general, a small number of wizards—wizards by vocation—may be strongly persuaded of the genuineness of the art; a much larger body mingles credulity in various proportions with fraud; and not a few are deliberate cheats. Some of the greatest masters of wizardry are dissatisfied with their own colleagues: that eminent shaman Scratching Woman said to Bogoras the traveller, "There are many liars in our calling."[501] On the other hand, the wizard who demonstrated the "pointing-stick" to Messrs. Spencer and Gillen, and having no object upon which to discharge its Magic, thought it had entered his own head and thereupon fell ill, was certainly a believer;[502] and so was the wizard who felt that he had lost his power after drinking a cup of tea, because hot drinks were taboo to him.[503] Now a cheat needs no explanation—at least no more on the Yenisei than on the Thames; and the variety of those who mingle credulity with fraud is too great to be dealt with. What chiefly needs to be accounted for is the persuasion of those who—in spite of so many circumstances that seem to make disillusion inevitable—are in some manner true believers—in the manner, that is to say, of imaginative belief, founded on tradition and desire, unlike the perceptual belief of common sense.

(*a*) Men under a vocation to wizardry, of course, begin with full belief in it. Probably they are possessed by the imaginative and histrionic temperament, which we have seen to be favourable to eminence as a wizard. Their vocation consists in the warm sympathy and emulation with which, before their own initiation, they witness the feats of great practitioners, and which generally imply a stirring of their own latent powers; just as many an actor has begun by being "stage-struck." A man of such temperament is prone to self-delusion not only as to his own powers, but in other ways. The wizard often begins by fasting and having visions; thereby weakening his apprehension of the difference between fact and phantasy. The fixed idea of his calling begets in his imagination a story of what happened at his initiation, manifestly false, but not a falsehood—a "rationalisation" according to wizardly ideas of what he can remember of that time. If initiated with torture, which he endures for the sake of his vocation, he is confirmed in it. When called upon to perform, he "works himself up" by music, dancing and whatever arts he may have learned or discovered, into a state of dissociation, during which his judgment of everything extraneous to his task is suspended; and his dramatic de-

[501] A. M. Czaplicka, *Aboriginal Siberia*, p. 180.

[502] *Across Australia*, p. 326.

[503] Spencer and Gillen, *Northern Tribes of Central Australia*, p. 481.

meanour uninhibited by fear or shame, unembarrassed by any second thoughts, makes, by vivid gestures and contortions and thrilling tones, a profound impression upon patients, clients and witnesses. His performances may derive some original traits from his own genius; but must generally conform to a traditionary pattern and to the consequent expectations of the audience. By practice he acquires—as for their own tasks all artists, poets and actors must—a facility in inducing the state of dissociation (more or less strict), in which work goes smoothly forward under the exclusive dominance of a certain group of ideas and sentiments. Whether, in this condition, he believes in himself and his calling, or not, is a meaningless question. Whilst the orgasm lasts there is no place for comparison or doubt. And since he really produces by his frenzy or possession a great effect upon the spectators—though not always the precise effect of curing a patient or of controlling the weather at which he aimed—we need not wonder if he believes himself capable of much more than he ever accomplishes. The temperament, most favourable to a wizard's success is not likely to be accompanied by a disposition to the positive or sceptical attitude of mind. Moreover, to the enthusiast for whom belief is necessary, it is also necessary to create the evidence. That the end justifies the means is not his explicit maxim, but a matter of course. Gibbon comments on "the vicissitudes of pious fraud and hypocrisy, which may be observed, or at least suspected, in the characters of the most conscientious fanatics."[504] After failures, indeed, or in the languor that follows his transports, there may come many chilling reflections; only, however, to be dispersed by an invincible desire to believe in his own powers and in the profession to which he is committed.

The "white" wizard may pacify a troubled conscience by reflecting that at any rate he discharges a useful social function; as, in fact, he does, so far as he relieves the fears of his tribesmen and gives them confidence. To understand the "black" wizard, we must turn to the dark side of human nature. That a man should resort to magic or sorcery to avenge himself or his kinsmen, or to gratify his carnality, jealousy or ambition, is intelligible to everybody; but that he should make a profession of assisting others for a fee to betray, injure, or destroy those with whom he has no quarrel, seems almost too unnatural to be credible. Yet it admits of a very easy explanation. The love of injuring and slaying is deeply rooted in us: men afflicted with homicidal neurosis are known to the asylums and to the criminal courts of all civilised nations; assassins on hire have often been notoriously obtainable. To slay in cold blood by violence, or even by poison, seems, however, less revolting than to slay by sorcery and obscene rites. But the fascination of this employment may be further understood by considering the attraction that secret power and the proof of their own cunning has for many people. To slay is sweet; but the ancient hunter depended more upon strategy than upon the frontal attack; and no strategy is so secret or needs so much skill as the Black Art. Finally, if sorcery is persecuted, it excites the contra-suggestibility which in some neurotics becomes a passion capable of supporting them at the stake. Hence the malevolent wizard may feel a vocation, may believe in his own powers; and, of course, he will be confirmed in his belief by the fear excited wherever his reputation spreads. If you put yourself in his place whilst practising some unholy rite, you may become

[504] *Decline and Fall*, ch. xvii—discussing the character of Julian.

aware that the secrecy, the cunning, the danger, the villainy and the elation of it exert a peculiar fascination, and that this is enhanced by foul and horrible usages, such as appeal to the perverted appetites of insanity.

(*b*) The deceit employed by a wizard in conjuring, ventriloquising, dressing up, keeping a "familiar," choosing favourable opportunities for his *séance* and inciting himself to frenzy, seems incompatible with sincerity; but whilst he knows such proceedings to be artifices, he also knows them to be necessary to the effect which he produces. For that effect, so far as it depends upon wizardly practices, not on such means as massage, or poisons, or drugs, is always subjective—an influence on other men's belief. Are we not demanding of him greater discrimination than he is likely to enjoy, if we expect him to see the hollowness of his profession, because some of the means by which he operates are not what his clients suppose them to be? If it be said that the wizard's stock excuses for failure—that there has been a mistake in the rites, or that another wizard has counteracted his efforts—are those of a man who has anticipated detection in fraud and prepared a way of escape, it may be replied that, according to accepted tenets concerning wizardry, these excuses are reasonable and not necessarily subterfuges.

The professional attitude may induce a man to exonerate himself and his colleagues in certain dubious dealings, for the sake of the public utility of their office on the whole; which is so manifest to him and to them, and is also acknowledged by the public. For a wizard's belief in his art is supported by the testimony of other wizards, in whom he also believes, and by the belief of the tribe generally in the power of the profession, even though he himself be not greatly esteemed. "Who am I," he will ask, "that I should have a conscience of my own?" And if this attitude is inconsistent with keen intelligence and megalomania, such inconsistency is not inconsistent with our experience of human nature.

(*c*) The effects produced by charms, spells and rites, simple or to the last degree elaborate, purely magical or reinforced by spirits, are always subjective, but are believed to have a much wider range. The wizard seems to make the sun rise when he summons it just in time every morning; to cause clouds to gather in the sky when he invokes them just before the rainy season; and so on. Such performances convince others, but seem to us poor evidence for any one who is in the secret. He is not, however, left without further evidence of three kinds:

(i) From the effects of natural causes that form part of his professional resources. Some of a wizard's practices are really good; e. g. in curing the sick he may employ massage, or sweat-baths, or skilful surgery, or medicinal drugs, or suggestion, and thereby succeed without any Magic; whilst he is incapable of clearly distinguishing these means from useless rites and incantations. He does not understand intimately why *any* method is efficacious, and therefore cannot understand the limits of his power. His whole art is empirical. Even in modern science explanation always ends sooner or later (and often pretty soon) in pointing to some connexion of phenomena which we are obliged to accept as a fact: the wizard is always brought to this pass at the first step. He has no generally acknowledged public standard of what may possibly happen: it is only in the mind of a natural positivist that a standard of common sense grows up by experience without explicit generalisation; and this standard is incommunicable. Hence the wizard is always trying experimentally to extend his power—of course on the model of his traditionary art; always desiring power, and believing that he has obtained, because he desires it.

(ii) The wizard's arts are justified by the action of natural causes set in motion by his clients. He prepares the hunter and his weapons for an expedition; the hunter does his best, and his success swells the reputation of the wizard. Similarly in agriculture, and in war. And in all these cases nothing is really due to the wizard, except the greater confidence his clients derive from his ministrations: the hunter's hand is steadier; the sower and the reaper work more cheerfully; and the warrior fights more courageously in the belief that his enemies are surely devoted to the infernal gods. But the wizard, with general acquiescence, claims far more than this, and rises in his own esteem as well as in the esteem of his tribe.

(iii) The persevering wizard is often aided by coincidences. An Australian squatter at Morton's Plains, after a drought, promised a native rain-maker half a bullock, a bag of flour and some tea, if he would fill his new tank for him before the morrow night. The rain-maker set his rites and spells to work, filled the tank and got the reward.[505] Whilst Messrs. Spencer and Gillen were with the Urabunna tribe, "the leading rain-maker performed a ceremony and within two days there was a downpour—possibly connected with the fact that it was the usual time for rain to fall in that part of the country." The reputation of the rain-maker was firmly established, and, no doubt, his self-confidence. The Australian wizard already mentioned, who thought that his Magic had entered his own head, claimed to have driven away a comet by means of his magic stones. Certainly the comet disappeared, and what other cause could any one point out? "At one time the gusts were very unpleasant and one of the men told a wind-man to make it stop. Accordingly he shouted out to the wind, and in a minute there was a lull; and no one doubted that this was due to the power of the wind-man."[506] Many similar cases might be given.[507] Striking coincidences are not very rare: there is an illogical prejudice that they are rare because they excite wonder. Moreover, as I have observed, so remote a resemblance to the event shamanised or prophesied may be regarded as a fulfilment, that fulfilment is not uncommon. In the interpretation of omens, where there is only the alternative of good or ill success, half the guesses must be right; and by the glozing of doubtful cases, more than half will seem to be right. And as for the effect of coincidence, Mr. Basil Thompson says, "Tongans never admit coincidences"[508]—that is to say, in our sense of the word: for them, in what we call coincidence, there must be causation; and this seems to be generally true of the

---

[505] Howitt, *Native Tribes of South-East Australia*, p. 398.

[506] *Across Australia*, pp. 14, 326, 366.

[507] See Haddon, *Reports of the Cambridge Expedition to Torres Straits*, VI. p. 210; Stefánson, *My Life with the Esquimo*, p. 88; Murdoch, Ethnological Results of the Point Barrow Expedition, in *Ninth Ann. Report of Am. Bureau of Eth.*, p. 431; Frazer, *Psyche's Task*, p. 55; Risley, *The People of India*, p. 77; Langloh Parker, *The Euahlayi Tribe*, pp. 48, 49, 82, 90; Dudley Kidd, *The Essential Kafir*, p. 116; E. Casalis, *Les Bassoutos* (2nd ed.), pp. 302-3; W. E. Roth, *Ethnological Studies in North-West Central Queensland*, p. 154.

[508] *Diversions of a Prime Minister*, p. 245.

untutored mind. Among the Churaches, the profession of shaman is generally hereditary; but a man may become a shaman against his will. It is enough "to make a lucky guess as to the issue of some event, and people flock to him for advice from all parts."[509] How many failures are necessary to discredit one lucky guess?

These three kinds of evidence in favour of the wizard's power—natural causes set in motion by himself, natural causes introduced by his clients, and sheer favourable coincidences—have so much the air of perceptual proof, or of an appeal to common sense, that the savage positivist who is able to resist them must have a more solid judgment than most of our educated civilised people. Judgment is an innate individual character, on which education has little effect, except in the special department of a man's training. A scientific expert, for example, may be an excellent judge of evidence in his own pursuit, and elsewhere quite helpless; for where he is strong it is not a set of rules but the mass of his special experience that guides him. That out of the mass of general experience, so disorderly and fragmentary as it is, some minds should have the power of extracting common sense, in spite of the misrepresentations of Magic and Animism, is very remarkable, and very fortunate for the rest of us.

That the three kinds of evidence which serve so well to confirm belief in wizardry are all of them—as to the connexion between a wizard's rites or spells and the event—entirely coincidental, gives some support to the hypothesis that coincidences are the foundation of the belief in Magic.

Bearing in mind, then, that a wizard's practices sometimes include real causes, and that his shallow knowledge disables him for discriminating between causation and hocus-pocus; that Magic or Sorcery is generally believed in by those about him, who seek his aid, or the aid of others of his class; that both they and he earnestly desire that his pretensions should be well founded; that he produces striking subjective effects; that in such cases his artifices are a condition of his success, and that a good many coincidences, complete or partial, seem to prove that his art has further extraordinary influence upon men and nature—it is no wonder that some wizards are deluded along with their dupes, especially neurotic enthusiasts or men of an imaginative and histrionic temperament.

To explain the possibility of some men being sincere in witchcraft is not to palliate the profession, much less the anti-social practices of witchcraft. For the most part those practices are deceitful. They are not the invention of savage society; society invents nothing; only the individual invents. They are the invention and tradition of wizards, who keep the secret so far as it is to their advantage: of wizards growing more and more professional, and trading upon the fears and hopes, the anxiety and credulity of their fellows. The spirit of superstition is common to the tribe, but its professional exploitation is the work of those who profit by it.

Observing with satisfaction that, even amongst savages, the positive mind can sometimes free itself from popular superstitions and penetrate the disguise of mystery-mongers, one asks why Nature could not produce whole tribes of men so minded, and spare the folly and horror and iniquity which take up so much space

____

[509] "Shamanism," *Journal of the Anthropological Institute*, XXIV. p. 154.

in the retrospect of human life. Because common sense is only related to actual experience, and could not appreciate the necessity of government and social co-ordination as the condition of all improvement in human life, until it already existed. Such co-ordination had, therefore, to grow up without being understood; and it did grow up under the protection of certain beliefs that induced the tribes of men to hold together and subordinate themselves to leaders: amongst which beliefs the superstitions exploited by wizards had no small part.

CHAPTER IX
TOTEMISM

§ 1. Meaning and Scope of Totemism

§ 1. *Meaning and Scope of Totemism.* — Frazer's definitions. The Clan-Totem, and observances connected with it

Of very much less importance in the history of culture than Animism or Magic, Totemism interests us by its strangeness. To be descended from a crocodile, or blood-brother to the crow, or "the same as a kangaroo" must be, we think, the grotesque notion of a lunatic. We never meet people who believe such a thing; it has no stronghold in our own breasts. So much the more surprising that it should, nevertheless, be widely entertained. It is, indeed, far from universal among mankind, probably much less ancient than Animism and certainly far less enduring. Where it has prevailed it is sometimes quite forgotten; and in the higher stages of human development it has no influence. But every student of early institutions finds it necessary to give himself some intelligible account of its nature and sources.

"A Totem," says Sir James Frazer, "is a class of material objects which a savage regards with superstitious respect, believing that there exists between him and every member of the class an intimate and altogether special relation."[510]

This definition is scientifically drawn so as to include what is common to all Totems and not to include any character that is not universally connected with them. It is true of the Totems of individuals (or guardian genii), very common among the Northern Amerinds; as well as of the Sex-Totems (say Bat for men and Owl for women) which occur in Australia; and of the Totems of clans found in many parts of the world, of which the Australian may be supposed most nearly to represent the original institution. When one speaks of Totems without qualification, one means these Clan-Totems, being incomparably the most important:

---

[510] *Totemism and Exogamy*, I. p. 3. The definition occurs in a reprint of an earlier essay. A later definition (IV. p. 3) runs: "Totemism is an intimate relation which is supposed to exist between a group of kindred people on the one side and a species of natural or artificial objects on the other side, which objects are called the totems of the human group." The relation appears to be one of friendship and kinship, on a footing of equality, not religious in Australia. I have, in this chapter, drawn freely upon the great mass of facts and speculations collected in *Totemism and Exogamy*; believing that in that work the author not only intended to present the evidence for his own conclusions, but had also the benevolent purpose of assisting the labours of those who might come after him. A heavy debt of gratitude is due; which, indeed, causes some embarrassment if ever one feels obliged to differ from him in opinion.

others probably derive from them.

"The Clan-Totem" (to quote the same source) "is reverenced by a body of men and women who call themselves by the name of the Totem, believe themselves to be of one blood, descendants of a common ancestor, and are bound together by common obligations to each other and by a common faith in the Totem."[511] This definition is also strict: whereas it is not uncommon for writers on Totemism to include in their notion of the Totem other characters which are accidents more or less often associated with it: as that the clan believes itself descended from the Totem; though in many cases the clan traces its origin to something that was neither Totem nor man, or regards the Totem animal as descended from their own human ancestress, or tells some story of the transformation of a man into an animal, or of an animal into a man, or of an ancestor's friendship with the Totem animal; for the institution is a copious source of explanatory myths. Again, it may be written that no member of a clan may kill or injure the Totem, or eat, or utilise it (if an animal or plant); and this is often, but not always true. If the Totem is water, or the most important food in the district—dugong, turtle, coconut, sago—abstention is impossible or intolerably inconvenient. Hence among the Kaitish a Water clansman when alone may drink; but if others are with him he may drink only when water is given him by a man of another Totem. And to eat a little of the Totem sacramentally, in order to confirm one's identity with it, may be allowed or (rather) required. Among the Warramunga the Snake clan may kill snakes. It may even be the clan's duty to destroy or drive away their Totem; as happens with the Mosquito clan of the Kakadus in North Australia, and with the Reptile clan amongst the Omahas. Similarly, the clan sometimes, but by no means always, imitate the Totem in character, in costume, in dances, or bear in tattoo or otherwise its badge to manifest the community of nature. They may be thought to have special magical powers to influence its fertility or to control its actions (actions of game or wind or rain), and may use these powers for the benefit of the tribe. At death the soul of a clansman may pass into, or may appear as, the Totem animal. The Totem may be the protector of its clansmen, and in some cases it seems to have become a god. These accidents of Totemism, however, are very irregularly diffused and some of them are rare.

Most important socially is the connexion between Totemism and Marriage-customs. In the great majority of cases, men and women of the same Totem may not intermarry; the Totem clans are said to be exogamous; but there are exceptions even to this rule. In many parts of the world—America, Africa, India, Indonesia, as well as Australia—tribes are divided into non-intermarrying or exogamous classes (moieties or phratries); sometimes the classes are subdivided, and even the sub-classes again (in parts of Australia), so that in all the exogamous classes are eight; and the rules concerning these classes are such as to prevent the marriage of brothers and sisters, parents and children and first cousins. The Totem clans are usually distributed amongst the Marriage-classes; being probably the older institution (whether or not originally exogamous), they may be said to have been subordinated by the formation of the classes; and in the matter of mar-

[511] *Totemism and Exogamy,* I. p. 4; cf. IV. pp. 3, 4. Perhaps the author no longer approves of the word "reverenced." Totem and clan are rather on a footing of equality.

riage they follow the class rules. But the Arunta with some neighbouring tribes of Central Australia, though divided into eight exogamous classes, have not subordinated the Totem clans; which, accordingly, are not exogamous. If Exogamy was originally the vital utility of Totemism, the institution is undermined by the Marriage-classes, whether the clans are subordinated to the classes and merely repeat their rules, or are not subordinated and lose their Exogamy. This may explain why the classes prevail more widely than Totems, and may be found where Totemism seems to have become extinct.

§ 2. Of the Origin of Totemism

> § 2. *Of the Origin of Totemism.*—Totemism not universal. Totemic names sometimes recent, generally ancient. Totemism has not the psychological necessity of Magic and Animism. Originates with the names of individuals or of groups?

It has already been said that Totemism does not prevail universally amongst mankind. There is very little evidence of its having existed amongst the ancestors of the Indo-European peoples; and it seems to be unknown to many of the most primitive of surviving tribes—the Boschmans, Veddas, Puranas (Borneo), Andamanese, Yaghans (Tierra del Fuego) and Californian Indians. It is not, therefore, something founded in human nature itself, but must have originated (whether in one or in several places) under particular conditions.

There is some probability that the earliest Totems were animals. Wherever Totems are found most of them are animals. A list of Totems recognised in North Australia, given by Spencer and Gillen,[512] comprises 202 altogether: Animals 164,[513] Plants 22, Inanimate 16. The animals (except insects) and plants are nearly all edible. To hunters animals must have been of all things the most interesting; next, certain plants, especially to women. Animals lend the greatest plausibility to any notion of blood-relationship. The inanimate Totems include some which it is very desirable to control by Magic, such as Water, Wind, Fire, Sun, Moon and the Boomerang.

Generally, no doubt, Totemism is ancient; but in some cases the existing Totems must be recent, as among the Bahima of Uganda.[514] Nearly all their Totems are different coloured cows, or some part of a cow, and must have been adopted since the advance to pastoral life—at a stage of culture, therefore, much above the Australian. "Split Totems," arising on the division of a clan by dividing its Totem (as the Omahas comprised Buffalo-heads, Buffalo-tails, etc.[515]), were probably formed by deliberate agreement, and had the incidental advantage that a clansman's food-taboo did not extend to the whole buffalo, the staple food of the tribe, but only to the head or tail.

Amongst the Australian aborigines, the group of beliefs and practices includ-

[512] *Northern Tribes of Central Australia*, App. B.
[513] The animals are: Human 2, other Mammalia 31, Birds 46, Reptiles 51, Amphibia 1, Fishes 8, Insects 24, Mollusca 1.
[514] *Totemism and Exogamy*, II. p. 535.
[515] *Totemism and Exogamy*, III. pp. 90-100.

ed in, or connected with, Totemism are of such intense and widespread social importance, that it must have prevailed amongst them for many generations. The northern Amerinds are so much in advance of the Australians in social organisation, culture and mentality, that if their Totemism has descended to them from a time when they lived at the Australian level, its history must go back not merely for many generations but for thousands of years. And if Egyptian gods, such as Hathor and Anubis, were formerly Totems, the retrospect becomes still longer. I am not aware of any direct evidence of the prehistoric existence of Totemism, such as we have, in some ancient burials, of the existence of Animism; but some palæolithic carvings or paintings may have had totemic significance.

It follows that any account of the origin of Totemism can only be hypothetical. Were this all, indeed, it would be on the same foot with Magic and Animism; but it is not all. That Magic should arise from belief in mysterious forces and from confusing coincidence with causation, or that Animism should result from a confusion between dreams and objective experience (with the help of Magic-ideas) is highly probable; because such errors are active to this day, and they seem to spring up in primitive minds by psychological necessity; though it may not be intrinsically necessary that the errors should be perpetuated and systematised as, in general, they have been. But the case of Totemism is different; for we do not see—at least, no one has yet shown—any sort of necessity why in certain cases clans should have borne the names of certain animals: and this is the root of the whole matter. Indeed, this practice, not being universal, cannot be necessary; and it may have had several different origins. Any relevant hypothesis, therefore, can claim no more than to agree with the known facts better than rival hypotheses; we cannot expect to deduce it from laws of human nature; whilst still another hypothesis just as good may any day be put forward by some speculative genius; and the doubt must always remain whether some important facts of Totemism have not been lost which, could they be recovered, would prove all our guesses to have been made in vain.

In spite of these discouraging considerations, several hypotheses have been proposed: this also is for us a sort of psychological necessity. They may be grouped into two classes, according as they assume the totemic names to have been originally names of individuals or of whole clans. All seem to assume that one explanation must hold good for all the cases.

Of hypotheses that trace totemic names to individuals there is, first, Spencer's; namely, that the name of an animal or plant was first given to an individual, and then inherited by his family; who after a time forgot his personality, remembered only their descent from such a name, and assumed that their ancestor must have been an animal or plant such as still bore that name. Secondly, there is the explanation offered by Prof. Franz Boas, that the first Totems were guardian spirits of individuals, and that these became Clan-Totems of their descendants. For this account it may be said that among the Northern Amerinds the belief in guardian spirits of individuals (generally some animal) is universally diffused, and perhaps of greater importance than the Clan-Totems, seeing that these are subordinate to the Marriage-classes: moreover, the Totems are rarely, if ever, believed to have been ancestors. On the other hand, in Australia, guardian spirits of individuals are rare, whilst Totemism is universal. So that, if we suppose only one origin of the institution, it is more reasonable to view the guardian spirit as derived from the Clan-Totem. In Borneo we find the guardian spirit with some traits similar to the American, but much less generally, whilst there is now no plainly marked Totemism: but there are several beliefs akin to those of Totemism which may be marks of its former existence; and, if so, the guardian spirit may also be one of its relics.[516] Thirdly, Frazer's hypothesis, that Totems originated in the fancies of pregnant women, who, ignorant of physiological causes, supposed that that which stirred within them must be some animal or plant that had entered them; so that the child when born could be no other than that animal or plant.

Of hypotheses which regard totemic names as from the first names of groups we have, first, Max Müller's, that they originated with clan marks.[517] But in Australia clan marks are not often to be found. Secondly, Professor F. B. Jevons', that the Totem was originally some animal adopted by the tribe as a friendly natural power, aiding them in the struggle for existence.[518] But, if so, this character seems to have been lost, or greatly attenuated in Australia, and in America belongs to the guardian spirit rather than to the Totem. Thirdly, Dr. Haddon's, that the Totem name was derived by a group from the animal or plant which was its principal food; but cases to support this suggestion are very few. Fourthly, Andrew Lang's, that group names were obtained in some way—perhaps imposed upon each group by others, and accepted; and that names of animals or plants having been obtained in any way, and the origin forgotten, just such beliefs concerning the relation of the group to its namesake would be likely to arise, as in fact we find amongst Totemists.[519]

For want of space to discuss all these doctrines I shall deal chiefly with those of Frazer and Lang.

§ 3. The Conceptional Hypothesis

§ 3. *The Conceptional Hypothesis of Frazer.*—Belief in Totems derived
   from the fancies of women as to cause of pregnancy. Criticisms

Sir J. G. Frazer, after very candidly relinquishing two early suggestions—by no means fanciful—concerning the origin of Totemism, as unsupported by sufficient evidence, has put forward a third—"conceptional Totemism"—which occurred to him upon the discovery by Messrs. Spencer and Gillen of the doctrine of totemic descent prevalent amongst the Arunta and allied tribes. These tribes are said not to be aware of the connexion between sexual intercourse and pregnancy. They say that a child is the result of the entry into a woman of the spirit of some pre-existing tribesman of this or that Totem; which, therefore, will also be the child's. What Totem it is depends upon the place where the woman first becomes aware of quickening; for there are certain places known to the natives where the people of such or

[516] Hose and McDougall, *Pagan Tribes of Borneo*, II. pp. 96-110.
[517] *Contributions to the Science of Mythology*, I. p. 201.
[518] *Introduction to the History of Religion*, p. 101.
[519] *Secret of the Totem* and *Social Origins*.

such a Totem "went into the ground" [perhaps were buried]; and in passing such a place any woman is liable to be impregnated by one of the discarnate spirits; who are always on the look-out for an opportunity to re-enter the mortal state. This is the real cause of pregnancy, for which marriage is merely a preparation.[520] A young woman who does not desire the dignity of a matron, when passing such haunted ground, runs crouching by, and cries out that she is an old woman; for facility in being deceived is a saving grace of spirits. In modified forms this doctrine of "no paternity and re-incarnation" is professed by tribes throughout the centre and north of the continent, in Queensland and in parts of West Australia.[521]

The Arunta doctrine of conception by animal or plant spirits cannot, however, be the origin of Totemism; because, as Sir James Frazer points out, the impregnating spirits are already totemic. One must, therefore, suppose (he says) an earlier state of things, in which a woman, ignorant of the true causes of childbirth, imagined at the first symptoms of pregnancy (by which the quickening seems to be meant) that she had been entered by some object, or by the spirit of some object, which had been engaging her attention at the time, or which she may have been eating—a wallaby, emu, plum or grass-seed—and later believed that the child she bare must be, or be an incarnation of, that object or spirit, and in fact nothing else than a wallaby, emu, plum or grass-seed with the appearance of a human being. If other women had similar experiences in connexion with other animals or plants, and if the descendants of their children remembered the stories, and considered themselves to be wallabies, grass-seed and so forth, the hypothesis would fully explain that identification of groups of men with groups of things which is characteristic of Totemism; and the other characters naturally follow. Such is the conceptional theory of Totemism, deriving that institution from "the sick fancies of pregnant women."[522]

Circumstances, which Sir James Frazer regards as very similar to those which he imagined as having prevailed at some former time amongst the Arunta, have been discovered by Dr. Rivers at Mota and Motlar in the Banks Islands. There many people are "by the custom of the island" not permitted to eat certain animals or fruits or even to touch certain trees; because they are believed to *be* those animals or plants—their mothers having suffered some influence from such animals or plants at conception or at some subsequent period of pregnancy. "The course of events is usually as follows: a woman, sitting down in her garden, or in the bush, or on the shore, finds an animal or fruit in her loin-cloth. She takes it up and carries it to the village, where she asks the meaning of the appearance. The people say that she will give birth to a child who will have the characters of this animal, or even (it appeared) would be himself or herself that animal."[523] She takes it to its proper home, tries to keep it, and feeds it; but after a time it will disappear, and is then believed to have entered into her. There is no belief in physical impregnation by the animal, nor of its invading the woman as a physical object; such an animal seems to be considered as "more or less supernatural, a spirit-animal, from the

[520] Spencer and Gillen, *Northern Tribes of Central Australia*, p. 330.
[521] *Native Tribes of Northern Territory of Australia*, p. 263.
[522] *Totemism and Exogamy*, IV. pp. 57-63.
[523] *Journal of the Anthropological Institute*, 1909, p. 173.

beginning." "The belief is not accompanied by any ignorance of the physical rôle of the human father." Apparently the prohibition against eating animals or plants thus connected with oneself rests on the idea that it would amount to eating one-self—a sort of cannibalism. One partakes of its physical and mental characters. But the resemblance to, and the taboo on eating, a certain animal are individual matters; there is no belief in their being passed on to one's descendants. In this alone the belief at Mota falls short of Totemism. "Yet it occurs in a people whose social system has no totemic features at the present time, whatever it may have had in the past."[524] Possibly former Totem-clans have been merged in secret societies, but there is no clear evidence of it. In Melanesia, Totemism occurs in Fiji, Shortland Islands, Bismarck Archipelago (probably), Reef Islands, Santa Cruz, Vanikolo and in some regions of the Solomon Islands, but not in the Banks Islands nor in the Torres Islands to the south.

This hypothesis that Totemism is derived from the fancies of women concerning the causes of their own pregnancy suggests several adverse considerations. In the first place, it is to me incredible that the Arunta are really ignorant of paternity; young women and children perhaps may be, but not the seniors. My reasons for thinking so are set out at length in the *J.R.A.I.*, 1819 (p. 146), namely, that the facts of childbirth are too interesting to be overlooked or misconstrued, and are well within the grasp of savage understanding; that those who think the Arunta capable of such stupidity have attended too exclusively to particular incidents of pregnancy, especially the quickening, and have not considered that there is a definite series of closely connected incidents; that there is testimony, not to be lightly put aside, that the old men know the truth in the case of human beings, and that knowledge of the parallel phenomena amongst animals is shared even by the Arunta children; that it is possible for knowledge to be repressed by dogma without being extinguished; that this is an old man's dogma, and that we must not assume that in Australia, any more than in Europe, what people are accustomed to say is good evidence of what they really believe;[525] that other tribes at the same level of culture, in South-East Australia, are so convinced of the importance of paternity that they say the child proceeds entirely from the father; that those who deny paternity show by their customs and myths that they are secretly aware of it; and, finally, that in some cases they have clear motives for maintaining the dogma and suppressing the truth.

Secondly, the observations of Dr. Rivers in the Banks Islands give not the slightest support to the conceptional hypothesis. For (*a*) the Banks Islands belief "is not accompanied by any ignorance of the physical rôle of the human father." (*b*) The belief is that the child born to a woman who has been visited by a plant or animal is in some way "influenced" by the experience; not, as with the Arunta, that it is entirely due to it (except for some "preparation" by the father). (*c*) Before

[524] *Journal of the Anthropological Institute*, 1909, p. 175.

[525] In the Gazelle Peninsula of New Britain, a man applies the name of "mother" to his real mother and also to his maternal aunts, who accept the relationship and may assert: "We all three of us bore him" (*Totemism and Exogamy*, I. p. 305 note). Is this what they believe, or what (following their system of class-nomenclature) they are accustomed to say?

the Banks Islands belief can give rise to Totemism there must be a belief in the continuous inheritance of the plant or animal influence; and not only is this absent, but there is a strong tendency to prevent it. A woman having been influenced by an eel, her child is an eel; but if that child be a girl, there is no further transmission of eel-like qualities; the girl, on becoming pregnant, may be influenced by a yam, and then her child will be a yam. This hinders the formation of a group of human beings mysteriously allied to an animal or plant, such as Totemism implies. But (*d*) the conceptional hypothesis refers the origin of Totemism to the ignorant imaginings of women themselves, who think they have been entered by this or that; whereas in the Banks Islands a woman's belief in the influence of an animal or plant upon her offspring is not prompted by her own fancy, but by a popular superstition. For when she carries the thing found in her loin-cloth to the village, "the people say" she will give birth to a child who will have the qualities of, or even will be that thing; and a child afterwards born may not eat or touch that thing "by the custom of the country." Had the Arunta, then, of pre-totemic days such a superstition and custom for the guidance of mothers? If so, the history of that superstition and custom must be more obscure than Totemism itself. But in the Banks Islands their origin may admit of a wide solution; for although it is said that no manifest traces of Totemism are to be found there now; yet, seeing that the Australians, Papuans, Polynesians and the Melanesians to the north all have Totemism or plain vestiges of it, the improbability that Melanesians in the Banks Islands never had it is very great; and it is reasonable to suppose that the superstition concerning the influence of animals or plants upon pregnant women, and the taboo upon the eating of such an animal or plant by the offspring, represent not a possible origin of Totemism, but a survival of it.

These considerations raise a further question as to the employment of the Comparative Method. Natives of the Banks Islands are far in advance of the Arunta in all the arts of life, as well as in relation to Totemism which they seem to have outlived. Is it admissible to take some trait of their life as an example of what may have existed amongst the Arunta at a stage of culture which is generally assumed to have been inferior even to the present? When the antecedents of an institution have been lost amongst any given people, and we set out to supply them from parallel cases amongst other peoples, must we not require the same relative order of development? If a social phenomenon is found in the Banks Islands, its possibility is proved; but strictly it was possible only where it occurred: elsewhere we can expect only something similar, according to the similarity of other relevant circumstances. Comparing the Banks Islands and their people with Central Australia and its people, one discovers hardly anything common to them. And Arunta tradition (whatever worth) shows no sign of anything like the southern Melanesian culture: the Alcheringa ancestors are represented as having been already Totemists. To assume, however, that the former condition of the Arunta was even lower than the present, may not be justifiable: social degeneration is not uncommon. There would be something to guide our judgment if we knew how recently the desiccation of their country approached its present severity. But, in any case, can we suppose it to have been at all like the Melanesian?

§ 4. ANDREW LANG'S HYPOTHESIS

> § 4. *Lang's Hypothesis.*—Names of animals or plants given to groups
> probably by other groups. Circumstances of origin having been
> forgotten, explanatory myths are invented with corresponding
> observances. Comments

In some very remote age—to summarise Lang's statement—at a level of cul-
ture inferior to that of existing Australians, distinctive names were acquired by
small groups of mankind. Since a group needs names for other groups more than
for itself (for itself it consists of "men" as contrasted with other kinds of animals),
names may at first have been bestowed upon each group by some other, or oth-
ers, in its neighbourhood—probably names of animals or plants—and accepted
by each; for no opprobrium attaches to such names. In *Social Origins* Lang offers
evidence concerning names (even depreciatory and mocking names) having been
conferred in this way and accepted; but in *The Secret of the Totem*,[526] he says that
how groups got their names is not essential to his theory. They may have been
given, or adopted, on account of a group's staple food (Haddon); or because of
some animal or plant characteristic of a group's territory; or for some fancied re-
semblance of its members to some animal. The important point is that, from the
first, they were names of groups—not derived from the names of individuals. At
the early period assumed for these events there was not a long enough memory
of individuals to make their names traditionary; and, indeed, the reckoning of
descent in the female line (which Lang regards as universally the most ancient
custom) must have prevented the inheritance of the names of male ancestors.

Whatever may have occasioned the first fixing of names, with the flight of time
the circumstances were forgotten; and groups of men and women found them-
selves with names—the names of animals or plants—without knowing why. The
bearing of a name in common with an animal or plant inevitably suggested to
the savage a mysterious connexion with the species—perhaps that they had the
same sort of soul. It gave rise to an explanatory myth, and the analogy of family
relationship suggested a blood-bond: the animal or plant must be one's ancestor,
brother, or primal ancestral form. From this idea follows a regard for it, respect,
reverence: it must not be killed, or eaten, or used in any way; it may be protected,
may be helpful; it is a Totem.

The connexion of Totemism with Exogamy (the custom of marrying outside
the group or kin) Lang conceives of in this way. Adopting a suggestion of Dar-
win's,[527] and the scheme of his cousin, J. J. Atkinson in *Primal Law*, that the pri-
mary human group consisted of a powerful male with one or more wives and
their children, he argues that the jealousy of the head of this family imposed the
rule—"No male to touch the females in my camp." The sons, therefore, as they
grew up, were driven out, and must find wives elsewhere. This was the begin-
ning of Exogamy, and it may have preceded the rise of Totemism; but Totemism,
once established, strengthened the custom of Exogamy by mysterious sanctions.
As the Totem might not be eaten, or in any way used or touched, so a woman of

[526] Page 125.
[527] See above, ch. ii. § 3.

the same Totem could not be married; and that not only within their immediate family-group, but not even by a male of any group having the same Totem.

In maintaining this hypothesis against those who would derive Totems from the names and traditions of individuals, Lang seems to me to lay too much stress upon the difficulty of establishing a tradition of descent amongst people who trace descent (as he would say) "on the spindle side." If the tradition began from a woman (as it might do), there is no difficulty; and even if it began from a man, it is conceivable that his women-folk should adopt it. Moreover, in the opinion of both Westermarck and Frazer, it has not been shown that the reckoning of descent in the female line is original and universal. Still, the further we push back the origin of Totemism the more difficult it is to understand the growth of a tradition of the descent and inheritance of the name and personal qualities of an individual; and this difficulty is avoided by an hypothesis which derives Totemism from the animal- or plant-names of groups of men and women. That such names were conferred upon each group by others in the neighbourhood is a reasonable conjecture;[528] being the earliest names of groups they cannot be called nicknames; and the names of animals or plants need in no way have been offensive. It is still more reasonable to urge that, having been adopted by a group, the circumstances of their acquisition would, in a few generations, be forgotten, and that they would then become the ground of myths and mysterious totemic beliefs. But does any one think that it will now ever be possible to decide with confidence where, when, how or why the names were given at first? I do not.

As to the origin of Exogamy, I cannot believe that the primitive human groups were such as Lang described; and, if not, some other origin of that custom must be sought.

§ 5. TOTEMISM AND MARRIAGE

§ 5. *Totemism and Marriage.* — Exogamy, Totemism and Marriage Classes. Westermarck's hypothesis as to Exogamy

Generally men and women of the same Totem cannot marry. Tribes, such as the Arunta, that do not observe this rule are so few that it is reasonable to consider them aberrant; so that in each case the non-coincidence of Totemism and Exogamy is a distinct problem.

Nevertheless, there is reason to think that these institutions have not the same origin. For several primitive tribes, some of them inferior in culture to the average Australian, have customs of Exogamy, or (at least) forbidding marriage between individuals of some certain description, who have not, and are not known ever to have recognised Totemism. Many tribes, again, who by their ethnological position

[528] It is reasonable to suppose that a group named other groups to distinguish those around them, before needing to name itself. It follows that probably each group sometimes bore a different name when spoken of by each of several neighbours. How amidst such confusion could single names be fixed? Perhaps because the group designated adopted one of them; or by the elimination of the other names through many causes in course of time, in generations, in hundreds of years. The march of progress was leisurely in those days.

may be supposed once to have entertained Totemism, have abandoned it, but still maintain Exogamy by means of Marriage-classes (phratries) or otherwise. Further, many nations of advanced culture cannot be shown ever to have been totemists, but have always (as far back as can be traced) enforced Exogamy so far as to prohibit marriage within certain degrees of kindred. And that the connexion between Totemism and Exogamy is not original but acquired, is indicated by the consideration that the most obvious tendency of Totemism would be to favour Endogamy (the practice of not marrying outside certain limits), on the obvious principle that as an animal kangaroo mates with an animal kangaroo, so a human kangaroo should marry a human kangaroo. This is so obvious that the opposite rule that a human kangaroo must not marry another one, but (zoological paradox!) only an emu or a witchety-grub, seems perverse, and only to be explained by the influence of some superstition or incidental custom. According to Arunta tradition, their ancestors in the Alcheringa were endogamous.

Whether Exogamy originated in the days of the hunting-pack—which is so far probable that the Boschmans observed it—or during the reconstitution of society after the breaking up of the packs, or even later, or in some regions at one period, in others at another, is, I fear, beyond our power of verifiable guessing. The best hypothesis as to the grounds of the custom is Westermarck's, namely, that an instinct of mutual avoidance grew up between near kin. This requires that at the time of its origination promiscuity of sexual relations should not have prevailed in the human stock, since that would have destroyed the conditions necessary to the rise of such an instinct. If promiscuity was ever widely practised, it must have been after the breaking up of the hunting-packs. That at some stage of human life, and apparently with some Australian tribes not a remote one, promiscuity was established, has been argued (on the ground of some Australian customs) with much plausibility; but in his *History of Human Marriage*,[529] Westermarck has examined this opinion very carefully, and concludes that it is not tenable. His reasoning seems to me good throughout; and, having nothing important to add to it, I refer the reader to his work.

Whether amongst anthropoids any instinctive avoidance prevails, preventing what we conceive of as incest, nobody knows. With their solitary families, the growth of such a disposition may be more difficult than amongst gregarious animals (such as our ancestors had become long before they could be called "human"), who find other families at hand to intermarry with; though the primitive human bands probably were not large. Savages now at the lowest level, such as the Veddas or Yaghans, rarely form parties of more than thirty or forty. The Boschmans, before their tribal habits were destroyed in the early years of last century, though sometimes assembling in large numbers for the great hunts by means of stockade traps, yet were usually scattered in groups of a few families. It is not likely that their remote forefathers consorted in larger numbers: eight or ten families may have been enough to co-operate in hunting, or in mutual defence. Within each family constituting such a band the tendency to Exogamy may first have manifested itself.

---

[529] Chs. iv., v., vi.

Westermarck's hypothesis concerning Exogamy was first published in the *History of Human Marriage*,[530] and has been re-stated in *The Origin and Development of Moral Ideas*.[531] In the former work he fully discusses the evidence as to the effects of the inter-breeding of near kin, and concludes that it is probably injurious. The evidence is conflicting, but his conclusion seems to me justifiable. And he rightly points out that if, amongst civilised nations, the mischief of inbreeding is not always manifest, it was probably much greater amongst primitive savages: (1) because the blood of the stock was purer; for in modern Europe (e. g.) every marriage brings together many different strains. (2) Because communities were then much smaller; so that under endogamous conditions whatever vice may beset inbreeding would, generation after generation, be perpetuated and exaggerated without relief. It may be added that with Endogamy the young folk are likely to begin to breed earlier—perhaps by two or three years—than they would with Exogamy; and there is no doubt that the marriage of immature individuals is highly injurious to the race.

But if inbreeding was injurious, Natural Selection favoured any family or band that practised Exogamy. That any should have done so on rational grounds, to avoid the observed evil effects of inbreeding, cannot be supposed. The motive must have been blind to the consequences, and may have taken the form of coldness toward those of opposite sex with whom one had grown up from infancy, or of aversion to the idea of marrying them. Such dispositions Natural Selection preserved, and they have descended to ourselves; for such was the beginning of the abhorrence of incest.

I conjecture that this feeling first showed itself within the family, and led the families of a band to exchange their daughters; and that later it extended to all members of the same band, and that wives were then sought from other bands. Probably wives were obtained sometimes by capture or enticement, sometimes by exchange so far as amicable relations with neighbours prevailed: for the evidence is far from showing that "marriage by capture" was ever a general custom; whilst our knowledge of the Australians and Boschmans shows that neighbouring bands of savages are not always hostile.

Such a state of things may have existed for ages before the rise of Totemism, and amongst races that never adopted Totemism. When names of animals were first given to, or adopted by, various groups, Totemism somewhere (perhaps in several places) resulted, as a belief in the magical or spiritual connexion between men and animals of the same name. But the bands that adopted Totemism were already exogamous, having an aversion to marriage with others of the same band; and the practice of Exogamy was thus brought under the mysterious sanction of totemic ideas. It would then be further extended to bar marriage with those of the same Totem in other groups.

Totemic sanctions may have been useful in confirming the Exogamy of some groups, but all superstitious aids to right conduct are liable to perverse issues, and at best they are second best. Totemism prevents consanguineous marriages, but

[530] Chs. xiv., xv., *Prohibition of Marriage between Kindred.*
[531] Ch. xl., *Marriage.*

also prevents marriage with thousands of people where no blood-relationship is traceable. If any races were able to perceive that the interest of Exogamy was the prevention of marriage between near kin, and then to keep account of kinship and govern themselves accordingly, they chose the better part.

Some exceptions to the rule that Totem-clans are exogamous may, perhaps, be explained by supposing that certain bands had not adopted Exogamy when they became totemists—may not this have happened amongst the Arunta?—and that they have since learnt Exogamy under other conditions from neighbouring people, or by conquest. Amongst the other possible conditions there are the remarkable Marriage-classes, or phratries that prevail in Australia, North America, and less regularly in other parts of the world. These Marriage-classes are considered by some ethnologists to be of deliberate institution—a reform for the regulation of Exogamy; and Spencer and Gillen, who knew the Australians so intimately, thought such a law—though its intricacy astonishes most Europeans and stumbles many—was not beyond their power of excogitation. Upon that point it would be absurd of me to have any opinion. But to suppose deliberate intention is contrary to the usual method of interpreting savage institutions: a savage language is a system of customs much more intricate and refined than the Marriage-classes, and not generally believed to have originated with the deliberate enactment of rules of grammar. I conjecture that those classes resulted at first from a grouping of exogamous Totem-clans which grew up by custom, and that the only deliberate work consisted in some minor adjustments of clan-relations. Marriage of cousins is prevented in Central and North Australia by the recognition of eight sub-classes; but the same result is obtained in other tribes by a custom which merely forbids it. Exogamous classes having been established in some tribes, may have been imitated in others.

One result of the classificatory marriage system, however it grew up, is the extended use of names of kinship to denote all individuals of the same or corresponding generation—"father" for all men who might by custom have married your mother; "brother" and "sister" for all men and women descended from those whom your father or mother might have married; "husband" or "wife" for any man or woman whom, according to custom, you might have married. When further progress has been made in culture, distinctive names are used to express blood-relationship and class-relationship. It may be worth considering whether, in Australia, some of the customs which have been supposed to bear witness to an original state of promiscuity are not really results of the classificatory system of naming relationship: marital rights having been claimed on the ground of the names "husband" and "wife" as used in that system.

§ 6. The Clansman and his Totem

§ 6. *The Clansman and his Totem*—perhaps believed to have the same
  soul

The relationship of Clansman to Totem may be conceived of as one of friendliness, protection, consanguinity, or even identity; and this last I take to be the case in the age when Totemism is most alive and powerful. But in what sense can a man be the same as an emu? He may be of the same name; but by itself that would be nothing. It is not the name, but the identity which the name has come to signify that must be considered. Some light may be shed upon the problem by the saying of a native to Spencer and Gillen, pointing to a photograph of himself: "That one is just the same as me; so is a kangaroo." The photograph might be "the same" as himself in the sense of resemblance; but in that sense the kangaroo is not the same. Some, indeed, who have speculated on the savage mind suppose that it is not only incapable of reasoning, but even of perceiving the facts before it, when under the influence of some strong belief; and I admit that this is sometimes true. But all a savage's actions in relation to his Totem show that he is aware of the difference: not least his efforts on certain occasions to help his imagination to establish identity by disguising himself and by imitating the actions of this strange other self, and by eating a little of it to insure physical identity at least to that extent. He also seeks to multiply it that others may eat their ration, and for any theory of his identity with the Totem, this must be a puzzle.

But a photograph may be the same as oneself in another sense than mere superficial resemblance: it may, like a shadow or reflection, be (or contain) a man's soul, or part of it. And similarly a kangaroo or other Totem may be conceived to be the same as a man, that is, as having the same soul. Perhaps this is as near as we can get to the Australian's meaning in the above-quoted confession of faith. It is reconcilable with the ceremonial eating of some part of the Totem; for that will convey spiritual as well as physical properties: and to reconcile it with the multiplication of the Totem that others may eat, I point to the biological necessity that each clan's Totem should be food for the other tribesmen. Where all edible animals and plants are Totems, how else can they subsist? But we have several times seen that biological necessity will place limits to a belief, and that excuses can be found for necessary actions which are in conflict with a belief. That the clansmen give their own Totem to the tribe (since they cannot defend it) is an ingenious compromise.

It is reported that amongst the Euahlayi tribe occur personal Totems (or guardians, rare in Australia) called Yunbeai, possessed chiefly by wizards. A man may eat his hereditary Totem, but not his Yunbeai; which in this privilege seems to have supplanted the Totem. His spirit is in the Yunbeai, and its spirit is in him.[532] They have, then, the same soul; and, although this belief is not strictly Totemism, it is probably derived from it. A clansman of the Yuin tribe (West Australia) had as his Totem the Black Duck, which warned him against enemies; and he related that once, whilst he slept, a Lace-Lizard man sent his Totem, which went down his throat and almost ate his Black Duck residing in his breast; so that he nearly died.[533] Were not his Black Duck and his soul the same?

This hypothesis agrees very well with a belief that one's body and soul descend from the same ancestor as the Totem's; and that at death one goes to, or becomes, the Totem; and excuses the fiction that the quickening of a pregnant woman may be caused by the entry into her of the spirit of some totem-plant or animal.

---

[532] Langloh Parker, *The Euahlayi Tribe*, p. 21.
[533] *Totemism and Exogamy*, I. p. 489.

On the Gold Coast and elsewhere in West Africa, a man has more than one soul, it may be as many as four; and one of them dwells with some animal in the bush: thence called his "bush-soul." Sir James Frazer's first hypothesis concerning Totemism was that it may have been derived from the notion of an external soul which may be deposited in anything (as thus in an animal in the bush) for safety. He now thinks the connexion of the "bush-soul" with Totemism uncertain.[534] If there has been any connexion, may it not be that the "bush-soul" is derived from Totemism, and that every Totem is a sort of "bush-soul"—that is, it has a soul which is the same (at least, of the same kind) as the clansman's?

§ 7. TOTEMISM AND MAGIC

§ 7. *Totemism and Magic.*—Magical properties of names. Transformation. Penalties on breach of observances. Control of Totems

The identity of a man with his name, as usually assumed by savages, whether his personal or his totemic name, is not itself a magical belief, but an inevitable result of mental association at a low level of intelligence: perhaps earlier than any notions that can properly be called magical. The name of a man, always thought of along with his other properties, seems to be as much one of them as a scar on his neck or any peculiar trait of visage or length of limb. This must be as old as naming. But such a complication of the name with other marks having been formed, it becomes the ground of magic beliefs and practices. To mention the name of a man or spirit insures his presence and participation in any rite, either acting or suffering; or where writing is known, his name on a piece of paper is as good as his nail-parings. The use of the name is not a mere animistic summons (which might be disobeyed), but an immediate instatement of the given individual. Such magic may enter into totemic observances.

The descent of the clan from the Totem-animal, or of the animal from a forefather of the clan, or of both from a *tertium quid*, involves metamorphosis; and this, again, is not itself a magic idea; for real metamorphoses are common in the life of birds, amphibia, insects, and it would be unreasonable to expect savages to perceive clearly that these are not parallel cases. There is a difference, however, between transformations that may be observed, such as that of a chrysalis into a butterfly, and those that have never been observed, but are merely imagined and asserted. The latter are more mysterious, and mystery is one character of magic. For example, the Witchety-Grub clan among the Arunta have as their mate a bird, the chantunga, which they will not eat because, they say, of old some full-grown witchety-grubs were transformed into these birds.[535] This change has a magical character, though no magical agency is assigned. But if any attempt were made to explain how the great change took place, recourse might be had to powers of magic. Even when agency is assigned, it is not always magical. In the earliest Alcheringa the two Ungambikula ("out of nothing") saw in groups by the shore of the salt water a number of inapertwa, rudimentary men, mere roundish masses, without organs or means of feeding, and these they cut out into men with stone

[534] Ibid., IV. p. 54.
[535] *Totemism and Exogamy*, I. p. 254.

knives, therefore not by magic.[536] But, again, a tribe on the Darling River (Wathi-wathi) have traditions concerning Bookoomuri who lived long ago, excelled in Magic, and transformed themselves into animals; and here the magical power is asserted, though the manner of its operation is indefinite. But the Bear clan of the Tshimshians (British Columbia) explain their position by the story that once upon a time an Indian, whilst hunting, met a bear, which took him to its home, where he stayed two years. On returning to his village he looked like a bear; but, having been rubbed with medical herbs, recovered human shape.[537] And here the magic is as explicit as in any recipe for a were-wolf, or that fallacious ointment with which Lucius achieved his memorable transformation.

Nor, further, has the prohibition to slay, injure or eat the Totem in the first place any magical significance; for it merely puts the Totem in the position of a clansman. But the situation, being strange and mysterious, acquires a magical atmosphere; and the enforcement of the taboo by penalties is unmistakably magical. The Untmajera (North Central Australia) have a legend of a Beetle-Grub man of former times who ate beetle-grubs, and thereupon broke out in sores, wasted away and died. Or one's hair may turn grey; or, according to the Samoan belief (not strictly totemistic), the forbidden food may grow inside one into the whole animal or plant to the destruction of its host. Such beliefs, resting on the analogy of poisons and their physiological consequences, are magical imaginations: the taboo has the same character as a conditional curse.

Similarly, the prohibition of marriage within the Totem-clan, if it originated (as I have supposed) with the fusion of Totemism and Exogamy in the customs of various early groups of men and women, is not based on Magic; but the penalties for breaking the taboo are magical. Thus amongst the Euahlayi and their neighbours men and women of the Iguana clan cannot intermarry, though coming from different parts of the country and without any traceable consanguinity; because, if they did, their children, inasmuch as their ancestors on both sides were the same animal, would "throw back" to the form or attributes of the iguana.[538] A grotesque anticipation of scientific ideas.

But the most remarkable connexion between Totemism and Magic occurs in those rites by which clansmen in several parts of the world, but especially in Australia, believe themselves able to influence their Totems: when these are edible, to multiply them; when noxious, to drive away or destroy them; or, as with the wind and rain, to control them for the general good. Spencer and Gillen[539] give astonishing descriptions of the rites of multiplication (or Intichiuma), carefully prepared and regulated, including disguisings of clansmen in the likeness of the Totems, drawings of the Totems on the ground, dances, incantations and ceremonies, sometimes representing traditional history—by which the tribesmen discharge this function of theirs. They rely chiefly on mimetic (exemplary) Magic which, by dramatising some natural process, brings it into real operation. In identifying

[536] *Native Tribes of Central Australia*, p. 388.

[537] *Totemism and Exogamy*, III. p. 13.

[538] Langloh Parker, *The Euahlayi*, p. 22.

[539] *Native Tribes of Central Australia*, ch. vi.; *Northern Tribes of Central Australia*, ch. ix.

themselves with the Totem, they exert their imaginations to the utmost, and to this end may eat a little of the Totem, at other times forbidden. This assumption that by eating a little of any animal, plant or human being, you become one with it, or acquire its qualities, or, further, that two men by eating together of the same food become allied (which is in a manner materially true, but absurdly interpreted), is another of those notions simpler than, and antecedent to, Magic, which provide a base for magical operations.[540] These solemnities last for months, and are carried out with conscientious diligence and earnestness: the infatuation is profound and universal. Here, as at most of the higher stages of culture, we find the most intense emotions of which men are capable excited by participation in communal imaginative exercises that have directly, in relation to their expectations, absolutely no result. Indeed, pre-occupation with vain employments tends to exclude all ideas that might be useful, that might lead (e. g.) to the increasing of food by the cultivation of plants or domestication of animals. Sir James Frazer has pointed out that a passage of the rites of the Grass-seed clan, in which grass-seeds are scattered about upon the ground, might have led to cultivation: but the mental state of the clan is unfavourable to cool observation. As for animals, it is some excuse for the backwardness of Australian culture that the Marsupialia do not comprise a single species that would repay domestication. Indirectly and undesignedly these performances have very useful consequences: they annually restore the unity of the tribe assembled from all parts for the great occasion; promote mutual good-will and a spirit of co-operation, for which they afford the chief opportunity; maintain the social organisation and the tradition of customs by increasing the influence of the Headmen, who have a leading part in everything that happens, and on whose authority all order and discipline depend; interrupt the monotony of savage life with variety of interests; stimulate ingenuity, and fill up the time, that might else be wasted in idleness or quarrelling, with artistic and dramatic recreation.

Upon these rites for the multiplication and control of the Totems, Sir James Frazer based his second hypothesis concerning the origin of Totemism, namely, that it was a system of co-operation amongst sections of a savage tribe for the magical supply of food, etc.: the Emu clan multiplying emus, the Kangaroo clan kangaroos, the Witchety-Grub clan witchety-grubs, and so forth.[541] But he afterwards reflected that such a design was beyond the conception of savages. And, no doubt, as a plan thought out and deliberately adopted as a whole, most ethnologists would consider it above the capacity of Australian aborigines. But if so—though not more difficult than the invention of the Classificatory Marriage System—it shows what complex arrangements, simulating design, may come into existence by the growth of custom; for the clans certainly do co-operate in the magical supply of food.

Whatever may have been the origin of Totemism the institution seems to have been utilised by some tribes in an ambitious attempt to control all nature by grouping (on very obscure principles, if on any) various classes of phenomena with the Totems, so that one clan or another is responsible for everything. Short of this, it

[540] There is, however, another possible reason for the eating by the clan or by its Headman of some portion of the food which they profess to supply to the rest of the tribe—namely, that it expresses a prior claim to some sort of proprietorship, which is then waived.

[541] *Totemism and Exogamy*, IV. pp. 55-7.

is plainly necessary to control the wind, rain, hail and lightning. The control of an animal Totem is not always benevolent toward the animals themselves. In the Kakadu tribe it is the duty of the Mosquito clan to save the rest from mosquitoes; they make imitation mosquitoes, dance and sing, and imagine they are killing them.[542] In North America similar beliefs and practices have been found both for encouraging and for discouraging the Totem, but occasionally and irregularly. The Bird clan of the Omahas, when birds threatened the crops, prevented their devastations by chewing corn and spitting it about over the fields; when mosquitoes were troublesome, the Wind people flapped blankets to raise a wind and blow the pests away; when worms attacked the crops, the Reptile clan (worms and reptiles are confused in primitive Zoology) countermined their approaches by pounding up some of them with a little corn into a soup and eating it.[543] The most remarkable American rites for the increase of food—the Buffalo-dances and Corn-festivals of the Mandans—were not totemic, but carried out by the whole tribe. The buffalo hunting-dance to bring the herd within reach, was continued, if necessary, for weeks—in fact until the animals came; so that the Magic was always effectual.

§ 8. Totemism and Animism

§ 8. *Totemism and Animism.*—Totems in Australia give warnings; are sometimes invoked in aid; the Wollunqua. Fusion of Totem with spirit of hero in Fiji; in Polynesia. Propitiation of guardian spirits, "elder brothers," species-gods in North and South America. Zoolatry in Africa; in Egypt

If the unity of clansmen with their Totem is very early conceived of as consisting in having the same, or the same sort of, soul, it is thenceforward essentially animistic. Yet this idea seems only very slowly to have led to any sense of dependence on the Totem as a spiritual power, or to any expectation that it would help or succour the clansmen, or (consequently) to the making of any appeal to it, except by magical coercion. Perhaps the earliest way in which the Totem was supposed to aid its clansmen was by omens; as a Black Duck man of the Yuin tribe (West Australia) thought that black ducks warned him against his enemies; but this is more characteristic of guardian spirits than of Clan-Totems. Occasionally in Australia we meet with something like a prayer to a Totem. On the Tully River (Queensland) we are told by Mr. W. E. Roth that before a man goes to sleep, or on waking in the morning, he utters in a low voice the name of the animal whose name he bears, or which belongs to his group; and that then, if edible, he will be successful in hunting it or, if dangerous, it will not hurt him without warning.

Professor Durkheim has an elaborate theory of the growth of divinities from Totems in Australia, especially in the example of Bungil, the Eagle-Hawk, a great phratry name-animal in several tribes.[544] He is a persuasive writer, but perverse and ingenious. Bungil receives neither prayer nor sacrifice (these, indeed, in the author's view are not necessary to religion), and there is nothing to show that he

[542] Spencer and Gillen, *Native Tribes North. Ter. Aust.*, p. 324.
[543] *Totemism and Exogamy*, III. pp. 104-5.
[544] *The Elementary Forms of the Religious Life*, II. ch. ix.

differs from the other glorified Headmen who are found in Australia. The most plausible of these superior beings is Byamee of the Euahlayi, who is not a Totem, but the source of Totems, which are derived from different parts of his body. At funerals prayers are addressed to him for the souls of the dead; and, again, at the close of the Boorah (initiation rites) for long life, inasmuch as the tribesmen have kept his law.[545] We are told that the nearest mission-station is a hundred miles off, and recently established; but on reading further that only those who have been initiated can go to Byamee's sky-camp, and that gross sinners are punished in the next life in Eleanbah Wundah, a place dark but for fires,[546] we cannot help reflecting that missionaries are not the only channels of sound doctrine.

The most authentic example of the rise of a Totem to something like divine rank is the Wollunqua, the great snake of the Warramunga, which differs from other Totems in being not a real animal but a mythological monster. It is not approached with prayer or sacrifice; but is the object of rites in part propitiatory, in part coercive, and is certainly regarded with superstitious awe much as a demon might be. To please the Wollunqua, the clan build a long mound and draw its representation upon it; which, however, afterwards meets with "savage destruction." On approaching Thapanerlu, the sacred pool where it lives, they whispered to it "to remain quiet and do them no harm."[547]

On the whole, funeral ceremonies, in Australia, to provide the dead with necessaries, food, utensils, warmth—even precautions against ghosts—come nearer to religious ideas than anything connected with Totemism. Among the Jupagalk (Victoria) a person when in great pain would call on some dead friend to come and help him, to visit him in a dream and teach a song against the evil magic that hurt him.[548]

In Yam Island (Torres Straits) there is a cult of two brothers, Maiou and Sigai, who are said to have come from Australia. They have shrines within a fence; women and uninitiated youths are not permitted to enter, and do not know that Maiou is the crocodile (Kodal), and Sigai the hammer-headed shark (Kursi); for they are always addressed and spoken of by their names as heroes, and not by their animal or Totem names. The shrines contain effigies made of turtle-shell representing the animals; and under each effigy is a stone in which the life or spirit of the Totem-hero resides. The natives, in the north-west monsoon, danced and sang before them for fine weather; and also on going to war, praying: "O Totem Sigai and Totem Maiou, both of you close the eyes of these men so that they cannot see us."[549] This is indisputably Religion; it is not, however, pure Totemism, but apparently a fusion of hero-worship with the Totemism of the heroes. Another hero of more recent date, Quoiam, is worshipped in the neighbouring island of Mabuaig. He

---

[545] Langloh Parker, *The Euahlayi Tribe*, pp. 458, 478, etc. In Eleanbah Wundah, they hold their right hands pressed against their sides, which A. Lang thought a remarkable image. It is, W. E. Roth tells us, gesture-language for sickness. (*Ethnological Studies in North-West Central Queensland*, p. 90.)

[546] *The Euahlayi*, pp. 4 to 8, and 78.

[547] *North. Ts. of C. Aust.*, p. 253.

[548] Howitt, *Northern Tribes of South-East Australia*, p. 435.

[549] Haddon, *Reports of the Expedition to Torres Straits*, V. pp. 37, 38.

came from North Queensland; and his house and cairn are still shown on a hill-top. His Totem was the shovel-nosed skate, but he has undergone no fusion with that animal. We may be inclined to infer that the hero can stand alone, whilst a Totem needs the alliance of a hero to anthropomorphise it.

Such an inference is, on the whole, confirmed by the state of religion in Fiji. There, amongst the coastal tribes, Totemism is decadent and irregular; though even on the coast of Viti Levu there are deities with animal attributes, and especially with the power of changing into animals; and the animal connected with a god must not be eaten by people of the district where he is worshipped.[550] In the mountainous interior Totemism still flourishes, and animal-gods are worshipped which have been assumed to have originated in Totems. Dr. Rivers tells us[551] that he formerly assumed this, but is inclined to revise his opinion. The Fijian Snake-god Ndengei was, according to tradition, a man who came to the island from else-where; probably he made a great impression and was apotheosised. His character as a Snake-god may be derived from the snake's having been his Totem. Probably god-like beings in Fiji were in many cases heroes, but a close relation with their Totem endued them with something of the animal nature. "The evolution would not be simply from Totem to god, but from hero and Totem together to god."

Gods present in animals, sometimes in plants, were acknowledged in Samoa, Tahiti, Hawaii, Tonga; and, in fact, Polynesia is the region where, if anywhere, Totems contribute largely to the divine population. Rivers will not deny (loc. cit.) that direct evolution of gods from Totems may have taken place; but he points out that in Samoa, for example, the Octopus-god (Ole Fe'e) was, according to tradition, brought to the island by a Fijian chief. Was then the mollusc or the chief the root from which the god grew up? In Savaii there were gods incarnate in men: one in an actual man who was a cannibal propitiated with human flesh; another, invisible to the people, though seen by strangers as a handsome young man wearing a girdle of leaves, was called the King of Fiji (Tuifiti). Other gods described by Turner[552] are Ole alii Fiti (chief of Fiji), who was manifest in an eel; and Tinalii (King of chiefs), who was associated with the sea-eel, octopus, mullet, and the ends of banana leaves. Fusion seems to have been common.

It must not, of course, be assumed that all animal gods are Totems. Among the ways in which animal gods may have arisen we cannot deny some place to Spencer's hypothesis, that heroes have sometimes been worshipped as animals because they bore animal names; and, after their death, the eponymous animals, ever present to men's eyes, superseded the heroes, and were connected with and transformed their legends. It is also conceivable that a hero has been worshipped in the form of an animal or plant, because he had announced that, after death, he would be in such an animal or plant; for at Ulawa (Solomon Isles) bananas were *buto*, things that might not be eaten, approached or beheld (according to Dr. Coddrington[553]), because an influential man had prohibited the eating of them, saying

[550] W. H. R. Rivers, *J. A. I.*, 1909, p. 158.

[551] *J. A. I.*, 1909, p. 163.

[552] *Samoa*, chs. iv., v.; especially pp. 28, 48, 62-3, 70, 75. Fiji had in some way deeply impressed the Samoan imagination.

[553] *The Melanesians*, p. 31.

that, after death, he would be in the banana; and with so much influence he might, in favourable circumstances, have become a Banana-god. And, again, in Professor Westermarck's opinion, "the common prevalence of animal worship is, no doubt, due to the mysteriousness of the animal world; the most uncanny of all creatures, the serpent, is also the one most generally worshipped."[554]

But these considerations strengthen the probability that a Totem may sometimes become a god; having the general respect of the clan to begin with. Some Totems having been deified with the assistance of heroes, others may perhaps be elevated by the force of analogy; or, once the conception of a spiritual being has been reached—chiefly (as we suppose) by reflection on dreams—and animals and even inanimate things have been thought to have spiritual doubles, if then the Totem is conceived to have a spirit, and even the same as the clansman's soul, if it is appealed to for assistance, if it sends omens, listens to prayer and accepts sacrifice, what is it but a god?

In North America the Totem seems nowhere to have been worshipped; and any tendency that may have existed to propitiate it was diverted by the superior fascination of the personal guardian-genius, to which sometimes costly sacrifices were made and even self-mutilations; as among the Mandans, who often cut off a finger to secure its favour.[555] On the other hand, a class of spirits was recognised in the "elder brother" of each species of animal (or of the most interesting species—bear, deer, snake, etc.—all of the totemic class), a being (in the words of an early missionary, 1634) "who is as it were the principle and origin of all the individuals," and "marvellously great and powerful":[556] it watches over the species and avenges its wrongs. In North-West America and throughout Siberia the Bear and the Raven are objects of religious reverence; not, indeed, as clan-totems, but for all men. Among the Gulf nations the Yuchis are Totemists, and a youth at his initiation is put under the care of his clan-totem, instead of a personal guardian-genius as among the northern tribes; he looks for protection, however, not to the living animals of the Totem species, but to superior beings, like the "elder brothers" of the species.[557] Similar to these must be the Beast-gods of the Zuni Indians, to whom they offer a portion of all game, praying that they will intercede for them with the Sun-Father. In South America, too, the Patagonians and Araucanians teach that each species of animal has a guardian spirit, who lives in a cave, and that the Indians themselves at death go to live with him. We can hardly doubt that in all these cases, the spirit-animals are in some way connected with totemic beliefs: if not gods, they are at least divine beings, and they exemplify a noble sort of mysticism that is natural to the Amerind imagination.[558]

Africa is the principal home of Zoolatry. The religion of the Bantu nations of South Africa is, indeed, ancestor-worship; and their serpent-cult seems to be an outgrowth of ancestor-worship (for they think that their dead return as serpents of various species according to rank); unless, indeed, it has been diverted to such

[554] *Origin and Development of Moral Ideas*, II. p. 590.
[555] *Totemism and Exogamy*, III.
[556] Quoted by Tylor, *Primitive Culture*, II. p. 244.
[557] *Totemism and Exogamy*, III. p. 311.
[558] On species-gods see Tylor's *Primitive Culture*, II. pp. 242-6.

a subordinate place from some more ancient superstition. In West Africa there are many Beast-gods, especially the leopard, hyena, crocodile and python. They do not, however, give much indication of totemic origin; and Sir James Frazer observes that, as the hereditary worship of animals in certain districts (as of the hyena at Accra) was not totemic, nor need similar practices have been so elsewhere.[559] Hence that the Egyptians worshipped certain animals, and that in the district of any animal's worship it was not killed or eaten, cannot prove that the worship was totemic, unless it be shown that Totemism is the only road to Zoolatry; for, if there are other ways, any animal that becomes divine will, naturally, not be killed or eaten. On the other hand, that the Egyptians were not Exogamists does not prove they were not Totemists; since some known Totemists are not Exogamists. The natural impression of a student who merely comes amongst other things to Egyptian Religion is that Totemism was one of its sources; but it is a subject on which, more strictly than on most, only a few specialists can form a judgment.

On the whole, the contribution of Totemism to religion seems to have been greatly exaggerated. Compared with the influence of dead heroes and ancestors, or with the personification of the greater manifestations of nature—Sky, Sun, Thunder—it has been ineffective, falling short of the production of high gods; or if, as in Polynesia, it seems sometimes to have come near to that achievement, it may be suspected that its success owed much to an alliance with hero-worship.

---

[559] *Totemism and Exogamy*, II. p. 574.

CHAPTER X
MAGIC AND SCIENCE

§ 1. Their Common Ground

§ 1. *Their Common Ground.*—Both assume uniformity of action. Differentiated in opposite directions from common-sense

It is not infrequently said that Science is derived from Magic, and the tenet is strengthened by eminent names; nor is it displeasing to some bystanders whose attitude toward Science is one of imperfect sympathy; but it seems to me to involve a misunderstanding of the matter. Magic and Science have, indeed, some common ground; for both are products of our poor human mind, which is sorely pestered in explaining its experiences by the notion of "forces" that somehow bring about events, and which cannot get on at all without assuming uniformities of relation. Magic supposes constant connexions of events due to the agency, force, influence or virtue of charms, rites and spells; which connexions, however, are found only to be tendencies of some events to excite others, inasmuch as they may be frustrated by counteracting charms, rites or spells. This reads like a caricature of scientific ideas. Not long ago, too, "forces" had a considerable vogue amongst scientists; and such mysteries as "vital force" and "psychic force" are still to be met with. But it is plain that we never know more than that under certain conditions a change takes place; and when we try to explain the change by analysing the conditions, we never find any "force" distinct from the collocation and motion of bodies or particles. "Force" may be technically and formally used in various propositions, but the idea never contributes anything to the explanation of events; whilst the fact that with many people it seems to do so, often makes it a nuisance. That it seems to carry some explanation with it is due to the continuous influence of Magic which, though always the antithesis of Science, was yet for very many ages associated with Science. Magic is entirely constituted by notions of force, sometimes violent, as in the discharge of an enchanted spear; sometimes subtle, like the efficacy of an opal; intangible, invisible, and operating at a distance through space and time, like a witch's spells that eclipse the sun or moon. These forces have only a one-sided relation to the workaday world; they meet with no resistance from what we take to be the "properties of matter," such as weight and impenetrability; but are themselves entirely exempt from natural law: what we call the "real world" has no hold upon them; they live in a world of their own. They are absolutely immeasurable; and hence the causation, which is certainly implied in the notion of their operation, is indefinite, and becomes vaguer and vaguer as the magical system develops; and all this is the opposite of what happens in the history of Science. In spite of having a necessary common ground in the human mind, Magic and Science are contrasted from the first, in their development grow wider and wider apart, in their methods and ideas more and more opposed. If either can be said to precede the other, it is Science (at least, in its earliest and crudest form) that precedes Magic.

We had better begin, however, by considering a third something which is earlier than either of them, and which I have called Common-sense: I mean the accumulation of particular items of positive knowledge (which, as such, is the first form of Science) acquired by primitive man, and in less measure by the higher brutes: facts about cold and heat, sunshine and rain, the powers of water and fire, the life of trees and animals, the properties of wood and stone, and so forth, which are unfailingly confirmed by further experience. Examination of the life of savages discovers that this positive knowledge of theirs amounts to a great deal, and that they are able to use it "and reason not contemptibly." From this Common-sense Science and a good deal of Magic are differentiated, and they expand at very unequal rates in opposite directions. Each of them starts from it; but whilst Magic rapidly distorts, perverts and mystifies it out of recognition in innumerable imaginations, Science slowly connects its fragments together, corrects, defines and extends it, without ever altering its original positive character. The difference between Magic and Science lies (as we have seen) in the causes that establish belief in them; in the character of their ideas—respectively, incoherent and vague, coherent and definite; and, as a consequence, in their respective falsity and truth.

§ 2. The Differentiation

§ 2. *The Differentiation.*—The Wizard a physician—genuine and magical drugs; a surgeon with some knowledge of Anatomy—effective remedies and the sucking-cure; of Psychology and suggestion; his Physiological Psychology. Knowledge of natural signs; Natural signs and Omens; Astronomy and Astrology. Rain-rites and Meteorology

Whilst Magic, amongst savage and barbarous people, is practised more or less by almost everybody, it is especially developed by the professional wizard, and in his art and tradition it is most conveniently studied. The wizard, or (at least) a leader amongst wizards, is a man of superior ability, penetration and enterprise; liable to be misled by a sanguine and ambitious temperament into extravagant imaginations and impostures, but with much more real knowledge than the rest of the tribe. He often takes pains to increase his knowledge, for it is the true basis of his power: "the power of the Angoqok," says Mr. Turner, writing of the Esquimo,[560] "has some basis in experienced weather-lore, and knowledge of the habits of animals, by which he advises hunters." But this knowledge is often the starting-point of his delusions, not altogether by any fault of his own, but as a result of his attempts to apply knowledge to new cases without any appreciation of the

[560] "Ethnology of the Ungava District," *Am. B. of Ethn.*, XI. p. 195. Other examples *ante*, ch. viii. § 3.

need of caution or of the conditions of sound inference and of proof and disproof. He never knows why he is right or why he is wrong. Hence, beside the modest edifice of his real knowledge, he builds out in one direction a few genuine additions warranted by sound inference and observation; whilst in the other direction he raises, largely by analogy, with the help of "sympathy" and spiritual powers, a towering structure of imaginations, which throws his little hut of Common-sense quite into the shade.

(*a*) For example, the wizard is often literally a medicine-man or physician, and knows the use of certain drugs; and he may discover other drugs and more uses for them, and in that direction lies Pharmacology. But in the other direction he adopts on altogether fanciful occasions a great many other recipes that serve no purpose but charlatanry and mystification. Pliny, much of whose *Natural History* is a handbook of ancient medicine, describes hundreds of remedies derived from animals, vegetables and minerals; and Burton[561] cites Galeottus as having enumerated 800 medicinal herbs and other drugs. Some of these were good and are still in use, but most were useless or worse than useless. The difference between these two classes of drugs depended on a difference of method in determining their uses: a difference that existed but was not yet understood (namely), on the one hand, proof by experience, giving in the smaller class the rudiments of medical science; and, on the other hand, acceptance on the strength of superficial likeness, or of the doctrine of qualities, virtues and signatures, which made the larger class essentially magical.

Thus all sorts of precious stones and metals were believed to be medicinal, not because they had been known to cure any disease, but because it seemed obvious in those days that precious things must have all sorts of desirable effects by some occult virtue. Gold, the most perfect of all substances (according to the alchemists), must in particular be a propitious and powerful restorative. So Chaucer says of his Doctour of Phisik:

> "For gold in phisik is a cordial,
> Therefore he lovede gold in special."

And throughout India at the present day gold is a trusty item in any prescription. Belief in the virtue of precious stones probably goes back to very early times; since we find that in Australia crystals are not only magically powerful but the great primary sources of Magic, by having which inside him the wizard acquires and maintains his power.

With herbs, again, whilst the utility of some, such as quinine or senna, was a matter of experience, others were equally prized out of pure fancy. Dracunculus, a plant spotted with various colours, like a viper's skin, was supposed to be a remedy for all kinds of snake-stings.[562] The Cherokees gave their children a concoction of burs to strengthen their memories; for as a bur will stick to anything, the mind of a man with bur inside him will cling to all kinds of useful information. The same Amerinds had other remedies which illustrate the character of magical physic. They concocted a vermifuge of the red fleshy stalks of chickweed,

[561] *Anatomy of Melancholy*, Part II. Sec. IV. Mem. 1, Subsec. 3.
[562] Pliny, XXV. c. 6.

which somewhat resemble worms, and therefore must have some influence upon them; and they steeped in this concoction a flint arrow-head, that its sharpness, communicated to the brew, might cut the worms in pieces. Biliousness, marked by the vomiting of yellow bile, was cured by four herbs—all yellow in root, or stalk, or flower. To ward off smallpox they ate the flesh of the buzzard: that bird being, in their opinion, exempt from smallpox, because its foul stench keeps the disease-spirit at a distance. To cure snake-bite, they said, rub the place in the direction contrary to that in which the snake coils itself (to the right); because this is the same as uncoiling it.[563] But here there seems to be some hiatus in the thought, for how does uncoiling the snake counteract its poison? One easily appreciates the exultation of the wizard to whom this idea first revealed itself, and his contempt for the dull process of working it out, when its place in the harmony of things was self-evident.

In some of these cases we find the assumption (tacit with primitive practitioners, but explicit in Mediæval Medicine) that "like causes like": the adhesiveness of the bur is communicated to the memory, the sharpness of the flint arrow-point to the vermifuge, the buzzard's immunity from smallpox to the eater of the buzzard. And this is intelligible: because, first, there are many examples (superficially considered) of like causing like, such as animal generation, the spread of fire; hot things heat, and cold things cool, and so forth: and, secondly, qualities such as stickiness and sharpness, are thought of by savages as fine material, like curses and ghosts, which may be transferred from one thing to another. But in other cases it is assumed that "like cures like," as chickweed cures worms, and yellow herbs biliousness (as in Europe turmeric was long believed to cure jaundice); and this is a very different matter—equivalent to "like expels or annuls like." In ordinary experience, there seem to be no obvious examples of it: but in primitive medical practice it is found that fomentation reduces inflammation, rubbing with snow is good for frost-bite, an emetic cures sickness, and castor oil diarrhœa; and such may be the experiential ground of these magico-medical fancies.

The power of herbs may depend upon rites observed at their gathering: when a Cherokee wizard pulled up a plant for medicine, he dropped a bead into the hole to compensate the earth for the theft;[564] and when a Greek physician gathered the *Panaces Asclepion*, which was a remedy for all diseases, he filled the hole with various kinds of grain by way of expiation.[565] In employing medicinal herbs it is also important to remember *when* they should be procured, as on the eve of the summer solstice, at the new or the full moon, or at the turn of the tide; *by whom*—a child or a virgin; and *where*—on a mountain-top or at a grave. Hierabotane was so potent that whoever rubbed himself with it obtained whatever he desired; and in gathering it, you first offered honey to the earth in expiation, then traced a circle around it with iron, and—taking care that neither sun nor moon should shine upon it—at the rising of the Dog Star, you pulled it up with the left hand, and dried separately in the shade the root, the stem and the leaves.[566] Indeed the con-

<hr>

[563] J. Mooney, "Sacred Formulas of the Cherokees," *Am. B. of Ethn.*, VII. pp. 323-39.
[564] J. Mooney, op. cit.
[565] Pliny, XXV. c. 11.
[566] Ibid., XXV. c. 59.

ditions under which a drug can be legitimately obtained so as to ensure its efficacy, may be so numerous, minute and exigent as to make the satisfying of them almost impossible; so we need not wonder if the remedy sometimes fails. Prescriptions often include the flesh or juices of dead bodies, or their pounded bones, or other foul and repulsive ingredients related to Black Magic—much trusted, and still traditional in some strata of this country, where the belief is inexpugnable that medicine, the nastier it is, is the more efficacious.

If any one wonders how such prescriptions can have held their ground for ages, it was because patients did not always die. Recovery was credited to the drastic medicine, and death to evil Magic; and the *vis medicatrix naturæ*, that staunch ally of honest physic, was sometimes too strong for the wizard's whole pharmacopœia.

(*b*) Again, the wizard is a surgeon, and knows something of the construction and working of the human body, and this is the beginning of Anatomy and Physiology. He was especially well informed in these matters in such a country as Fiji, where he had access to two great sources of anatomical knowledge—frequent wars and cannibalism. He also knows certain ways of treating wounds and other lesions, such as bandages, ligatures, splints, slings, massage and fomentations, which all admit of rational development and have been continuously practised to this day. Could he be content to abide by the facts, all might be well; but he is tempted to extend his methods in various directions to cases which, on very slight grounds, he believes to be similar. The best known example of the erroneous extension by analogy of a sound method is the sucking-cure. It is, or has been, practised all over the world, and obviously rests on the proved utility of suction in extracting from the flesh thorns or poisons. In Australia snake-bite is sometimes cured by sucking the wound and rinsing the mouth with water.[567] But the operation is gradually applied to other cases until, whatever pain you suffer, it is attributed to something like poison, or a thorn (or, later, a spirit), that has got inside you, though by an invisible wound, and may be sucked out. The wizard, accordingly, undertakes to suck it out, and he sometimes exhibits it to you—a piece of wood or bone, which he brought to your bedside in his waistband. Sometimes a medicine-man enjoys great suctorial powers by having a lizard in his own body.[568]

For getting a foreign body out of a man a method alternative to suction is pressure. Mr. Howitt[569] reports a remarkable prescription for curing headache. Cut out of the ground a circular turf, place the sufferer's head in the hole and the turf upon his head; then sit or stand upon it. He may presently declare that he feels relief; but perhaps he only desires it. It is a fact that a patient sometimes feels better after such treatment, though the cause of his pain was nothing that could possibly yield to suction or pressure: that is to say, his mind yields to suggestion. But not all savages are equally suggestible, any more than we are. Dr. Coddrington says[570] that, in Pentecost Island, witches profess to cure pain with a leaf-poultice, and in

---

[567] A. W. Howitt, *Native Tribes of South-East Australia*, p. 384.
[568] Spencer and Gillen, *Across Australia*, p. 339.
[569] *Native Tribes of South-East Australia*, p. 381.
[570] *The Melanesians*, p. 199.

taking it off to remove with it the cause of pain, perhaps a snake or a lizard. "But," said a native, "no one sees the things but the woman, and the pain remains"—one of those troublesome sceptics! Yet it is possible that had he just undergone the operation, he would not have denied that the pain was better. There is a state of mind between suggestibility and sane judgment, namely, assentation: unwillingness or unreadiness to form or state one's own opinion, and, consequently, an appearance of acquiescing in another's assertion. There is confusion and conflict, from which assent is the easiest relief. This state of mind for the immediate purpose of medicine-man or orator may serve as well as suggestibility; but may soon pass off when the patient recovers his faculties, and should be distinguished from the suggestibility that takes a relatively permanent impression from the pretensions of a mountebank. The power of suggestion, however, is one of the facts that the wizard has observed, and he counts upon its aid. He has also learnt to practise hypnotism; and seeing how mysterious these things have been to the most enlightened moderns, we need not wonder that he employs them in magical therapeutics—dancing, drumming, shouting to overpower his patient and to incite himself to put forth his utmost energy. Nowhere, probably, in the whole range of his art, is the difference between Reality and Magic so obscure to himself.

The wizard, then, acquired in his medical functions (and in others) a certain empirical knowledge of some obscure facts in Psychology, and this knowledge persisted in his profession in shady quarters to our own time; but with the growth of positive Science, its mysteriousness was mistaken for quackery, until quite recently, when the facts forced themselves on the attention of some men, who needed great courage to confess their conviction. A crude Physiological Psychology, too, resulted from savage observation of a connexion between the agitations of body and mind. Very early sundry mental powers—skill, courage, affection—are located in special parts of the body—the heart, spleen, kidneys, bowels—as they still are in popular language. Apart from the bare observation that the bowels and heart are disturbed during emotion (which is true and important), these doctrines are not Science; nor are they exactly Magic, but belong to the region of ideas ancillary to Magic—ideas of qualities as material things. The savage, always eager to apply his supposed knowledge to practice, utilises his Physiological Psychology for the improvement of his mind, and misses no opportunity to make a meal upon an enemy's (or perhaps a relative's) heart or spleen or kidney or tongue or eye, in order to appropriate the quality for which the deceased had been conspicuous.

(c) Savages (as we have seen in the chapter on Omens) are familiar with a great many natural signs by which to judge of things not now present, but that have happened, or are about to happen. Every hunter must have a great stock of such knowledge, inasmuch as the pursuit of game entirely depends upon it. This knowledge of natural signs is, on the one hand, a genuine contribution to Natural History; it increases, is handed down from generation to generation, and forms the nucleus of Botany and Zoology. But, on the other hand, there is reared upon it, under the influence of hope and fear, the belief in Omens that give warning of good or ill success in all the affairs of life. Omens, at first merely signs mysteriously connected with events, are later regarded as the sendings of spirits or gods, whose oracles forecast the fate of heroes and nations. At first, perhaps, the wizard may do no more than other tribesmen to promote this particular superstition; but it is he who works out the great art of Divination, without which Omens would have been a matter of much less consequence.

The most famous branch of Divination, namely, Astrology, was the invention of a comparatively late age, and it was, of course, long preceded by the discovery of the rudiments of Astronomy as part of the common sense of agriculture: some knowledge of the regularity of the motions of the sun and moon and of the constancy of the stars in contrast with the planets. This is plainly presupposed by the comprehensive system of predictions based on sympathetic Magic, arbitrary assumptions and fanciful analogies which, for the last four or five thousand years, has promised to disclose to any mother the career of her infant, or to any monarch the future of his kingdom. But what now seems fanciful or arbitrary once seemed reasonable. The sun manifestly rules all things; the waxing and waning of the moon must strengthen and weaken all things; the signs of the Zodiac are certainly connected with the seasons; the planets partake of the nature of the gods.[571] If there are gods they must, as the Stoics argued, have some way of communicating with men; and what way can be more congruous with their nature than by writing on the face of the heavens? But generally the ideas of Astrology were magical rather than animistic. Having determined the powers and dispositions of the heavenly bodies, let us consider only what must necessarily follow from their influences in conjunction or opposition and various relations in trine, quartile and sextile. Thus they dreamed and speculated, but at the same time made many exact observations on the sky. And so Astronomy made some progress in spite of Magic.

(*d*) More widely prevalent than Astrology and far more ancient is the art of controlling the weather, especially rain; for rain, from its uncertainty in many countries and its indispensableness, is a matter of deeper interest and anxiety than even the sun himself. "Rain-making," as it is called, common in Australia and other regions of lowly culture, survives when society has risen to higher levels, becomes the function of the most eminent wizards or priests, sometimes the duty of kings, and is not extinct amongst ourselves. But from what knowledge of fact or common sense can "rain-making" be derived? I conjecture it was from facts observed in the behaviour of fire.

The making of fire was the first great chemical experiment and the foundation of all Chemistry. Having made fire, the most wonderful of all achievements, there would be little excuse for astonishment if men had then thought they could also make rain; but probably they never thought so. It seems to me a misconception of rain-rites to describe them as endeavours to "make" rain; for they plainly aim not at making, but at inducing, instigating or propagating it. The Swazies, we are told explicitly, try to procure rain by throwing water high into the air, expecting that the falling drops will stimulate the clouds in sympathy with them.[572] Savages may be said to "make" fire; for until they rub their sticks, or knock their flints

---

[571] For Proclus' defence of Astrology see Whewell's *History of the Inductive Sciences*, Book IV. ch. iii., 1st ed., pp. 298-300.

[572] Dudley Kidd, *The Essential Kafir*, p. 114.

together, it does not exist. But in the so-called "making" of rain there is nearly always some water to begin with; and the essence of a rain-rite is the splashing of water into the air, or the pouring of it out, sometimes on a particular stone, or on a particular person, with many variations. In rare instances the water has been forgotten: the Kurnai, instead of water, let blood, and throw down into the air for clouds; but in another rite they fill their mouths with water and squirt it out in one direction or another (according to the clan) and sing a spell: to stop the rain they throw up fire-sticks.[573] Those who practise such rites hope that the spilling of a little water will bring on a great downfall or outpouring of water, namely, rain; and this agrees with the fact that a wizard will not operate except when the rainy season approaches. Now this inducing of much by little is not, indeed, analogous to the *making* of fire; but it is analogous to the spread or propagation of fire; when, having produced a few sparks, these spread through tinder to the firewood, and thence a conflagration may be communicated to the prairie or to the forest. My conjecture is, then, that not the making (which is never attempted) but the inducing, or propagation of rain is based on the analogy of the propagation of fire, and belongs to the class of exemplary or incentive rites; which are to be understood not as intending the direct causation of events, but rather as instigating Nature to bring it about: the class described in Chap. IV. § 8, such as the furthering of crops by fertility-rites, or the ensuring of successful hunting or warfare by a dramatic dance.

Rain-rites being very apt to fail of their purpose, the wizard is in danger of losing his reputation, or of some worse fate. His attention is, therefore, drawn to the signs of the weather, the character and course of the seasons, the connexion of rain with the aspect of the sky and direction of the wind; so that he learns to operate for rain only when rain may reasonably be expected. He has then laid out the rudiments of Meteorology, but by observation, not by hocus-pocus.

§ 3. Why Magic seems to be the Source of Science

§ 3. *Why Magic seems to be the Source of Science.* —Conducted for ages by the same people, and develops faster

In no case, then, is Science derived from Magic, but Science on the one hand and Magic on the other are differentiated from Common-sense,[574] and Science is much nearer akin to Common-sense than Magic is, being of the same substance and only formally different. And in that sense it is earlier than Magic, and sometimes formally earlier, as in the case of Astronomy and Astrology. The illusion that Magic is the earlier is due to the misinterpretation of two facts: (*a*) Magic and Science are, for the most part and during many ages, worked out by the same men—magicians or priests; and all that they do is mistaken for Magic, even by themselves. And (*b*) Magic in most of its branches undergoes immense development, whilst the Sciences remain rudimentary; grows old and even decrepit, whilst they

---

[573] A. W. Howitt, *Native Tribes of South-East Australia*, pp. 397-9.

[574] I do not mean that Magic is always a *direct* derivative of Common-sense: we have seen (ch. vi. § 5) that it sometimes comes from Animism by retrogradation, and (elsewhere) often from coincidences.

are still in infancy; so that, on first emerging into public notice, they seem to issue from the matrix of Magic.

The reasons for the relative backwardness of Science, again, are chiefly three: (*a*) For ages it is in the hands of wizards who, though highly valuing knowledge, are mainly eager for power and prophecy. It is true that Science gives power, and the hope of power is a reasonable incentive to the study of Science; but it must be a remote incentive, in the actual work of research rigorously excluded. There, unless truth is the sole end in view, the procedure will not be clean, will be confined to immediate utility. But this is a recent discovery. The wizard has no such ideas: he is governed by his desires and traditions. Hence for verification he is content with coincidences; negative instances he neglects, or regards failure merely as an occasion for excuses. He accepts connexions of events remote in space and time, and is very slow to see the necessity of connecting events in the closest possible sequence. Moreover, having no understanding even of the facts he knows (such as the making of fire), the mysteriousness of any relation of events constitutes no objection to his acceptance of it; as the magical side of his practice grows, so does its mystery; until at last mysteriousness is a strong recommendation, and becomes a character of the apperceptive mass that assimilates and confirms all magical beliefs. This state of mind always offers strong resistance to positive explanation.

(*b*) Another reason of the backwardness of Science is the slow elucidation of the idea of Causation—long obscured by the impressiveness of coincidence and by fallacious imaginations of magical and spiritual forces: a process still incomplete. Until this idea had made considerable progress in definiteness (in antiquity, say, with Archimedes, and in modern times with Galileo), it was impossible that the indispensableness of analysis and elimination should be understood, that absolute respect should be felt for negative instances and that any gap in a series of events should always be regarded as an instant problem. And, finally (*c*), for scientific progress it was necessary that reasoning by analogy should be abandoned, and a methodology discovered of parallel and equational reasoning, with the apparatus that makes exact investigation possible.

As the Sciences grow in comprehensiveness, precision and solidarity, they constitute their own apperceptive mass, assimilation with which is the supreme test of all relevant beliefs; and this, together with a methodology that has become a habit of mind, tends to establish a social atmosphere in which Magic is no longer thinkable. Exact habits of thought in commerce and industry contribute greatly to this result. So we are tempted to ridicule our benighted predecessors; but a study of the conditions of their life shows that darkness was no more their fault than illumination is our merit.

The nearest approach that can be truthfully made to the position that Science is derived from Magic, is to say that the scientist is derived from the wizard (or wizard-priest), on that side of his activity in which he relied upon fragments of positive knowledge; but this was, in nature, always opposed to his Magic. In the course of thousands of years some men grew more interested in the positive than in the magical side of their profession, and became scientists; whilst others adhered to the fanciful and mystical. It is remarkable that, as sceptics occur in the most unsuspected quarters, so pure scientists may sometimes be found as an institution in barbarous or even savage communities. In a Bantu tribe there is a class of doctors that claim no powers by the aid of spirits or Magic, but without any ceremony dispense a few well-known drugs—aloes, nux vomica, castor-oil, fern-root, rhubarb, and the bark of various trees, purgative or emetic.[575] The Kanyahs of Borneo have a weather-prophet to determine the right time for sowing; he is not expected to cultivate padi, but is supplied with it by the rest of the village. Not knowing how many days there are in a year, and finding that the seasons do not correspond with any certain number of lunar months, he depends entirely upon observation of the altitude of the sun by means of an upright pole, whose upper end is carved into a human figure.[576] Except the carving on his pole, there is nothing to indicate that either Magic or Animism perturbs the method of this Astronomer Royal. Hence the adventure, though most wonderful, is not unexampled in a humbler world, by which eminent citizens amongst the Greek laity, with minds almost free from Magic and Animism, established for ever Philosophy and the Sciences as liberal studies.

§ 4. ANIMISM AND SCIENCE

§ 4. *Animism and Science.*—Naturally opposed as caprice to uniformity; but, indirectly, Animism is the great nurse of Science and Art. Animism and Philosophy. Conclusion

Animism is opposed to Science, as well as to Magic,[577] by its rejection of uniformity. A spirit, indeed, has some character (though it may be very faintly marked); for he is, or is assimilated to, a human ghost. But although he is supposed to have reasons or motives for his actions, they are often unintelligible. Until he is brought under the control of magical rites and formulæ, he may reject offerings and prayers, as if by pure caprice or free-will. His interventions are incalculable. Hence he may be the unseen agent in anything that happens; and the habit is formed of putting upon him, or one of his kind, every occurrence whose cause is not obvious: diseases, deaths, storms, droughts, noises in the forest, unusual behaviour of animals. A spirit-being with its body of soul-stuff capable of taking any shape, a material thing exerting mechanical power, there is nothing that may not be imputed to it. But being entirely imaginary, its supposed agency can only satisfy the imagination by the assimilation of each intervention by the animistic apperceptive mass. It is never seen or known to do any one of the actions attributed to it; for the understanding, based on perception and the classification and analysis of perceptions, it is nothing. Moreover, so far as the actions of a spirit are of free-will, or motiveless, or pure caprice, there is no distinct imagination of even a spiritual cause. When a man, suffering from disease, or hearing an unfamiliar noise, refers it to a spirit, there is usually nothing in his mind but the word of vague meaning and a feeling of awe, wonder, or dread. He gets no further in the understanding of the fact, and curiosity is paralysed. To say "a spirit did it" becomes, therefore, a means of avoiding the labour of explanation; it is a good example of the "principle

[575] Dudley Kidd, *The Essential Kafir*, pp. 134-5.
[576] Hose and McDougall, *Pagan Tribes of Borneo*, I. p. 106.
[577] *Ante*, ch. vi. § 3.

of least effort." But in another direction his wits may get to work. He is full of fear, and objectless fear must invent a danger, which is easily done by supposing that the spirit has been actuated by wrath. Then something must have been done to enrage him: a taboo has been broken, his rites have been neglected, sin has been committed — according to the customary ideas of the tribe. There must be lustration, propitiation, expiation, perhaps with horrible cruelty. Again, then, shall we say the man has been diverted from the important inquiry into the causes of disease or drought? But this is laughable: how can he set about such a task? It is the tragedy of the world that for thousands of years the speculative powers of man — of some men — expanded without any power, except in the classical age, of discriminating sense from nonsense. Therefore, looking back, we see everywhere else superstition and the kingdom of darkness.

Animism can never have directly enriched Science with a single natural law; but, indirectly, it has instigated many investigations. With the development of Religion, the building of temples and the regulation of sacrifices and festivals according to their seasons, necessitated at least the empirical study of Geometry, Arithmetic and Astronomy; and the preservation of the ancient language of the sacred formulæ of ritual required a knowledge of prosody, phonetics and grammar. For thousands of years erudition was confined to the priestly orders. They also practised, or were the chief patrons of, all the fine arts, Architecture, Sculpture, Painting, Music and Poetry; and by their connexion with government they left in Egypt and Assyria, in monuments and inscriptions, History, or the materials of History. Indirectly, the progress of mental culture, both in learning and in æsthetics, has depended almost entirely on the development of Animism; and this in turn has depended on the aid which Animism gave to government and to the extension of law and order, however imperfect, over wide regions of the earth. This is the fundamental utility which, first, Magic and, afterwards, Animism subserve, and for the sake of which — unconsciously, of course — they arise and prevail. Mankind has been subdued through imagination; because the peoples that had the cast of imagination requisite for their political organisation and co-operation had an advantage over others.

We must qualify this by observing that other imaginations, such as devotion to the Family and Patriotism, with a much surer hold than Animism has upon experience, have had a great and growing influence upon the solidarity and civilisation of some branches of the human race, especially the Nordic.

Philosophy has derived from Animism most of her problems — free-will and predestination, final causes, creation and miracles, emanation and intuition, idealism and materialism, immortality, the being and attributes of God, eternity, infinity — in some of which, indeed, magical ideas are deeply concerned: all of them the exercise of the most eminent minds, exercise so delightful and so disappointing. Considering their source, we cannot wonder that these problems remain problems, and that philosophical discussion has, of late years, turned from them to questions concerning the theory of knowledge.

A student of human origins is under no obligation to predict the future. Fortunately: for several considerations make the task appear altogether impossible. Of these I will mention three: (*a*) Whereas nations have hitherto submitted to, and enforced, law and order, and undertaken costly works of utility or splendour, in large measure under the influence of animistic illusions, it is now everywhere noticeable in the more civilised countries, that these illusions are being dissipated, and it is very difficult to judge how people will behave when they are gone. It is, indeed, true that our ordinary working life has always depended chiefly on common sense, a knowledge of facts within the range of ordinary experience and memory. Animistic or magical rites and ceremonies associated with the working-life may have increased the confidence and encouraged the co-operation of labourers, but were not indispensable; although the association of Magic with industry seems sometimes to have become so close, that to forget the Magic was to destroy the industry. When, however, we turn to those conditions of social life that are beyond the purview of common sense, such as the preservation of tribal tradition and solidarity, and future prosperity, loyalty to the king and obedience to his officers, it is plain that something else than common sense was needed to reinforce the interest of the whole against the tendency of the individual's self-assertion to overcome his social dispositions, and that this control was found chiefly in Religion. It is also true that at present, whilst some beliefs concerning supernatural things are being lost, others are being resuscitated; but the lapsing beliefs are noble and venerable and have exerted great public power and authority; whilst those now eagerly propagated, are the raw infatuation of quacks, on a level with the Animism of an Australian medicine-man and, indeed, much inferior to his, as having no moral influence or authority. What must come of this is so dubious, as to discourage one about the future of the world.

(*b*) Reflection on the levity with which imagination-beliefs are let slip and lost, or received and adopted, upon no evidence either way, from mere shallowness of soul, brings forward a second consideration that makes the future impredictable, namely, the low average development of mankind in both intellect and character. This is the consequence of our having depended, probably from the very beginning, on leaders. A pack or tribe needed enough variability to produce able leaders and enough average ability to follow and support them in a crowd. Natural Selection, therefore, has operated first in producing variability; and all tribes, even the lowest, produce relatively eminent men. The average intelligence or ability of the crowd, in which individuality is liable to be lost, is much less important. The result is that each nation has its military affairs, organisation of industry, science, invention, literature and art provided for it by a small number of citizens; the rest fill the ranks, and learn what they are taught. Thus arranged, the leading nations have of late years made wonderful progress in science and in everything that can be done by machinery; but there is no reason to suppose that anything has been done towards raising the average intelligence and character; and in default of that, in my judgment, nothing has been done to advance civilisation. The world is no safer against war, revolution, demagogy, despotism, degeneration. The greatest improvements have been made in means of destruction; next we may put the invention of flying machines; and their chief use has been destruction. Destruction now pauses, not because the antagonists are satiated; they are only exhausted; and there is more hatred in the world than was ever known before. How then shall we judge of things to come?

(*c*) Speaking of the average man, we usually think of the European and North American average; but in considering what changes may be expected in the world, the people of India (800,000,000), China (350,000,000), and the millions of the rest of Asia, the Eastern Archipelago, Africa and South America cannot be left out; and to include them does not raise the average. What will be their contribution to history? There are two rational proposals for raising the average, namely, eugenics and deliberate elimination of the unfit; and there are 1,600,000,000 on whom to operate.

Any one who anxiously desires to foresee the future of our race is in a position to sympathise with the ancients. Go, inquire at Delphi or Dodona; or sleep in Stonehenge, or at the tomb of Merlin, or by the barrows at Upsala, and dream of things to come; or consult the stars, cast the nativity of Lycopithecus, and read in heaven the fate of his posterity. If these methods are not very hopeful, any one of them is as good as guessing. The only safe reflection is that he who lives longest will see most.

INDEX

I

J

K

L

M

Lector House believes that a society develops through a two-fold approach of continuous learning and adaptation, which is derived from the study of classic literary works spread across the historic timeline of literature records. Therefore, we aim at reviving, repairing and redeveloping all those inaccessible or damaged but historically as well as culturally important literature across subjects so that the future generations may have an opportunity to study and learn from past works to embark upon a journey of creating a better future.

This book is a result of an effort made by Lector House towards making a contribution to the preservation and repair of original ancient works which might hold historical significance to the approach of continuous learning across subjects.

HAPPY READING & LEARNING!

LECTOR HOUSE LLP
E-MAIL: lectorpublishing@gmail.com